CATEGORIES, CONSTRUCTIONS, AND CHANGE IN ENGLISH SYNTAX

A pioneering collection of new research that explores categories, constructions, and change in the syntax of the English language. The volume, with contributions by world-renowned scholars as well as some emerging scholars in the field, covers a wide variety of approaches to grammatical categories and categorial change, constructions and constructional change, and comparative and typological research. Each of the fourteen chapters, based on the analysis of authentic data, highlights the wealth and breadth of the study of English syntax (including morphosyntax), both theoretically and empirically, from Old English through to the present day. The result is a body of research which will add substantially to the current study of the syntax of the English language, by stimulating further research in the field.

NURIA YÁÑEZ-BOUZA is a Senior Lecturer in English Language at the University of Vigo and Honorary Research Fellow at the University of Manchester.

EMMA MOORE is a Professor of Sociolinguistics at the University of Sheffield.

LINDA VAN BERGEN is a Lecturer in the department of Linguistics and English Language at the University of Edinburgh.

WILLEM B. HOLLMANN is a Senior Lecturer at Lancaster University.

STUDIES IN ENGLISH LANGUAGE

General editor
Merja Kytö (Uppsala University)

Editorial Board
Bas Aarts (University College London),
John Algeo (University of Georgia),
Susan Fitzmaurice (University of Sheffield),
Christian Mair (University of Freiburg),
Charles F. Meyer (University of Massachusetts)

The aim of this series is to provide a framework for original studies of English, both present-day and past. All books are based securely on empirical research, and represent theoretical and descriptive contributions to our knowledge of national and international varieties of English, both written and spoken. The series covers a broad range of topics and approaches, including syntax, phonology, grammar, vocabulary, discourse, pragmatics and sociolinguistics, and is aimed at an international readership.

Already published in this series

Christiane Meierkord: *Interactions across Englishes: Linguistic Choices in Local and International Contact Situations*
Haruko Momma: *From Philology to English Studies: Language and Culture in the Nineteenth Century*
Raymond Hickey (ed.): *Standards of English: Codified Varieties around the World*
Benedikt Szmrecsanyi: *Grammatical Variation in British English Dialects: A Study in Corpus-Based Dialectometry*
Daniel Schreier and Marianne Hundt (eds.): *English as a Contact Language*
Bas Aarts, Joanne Close, Geoffrey Leech and Sean Wallis (eds.): *The Verb Phrase in English: Investigating Recent Language Change with Corpora*
Martin Hilpert: *Constructional Change in English: Developments in Allomorphy, Word Formation, and Syntax*
Jakob R. E. Leimgruber: *Singapore English: Structure, Variation, and Usage*
Christoph Rühlemann: *Narrative in English Conversation: A Corpus Analysis of Storytelling*
Dagmar Deuber: *English in the Caribbean: Variation, Style and Standards in Jamaica and Trinidad*
Eva Berlage: *Noun Phrase Complexity in English*
Nicole Dehé: *Parentheticals in Spoken English: The Syntax-Prosody Relation*
Jock O. Wong: *The Culture of Singapore English*

Marianne Hundt (ed.): *Late Modern English Syntax*
Irma Taavitsainen, Merja Kytö, Claudia Claridge and Jeremy Smith (eds.): *Developments in English: Expanding Electronic Evidence*
Arne Lohmann: *English Coordinate Constructions: A Processing Perspective on Constituent Order*
Nuria Yáñez-Bouza: *Grammar, Rhetoric and Usage in English: Preposition Placement 1500–1900*
Anita Auer, Daniel Schreier and Richard J. Watts (eds.): *Letter Writing and Language Change*
John Flowerdew and Richard W. Forest: *Signalling Nouns in English: A Corpus-Based Discourse Approach*
Jeffrey P. Williams, Edgar W. Schneider, Peter Trudgill and Daniel Schreier (eds.): *Further Studies in the Lesser-Known Varieties of English*
Jack Grieve: *Regional Variation in Written American English*
Douglas Biber and Bethany Gray: *Grammatical Complexity in Academic English: Linguistic Change in Writing*
Gjertrud Flermoen Stenbrenden: *Long-Vowel Shifts in English, c. 1050–1700: Evidence from Spelling*
Zoya G. Proshina and Anna A. Eddy (eds.): *Russian English: History, Functions, and Features*
Raymond Hickey (ed.): *Listening to the Past: Audio Records of Accents of English*
Phillip Wallage: *Negation in Early English: Grammatical and Functional Change*
Marianne Hundt, Sandra Mollin and Simone E. Pfenninger (eds.): *The Changing English Language: Psycholinguistic Perspectives*
Joanna Kopaczyk and Hans Sauer (eds.): *Binomials in the History of English: Fixed and Flexible*
Alexander Haselow: *Spontaneous Spoken English: An Integrated Approach to the Emergent Grammar of Speech*
Christina Sanchez-Stockhammer: *English Compounds and Their Spelling*
David West Brown: *English and Empire: Language History, Dialect, and the Digital Archive*
Paula Rodríguez-Puente: *The English Phrasal Verb, 1650–present: History, Stylistic Drifts, and Lexicalisation*
Erik R. Thomas (ed.): *Mexican American English: Substrate Influence and the Birth of an Ethnolect*
Thomas Hoffmann: *English Comparative Correlatives: Diachronic and Synchronic Variation at the Lexicon-Syntax Interface*
Nuria Yáñez-Bouza, Emma Moore, Linda van Bergen and Willem B. Hollmann (eds.): *Categories, Constructions, and Change in English Syntax*

Earlier titles not listed are also available.

CATEGORIES, CONSTRUCTIONS, AND CHANGE IN ENGLISH SYNTAX

EDITED BY

NURIA YÁÑEZ-BOUZA
University of Vigo

EMMA MOORE
University of Sheffield

LINDA VAN BERGEN
University of Edinburgh

WILLEM B. HOLLMANN
Lancaster University

with the assistance of Ayumi Miura

CAMBRIDGE
UNIVERSITY PRESS

University Printing House, Cambridge CB2 8BS, United Kingdom

One Liberty Plaza, 20th Floor, New York, NY 10006, USA

477 Williamstown Road, Port Melbourne, VIC 3207, Australia

314-321, 3rd Floor, Plot 3, Splendor Forum, Jasola District Centre, New Delhi - 110025, India

103 Penang Road, #05-06/07, Visioncrest Commercial, Singapore 238467

Cambridge University Press is part of the University of Cambridge.

It furthers the University's mission by disseminating knowledge in the pursuit of education, learning and research at the highest international levels of excellence.

www.cambridge.org
Information on this title: www.cambridge.org/9781108411424
DOI: 10.1017/9781108303576

© Cambridge University Press 2019

This publication is in copyright. Subject to statutory exception and to the provisions of relevant collective licensing agreements, no reproduction of any part may take place without the written permission of Cambridge University Press.

First published 2019
First paperback edition 2022

A catalogue record for this publication is available from the British Library

ISBN 978-1-108-41956-7 Hardback
ISBN 978-1-108-41142-4 Paperback

Cambridge University Press has no responsibility for the persistence or accuracy of URLs for external or third-party internet websites referred to in this publication, and does not guarantee that any content on such websites is, or will remain, accurate or appropriate.

Contents

List of Figures   *page* ix
List of Tables   xi
List of Contributors   xiii
Acknowledgements   xix

Introduction: Analysing English Syntax Past and Present   1
Nuria Yáñez-Bouza, together with Emma Moore, Linda van Bergen, and Willem B. Hollmann

PART I: APPROACHES TO GRAMMATICAL CATEGORIES AND CATEGORIAL CHANGE   23

1. What Is Special about Pronouns?   25
   John Payne

2. What *For*?   54
   Bas Aarts

3. Whatever Happened to *Whatever*?   81
   Dan McColm and Graeme Trousdale

4. Are Comparative Modals Converging or Diverging in English? Different Answers from the Perspectives of Grammaticalisation and Constructionalisation   105
   Elizabeth Closs Traugott

5. The Definite Article in Old English: Evidence from Ælfric's *Grammar*   130
   Cynthia L. Allen

PART II: APPROACHES TO CONSTRUCTIONS AND
CONSTRUCTIONAL CHANGE   147

6. How Patterns Spread: The *To*-Infinitival Complement as
   a Case of Diffusional Change, or '*To*-Infinitives, and Beyond!'   149
   Bettelou Los

7. *Me Liketh/Lotheth* but *I Loue/Hate*: Impersonal/Non-Impersonal
   Boundaries in Old and Middle English   170
   Ayumi Miura

8. *That's Luck, If You Ask Me*: The Rise of an Intersubjective
   Comment Clause   190
   Laurel J. Brinton

9. Misreading and Language Change: A Foray into Qualitative
   Historical Linguistics   210
   Sylvia Adamson

10. The Conjunction *and* in Phrasal and Clausal Structures in
    the *Old Bailey Corpus*   234
    Merja Kytö and Erik Smitterberg

PART III: COMPARATIVE AND TYPOLOGICAL APPROACHES   251

11. The Role Played by Analogy in Processes of Language Change:
    The Case of English HAVE-*to* Compared to Spanish
    TENER-*que*   253
    Olga Fischer and Hella Olbertz

12. Modelling Step Change: The History of WILL-Verbs in
    Germanic   283
    Kersti Börjars and Nigel Vincent

13. Possessives World-Wide: Genitive Variation in Varieties
    of English   315
    Benedikt Heller and Benedikt Szmrecsanyi

14. American English: No Written Standard before the Twentieth
    Century?   336
    Christian Mair

References   366
Index   399

Figures

1.1	The main semantic relations	page 32
3.1	Distribution of *whatever* by function in COHA	91
3.2	Distribution of *whatever* in chunks in COHA	92
3.3	COHA VNC dendrogram	92
3.4	Distribution of *whatever* by function in COCA	93
3.5	Distribution of *whatever* in chunks in COCA	94
4.1	Model of a constructional hierarchy	109
4.2	Partial constructional network of eModE comparative modals	126
4.3	Partial constructional network of lModE comparative modals	127
8.1	Distribution of *if you ask me* by genre in COCA (1990–2015)	195
8.2	Distribution of *if you ask me* by period in COCA (1990–2015)	196
8.3	Postulated development of *if you ask me* from full biclausal structure	202
11.1a	The traditional scenario	254
11.1b	Our scenario	254
13.1	Distribution of genitive variants by variety in nine varieties of English	323
13.2	Distribution of genitive variants by genre in the entire dataset vs. the distributions in ICE-New Zealand and ICE-Philippines	324
13.3	Distribution of genitive variants by possessor animacy in the entire dataset vs. the distributions in ICE-Canada and ICE-Hong Kong	325
13.4	*S*-genitive proportion as a function of possessor length in nine varieties vs. the distributions in ICE-Canada and ICE-Great Britain	325

13.5	*S*-genitive proportion as a function of possessum length in nine varieties of English	326
13.6	Distribution of genitive variants by final sibilancy in the entire dataset vs. the distributions in ICE-Hong Kong and ICE-Philippines	327
13.7	Distribution of genitive variants by givenness of the possessor head in the entire dataset vs. the distributions in ICE-Canada and ICE-Hong Kong	328
13.8	*S*-genitive proportion as a function of text frequency of the possessor head in nine varieties of English	329
13.9	*S*-genitive proportion as a function of overall frequency of the possessor head in nine varieties of English	329
13.10	*S*-genitive proportion as a function of type-token ratio of the corpus texts in nine varieties of English	330
13.11	Conditional inference tree showing predictor splits that significantly (p < 0.01) influence genitive distribution in nine varieties of English	332
14.1	Move from *-our* to *-or* spellings in AmE (*Ngram Viewer*, AmE, 1800–1900)	342
14.2	Variation between *-our* and *-or* spellings in BrE (*Ngram Viewer*, BrE, 1800–2000)	344
14.3	The establishment of *toward* as the US norm (*Ngram Viewer*, AmE, 1870–1930)	345
14.4	Frequency of *had gotten*, followed by article (COHA, 1900s–2000s)	347
14.5	Frequency of *had got*, followed by article (COHA, 1900s–2000s)	347
14.6	*Had got* vs. *had gotten* in *get back* and *get over* (*Ngram Viewer*, AmE, 1950–2000)	349
14.7	*To-* and bare infinitives in British and American English (c. 1930–2006)	351
14.8	*Help* followed by *to*-infinitive, 1810s–2000s (COHA)	355
14.9	*Help* followed by bare infinitive, 1810s–2000s (COHA)	355
14.10	*Help* + *to*-infinitive: non-*horror aequi* environments, 1850s–1940s (COHA)	356
14.11	*Help* + bare infinitive: non-*horror aequi* environments, 1850s–1940s (COHA)	356
14.12	*To help* + *to*-infinitive, 1850s–1940s (COHA)	357
14.13	*To help* + bare infinitive, 1850s–1940s (COHA)	357

Tables

1.1	*Of*-PPs and the genitive alternation	page 50
3.1	Distribution of *whatever* in the COCA corpus per decade	89
3.2	Distribution of *whatever* in COHA per million words	93
3.3	Distribution of *whatever* in COCA per million words	94
4.1	Occurrence of auxiliaries with BETTER, RATHER, and SOONER in OBC	120
4.2	Differences between BETTER and RATHER, SOONER in OBC	125
5.1	SE with direct arguments	138
5.2	*Cyning* as a subject in Ælfric's *Grammar*	138
5.3	*Cyning* as the object of a preposition in Ælfric's *Grammar*	143
7.1	Tokens in YCOE	180
7.2	Tokens in PPCME2	180
7.3	Unambiguous Cause-subject constructions in YCOE	181
7.4	Unambiguous Cause-subject constructions in PPCME2	181
7.5	Animacy of the Target of Emotion in YCOE	186
7.6	Animacy of the Target of Emotion (other than God) in YCOE	187
7.7	Animacy of the Target of Emotion in PPCME2	187
8.1	Complements of direct condition *if you ask me* in COCA (random sample of 200)	194
8.2	Position of indirect condition *if you ask me* in COCA (random sample of 200)	195
8.3	Corpora and text collections used in this study	199
8.4	Syntax of *if you ask me* over time in COHA	203
10.1	Categories of witnesses sampled	238
10.2	Co-ordination with *and* by period	242
10.3	Co-ordination with *and* by gender	243
10.4	Co-ordination with *and* by period (female witnesses)	244

10.5	Co-ordination with *and* by period (male witnesses)	244
10.6	Co-ordination with *and* by social class	245
10.7	Co-ordination with *and* by period (higher-class witnesses)	246
10.8	Co-ordination with *and* by period (lower-class witnesses)	246
10.9	Co-ordination with *and* by gender (period 1)	249
10.10	Co-ordination with *and* by gender (period 2)	249
10.11	Co-ordination with *and* by class (period 1)	249
10.12	Co-ordination with *and* by class (period 2)	250
11.1	HAVE, MUST, and BE with *nede*	262
11.2	Frequencies of verbal expressions of modal necessity in spoken Modern Spanish	265
11.3	The quantitative relations between possession-based expressions of necessity	275
12.1	Present tense of Old Icelandic WILL	291
12.2	Structural properties of WILL	299
12.3	Desirability and its source as intersecting features	302
14.1	Complementation of *prevent* in the Brown family of corpora	359
14.2	*To-* vs. bare infinitives after *help* in British and American English, 1800–2006 (ARCHER and Brown family)	362
14.3	Proportion of *to-* vs. bare infinitives after *help* in British and American English, 1930–2006 (Brown family)	363
14.4	Frequency of *to help* as percentage of all verbal uses of *help*, 1850s–1940s (COHA)	363
14.5	Percentage of *horror aequi*, 1850s–1940s (COHA), as computed from Figure 14.12 and Figure 14.13	363
14.6	Frequency of non-finite complements of *help* and *prevent* in B-LOB, LOB, F-LOB, and BE06	364
14.7	Frequency of non-finite complements of *help* in B-Brown, Brown, Frown, and AmE06	365

Contributors

BAS AARTS is Professor of English Linguistics and Director of the Survey of English Usage at University College London. His publications include: *Syntactic Gradience* (2007), *Oxford Modern English Grammar* (2011), *The Verb Phrase in English: Investigating Recent Language Change with Corpora* (edited with Joanne Close, Geoffrey Leech, and Sean Wallis, Cambridge University Press, 2013), *The Oxford Dictionary of English Grammar* (edited with Sylvia Chalker and Edmund Weiner, 2nd edn. 2014), *The Oxford Handbook of English Grammar* (edited with Jill Bowie and Gergana Popova, forthcoming), as well as book chapters and articles in journals. He is a founding editor of the journal *English Language and Linguistics* (Cambridge University Press).

SYLVIA ADAMSON is Emeritus Professor of Linguistics and Literary History in the School of English at the University of Sheffield and a Professorial Affiliate in the Department of Linguistics at the University of Cambridge. Her research and publications range across the fields of literature, language, and linguistics, with particular interests in grammaticalisation, subjectivity, narrative, rhetoric, and the history of English from 1500.

CYNTHIA L. ALLEN is a Fellow Emerita at the Australian National University and a Fellow of the Australian Academy of the Humanities. Her career investigating syntactic change in English began with her PhD from the University of Massachusetts at Amherst researching topics in the diachronic syntax of English. Her publications include monographs and articles investigating the relationship between morphological and syntactic change, especially in the transition from Old to early Middle English.

KERSTI BÖRJARS is Professor of Linguistics at the University of Manchester and Professor (II) of Nordic Languages at Oslo University. Her research is focused on morphosyntax and diachronic linguistics and she uses Lexical-Functional Grammar for analysis.

LAUREL J. BRINTON is a Professor of English Language at the University of British Columbia, Vancouver. Her research interests include grammaticalisation and lexicalisation, historical pragmatics, phrasal verbs and composite predicates, and verbal aspect. Her most recent publications include the edited textbook *English Historical Linguistics: Approaches and Perspectives* (Cambridge University Press, 2017) and the monograph *The Evolution of Pragmatic Markers in English: Pathways of Change* (Cambridge University Press, 2017) as well as five readers in *The History of English* co-edited with Alexander Bergs (2017). She is co-editor of *English Language and Linguistics* (Cambridge University Press).

OLGA FISCHER is Emeritus Professor of Germanic Linguistics at the University of Amsterdam. She is a contributor to *The Cambridge History of the English Language*, vol. II (Cambridge University Press, 1992), co-author of *The Syntax of Early English* (Cambridge University Press, 2000), and author of *Morphosyntactic Change: Functional and Formal Perspectives* (2007). She has edited many books and published widely in international journals and handbooks on syntactic change, grammaticalisation, analogy, and iconicity. She is an initiator and co-editor of the Iconicity Research Project and of the 'Iconicity in Language and Literature' series.

BENEDIKT HELLER is Postdoctoral Researcher at Justus Liebig University, Giessen. During his PhD, which he obtained from KU Leuven, he focused on syntactic variation in English around the world. Heller is most interested in quantitative approaches to linguistics and is currently working on data-driven methods to describe variation in World Englishes.

WILLEM B. HOLLMANN is a Senior Lecturer at Lancaster University. Having obtained his PhD from the University of Manchester, where he focused on causative constructions, he currently does research on aspects of cognitive-typological linguistic theory, often using synchronic and diachronic corpus evidence. He also has an interest in sociolinguistics and dialect grammar, particularly the British English dialect of Lancashire.

MERJA KYTÖ is Professor of English Language at Uppsala University, Sweden, specialising in English historical linguistics, corpus linguistics, historical pragmatics, and manuscript studies. She has participated in the compilation of the *Helsinki Corpus of English Texts* and *A Corpus of English Dialogues 1560–1760*. She co-edited *Nineteenth-Century English: Stability and Change* (Cambridge University Press, 2006) and *Corpus Linguistics: An International Handbook* (2008). She was associate editor of the *Records of the Salem Witch-Hunt* (Cambridge University Press, 2009), co-author of *Early Modern English Dialogues: Spoken Interaction as Writing* (Cambridge University Press, 2010), and co-editor and co-compiler of *An Electronic Text Edition of Depositions 1560–1760*, a manuscript-based corpus accompanying the volume *Testifying to Language and Life in Early Modern England* (2011). She recently edited *English Corpus Linguistics: Crossing Paths* (2012). She is co-editor of the *ICAME Journal* and associate editor of *Studia Neophilologica*. Her current research projects include work on intensifiers in early speech-related texts.

BETTELOU LOS is Forbes Professor of English Language at the University of Edinburgh. She has held teaching and research positions at the University of Amsterdam, the Vrije Universiteit Amsterdam, and Radboud University Nijmegen. She published *The Rise of the To-Infinitive* (2005) and *A Historical Syntax of English* (2015). She edited, with Ans van Kemenade, *The Handbook of the History of English* (2006), and, with Anneli Meurman-Solin and María José López-Couso, *Information Structure and Syntactic Change in the History of English* (2012). She co-authored *Morphosyntactic Change: A Comparative Study of Particles and Prefixes* (Cambridge University Press, 2012). Her research interests are diachronic syntax, the history of English, and the role of information structure in syntactic change.

CHRISTIAN MAIR has been a Professor of English Linguistics at the University of Freiburg in Germany since 1990. His research over the past three decades has focused on the corpus-based description of modern English grammar and on variability and change in Standard Englishes world-wide. It has resulted in the publication of several monographs (among them *Infinitival Complement Clauses in English: A Study of Syntax in Discourse*, Cambridge University Press, 1990; and *Twentieth-Century English: History, Variation and Standardization*, Cambridge University Press, 2006) and more than one hundred contributions to scholarly journals and edited works. Mair's current research focuses on the role of global English in a multilingual world, on multilingual and nonstandard language practices in computer-mediated communication, and on the sociolinguistics of diaspora and migration. From 2011 to 2014 he served as President of ISLE, the International Society for the Linguistics of English.

DAN MCCOLM is a PhD student at the University of Edinburgh under the supervision of Dr Graeme Trousdale and Dr Nik Gisborne. His thesis investigates the diachronic development of the *way*-construction in English, German, and Dutch. His research interests focus on corpus linguistics, historical linguistics, and statistical analysis techniques of corpus data.

AYUMI MIURA is Associate Professor at the Graduate School of Language and Culture, Osaka University, Japan. She obtained her PhD at the University of Manchester, and a revised version of her thesis was published under the title *Middle English Verbs of Emotion and Impersonal Constructions: Verb Meaning and Syntax in Diachrony* (2015). She is primarily interested in the crossroads of syntax, semantics, and lexicography in the history of English, especially Old and Middle English. She maintains the website 'HEL on the Web', a collection of online resources useful for studying, teaching, and researching the history of the English language.

EMMA MOORE is Professor of Sociolinguistics at the University of Sheffield. Her research explores how individuals and communities use language to construct social styles and identities. Much of her published research has focused on the morphosyntax used by adolescents, but the methods and forms of analysis have enabled her to address the relationship between language and social factors more generally. Her most recent work comes out of an AHRC research grant exploring language, variation, and change on the Isles of Scilly. She has published in the *Journal of Sociolinguistics*, *Language Variation and Change*, *Language in Society*, and most recently in *Language*. She is a co-editor of the volumes *Language and A Sense of Place: Studies in Language and Region* (2017) and *Social Meaning and Linguistic Variation: Theorizing the Third Wave* (forthcoming), both published with Cambridge University Press.

HELLA OLBERTZ completed her PhD on verbal periphrases in Spanish at the University of Amsterdam in 1996. Presently, she is Visiting Professor at the State University of Feira de Santana (Brazil) and Guest Researcher at the University of Amsterdam. She works on grammaticalisation, mainly in Spanish and Portuguese, with particular interest in modality, aspect, and related fields.

List of Contributors

JOHN PAYNE is currently Professor of Linguistics in the Division of Linguistics and English Language at the University of Manchester. His principal areas of interest are English syntax and semantics, linguistic typology, and grammatical theory. He was a contributor to *The Cambridge Grammar of the English Language* (Cambridge University Press, 2002), co-authoring the chapters on nouns and noun phrases, and on co-ordination and supplementation.

ERIK SMITTERBERG is a Reader in English and a Senior Lecturer in English Linguistics at Uppsala University, Sweden. His main research interests are language change, late Modern English syntax, Modern English punctuation, and corpus linguistics. He is the author of *The Progressive in 19th-Century English: A Process of Integration* (2005) and a co-editor of *Nineteenth-Century English: Stability and Change* (Cambridge University Press, 2006). He has contributed chapters to a number of recent handbook projects, among them *The Cambridge Handbook of English Corpus Linguistics* (edited by Douglas Biber and Randi Reppen, Cambridge University Press, 2015) and *The Cambridge Handbook of English Historical Linguistics* (edited by Merja Kytö and Päivi Pahta, Cambridge University Press, 2016). He is also the compiler of *The Corpus of Nineteenth-Century Newspaper English* (CNNE). He is currently working on colloquialisation phenomena in late Modern English.

BENEDIKT SZMRECSANYI is Associate Professor at the Department of Linguistics at KU Leuven. His research interests focus on variation studies (synchronic and diachronic), probabilistic grammar, language complexity, geolinguistics, and dialect typology. Recent books include *Grammatical Variation in British English Dialects: A Study in Corpus-Based Dialectometry* (Cambridge University Press, 2013) and *Aggregating Dialectology, Typology, and Register Analysis: Linguistic Variation in Text and Speech* (edited with Bernhard Wälchli, 2014).

ELIZABETH CLOSS TRAUGOTT is Professor Emerita of Linguistics and English at Stanford University. She obtained her PhD in English Linguistics at the University of California, Berkeley, with a focus on exploring how the history of English syntax could be analysed in terms of transformational grammar. She has co-authored books on linguistics and literature (with Mary Pratt), grammaticalisation (with Paul Hopper), and constructionalisation (with Graeme Trousdale). Her current research focuses on ways to bring construction grammar to bear on accounts of the development of pragmatic markers in English.

GRAEME TROUSDALE works as a Senior Lecturer in the department of Linguistics and English Language at the University of Edinburgh. His research interests are in cognitive linguistics and language change, particularly in the history of English. He is the author of *An Introduction to English Sociolinguistics* (2010), co-author of *Constructionalization and Constructional Changes* with Elizabeth Closs Traugott (2013), and the co-editor of *The Oxford Handbook of Construction Grammar* with Thomas Hoffmann (2013).

LINDA VAN BERGEN is a Lecturer in the department of Linguistics and English Language at the University of Edinburgh. Most of her research to date has focused on aspects of the syntax of early English that are related to word order and/or negation, which has led to publications on the behaviour of Old English pronouns, the *ne*+infinitive construction, and the dialectal distribution of negative contraction in Old English. In addition, she has published work on late Modern English syntax, specifically early progressive passives.

NIGEL VINCENT is Professor Emeritus of General and Romance Linguistics at the University of Manchester. His research interests lie in the history of Latin and the Romance languages, in particular Italian and the dialects of Italy, and in the analysis and formal modelling of the mechanisms of morphosyntactic change within the framework of Lexical-Functional Grammar. He is a Fellow of the British Academy and a Member of the Academia Europaea. He has held an Erskine Fellowship at the University of Canterbury (New Zealand) and visiting posts at the Universities of Copenhagen, Pavia, and Rome III.

NURIA YÁÑEZ-BOUZA is Senior Lecturer in English Language at the University of Vigo, where she held a position as Senior Research Fellow 'Ramón y Cajal'. She also holds an Honorary Research Fellowship at the University of Manchester, where she worked as a lecturer after obtaining her PhD. Her main research interests lie in historical sociolinguistics, prescriptivism, and corpus linguistics, with a focus on the eighteenth century. She is the author of *Grammar, Rhetoric and Usage in English: Preposition Placement 1500–1900* (Cambridge University Press, 2015), and has collaborated in various projects involving the compilation of historical corpora and databases, such as ARCHER, *Eighteenth-Century English Grammars Database*, *Eighteenth-Century English Phonology Database*, *Mary Hamilton Papers*, and *APU Writing and Reading Corpus 1979–1988*.

Acknowledgements

The editors wish to thank Merja Kytö for her encouragement, support, and judicious advice throughout, and for accepting the book in the Studies in English Language series. We are very grateful to Helen Barton of Cambridge University Press, for both her constant assistance and her unfailingly positive attitude. We especially thank all contributors, who have generously given so much of their time during the production of this volume. We also thank all reviewers, whose constructive comments on individual chapters have been so useful and illuminating: Anita Auer, Bert Cornillie, Hendrik De Smet, Nikolas Gisborne, Caterina Guardamagna, Jane Hodson, Minna Nevala, Catherine O'Connor, Gabriel Ozon, Ann Taylor, Elizabeth Closs Traugott, Rob Truswell, Daniël van Olmen, Graham Williams, and Ilse Wischer.

Finally, we are particularly indebted to Ayumi Miura for her invaluable contribution as editorial assistant on the project, not only in her conscientious work checking references, house-style editing, and proof-reading, but also in making many suggestions for improvements to the content and coherence of the volume.

Introduction: Analysing English Syntax Past and Present

Nuria Yáñez-Bouza,
together with Emma Moore, Linda van Bergen,
and Willem B. Hollmann

This book is an exploration of categories, constructions, and change in English syntax. A great many books are published on the syntax of English, both monographs and edited volumes, and yet another may seem unnecessary. However, we felt more than justified in adding to the sizeable literature here for two reasons. The first, to borrow from Richard M. Hogg and David Denison's justification for *A History of the English Language*, is that 'one of the beauties of the language is its ability to show continuous change and flexibility while in some sense remaining the same. And if that is true of the language, it is also true of the study of the language' (2006: xi). Central to our book is a focus on the syntax of the English language, through a wide variety of orientations that a collective work makes possible. Thus the volume aims to embrace the wide variety of approaches and methodologies in the current analysis of English syntactic structure, variation, and change, both past and present, through a careful curation of new case studies by established and emerging scholars in the field. Such breadth of scope, together with a specific focus on English syntax, sets the collection apart from most others.

The second reason is that this book is dedicated to David Denison, Professor Emeritus of English Linguistics at the University of Manchester, former Smith Professor of English Language and Medieval Literature, Honorary Doctor of Uppsala University, and Fellow of the British Academy, but above all, academic supervisor, colleague, and friend to the editors and contributors. This volume offers chapters based on original research and serves to celebrate David's rich, diverse, innovative, and inspiring work over the years as well as his legacy as supervisor, colleague, and greatly valued friend. Each of the editors was fortunate enough to be supervised by David. Our time at the University of Manchester coincided with the 'Langwidge Sandwidge', an informal lunchtime meeting where staff and students met 'to socialise and to share interesting nuggets of data, perplexing questions of theory, or trial drafts of work-in-progress' (Sylvia Adamson, personal communication). Although David was never any less than very generous with his time, this gave his students and colleagues even more access to his kindness (manifested in the sharing of his chocolate biscuit tin) and his keen intellect (which was always worn lightly). Not all scholars are able to be both conscientious and convivial, but this combination has endured throughout his career. When we were writing this introduction, Bettelou Los reminded us of David's love of a 'shindig': occasions that were not just sociable – they often resulted in compelling and significant research outputs (see, for instance, Denison and Vincent 1997). David encouraged us to start with the data, to work with others to best understand it, and, in doing so, to continue inching the field forward. In the words of Olga Fischer (personal communication), he has always been 'good at the nitty gritty', with a 'keen eye for any new constructions arising in English'. Whilst not a Festschrift, we think that this volume reflects all of David's best characteristics.

The fourteen chapters herein, written by nineteen scholars, are grouped into three parts: (I) approaches to grammatical categories and categorial change (five chapters); (II) approaches to constructions and constructional change (five chapters); and (III) comparative and typological approaches (four chapters). The contributors in Part I all deal with the fuzzy status of different grammatical categories and explore syntactic change across categories: **John Payne** on the special status of pronouns in the *of*-PP of genitive constructions; **Bas Aarts** on the analysis of *for* as a preposition or as a subordinator/complementiser; **Dan McColm and Graeme Trousdale** on the recent development of *whatever*; **Elizabeth Closs Traugott** on the converging and diverging development of the comparative modals BETTER, RATHER, and SOONER; and **Cynthia L. Allen** on the existence of the definite article in Old English (OE). The chapters in Part II are concerned with factors involved in English syntax and syntactic change that often go beyond the strictly syntactic. Thus, **Bettelou Los** revisits the way in which patterns spread with regard to the *to*-infinitival complement as a case of analogy and diffusional change; **Ayumi Miura** explores the interface between syntax and lexico-semantics with regard to impersonal and non-impersonal constructions in OE and Middle English (ME); **Laurel J. Brinton** examines the rise of the intersubjective comment clause *if you ask me* in terms of its syntax and pragmatics; **Sylvia Adamson** addresses the role of misreading and prescriptivism in language change from the perspective of literary and textual criticism; and **Merja Kytö and**

Introduction: Analysing English Syntax Past and Present 3

Erik Smitterberg investigate the role of sociohistorical factors in the use of the conjunction *and* and its double function in phrasal and clausal structures. The shared focus in Part III is on the analysis of English syntax from a comparative and typological approach, comparing British English with other varieties of English and with other Germanic languages, as well as Romance. **Olga Fischer and Hella Olbertz** reconsider the role of analogy by comparing the case of English HAVE-*to* and Spanish TENER-*que*; **Kersti Börjars and Nigel Vincent** analyse the history of WILL-verbs in various Germanic languages in addition to English such as Danish, Dutch, German, Icelandic, and Swedish; **Benedikt Heller and Benedikt Szmrecsanyi** investigate genitive variation in nine varieties of English; and **Christian Mair** closes the volume with a corpus-based analysis of a number of variants in American and British English.

One of the (many) strengths in David Denison's work is his artful ability to explore the syntax of English by combining synchrony and diachrony. Back in 1993, he observed that a 'renewed interest' in historical change brought together the two traditions of diachronic and synchronic linguistics, and that '[t]he explicitness of current linguistic theory should provide better explanations of historical change, while historical facts can play their part in testing and shaping linguistic theory' (Denison 1993: ix). Both synchronic and diachronic work on English syntax are currently thriving, and the range of research being done in this field would not be adequately reflected if we were to restrict the volume to either Present-day English (PDE) syntax or to historical work. In an attempt to remain faithful to Denison's core approach, we offer a number of case studies concerning the syntax of English that are synchronic (Aarts, Heller and Szmrecsanyi, Payne), that trace the recent history of English (Brinton, Mair, McColm and Trousdale), and that deal with the earlier history of English (Adamson, Allen, Fischer and Olbertz, Kytö and Smitterberg, Miura). In this way we also adhere to one of the guiding principles of *The Cambridge History of the English Language* series of volumes in that 'a satisfactory understanding of English (or any other language) cannot be achieved on the basis of one of these [i.e. synchrony or diachrony] alone' (Hogg 1992: xvi).

A second major strength in Denison's work is his dexterity in combining theoretical considerations with traditional philology, and, furthermore, combining these with meticulous analyses of data made possible by methodological advances in recent corpus linguistics. As he himself put it, before the 1970s '[h]istorical syntax was largely synchronic, concerned as it often was with the description of patterns in one author or text or period', but increasingly, as new and more corpora became available, these resources 'were mined for the relative frequency of rival [syntactic] patterns' (Denison 2012: 247). Denison himself comments on his 'eclectic' methodology in his 1993 book: '[n]o linguistic discussion is ever wholly value- or theory-free, of course, but my choice of an eclectic approach is deliberate' (1993: x). Similarly, our aim has not been to present a volume that focuses on a specific theoretical approach; rather, we aim to show the wealth and breadth of the study of syntax (including morphosyntax where relevant), both theoretically and empirically. So, chapters concerned with theory address the state of the art in the study of English syntax from the perspective of grammaticalisation and intersubjectivity (Börjars and Vincent, Brinton, Mair, Traugott), gradualness (Allen, Los), Lexical-Functional Grammar (Börjars and Vincent, Payne), Construction Grammar (McColm and Trousdale, Traugott), analogy and diffusional change (Fischer and Olbertz, Los), historical sociolinguistics (Kytö and Smitterberg), and literary and textual criticism (Adamson). Comparative and typological approaches also feature prominently, including analyses of (morpho)syntactic features in national and regional varieties of English (Heller and Szmrecsanyi, Mair) and in other Germanic (Börjars and Vincent) and Romance languages (Fischer and Olbertz). Methodologically, this volume includes studies conducted using traditional methods such as conscientious philological work (Adamson, Allen), thorough work based on large corpora (Brinton, Kytö and Smitterberg, Mair, McColm and Trousdale), alongside work with newly applied methods such as conditional inference trees in probabilistic grammar (Heller and Szmrecsanyi), and dictionaries for the study of historical syntax (Miura). All in all, the chapters provide materials for investigating some of the central topics currently under discussion in English syntax, relating to both data and analysis (see Denison 1993: ix).

Empirically, in addition to the types of change dependent on internal factors and factors below the level of conscious awareness, there are changes brought about or influenced by external and social factors, including the speaker's conscious choice of competing variants. As Barbara Strang has noted, 'the possibilities of variation, the matrix of change, in grammar, are very great indeed' (1970: 69), and in Hogg and Denison's words, '[f]rom the continual, dynamic interaction of internal and external factors comes what is by any standards a richly varied language' (2006: xii). Hence the present volume includes contributions that consider some of these latter kinds of factors, namely gender and social class (Kytö and Smitterberg), prescriptive norms (Adamson), and the role of standardisation (Mair). Overall, the emphasis is laid naturally on the syntax of written language, but an attempt has also been made to consider speech-based or speech-like data in some of the chapters, both in earlier historical periods (Kytö and Smitterberg, Traugott) and in recent English (McColm and Trousdale). Rissanen observed that '[i]t is a constant source of frustration for the language historian that all observations and analyses of early periods have to be based on written evidence only, while the importance of speech in the development of the language is self-evident' (1999: 188). Yet Rissanen also pointed out that 'by a careful comparison of texts which stand at different distances from spoken language [...] it is possible to present hypotheses about whether a certain construction is favoured or avoided in the spoken language of the period' (1999: 188).

As previously mentioned, the contributions in each part share a focus on syntax from a similar angle, yet they vary in terms of the feature(s) examined, the theoretical perspective, and the methodology adopted. Our ultimate aim is to maintain and stimulate interest in a widely investigated subject in which much work has been done and yet much more remains to be done; the varied range of perspectives within each part allows us to achieve this. We believe that the result is a body of research which substantially adds to the current study of the syntax of the English language.

What follows is an outline of each chapter in the volume, summarising the main objectives, methods, and results.

Part I

Part I concerns approaches to grammatical categories and categorial change, with contributions addressing the 'fuzzy' status of various grammatical categories and exploring syntactic change across categories.

John Payne opens the volume with research into PDE which questions old categorial distinctions. He raises the issue of what is special about pronouns, in particular (the restrictions in) the use of personal pronouns in the genitive construction with *of*-PP, which contrasts with the alternative patterns *s*-genitive and oblique genitive, as in **the brother of him, his brother, that brother of his*, respectively. More precisely, he provides a new corpus-based study of 'the semantic relations permitted to the *of*-PP construction as a totality' which offers an innovative approach: the restriction lies not in the head of the construction, as is common in previous work (see Heller and Szmrecsanyi this volume), but in the personal pronoun dependent. This approach, it is argued, allows us to identify semantic relations between the head and the dependent where the genitive alternation is not possible, whereas recent studies based on sophisticated regression models naturally exclude truly categorical contexts and contexts in which variation is not attested. The data are drawn from the *British National Corpus* (BNC*web*), both spoken and written material (1960–1993). In terms of relative token frequency, the results show that three semantic relations predominate: (i) quantity, as in *And there was a rare lot of them*; (ii) theme, as in *Some even had photographs of it on their walls*; and (iii) location, as in *she had fallen on top of him*. A further two are relatively frequent: (iv) part-whole, as in *You are that part of me that I cut off*; and (v) property, as in *too stunned by the sheer beauty of it all*. The remainder are 'a diverse residue of other examples', including sixteen different subsets, some of which are attested with just a single example. The analysis provides new insights not only with regard to the semantic relations participating in the genitive alternation between *of*-PP and *s*-genitive (e.g. theme, location, part-whole, property), but it also sheds new light on the behaviour of semantic relations in which there is no alternation and only the *of*-PP is attested (e.g. quantity, subset, collection, container). Thus, this case study qualitatively confirms claims made in previous research that 'the set of semantic relations available to the *of*-PP construction is a superset of those available to the *s*-genitive'. As far as the status of pronouns is concerned, Payne's data argue against Lyons' (1986) intuitive judgement that personal pronouns only reluctantly occur as dependents in *of*-PP constructions, showing rather that they can occur in a wide range of semantic relations, including those in which the *s*-genitive is prone to occur.

Like Payne, **Bas Aarts** deals with PDE and also revisits old categories, in this case taking the range of functions of English *for* as the basis of his study. He proposes an analysis of the lexical item *for* as always being a preposition, which can then take part in constructions with phrase complements or clausal complements. He does not find previous analyses of *for* as a subordinator or complementiser convincing, and considers some of the labels used in the literature ambiguous. The chapter first offers a detailed account of the guises of *for* in a wide array of constructions: (i) [*for* + NP], the traditional conception of the item as a preposition, whether as a complement, as in *You can't blame her for that really, can you?*, or as an adjunct, as in *Hold it for a moment*; (ii) *for* + finite clause, commonly seen as a formal subordinating conjunction, as in *'I'm afraid I've always been bad at names,' she told him for she'd no recollection of him*; (iii) [*for* [NP *to* VP]], which can occur syntactically as a subject or subject predicative, as in *The idea was for me to see the material*; as the complement or modifier of a head (typically verb, adjective, noun), as in *where the Mayor has given permission for them to sleep*; or as the focus element in a pseudocleft construction, as in *What I want is for it to continue the way it is at the moment*. Before presenting his own analysis, Aarts discusses the labels and arguments put forward in the literature and critically reviews a number of works. He takes issue in particular with Huddleston and Pullum *et al.* (2002) and Radford (2004) for considering *for* to be a subordinator, questioning each of their arguments on syntactic and/or semantic grounds. In his view, there are strong reasons in favour of categorising *for* as a preposition instead of a subordinator. Aarts' analysis simplifies the lexicon entries for a number of verbs, as illustrated with *long* and *prefer*, and the treatment of the constructions [*for* [NP *to* VP]] and [*for* [(NP) V-*ing*]], solving the close parallelism in the syntactic role of *for* and *that* in sentences such as *That's the best course for you to take* and *That's the best course that you can take*. Furthermore, it simplifies the historical account of *for* ... *to* constructions without resorting to theories of reanalysis from preposition-*for* to subordinator-*for*.

Dan McColm and Graeme Trousdale study the fuzzy category of interjections; in particular, the development of *whatever* as a new interjection and discourse marker in the recent history of English, within a Construction Grammar framework. Methodologically, the authors offer a quantitative and qualitative analysis of data drawn from the *Corpus of Historical American English* (COHA, 1810–present) and the *Corpus of Contemporary American English* (COCA, 1990–2017); the qualitative analysis is supplemented with data from the ENCOW16A subcorpus of *Corpora from the Web* (2012–2014). The three corpora were searched for *whatever* plus a number of additional variants, such as *wev* and *whatev(s)*. In addition, in ENCOW16A the authors observe forms such as *whoevs*, *howev*, *whenev*, and *wherev* which also function as discourse markers. This study has two main aims: first, to complement previous work by Brinton (2017) on the pathways of change in the evolution of pragmatic markers, and, second, to extend the discussion by means of a quantitative analysis of the patterns identified which can help us distinguish interjections from other word classes.

Theoretically, the authors argue that the form and function of *whatever* in contemporary English is not satisfactorily explained by the processes of grammaticalisation, lexicalisation, or intersubjectification alone, since the diachronic path followed from *whatever* > *whatevs* > *wevs* is atypical, and, besides, according to Brinton (2017), there are two potential syntactic sources for the development of its pragmatic function – a type of general extender and a clause of the type *whatever you say/think*. Instead, McColm and Trousdale carry out a closer inspection of this fuzziness from the perspective of constructionalisation, looking at aspects of the nature of directionality in language change and considering what the authors here refer to as *bolstering*. The study is thus driven by research questions highlighting the central quantitative and qualitative aspects of developments in the recent history of the forms.

Before dealing with the data and the results, the chapter offers an account of the forms and functions of *whatever* in PDE. The authors classify the use of *whatever* into nine different types. The diachronic trends and the synchronic distribution of the item and its variants reveal that some functions of *whatever* have decreased in frequency (e.g. exhaustive conditional, as in *Whatever was the purpose of his visit, it was not long continued*); some have increased their use (especially the reduced forms, as in *No one ever made the argument you just summarized there, so whatevs*); while some others have remained frequent (relative determinative, as in *I will partake of whatever you have for supper*). All in all, McColm and Trousdale argue for 'an approach to grammatical change which privileges a view of language as a conceptual network of constructions at various levels of generality, and change as a change to the links between nodes in that network'.

Elizabeth Closs Traugott focuses on categorial change of the comparative modals BETTER/RATHER/SOONER. Her chapter explores the historical syntax of each form and complements accounts of the development of these from a grammaticalisation perspective (reported in the literature) with a constructionalisation perspective. The former approach suggests that by means of reduction and erosion the three comparative modals have converged overall, that is, they have evolved in the same direction and thus are part of the same category in PDE, taking discrete micro-steps and changing one feature at a time. The Construction Grammar approach, however, points to a different perspective on directionality, in particular that BETTER has diverged from the path followed by RATHER and SOONER. The theoretical question raised and addressed by Traugott is thus how to conceptualise these diachronic syntactic changes. The underlying argument is that historically each of these changes is considered a 'constructional change', and that the accumulation of these constructional changes 'may lead to constructionalisation', that is, 'the development of a form$_{new}$-meaning$_{new}$ construction'. The three research questions raised in the chapter evolve around the evidence for the emergence of the three micro-constructions under consideration, the type of subschema relationship between the three constructions, and the kind of contribution added by a constructional approach to a grammaticalisation approach to the data.

The evidence discussed by Traugott is rich and varied, including the *Middle English Dictionary* (*MED*), *A Corpus of English Dialogues 1560–1760* (CED), the *Corpus of Early English Correspondence Sampler* (CEECS), and the *Old Bailey Corpus* (OBC). On the rise of the comparative modals, Traugott argues that RATHER was constructionalised as a modal by Shakespeare's time, and that its use often involved negative semantic prosody. Similarly, SOONER seems to be well established as a modal in the sixteenth century and also shows a tendency for being used with negative semantics. Slightly different is the emergence of *had better*: its comparative modal meaning is not entrenched until the early eighteenth century, when the new meaning is paired with the new form (i.e. a case of constructionalisation). In a second step, the author considers the late Modern English (lModE) period, a crucial era for exploring the directionality of change and how the micro-constructions were organised. A clear picture emerges here, in that *had* occurs with the three modals, but the differences observed in their historical distribution point to RATHER and SOONER forming a subschema together, vis-à-vis BETTER. In the course of their development, the three comparative modals have become more similar in terms of their formal reduction but distinct in terms of their semantics. Regarding the analytical frameworks, constructionalisation has the added value of considering semantics as well as a formal analysis. Crucially, this leads to different clines: BETTER > SOONER > RATHER in the grammaticalisation approach; BETTER > RATHER > SOONER in the constructionalisation approach.

The final chapter in Part I is also diachronic in nature, but focuses on OE. Like Payne, **Cynthia L. Allen** is concerned with categories within the noun phrase, and, like Payne and Aarts, she revisits old labels with new data and from a new theoretical angle. The category involved here is the 'definite article'. More precisely, this chapter addresses the question whether this category already existed in OE by considering new evidence on the use of SE. A crucial point is made by the author at the start: the fact that surviving OE texts do not document an element which behaves exactly like what in PDE is labelled 'definite article' does not necessarily imply that OE did not have this category. The two inspiring sources for Allen's research are Crisma (2011) and Denison (2006). According to the former study, the definite article was in regular use in OE prose from the late ninth century onwards, consistently in some syntactic positions, variably in others. The latter study is relevant for the pathway of change of this category. In Denison's re-examination of the similarities and differences in OE between a number of categories such as pronouns, adjectives, and determiners, he argues that the boundaries across categories are blurred in OE, and that in ME they continue to be so, developing not through sudden reanalysis but through incremental change.

In her chapter Allen turns to Ælfric's *Grammar*, a late OE text which is not often used for evidence on syntax, given that it is a grammar of Latin, not of English. Allen meticulously checked the English translations of Latin sentences in the *Grammar* that lacked any determiner, arguing that Ælfric's use of SE in such cases gives evidence that can help us to identify contexts in which he considered its use to be essential. This method contributes to previous work in early English by presenting negative evidence that cannot be retrieved in corpus studies. The qualitative analysis, based on a careful philological study of each instance documented in Ælfric's *Grammar*, supplementary data from Ælfric's homilies, and a case study of the noun *cyning*, corroborate Crisma's (2011) claims. On the one hand, definiteness was marked obligatorily for subjects and objects ('direct arguments') in the *Grammar*. Allen thus argues that the reverse can also hold true, that is, the absence of SE is likely to imply that 'Ælfric intended his readers to understand an indefinite interpretation'. On the other hand, the use of the definite article SE was optional and variable in the context of prepositional objects (PObj), which in some ways behave differently from PDE; their use is difficult to pin down to one particular reason or context, be it lexical or grammatical. A search for the definite count noun *cyning* indicates that definiteness marking of *cyning* was more or less the rule at a time when such marking exhibited more variation with other nouns as PObj. Thus Allen recalls and supports Denison's argument that the increasing use of definite articles in this kind of construction may have developed through gradience rather than through an abrupt change in the use of the definite determiner in general.

Part II

Part II in this volume concerns approaches to constructions and constructional change; more precisely, the chapters here consider diverse factors involved in English syntax and syntactic change that often go beyond the strictly syntactic.

Starting with the *to*-infinitive construction, **Bettelou Los** investigates how different types of analogy can account for the diffusional change of the *to*-infinitival complement in the early stages of English. Although some of the stages are not directly observable because they occurred before the recorded period of OE, Los argues that the distribution of the construction in OE makes it possible to identify the niche in which it had originated and to construct a scenario for its spread. In essence, this chapter revisits previous work by Los (2005) in light of new insights from De Smet's (2013) recent study of the spread of complementation patterns in the gerund construction during the early Modern English (eModE) period. Los claims that the four successive stages proposed by De Smet can be applied to the spread of the *to*-infinitive. Furthermore, Los postulates that this account of change by means of analogy may also shed new light on the rise of the *to*-infinitival Exceptional Case-Marking (ECM) construction, which is here presented as Stage V.

The account in this chapter explains how patterns of complementation spread through gradual diffusion from (I) *narrow paradigmatic analogy*, to (II) *semantic analogy*, to (III) *indirect paradigmatic analogy*, and to (IV) *broad paradigmatic analogy*. According to Los, the process included 'abrupt gearshifts' when new classes of verbs started to appear with the *to*-infinitive complement. The author notes a number of parallelisms with the gerund, notably that both involved nominalisations and developed into clauses. Unlike the gerund, however, the initial niche for the *to*-infinitive involved an adjunct rather than a complement, so Los first accounts for the development from adverbial clause to complement clause through a process of pragmatic implicature. Embarking on the analysis of the pathway of diffusional change, Stage I involves verbs of spatial manipulation in a development parallel to the categorisation of bare abstract nouns in the account of gerund complementation. Stage II involves verbs of 'firing up' through an extension of the meaning of these verbs in a metaphorical manner. Stage III is somewhat more complex, as it involves the gradual extension of the *to*-infinitive as a complement of verbs that share the semantics with verbs of directive meaning but that did not collocate with a *to*-PP in OE; this stage involves in particular verbs of Commanding and Permitting. Stage IV is another gearshift with an extension to the expression of 'dependent desires'. Los identifies here a case of broad paradigmatic analogy which involves taking the *to*-PP and the *to*-infinitive to the domain of the subjunctive clause characteristic of the complementation pattern of verbs such as fearing, promising, ordering, hoping, expecting, or insisting. Finally, in her account Los adds one more stage in the development of the *to*-infinitive construction, also involving analogy. This is the ECM construction which emerged in late ME, involving verbs of Thinking and Declaring.

Ayumi Miura's chapter sheds new light on the extensively studied topic of impersonal constructions in the early history of English. Her approach is innovative in that it focuses on the interface between syntax and semantics, and it considers impersonal and non-impersonal verbs as well as near-synonymous phrasal impersonal counterparts. Under investigation here are the verbs *like, loathe*, which are impersonal, *love, hate*, which are non-impersonal, and the phrasal impersonals *have lief, be lief, be loath*. Miura's aim is to assess the role of four factors previously identified as playing a determining role in establishing boundaries between impersonals and non-impersonals in ME (Miura 2015), and to assess how they interact for a particular verb to occur or not in an impersonal construction. The four factors under examination are causation, transitivity, duration of emotion, and animacy of the Target of Emotion, and the scope in the present investigation extends back in time to the OE period in order to determine whether the same principles can be generalised for OE and ME, and whether they can be generalised to near-synonymous phrasal impersonals which emerged in ME. The data are drawn from various historical sources, namely the *Dictionary of Old English Web Corpus* (DOEC), the *York-Toronto-Helsinki Parsed Corpus of Old English Prose* (YCOE), the second edition of the *Penn-Helsinki Parsed Corpus of Middle English* (PPCME2), and the *MED*.

According to Miura, causation is the most important factor, a second relevant factor being the animacy of the Target of Emotion, for drawing the boundaries between impersonal and non-impersonal predicates. The other two factors, transitivity and duration of emotion, may be understood as secondary, yet they do play a role in the semantic-syntactic distribution of impersonal verbs and phrases. According to Miura, the parameter 'duration of emotion' correlates particularly with causation because causative psych-verbs are normally relatively punctual whereas non-causative ones typically involve long-term states; the role of this factor is examined in relation to the co-occurrence of the verbs and phrases with temporal adverbs. Although the data are at times scarce, it can be observed that the general trends mostly hold true for OE and also for the ME near-synonymous phrasal impersonals. All in all, Miura's investigation on the syntax-semantics interface of impersonal verbs and phrases in early English makes a significant contribution to our understanding of the development of impersonal constructions.

In **Laurel J. Brinton**'s chapter the focus moves on to pragmatics (see also McColm and Trousdale this volume). The author investigates the diachronic development of the syntactic construction *if you ask me* into a pragmatic marker; from a clause serving as a protasis in a direct condition to a comment clause of a parenthetical nature; and from a literal meaning where a question had been posited to a purely pragmatic meaning with no actual question, functioning as an epistemic hedge conveying negative politeness face-saving strategies. In contemporary English, the construction is parenthetical, structurally independent, and generally placed between commas, with relative flexibility of word order in the sentence; its internal structure is elliptical (lacking the complement of the verb *ask*), and prosodically it is also independent. A corpus-based analysis of Present-day American English, based on a sample from COCA, confirms the trends for indirect condition *if you ask me*, clearly in contrast with the syntactic structure of the direct condition *if you ask me*, which takes a complement argument and tends to occur in a more fixed initial position in the sentence (e.g. *And if you ask me to explain that, I'm going to have to demur*).

The data also point to a relatively stable frequency from 1990 to 2015, and to a higher frequency of *if you ask me* in more colloquial, oral genres, thus being considered a 'speech-like' construction in contemporary English. This sort of indirect condition is common in the history of English. On the one hand, they are 'expressions of epistemic modality', with a hedging function that softens the strength of the utterance. On the other hand, Brinton suggests that the indirect *if*-conditions serve as politeness forms, aimed at diminishing the threat to the interlocutor's face, as in *No, she looked half-starved if you ask me*. A further important issue raised in Brinton's chapter is the pathway of change of *if you ask me* in the history of English, for which she consulted a variety of well-known large-scale corpora containing British and American sources; the *Oxford English Dictionary* (*OED*) and *Google Books* were also surveyed. The earliest evidence of *if you ask me* is documented in the mid-sixteenth century, but it is not until the late nineteenth century that we observe unambiguous comment clauses with indirect condition *if you ask me*, as in *Well, it is the trick of the trade, if you ask me*. Given the dual elliptical nature of the construction as a comment clause – the lack of a complement structure required by the valency of *ask* and the lack of the main clause – the question posited here relates to the chronological order in which the elements were elided. The author tentatively concludes that insubordinated clauses are likely to have developed from a full biclausal structure, the deletion of the complement probably having occurred first. As for the pathway of semantic change, it is proposed that *if you ask me* develops from content meaning to procedural meaning, bearing in mind that the literal meaning is still used in PDE.

We turn now to **Sylvia Adamson**'s contribution, where she discusses a misreading resulting from cognitively internalised prescriptive rules. Adamson argues for the revival of the traditions of 'philologically oriented language studies', away from the boom in large-scale research focused on quantitative analyses and the use of statistical tools. She presents a novel approach that combines qualitative historical linguistics with literary criticism and textual criticism, as well as with recent developments in sociolinguistics. In particular, she is concerned with the evidential value of reading practices – and more precisely *mis*readings – in terms of what these can tell us about how far prescriptive rules have influenced the interpretative habits of a speech community and about the relation between grammatical change and cultural change. Interestingly, Denison (1998: 95) has noted with regard to potential sources of language change in the recent history of English that '[m]ost, perhaps all, linguistic changes start out as "mistakes" relative to the standards of the time (though often not noticed at first)', and that '[a]n aberrant usage therefore represents one of three broad possibilities: an incipient change which will in the long run prove successful, a possible change which does not get generally adopted, or simple error'.

Adamson understands *misreadings* in relation to mistranscriptions of a text, (conscious or unconscious) misquotations, and editorial corrections of a text, and she argues that a text-based approach characteristic of literary studies can provide suitable models for the role of misreadings 'as a window on cognition'. She is first concerned with the case-study method in literary criticism, where misreadings can be taken as creative transformations of earlier precursor texts, psychological motivations playing a key role. Adamson then turns to textual criticism, and more specifically textual reconstruction, whereby misreadings are viewed as deformations of text rather than creative transformations. She draws attention to the concept of *banalisation*, whereby a transcriber or editor tends to simplify the text by selecting the most banal or familiar form of expression. Moving then to the arena of qualitative historical linguistics, Adamson hypothesises that '[b]analisation is evidence that a grammatical change has become an internalised rule for the individual speaker'. To illustrate the point, she explores the regulation of the relative markers, specifically the animate/inanimate distinction between *who* and *which*, and the third-person anaphoric pronouns *he/she/it*. Going beyond the traditional approach that compares norms and usage, this chapter addresses the internalisation of externally imposed rules. Among the examples given of apparent changes in linguistic behaviour are the restriction on *that* vs. *which* in relative clauses, and a change in an individual from generic *he* to non-generic *he*. Historical data used as evidence by Adamson come from the reading of a line of Shakespeare, particularly whether the antecedent of *who* should be *heart* or *ghost* and the possibility that it involved personification. The final technique discussed by Adamson is the text-to-context method taken from literary studies: widening the scope to the textual, cultural, and intellectual context in which a text is produced can shed light on the original pragmatic purpose and its syntax.

The last chapter in Part II, by **Merja Kytö and Erik Smitterberg**, examines the syntactic use of the conjunction *and* as a phrasal and clausal linking device from the perspective of historical sociolinguistics, looking at variation and change in the lModE period as conditioned by two key social factors: gender and socio-economic group. Differences in text category and medium are also key to this investigation. The authors take two starting points: on the one hand, the synchronic correlation in PDE between clausal co-ordination and oral/spoken language, and between phrasal co-ordination and literate/written language; on the other hand, the diachronic cline towards colloquialisation observed in previous research in a variety of written genres. Thus it is hypothesised that (i) if the genre norms change following the historical drift towards orality, given the distribution of the clausal and phrasal patterns in PDE, we would expect an increase in the use of clausal co-ordination during lModE; (ii) if this evolves as a change from below the level of consciousness, we would expect women to lead the change to a greater extent than men; and (iii) if education and exposure to the written norm play a role, as they often do in lModE, we would expect higher social groups to show a preference for the phrasal use of the conjunction *and*.

Methodologically, the study draws data from a speech-based genre, the trial proceedings of the *Old Bailey Corpus* (OBC), and in particular from the language of witnesses. The analysis focuses on two linguistic variables: clausal *and*, as in *I ran after him for about 200 yards, came up to him, seized him, and knocked him down*; and phrasal *and*, as in *when she has addressed the prisoner in an angry and passionate manner*. The so-called *V and V* construction (e.g. *I went and enquired*) and ambiguous examples are also paid attention to. The results are quite consistent throughout and point to a cline towards a more frequent use of the speech-like clausal conjunction *and* from the early (1753–1785) to the late periods (1850–1881). This is consistent in both female and male witnesses, and in both higher-class and lower-class witnesses. Crucially, this cline runs in parallel with the decrease in frequency of the more written-like use of the conjunction *and* as a phrasal marker. The authors suggest that this may be indicative of the process of colloquialisation as documented in other written genres in the lModE period. The formality of the setting of the courtroom discourse here is thus thought to play a role, since a more formal setting would call for a parallel tendency to favour the norms developing in written genres. A second explanation may lie in the nature of the spoken genre itself: that a speech-based text type favours the increasing use of an oral-like feature such as clausal-*and*, on the grounds that 'speech is the locus of most language change'. Hypotheses (ii) and (iii) above are also confirmed.

Part III

In this, the final part of the volume, the focus turns to comparative and typological approaches, with British English examined alongside other varieties of English, Germanic languages, and Romance.

The first two chapters in this part take a cross-linguistic comparative approach. As with the above chapter by Los (Part II), **Olga Fischer and Hella Olbertz** discuss at length the role of analogy in relation to a specific grammaticalised construction in the early history of English. They take the premise that analogy may determine the outcomes of grammaticalisation to a great extent. Their object of study is HAVE-*to*, and its development is compared to the Spanish construction TENER-*que* (literally 'have which'), and, in particular, to the development of a possessive verb into a modal verb of obligation/necessity. The chapter is theoretically oriented in various ways. First, the authors revisit Fischer's earlier challenge to the traditional view of the role of word order change in this development in English (i.e. cause rather than result), in the sense that, as pointed out in Fischer (2015), word order may not be *the only* cause of change, although its relevance is not discounted. Second, the authors look closely at other constructions with similar formal and semantic characteristics and assess the role these neighbouring constructions may have played in the process of change, notably in terms of both semantic and structural analogy. Fischer and Olbertz contend that such analogical support from other constructions helps to establish the 'necessity' meaning acquired by HAVE-*to* in English, and by TENER-*que* in Spanish. Third, frequency is of great importance, and both languages shared the potential for analogical change

Introduction: Analysing English Syntax Past and Present 17

in that a lexical item expressing 'need' was frequently associated with the developing Aux-V construction, bringing the necessity meaning to the context. Furthermore, the traditional scenario of the process of grammaticalisation is replaced by one which goes beyond the unidirectional pathway from functional change to syntactic surface change, so that it works bidirectionally, and in addition is affected by synchronic internal (grammar) and external (socio-cultural) conditions co-determining speakers' way of processing their utterances.

Regarding the pathway of English HAVE-*to*, the authors summarise their account of how various structures contributed to this development, with supporting quantitative evidence to show the importance specifically of the structures involving the noun *nede* 'need' and its adverbial counterpart *nede(s)*. Synchronically neighbouring constructions are seen to have shared formal and semantic features with each other, and by means of analogical processes they 'co-determined the formal and functional development of HAVE+*to* into a semi-modal auxiliary expressing external necessity', rather than, for instance, expressing futurity. The grammaticalisation process of Spanish TENER-*que* involves some different analogical circumstances, yet it resembles English HAVE-*to* to a great extent. Fischer and Olbertz survey the history of HAVE-*to* and TENER-*que* and their variant constructions, and describe similarities and differences in the developments. In order to enrich the comparative syntactic account of the constructions in English and Spanish, the authors briefly address the asymmetry with Dutch and German, two languages with different pathways. Both of these have what is called the weak possessive construction with potential for the rise of a necessity meaning, yet only in certain contexts. Overall, this chapter makes an important contribution to the field in that it highlights the determinants of grammaticalisation phenomena and the role played by analogy in morphosyntactic developments.

Kersti Börjars and Nigel Vincent also present a cross-linguistic analysis, this time involving Germanic languages and looking at the development of what they label WILL-verbs. Empirical evidence is drawn from English, Danish, Dutch, Icelandic, and Swedish, all of which have WILL-verbs which can be traced back to the Proto-Indo-European root **wel-* 'want, wish'. The authors' aim is not to provide a detailed historical account of each of these languages, but to trace global patterns and to compare developments across four historical trajectories. The authors diverge from the difficult question of *why* language change occurs in some environments and not others and instead offer insight into *what* causes items to change in some environments but not in others (see also Miura this volume). This set of verbs offers 'fertile ground' for this investigation, given that in some of these languages the original lexical meaning is largely preserved, in some it has been lost and has developed into modal or temporal meanings, and in others it exists at an intermediate stage. The authors propose in particular that developments occur as a consequence of interaction between changes in both form and function, but note that change to form and function may happen at different rates, and that these two dimensions may interact in ways which are difficult to model.

The chapter opens with a detailed description of the formal and structural properties of the different WILL-verbs, specifically of the categorial properties of the verbs themselves and those of their complements. Börjars and Vincent conclude that, diachronically, WILL is quite similar to lexical verbs in terms of form distinctions across Danish, Dutch, Icelandic, and Swedish. In terms of structure, there is also little change historically in these four languages, while English has been affected by considerable structural developments over time. The authors discuss semantic properties in some detail, proposing a revision of the traditional semantic pathway in grammaticalisation: Desire > Willingness > Intention > Prediction. They argue that the cline should be reconceptualised as a cline from Desire to Prediction with 'a bifurcating diachronic route' for Intention and Willingness instead of a single trajectory; in particular, mapping the historical development of Germanic languages against the linear trajectory singles out 'willingness' as a distinct feature, interpersonal contexts serving as the triggering factor. The essence of the chapter lies in the authors' attempt to model the observed micro-steps of change within the theoretical framework of Lexical-Functional Grammar (LFG). They consider this approach to be appropriate because it allows for shifts in form and for changes in meaning independently of each other, and also for domains to change at different paces in different languages. The account presented by Börjars and Vincent addresses relevant issues for the cline from Desire to Intention to Prediction, such as the role of Independently Referring Expression, Anaphoric Subject Pronoun, (Quasi-obligatory) Anaphoric Control, Functional Control, and Raising. In conclusion, the authors emphasise the importance of considering smaller intermediate steps in studying semantic clines, and illustrate this with a more fine-grained comparative analysis of English and Danish.

The two remaining chapters in Part III present comparative studies dealing with syntactic variation and change in different varieties of

English. The research described in **Benedikt Heller and Benedikt Szmrecsanyi** nicely complements Payne's study (Part I) on genitive variation, this time offering a large-scale, synchronic, and comparative analysis of probabilistic genitive grammars in nine different varieties of English from around the world. Syntactic variation is here restricted to PDE, as documented in the *International Corpus of English* (ICE); to two variants, namely the *s*-genitive and the *of*-genitive; and to choice contexts in which the two constructions are interchangeable (i.e. excluding categorical uses of the construction), such as *the university's activities* and *the activities of the university*. The framework is Probabilistic Grammar, enriched by an understanding of World Englishes, with the aim of exploring variability in the hidden – though cognitively 'real' – probabilistic constraints that fuel variation within and across speech communities. The questions motivating the research here are to which extent varieties of English have different grammars for genitive choice, and what probabilistic constraints tend to make a difference across the varieties. Like other work in Part III, this chapter not only provides insights into syntactic variation but also considers what syntactic theory can add to our understanding of cognitive, sociolinguistic, and grammatical processes.

Methodologically, Heller and Szmrecsanyi present a highly sophisticated variationist method of analysis. This is based, on the one hand, on rich annotation comprising multiple conditioning factors previously identified in the literature: possessor animacy, constituent length (of both the possessor and the possessum), final sibilancy, information status of the possessor head (including givenness, thematicity, and overall frequency), and lexical density. On the other hand, the multifactorial analysis is plotted on a conditional inference tree, which reveals the extent to which the varieties under study share a core grammar that is explanatory across different varieties, and the degree to which individual probabilistic constraints are stable (rather than malleable) across varieties. The nine varieties under scrutiny comprise four Inner Circle varieties – British English (*br*), Canadian English (*can*), Irish English (*ire*), and New Zealand English (*nz*); two advanced Outer Circle varieties – Jamaican English (*ja*) and Singapore English (*sin*); and three other Outer Circle varieties – Hong Kong English (*hk*), Indian English (*ind*), and Philippine English (*phi*). From the main findings, the authors first observe that the *s*-genitive variant is attested more frequently in (native) Inner Circle varieties than in the indigenised L2 varieties of the Outer Circle, with two outliers (*sin, hk*). This is explained in relation to the language acquisition mode in the outlier varieties. Second, the cross-varietal comparison between written and spoken texts points to three different groups: some varieties show a preference for the *s*-genitive in spoken texts (*nz, can, ire, sin*); some document a lower frequency of this variant in the spoken medium (*phi, hk*); and some others display no particular difference for this extralinguistic factor (*br, ja*). Third, the linguistic constraints on syntactic variation for the genitive alternation display the expected effects. The multifactorial mapping of the linguistic factors points to the relevance of possessor animacy, constituent length, and final sibilancy. Finally, two main groups of varieties are distinguished: *br, ind, ja,* and *phi* vs. *can, hk, ire, nz,* and *sin*.

The final chapter in Part III is also concerned with national varieties of English, this time focusing on American English and British English, and attending not only to synchronic variation but also to diachronic developments since the early nineteenth century. Taking as a starting point Edgar Schneider's 'Dynamic Model' for the emergence of new varieties of English, **Christian Mair** aims to pinpoint the chronology of a number of standardisation processes in American and British English. Specifically, he is concerned with Phase 4 *endonormative stabilisation*, dating between 1828/1848 and 1898, and Phase 5 *differentiation*, dating from 1898, in order to assess the alleged claim that British and American English diverged in the nineteenth century, and that the former has undergone a certain level of Americanisation during the twentieth century. Mair's approach is enlightening in that it goes beyond the one traditionally taken in the literature on differences in pronunciation and vocabulary: he explores the history of various linguistic features at the level of orthographic, morpholexical, and syntactic variation, the last in greatest detail. This new perspective, moreover, is strengthened by means of an integrative approach in which the author combines close philological scrutiny of individual examples with statistical evidence from large-scale and smaller corpora.

Three variables are examined with regard to orthographic standardisation. First, the use of *-or* for *-our* in American English (e.g. *color/colour*) is taken to illustrate endonormative stabilisation because of its rapid integration into the national variety at the expense of the British *-our* variant, in particular during the decades of the 1830s to 1850s. Further spelling phenomena investigated include the *-er* vs. *-re* spellings (e.g. *center/centre*) and the word-final single consonant in unstressed syllables before vowels, as in *traveler* and *worshiping*. The two morpholexical variants under consideration are the preference in American English for *toward* vs. British English preference for *towards*, and the past participle *gotten* vs. *got*. The trend favouring *toward* in American English is apparent from the late 1890s, which fits nicely with Schneider's chronology of Phase 4 and

Phase 5. The distributional patterns of *towards/toward* in British English do not show change during the nineteenth century, and the Americanisation in favour of *toward* is only notable from the 1960s. The account for *gotten* and *got* is more complex. Mair argues that the perception of *gotten* as a long-established Americanism is in fact a misperception, possibly resulting from the salience of the form to British English ears, historically accustomed to a preference for the form *got*. Syntactic variation between the two national varieties is studied with regard to complementation patterns of the verbs *help* and *prevent*. Regarding the latter, the *from*-less construction (e.g. *it was necessary to distract Jones's mind in this way to prevent him killing himself*) continued to increase in frequency in British English, as it had done in both varieties during the nineteenth century, while it decreased in American English to the verge of becoming obsolete. The analysis of the four complementation patterns with *help* – *help* (+NP) (+*to*) + infinitive – revisits Mair's (2002) findings that the regional contrast observed in data from 1961, in which American English shows a preference for the bare infinitive pattern and British English for the *to*-infinitive pattern, had almost levelled out in the 1991/1992 data, so that British English now also prefers bare infinitives. The claim here is that this is not a straightforward case of Americanisation, but rather that grammaticalisation and the *horror aequi* factor (i.e. the avoidance of the construction *to help* + *to*-infinitive, e.g. *I was Calld up at 5 to help dress John*) play a crucial role in the increasing frequency of bare infinitives in both varieties.

This discussion above has outlined the studies contained in this volume. The range reflects the breadth of research currently being undertaken on English syntax. It suggests that there is no single approach currently driving research in the syntax of the English language, but we hope that the depth and diversity of the research presented in this volume provide an apt and vivid illustration of what Barbara Strang (1970: xv) has called 'the inexhaustible richness and variety of the subject'.

PART I

Approaches to Grammatical Categories and Categorial Change

CHAPTER I

What Is Special about Pronouns?

John Payne

1.1 Introduction[*]

The observation that personal pronouns typically sound highly unnatural as the object in *of*-PP dependents of English noun phrases dates back at least to Lyons (1986: 136). In a table comparing the frames [NP's N], [(Det) N of NP], and [(Det) N of NP's], he systematically excludes accusative pronouns from the NP position in the second of these. We will employ the terms used by *The Cambridge Grammar of the English Language* (Huddleston and Pullum *et al.* 2002) for these three constructions: *s*-genitive, *of*-PP, and oblique genitive respectively. Some characteristic examples are given in (1).

(1) a. his car ~ *the car of him ~ that car of his
    b. his brother ~ *the brother of him ~ that brother of his
    c. his hand ~ *the hand of him ~ that hand of his

(Lyons' (1986) judgements)

Note that the oblique genitive is only exceptionally found when the determiner is the definite article *the*: to control for this, the determiner is switched in these and subsequent examples to the demonstrative *that* in this construction. In (1a), we see the head noun *car* which Lyons, following a widely accepted formal semantics tradition established by Partee (1997), treats as non-relational. The semantic relation between the head noun and the dependent NP is, according to Partee, inferred contextually (a so-called 'free R' interpretation). In the case of the head noun *car*, this might well be straightforward possession or control ('the car that he owns/drives'), but could potentially include other

---

[*] I am grateful to audiences at the University of Lyon (2014), the University of Vienna (2015), and two reviewers for valuable comments which have shaped the final version of this chapter. The views expressed are of course my own.

relations, for example the one observed in 'the car that he designed'. By contrast, in (1b)–(1c) we see relational nouns, ones for which the interpretation of the semantic relation involved is inherent in the meaning of the noun itself (a kinship relation for *brother*, and a bodypart relation for *hand*).

The behaviour of personal pronouns in the *of*-PP construction is contrasted by Lyons with the behaviour of 'full NPs', in particular one-word proper names. Corresponding to the pronoun paradigm in (1), we have instead, if we follow Lyons' judgements, the paradigm in (2).

(2) a. John's car ~ *the car of John ~ that car of John's
    b. John's brother ~ the brother of John ~ that brother of John's
    c. John's hand ~ the hand of John ~ that hand of John's

The key claim made is that the *of*-PP is blocked in the free-R cases, but permitted when the head noun is relational. Further factors are of course relevant, as Lyons observes. In particular, the *of*-PP construction becomes more acceptable in the free-R cases when the NP is 'heavy', as in (3).

(3) the car of the people next door   (Lyons 1986: 134)

More to the point, however, developing a thread of animacy distinctions started by Hawkins (1981), Lyons notes that a pronoun dependent becomes more acceptable when specific inanimate part-whole relations are involved. Thus, with the exception that inanimates are not permitted at all in the oblique genitive construction, the head noun *funnel* behaves just like *car* (Lyons 1986: 135).

(4) a. the ship's funnel ~ the funnel of the ship ~ *that funnel of the ship's
    b. its funnel ~ *the funnel of it ~ *that funnel of its

By contrast, with nouns like *bottom* and *peak* (of a mountain), or *mouth* (of a river), while the oblique genitive remains impossible, the *of*-PP construction is actually preferred to the *s*-genitive frame, and the possibility of a pronoun in this frame is not excluded. Lyons does not give the full paradigms, but, using *mouth* as an example, we can extrapolate his judgements as follows:

(5) a. ?the river's mouth ~ the mouth of the river ~ *that mouth of the river's
    b. ?its mouth ~ ?the mouth of it ~ *that mouth of its

The validity of these contrasts, which are based on intuition, is somewhat unclear. However, it is an important observation that pronouns might indeed not be totally impossible in the *of*-PP construction.

The genitive alternation, with a dominant focus on the alternation between the *s*-genitive and *of*-PP constructions, has been the subject of much detailed research (for a complete survey, see Rosenbach 2014). Of particular interest is the fact that the more recent large-scale psycholinguistic and corpus studies (Rosenbach 2002; Börjars *et al.* 2013a; O'Connor *et al.* 2013) appear to support the general picture of the behaviour of pronouns in these constructions established by the early studies. The *s*-genitive construction strongly favours animate, short, and definite (or easily accessible) NPs, and personal pronouns appear almost categorically excluded from the *of*-PP construction whenever the *s*-genitive alternative is permitted. For instance, in the corpus investigation of O'Connor *et al.* (2013) it is established that, once intrinsically non-alternating cases of both *s*-genitive and *of*-PP are eliminated, 99 per cent of pronoun dependents (3,582 tokens) occur in the *s*-genitive, and 1 per cent (26 tokens) occur in the *of*-PP construction. The corresponding figures for proper nouns show much greater variation: 56 per cent (637 tokens) in the *s*-genitive, and 44 per cent (504 tokens) in the *of*-PP construction.

The contrast with the oblique genitive also turns out to be well-founded. In a qualitative analysis restricted for comparative purposes to examples exhibiting a narrow range of common semantic relations where all three constructions are in principle possible, including possession and bodypart relations as illustrated in (1)–(3), Payne and Berlage (2014) found that none of the examples in the *of*-PP sample are actually pronominal. By contrast, 93 per cent of the *s*-genitives are pronominal, and 81 per cent of the oblique genitives.

The consequences of this imbalance in distribution are, from a methodological perspective, quite striking. Pronoun cases have to be excluded from a standard regression analysis of the factors involved in the variation, since their behaviour is, from a statistical perspective, (almost) categorical. Nevertheless, as O'Connor *et al.* (2013) observe, their exclusion for this methodological reason is in one sense unfortunate: pronouns combine all the most important factors which favour the *s*-genitive construction. They are predominantly animate in this construction (88 per cent have human referents); they are not 'heavy' (having a word-length of one); and not only are they definite, they are by far the most accessible of all nominal categories (in the sense of Ariel 1990). Thus the regression methodology in effect bars from consideration the class of examples which most dramatically support the overall conclusions concerning the factors involved in the variation. What is more, as Rosenbach (2014) observes, it also excludes from consideration, in contrast to truly categorical contexts, any area of variation which does indeed exist. To the handful of invented examples with part-whole relations discussed by Lyons, and the single example with a location relation (*to the left of it*) cited by O'Connor *et al.* (2013: 101), Rosenbach adds three further attested examples (provided by a reviewer of her article) which illustrate what we will call the property relation: *the strength of him, the cleverness of me*, and *the size of me*. Note that the location and property relations freely admit examples with animate dependents (e.g. *to the left of me*). The precise semantic relation, rather than animacy per se, is thus the key factor.

In this chapter, we report on a detailed corpus-based investigation of the occurrence of personal pronouns in the *of*-PP construction. The preliminary aim is to provide a new empirical account of the semantic relations permitted to the *of*-PP construction as a totality. The aim is then not, as in the regression models, to identify the relative importance of disparate factors such as length, animacy, and accessibility in predicting the choice between the *of*-PP and *s*-genitive constructions. As we have noted above, personal pronoun dependents are, in usable corpus sizes, virtually never found in the *of*-PP construction in cases where the semantic relation involved is one of the semantic relations which strongly favour the *s*-genitive, e.g. the possession, bodypart, and kinship relations identified by Lyons in (1) above and proposed by Rosenbach (2002) as prototypical of this construction. Instead, by restricting our attention solely to personal pronoun dependents, we are able to focus on the full range of semantic relations which the *of*-PP construction straddles. That is, although the investigation places a restriction on the dependent and narrows down the example set in this way, it does not place any restriction on the head noun. To our knowledge, this is the first empirical investigation with this perspective (the investigation of *of*-PP dependents following anaphoric *one* in Payne *et al.* (2013) places a restriction on the head rather than the dependent). The focus is perforce rather different to that of the regression models, where the semantic relations encompassed are inevitably limited to those where the genitive alternation is indeed possible.

In the first instance, the investigation is intended to cast light on the nature of the *of*-PP construction. Given the totality of the semantic relations encompassed, can it indeed be considered a single 'construction' in the sense of Goldberg (1995, 2006)? Do the semantic relations have a semantic core based on the part-whole relation (see for example the discussion in Stefanowitsch 2003: 431)? Or are we possibly dealing with a set of entirely separate constructions? One claim in the literature along these lines is that there are at least two distinct prepositions *of*, one introducing the dependents of relational nouns, which is essentially meaningless since the semantic relation is provided by the head noun, and the other introducing the dependents of non-relational nouns (see for example Oga 2001; Panagiotidis 2003). Barker (1998), whilst (incorrectly, see example (3) above) discounting the possibility of *of*-PPs as dependents of non-relational nouns, identifies what he considers a further distinct *of*, one which he believes to occur in partitive constructions (as well as oblique genitives). How many more are there, or is there any point in distinguishing them?

The restriction of the investigation to personal pronoun dependents, in addition to providing a practical corpus size, also effectively controls the length and accessibility of the dependent. This has the immediate advantage of removing these otherwise potent variables from the equation. In particular, the frequency with which personal pronoun dependents occur then gives us a measure of the degree to which individual semantic relations are favoured in the *of*-PP construction. In the end, the investigation provides an insight not only into those relations which take part in the genitive alternation (several of which are to some degree disfavoured in the *of*-PP construction), but also into the behaviour of relations which alternate but do not figure prominently in studies specifically targeted at the genitive alternation, as well as those which do not alternate at all. Finally, as indicated in the title of this chapter, it will be possible to make some observations on the nature of pronouns. Is there something special about pronouns which in effect blocks them from the genitive alternation and prevents them, as noted by Lyons, from occurring in the *of*-PP construction when semantic relations prototypical to the *s*-genitive are involved?

1.2 Methodology

The corpus selected for the investigation was the *British National Corpus* (BNC*web* (CQP-Edition), henceforth BNC), consisting of approximately 100 million words of British English from the period 1960–1993, approximately 90 per cent of which consists of written text and the remainder spoken. Both the written and spoken sections of the corpus were used, and all examples cited are followed by the BNC text identifier code.

The search string was any noun followed by *of* and a personal pronoun (BNC tag PNP, i.e. including personal pronouns such as *you* and *yours*, but excluding pronominal determiners such as *your*). This produced 25,163 hits, from which a random sample of 1,000 tokens was extracted. Of these, 172 were immediately discarded as representing entirely different constructions. Since the PNP tag does not distinguish between accusative (*you*) and independent genitive (*yours*) forms, these included eighty examples of the oblique genitive construction, such as ... *any money of yours* ... [HAJ 492]. A further ninety-two examples of other types were also discarded. First of all, there were occasional instances involving pronouns such as *her* where the BNC automatic tagger was unable to distinguish a pronominal determiner from an accusative pronoun, as in ... *large parts of her [sic] manufacturing industry* ... [FA0 142]. Amongst the cases that were genuinely accusative, particularly frequent were examples in which the PP represented a complement of a prior verb rather than of the immediately preceding noun, as in ... *expected excessively high standards of her* ... [BNF 1334]. A variety of further isolated types then had to be excluded, such as ... *the pages of It* ... [HA1 773], where the pronoun represents the name of a popular magazine, and ... *the long and the short of it* ... [H0F 3140], an idiomatic expression where the head is an adjective rather than a noun.

In order to get to a final sample of free-standing nouns for analysis, two further types of example were then discarded. These were cases in which the noun followed by the pronominal *of*-PP was a component of a broader idiom, essentially a multi-word verbal idiom or a prepositional phrase idiom. Instances of multi-word verbal idioms were particularly frequent, totalling 106 examples, and are illustrated in (6).

(6) a. ... a plan took hold of her ... [FNT 3265]
    b. ... he intended to make fun of us ... [ABM 466]
    c. ... she caught a rash and unguarded glimpse of it [EFP 883]
    d. ... the children think the earth of you [A6N 1918]

In such examples the pronoun can be considered, at least functionally, as the object of a multi-word verb which includes the preposition, rather than as a complement of the noun within it. Multi-word verbs of this type can be quite variable in their syntactic properties, in particular their potential for passivisation. However, a passive which takes the nominal and *of*-PP together as object of the verbal head is invariably the least plausible option.

More interesting are the prepositional idioms, numbering twenty-five. These are illustrated in (7).

(7) a. in awe of her [ECM 1282]
    b. for the fun of it [F9R 272]
    c. for the love of it [K57 1935]
    d. for the life of me [FU6 1689]
    e. in the course of it [EFN 186]

Such expressions are in varying degrees idiomatic, and do not allow the full range of syntactic manipulation normally allowed to P + NP constructions, for example the addition of modifiers (Huddleston and Pullum *et al.* 2002: 618–23). One particular manipulation that is often excluded is the substitution of a genitive determiner for the *of*-PP. We do not have, for example, *for its fun or *for its love in the intended sense. In other cases, the determiner variant is comparatively rare: a BNC search reveals just one example each of a substitutable *in its awe* and *for my life*. The noun *course* in the expression *in the course of* seems to be bleached in meaning, and the whole can be replaced by the single preposition *during*. Although examples of *in its course* are found, they involve a more literal sense of the noun *course*. For example, in . . . *sociologists tend to see human behaviour as shaped in its course by the social context of human life* [HPU 63], *course* could be replaced by a noun such as *flow*. These prepositional idioms are therefore cases in which *of* + PP is either the only or the preferred variant, and pronominal objects simply follow the pattern.

A decision had to be taken whether to exclude at this point locative expressions like *in front of*. This expression is the most fossilised of a set of similar locative expressions such as *on top of*, *at the side of*, *at the bottom of*, *to the east of*, etc. A clear syntactic difference between all of these, including *in front of*, and the prepositional idioms in (7) is that the *of*-PP is omissible: we have *in front*, *on (the) top*, *at the side*, *at the bottom*, *to the east*, etc. The initial preposition can also be varied, especially in the less fossilised cases, e.g. *at the side, to the side*. As Huddleston and Pullum *et al.* (2002: 620-2) argue, the syntactic structure of these PPs contains an initial simple preposition and a following NP, viz. [$_{PP}$ *in* [$_{NP}$ *front* [$_{PP}$ *of* NP]]]. All such locative expressions were therefore included for subsequent analysis.

One final exclusion consisted of two examples in which the pronoun in the *of*-PP was the initial co-ordinate in a co-ordination:

(8) a. . . . a criticism of [him and the regime] [ADD 762]
    b. . . . letters predicting the deaths of [him and his relations] . . .
    [K55 3326]

The length of the co-ordinations (four words in each case) is a clear factor favouring the use of the *of*-PP construction as opposed to the *s*-genitive, and such examples cannot be used in a direct comparison with the non-coordinated pronoun cases.

Having thus excluded a total of 315 examples from the original random selection of 1,000, we were left with a sample of 685 for further analysis.

Figure 1.1 The main semantic relations

These were coded for the semantic relation holding between the head noun and pronoun in the *of*-PP.

1.3 Semantic Relations

The overall distribution of semantic relations is shown in Figure 1.1. It is immediately clear that in terms of token frequency three relations predominate: (i) quantity (27 per cent), (ii) theme (24 per cent), and (iii) location (20 per cent). Two others are relatively frequent: (iv) part-whole (10 per cent) and (v) property (6 per cent), while there is a diverse residue of other examples (13 per cent). In these figures, certain relations which at a more delicate level might be considered as separate are grouped together (cf. the groupings in Payne *et al.* 2013). For example, the theme (or object-like) relation is taken to include not only the undergoers of nominalisations but also the depiction relation (objects of 'picture' nouns). The full detail of such more delicate distinctions can be found in the discussion of each higher-level grouping. We now consider these in turn in Sections 1.3.1 to 1.3.6.

1.3.1 Quantity

Included in this category as head are various kinds of quantificational or collective noun, the three most frequent being *lot* (forty-seven examples), *rest* (thirty-nine examples), and *part* (twenty examples). Following the classification in Payne and Huddleston (2002: 349–52), quantificational nouns follow a fixed verb-agreement pattern, either singular only (*part of it was*...), plural only (*dozens of them were*...), or number-transparent, that is, verb-agreement is determined by the number of the *of*-PP (*a lot of it was*... /*a lot of them were*...). Singular collective nouns, on the other hand, allow the possibility of both singular and plural verb-agreement depending on a variety of semantic and contextual factors (*a group of them was*... /*a group of them were*...).

Lot, a number-transparent quantificational noun, is illustrated in (9).

(9) a. Central government may assign a local authority a large guideline figure for capital expenditure but also assume it will finance **a lot of it** from sales of council houses, for example, and hence give a small credit approval. [G1C 550]
  b. And there was **a rare lot of them**. [G09 383]
  c. She could have murdered **the lot of them**, Irish comedian included. [FB0 1145]

The noun *lot* is, as demonstrated in detail by Brems (2011), one of a group of similar nouns whose original meaning has been blanched to the extent that they can have purely quantificational force (with the noun in its original sense simultaneously preserved). *Lot* is distinct from the others (*heaps, loads, piles, stacks*, etc.) in that the quantificational force is available in the singular. The expression *a lot of X* shows a considerable degree of lexicalisation. Nevertheless, evidence that *lot* maintains its nominal status, i.e. that the structure of the bold NP in (9a) remains [$_{NP}$ *a* [$_{Nom}$ *lot* [$_{PP}$ *of it*]]], is provided by (9b), in which there is (admittedly rare) adjectival modification, and possibly also (9c), in which the determiner is alternated to *the*. Example (9c), as pointed out by a reviewer, might though represent a distinct idiom with its own meaning (something like 'all of X').

The noun *rest* is a straightforward number-transparent quantificational noun – see (10). Number transparency (note not person transparency) is clearly demonstrated by the difference between (10a), where the *of*-PP contains singular *you* and the agreeing verb-form is *does*, and (10b), where we have plural *us* and the agreeing verb-form *were*.

(10) a. Does **the rest of you** taste as sweet, I wonder? [HA6 2782]
  b. **The rest of us** were left to reproach ourselves for what had happened. [H8T 962]

The noun *part* appears to be a quantificational noun which solely allows singular verb-agreement (**part of them were*). In the examples in our sample, only the singular *part* was observed, and there was no determiner (clearly distinguishing this form formally from the count noun *part*). What is more, in the majority of examples, *part* could reasonably be substituted by the quantifier *some* (even if *part* is more natural in the given context and some residue of its original meaning is preserved) – see (11).

(11) a. The works, which have just started, will cost £191,000 and involve making the early-Victorian listed building wind and water tight and restoring **part of it** for use by the Brechin Railway Preservation Society. [EFV 49]
 b. Then Paula died, and Sam disappeared, and I can't find him on Belial, and I can't find him on Moloch, and **part of me** is frightened that he might be dead, and **part of me** is frightened that he's not. [G1M 1704]

In a handful of examples, this non-count *part* has a metaphorical interpretation, and is not substitutable by *some*, as in (12).

(12) Whether I will be **part of it** will depend on the new manager Rovers are appointing next week and whether it is a man I like and could work with. [CEP 5825]

The interpretation of *be part of* here is something like 'be (to some degree) connected with', and the whole might possibly be considered a verbal idiom, similar to those in (6). However, *part of X* in these examples seems to fit with any predicative verb (e.g. *it didn't form part of it*), and therefore is independently interpretable as a noun phrase. For this reason, we include such examples in the count.

It should be noted that the count noun *part* has a quantificational use equivalent to those in (11), in which case it occurs with a determiner and frequently a modifying adjective, as in (13).

(13) As regards the substantial outside assistance to the Western Isles, one wonders whether **a small part of it** might not usefully be redirected to subsidising the high costs of transport between them and the mainland. [AL9 274]

The presence of the adjective obviously forces the variant with a determiner, as in (13). With no adjective, the count form can be replaced by the non-count one. In our sample, however, none of these count examples was observed.

Other quantificational or collective nouns which occur more than twice in the sample are *bit(s)* (eleven examples), *number(s)* (eight examples), *majority* (six examples), *pair* (six examples), *proportion* (five examples), *percent* (four examples), and *half* (three examples). The remainder are: *amount, bags, batch, couple, crop, deal, degrees, feet, flocks, fraction, gallons, gulp, handfuls, load(s), pennorth, piles, quantity, quarter, sack, series, set, side(s), stone, string, subset, succession, sum, waterfall, whole, wisps*. Some, like *degree, gallon, handful, pennorth,* and *stone,* are straightforward measure terms. Others, like many quantificational nouns, have obvious non-quantificational origins, but were judged here to have developed a quantificational sense. The noun *crop*, for example, was used to denote a large quantity of acne spots (14a), and *waterfall* to denote a large quantity of diamonds in a necklace (14b).

(14) a. She had **a crop of them** now that she couldn't get rid of, even though she was using that acne treatment that worked wonders for the girl on the telly advert. [ACB 280]
b. Not just a rain of diamonds (and they were hardly common, Mama had explained), but **a whole waterfall of them**. [FPH 2097]

Also of note is the somewhat idiomatic use of the definite article with *half of it* in typically negative contexts such as (15a), and a positive counterpart with *sum of it* in (15b).

(15) a. No people don't know **the half of it**. [HML 108]
b. Only Caswell and I know **the full sum of it**. [HGV 6108]

Here, the implication of (15a) is not just 'less than half', but 'considerably less than half', or indeed 'very little'.

1.3.2 Theme

In this category we include three types of example. In the first type, totalling 115 examples, the head noun is a noun corresponding to a transitive verb, typically a nominalisation, in whose argument structure the *of*-PP represents an object-like argument (theme or patient). In the second type, totalling twenty-six examples, the head noun is a picture noun for which the *of*-PP represents the depicted item. We take this type to include specifically visual representations. And in the third type, totalling twenty-three examples, the head noun is a noun corresponding to an intransitive verb, again typically a nominalisation, in whose argument structure the *of*-PP represents an unaccusative (theme or patient) argument. In sum, in this category, the *of*-PP represents an object-like or theme-like argument.

The first type, where the nominalisation is transitive, is illustrated in (16).

(16) a. There is the learning, and there is **the critical evaluation of it**. [GoR 1236]
b. We shall accept Halliday's three functions, although not **his precise interpretation of them**. [EWA 1543]
c. Mozart was often able to report **performances of it** back to his father. [ANJ 339]

The nouns involved in this type are very varied, and none occurs with a frequency of greater than six occurrences. This type therefore represents a very productive source of pronominal *of*-PPs. The noun *lack*, as in *the lack of it*, occurs six times, and *sight*, as in *the sight of her*, five times. The standard pattern is for the head noun to be a transparent nominalisation; however, occasionally the noun itself must be taken to be the basic form, as in (17). Here the corresponding verb, *monopolise*, is clearly the derived form.

(17) AIDS (acquired immune deficiency syndrome) was first called GRID (gay-related immune deficiency) and, by homosexuals themselves when they thought they had **a monopoly of it**, the Gay Plague. [B71 1661]

Picture nouns are illustrated in (18).

(18) a. Some even had **photographs of it** on their walls. [ASV 243]
b. There is **a portrait of her** at St Anne's College. [GT4 299]
c. ... the tallest rioter is carrying **an effigy of you**. [HPY 900]

In several cases belonging to this type, e.g. *photograph* as in (18a), the noun denoting the type of representation corresponds to a verb which denotes the creation of that representation. However, as is obvious from (18b) and particularly (18c), this is not invariably the case. A portrait is a very specific kind of representation, focusing on the face, while the verb *portray* has no such specificity. And in the case of nouns like *effigy*, there is no corresponding verb at all.

In terms of frequency, the most common picture nouns in our sample are: *picture* itself (seven examples), *photograph* or *photo* (six examples), *image* (four examples), and *portrait* (two examples). Others with a single occurrence are: *drawing, dream, effigy, film, sketch, statue,* and *video*.

Finally, the unaccusative cases are illustrated in (19).

(19) a. He thought he heard **the clatter of it** in the roads. [G62 564]
  b. The public got **a very early taste of it** in the late 1970s when he was invited to play in the World International single wicket competition at The Oval. [CBG 1610]
  c. If they say no, it might not be because they don't like **the sound of it** but because their lists are already full and they are unable to take on any more. [CG3 2094]
  d. That should have been **the end of it** but it most certainly was not. [G39 110]
  e. If that was **the way of it**, she'd not say another word ... [C85 607]

Some of the examples literally denote impressions of the senses, e.g. *clatter* in (19a), and similarly *smell* (*the smell of it* [smoke]), *splatter* (*the splatter of it* [water]), and *taste* (*the taste of it* [beer]). However, *taste* is also used in a metaphorical way to denote an initial impression, as in (19b). The two most frequent head nouns are *sound* (seven occurrences) and *end* (six occurrences). Although *sound* potentially has a literal sense interpretation, all the examples of the sample display the metaphorical use in (19b). And similarly, *end* in the expression *the end of it* in (19d) denotes something like 'final event'.

In the majority of cases, the noun in all these examples corresponds to an intransitive verb which has a causative counterpart. The exception is *way* in (19e), where the somewhat fixed expression *way of it* denotes something like 'way it went'. The role of the argument here seems to be that appropriate to a motion verb, i.e. theme, and this example was therefore included in this type.

1.3.3 Location

Location is the third most frequent category overall, with 139 examples. It is however dominated by *front* (ninety-five examples), *top* (twenty-one examples), and *side* (eleven examples).

Front and *top* are undoubtedly the most syntactically frozen of the locative head nouns, and in fact all the examples in the sample take the somewhat fossilised form *in front of X* or *on top of X*, as in (20).

(20) a. The snow on the path **in front of us** was flawless; behind, it was as churned up as a freshly-harrowed field. [BNU 2124]

b. She said that the baby had suffered a fit, and she had fallen **on top of him**. [A96 83]

The use of *front* in this locative sense is, however, not totally fossilised, as can be seen from the examples in (21).

(21) a. A gentleman here **in the front of me** now, twenty one pounds. [G5A 565]
b. No piece of chalk had moved **across the front of me**. [HYD 81]

Both examples are from the spoken English section of the wider BNC. In (21a), said by an auctioneer during an auction, we see a variant with the definite article. In (21b), from a university philosophy discussion class, the preposition is altered to *across*, also triggering the use of the definite article. Such examples are no doubt comparatively rare, but they do attest to the limited syntactic flexibility of the noun *front* in this pattern.

The noun *top* exhibits a similar limited degree of flexibility, as can be seen in examples such as (22).

(22) There are times when barbel are so preoccupied with whatever business they have at hand, whether it be feeding, spawning, or just browsing, you can stand on the river's edge right **over the top of them** and watch them without them taking fright and scurrying off. [BoP 363]

This example, from the wider written section of the BNC, varies the preposition to *over*, again triggering the definite article. The sense is still clearly a locative one, indicating the location of the observer.

When we turn to the locative noun *side*, we see that the presence of a determiner is obligatory and the choice of determiner is not restricted to the definite article. Even in the sample, examples were found with *the*, *one*, *either*, and *each*. Also, the preposition can be more freely varied, typical choices being *on*, *at*, or *by*, or omitted altogether. This flexibility is illustrated in (23).

(23) a. I had a fellow come rushing out to me, point duty outside Legs o' Man pub one night, when I was directing traffic, puts a bottle of beer down **by the side of me**. [B24 2581]
b. And then the moment had passed, and tall and tanned and fit in the sunshine she had walked down the green street with the gardens **either side of her**, and had known by an instinctive glance that her mother still lived there, that nothing had changed. [A6J 52]

c. She came to a little patch of sand, the bottom of a miniature canyon, and **on the far side of it** there was a smooth grey rock, sliced neatly off at the top to make a platform. [H8X 1283]

As can be observed in (23c), this flexibility extends to the inclusion of a modifier.

The other, less frequent head nouns allocated to this category were: *middle* (five examples), and *back, bottom, centre, east, left, way* (one occurrence each). Typical examples are shown in (24).

(24) a. But the Jenkins family, part of the great mass, were trapped **in the middle of it**. [CL2 116]
 b. **To the left of them** was a complex of nets and cages in which the leopards, lions, cheetahs and tigers lived. [FP3 277]
 c. New ideas and a 'revolution of aspiration' through higher real wages around the 1850s may have persuaded populations that economic advancement was possible away from subsistence agriculture into manufactures, services, and cash agriculture and that large families stood **in the way of it** (Lesthaeghe 1983). [EDK 475]

1.3.4 Part-Whole

This category includes a wide variety of head nouns denoting a part of something, ranging from very general nouns such as *part, portion*, or *section* to very specific nouns relating to particular wholes, e.g. *suburb* (of a city).

Perhaps not surprisingly, the most frequent noun in this category is the noun *part* itself, with thirty-one occurrences. The distinction between *part* as a component of something and *part* as a quantitative noun (cf. Section 1.3.1 above) is mostly straightforward to draw: *part* as component is a standard count noun and never occurs in the singular without a determiner. It also has a regular plural *parts*. We do indeed also observe what we judge to be quantitative senses of *part* with a determiner, but these typically also contain quantitative modifiers like *small* (see (13) above). The use of *part* in the part-whole relation is illustrated in (25).

(25) a. You are **that part of me** that I cut off, and I never have been and never shall be whole without you. [K8S 2149]
 b. The finished product (or **parts of it**) can be printed out either dot matrix, inkjet or laser printer and it is the output which lets this program down. [HAC 5413]

We note also the idiomatic uses of *part* in the two examples in (26).

(26) a. Well, he made like he wanted **no part of me** at all. [FAP 2947]
 b. It's become **a part of me**. I could never leave. You only see the negative side of Beirut on the news back home. [EF1 128]

The expression *no part of X* denotes 'no involvement with X' and occurs with verbs of wanting (e.g. *want* and *desire*), as well as *have* (*I will have no part of it*). The expression *a part of X* in (26b), following a predicative verb, closely resembles the undetermined *part of X* in (12), and the determiner could easily be omitted with the same force.

Other general nouns similar to *part*, but with a much lower frequency of occurrence, are *half* (two examples), *fragment*, *portion*, and *section* (one example each) – see (27). Like *part*, *half* also has an undetermined quantitative use: the examples included here denote literal halves, and are accompanied by a determiner.

(27) a. The Count himself appears on horseback on the right-hand side of the portal, above a capital, while counterbalancing him on the left is a monster devouring a man (only **the bottom half of him** remains to go down). [FA2 590]
 b. **This fragment of it** survives, however, because it is quoted by Jerome – significantly in his Commentary on the messianic prophecy of Isaiah 11:1. [G3A 599]
 c. In this it is related to the heads of the Two Nudes painted a few months earlier, but as opposed to them, it is more completely mask-like, and every area or **section of it** is clearly defined and forms a self-contained unit. [GUJ 467]

Included in this category are various nouns which define a part by its location as part of the whole. These are: *end* (five examples); *back* (three examples); *edge*, *front*, and *side* (two examples each); *bottom*, *centre*, *corner*, *heart*, and *surface* (one example each). The focus here is on the part itself, as defined by its location within the whole, rather than on the relative location of some external entity as in the examples in Section 1.3.3. The contrast is particularly clear with the noun *front*, which in the relative location sense is obligatorily the complement of a preposition and typically lacks a determiner. Compare for example *He was in front of the house* (relative location) and *The front of the house was painted white* (part-whole). Attested examples from the sample are given in (28); note that in (28c) the writing is actually on the front of a station wagon.

(28) a. All the way across not one stone moved or even trembled as she jumped on to it or swayed on top of it or clutched at **the sides of it**! [BoB 853]
b. The basket was about a metre deep and **the back of it** had been built right up high so as to support the bank of flowers. [J19 411]
c. Across **the front of it** was painted 'Keep your distance' in mirror writing. [HR7 2891]

The remaining nouns in this category denote specialised parts and occur just once: *doorway* (of a church), *leg* (of a cart), *lesson* (of a summer course), *line* (of a face), *note* (of Fauré's chamber music), *offshoot* (of the IRA), *suburb* (of Neuhausen), *terms* (of a notice). Illustrative examples are given in (29).

(29) a. King Alchfrith also built St. Peter's church which was the first church in Stamford and all Mercia. It was built on the site of the *forum* of Hengist's Roman-style town in front of the great castle. Writing in his diary, William Stukeley takes his friend 'Panagius' to see **a supposed doorway of it**. [CBB 191]
b. Gabriel Fauré's chamber music constitutes one of the glories of French music, and virtually **every note of it** appears on two 'Rouge et Noire' sets in superb performances by Jean-Hilippe Collard, in company with artists such as Augustin Dumay, Frédéric Lodéon, and the Parrenin Quartet. [BMC 646]

1.3.5 Property

In this category, totalling forty examples, are included a semantically wide-ranging group of head nouns which attribute some general property to the *of*-PP. No particular head noun or set of head nouns predominates here, suggesting that this, like the theme category, represents a productive source of pronominal *of*-PPs.

The wide variety of attributable properties can be seen from the following list, the vast majority of which occur just once in the sample: *absurdity, advantage, balance, beauty, cheek, cheerfulness, colour, commercialism, complexity, costs, emptiness, fragrance, glare, hardness, heaviness, injustice, irony, joy, level, liabilities, limitations, measure, nature, numen, peace, purity, quality, rhythm, risk, ruthlessness, seriousness, shape, strain, texture, truth, usefulness*. As can be seen from this list, these range from concrete (e.g.

colour, glare) to more abstract (e.g. *advantage, beauty*). Some examples are provided in (30).

(30) a. Her fingers dug deep into his shoulders as she clung to him, caught up in a maelstrom of sensation, too stunned by **the sheer beauty of it all** to register more than the most fleeting second of pain. [JY5 3208]
b. Well they are grey looking cos that's **the colour of them**. [FYM 380]
c. He had talked wildly about the meaning of life, **the emptiness of it all**, the lack of scope offered by the Guardian Building Society. [ASS 1351]
d. Compare it with other theories, try and look for **the limitations of it**. [JT1 259]

It is worth noting that in the particular examples found in the sample, four of these property head nouns, namely *absurdity, injustice, irony*, and *truth*, seem to appear in what might be treated as mildly formulaic uses – see (31).

(31) a. I smiled to myself at **the absurdity of it**. [ADY 2411]
b. **The monstrous injustice of it** took her breath away. [H7W 244]
c. **The irony of it** struck her forcibly and her gurgling laughter broke out. [HGV 3467]
d. You've had a nasty shock and that's **the truth of it**. [CJF 2410]

Phrases such as *The absurdity of it!, The injustice of it!*, and *The irony of it!* can also be used in isolation as exclamative comment attributing the relevant property to a particular situation. In the case of *the truth of it*, the formula appears to be the whole phrase: *That's the truth of it*.

1.3.6 Other Relations

The remaining semantic relations to which the examples were assigned are listed in this section, in decreasing order of frequency. Only three have a frequency of greater than ten (aspect, source, time), and several are represented by just a single example.

1.3.6.1 Aspect

This reasonably frequent category, with twenty-two examples, includes cases where the head noun denotes some kind of aspect or manifestation of the *of*-PP. The predominant head nouns in this category are *side* (six occurrences, in the metaphorical sense where it can be substituted by *aspect*), *aspect* itself (five occurrences), *version* (three occurrences), and *copy* (two occurrences). The other nouns allocated to the category are *detail, facet, form, instance, look*, and, in a metaphorical sense, *ghost*. These are illustrated in (32). Note that in (32d) the phrase *by the look of him* has a somewhat formulaic character.

(32) a. You have to look at things like lighting, the height, colour and texture of the various plants or furnishings, and how you want to use the area – all **the practical aspects of it**. [HSK 18]
 b. Let's clarify **that side of it**. [KRL 784]
 c. When, infrequently, he wanted to write in 'some simple metre', he did so; but when more often he wanted to get away from standard metres, he left them behind altogether, **no ghost of them** lurking behind his arras. [A1B 1715]
 d. By **the look of him** he might well have left a genuine World War Two leather bomber jacket in the bedroom. [AoR 2632]

1.3.6.2 Source

In this category, totalling seventeen examples, we include instances in which the *of*-PP denotes in some sense the source or cause of the entity denoted by the head noun. This is admittedly a diverse category which could potentially be further disaggregated. It will include, for example, both the source of something relatively concrete, e.g. light, as well as the stimuli of a variety of mental states. The head nouns included here are *thought* (four occurrences), *memory* (three occurrences), *news* (two occurrences), *enchantment, humiliation, light, memento, scent, shame, symptom*, and *word* (one occurrence each). This category is illustrated in (33).

(33) a. One of **my favourite memories of her** goes back a few years to when she was playing Martina Navratilova in New England. [CKM 735]
 b. It's good to have **news of you** at last! [K1X 3800]
 c. **The shame of it** may have caused the slight stroke that overtook him, or perhaps it preceded the disaster. [H7H 1920]

1.3.6.3 Time

We include here temporal parts in terms of location, namely *end* (six occurrences) and *beginning* (two occurrences); temporal parts in terms of interval measures, namely *minute* (three occurrences); and also relative temporal location (*in front of*, with four occurrences).

(34) a. She made a mental note to check the tariff later with the receptionist – there would be little point in living so comfortably for a few weeks if the bill swallowed most of her wages at **the end of it**. [HA9 1863]
   b. 'It was a fantastic experience and I loved **every minute of it**,' says Ball. [HAE 1424]
   c. Knowing that she had a long day **in front of her**, Laura decided to follow her friend's good example. [JXX 106]

For reasons of transparency it was decided to keep these fifteen temporal examples as a separate category. However, another plausible option would be to reallocate the temporal part examples as a subtype of the part-whole category (from which all temporal examples were excluded), and similarly the relative temporal location examples could be assigned to a subtype of the location category.

1.3.6.4 *Member*

In these examples, totalling five occurrences, the head noun denotes an entity which is a member of the set denoted by the *of*-PP. The most frequent head noun is *member* itself (four occurrences), but note *officer* (one occurrence) in example (35). These examples might be considered a special case of the part-whole relation, but again for transparency we keep them separate.

(35) The settlement brought great relief to the whole of the Public Relations Department and clearly **the indigenous officers of it** needed to be trained for the new situation. [CDC 1449]

1.3.6.5 *Content*

Here, the head noun denotes a concept and the *of*-PP the content of it. The nouns found were *idea* (three examples, see (36)) and *impression* (two examples).

(36) Rhoda could not see the heavenly dust, but liked **the idea of it**. [HGJ 767]

1.3.6.6 *Similitude*

This category is illustrated by the noun *like*, either in the singular or plural, in the formulaic expression *the like(s) of X*. The only head noun found was *like* itself, with five occurrences – see (37). Semantically, as pointed out by a reviewer, the expression *the likes of X* always includes the referent of *X* within the set identified by the NP.

(37) She was not, she told Mrs Arbuthnot, prepared to work for **the likes of her**. [CDY 790]

1.3.6.7 Purpose
In this set, the head noun denotes the purpose of the entity denoted by the *of*-PP. Three head nouns were found, totalling four occurrences: *point* (two examples, see (38)), *purpose* (one example), and *object* (one example).

(38) If a ban makes no difference, what is **the point of it**? [K54 3398]

Note that the head noun *object* was also allocated, in a different sense, to the focus relation (Section 1.3.6.15 below).

1.3.6.8 Kin and Interpersonal
Here we group together two relations which are prototypically found in the *s*-genitive construction (Rosenbach 2002), namely kinship and interpersonal relations. In our sample, kin terms are represented by *father* (two examples) and *parent* (one example), and the interpersonal relation is represented by *friend* (one example) – see (39).

(39) a. And **the father of them all** David Smith is represented by a selection of sculptures all this month (and next, too) at Knoedler. [EBT 2626]
b. We meet **friends of him**, of Valentin, and also it rains and rains ... [FPH 4021]

It is interesting that in all four examples there is some factor which either forces or predisposes towards the use of the *of*-PP construction, even with a pronoun. One is the use of pronominal forms with *all*, as in (39a). These, like pronominal forms with *both*, are treated by Huddleston and Pullum *et al.* (2002: 427–8) as single grammatical words, forming a set of universal personal pronouns which only have accusative forms and therefore no genitive counterparts. The second is the addition of a supplementary *of*-PP, e.g. *of Valentin*, as in (39b).

1.3.6.9 Collection

In this set, constituting three examples, the head noun denotes a collection of the entities denoted by the *of*-PP. Two head nouns were found: *gang* (two occurrences) and *circle* (one occurrence) – see (40).

(40) a. Felix remembered **the gang of them** at the beginning of the World War, with Stephen stomping around reviling the call-up, deciding on conscientious objection for himself, shaking off the hand of any acquaintance who tried to help him speed over a dangerous crossing, and talking about the anti-militarist statement he would make to the court. [FRH 2522]
 b. At last she felt stones. **A small circle of them**, enclosing a heap of cold ashes and dried leaves. [HH1 1544]

The collection can be either animate, as in (40a), or inanimate, as in (40b). Because their meaning was judged not to be quantitative, the nouns in these examples are treated separately from the quantitative collective nouns in Section 1.3.1.

1.3.6.10 Doubt *Idioms*

Here we have another formulaic expression, this time involving negation of the head noun *doubt*. Two variants were found: *not a doubt* (one example) and *no doubt* (one example):

(41) The men lay more quietly; some, **not a doubt of it**, still alive, some even lying mort until it should be safe to rise and go. [HGG 1396]

1.3.6.11 Result

The head noun denotes the result of an event denoted by the *of*-PP. There are three head nouns with one occurrence each: *result*, *outcome*, and *effect* – see (42).

(42) a. ... this Swedish consensus is a precedent to the development of certain institutional forms rather than **a result of them**.
 [CLE 61]
 b. **The outcome of it** was that the Spencer Union was formed, ...
 [FY1 372]

1.3.6.12 Subset

In this case, the head nominal denotes a subset of the entities denoted by the *of*-PP. In (43), the sole example in the sample, the subset relation is licensed by the superlative adjective.

(43) **THE HOTTEST rock 'n' roll movie jukebox of them all**, Scorsese graphically captured the earthy street punk life of small-time Little Italy hoods with great improvised acting skits and a wired, combustible sound track. [CHA 3091]

1.3.6.13 Component

Here the head noun denotes the composition of the entity denoted by the *of*-PP. This relation is represented by one example with the head noun *fabric*, namely (44). This relation must be distinguished from the relation called 'composition' in Payne and Huddleston (2002: 477), where the head denotes the entity and the *of*-PP denotes the component, e.g. *dress of silk*.

(44) And if you think of a [sic] **the main fabric of them**, they're quite flimsy. [KNF 86]

1.3.6.14 Container

In this relation the head noun denotes an entity containing the entity denoted by the *of*-PP. Again it is illustrated by a single example (45), with the head noun *dish*. The product in (45) is pâté, and it would seem that *dish* is to be interpreted literally here, as a plate or bowl, rather than as food prepared in a certain manner.

(45) Because his wife had made **dishes of it** as first-night presents for the cast, apart from Titania, who was on a diet and would have to be dealt with in some other way. [FSP 455]

1.3.6.15 Focus

In this case the head noun denotes the focus of the entity denoted by the *of*-PP, see (46). The actual head noun illustrating this relation is *object* (one example). We might have called this relation the object relation, but chose 'focus' instead in order to obviate confusion with the purpose sense of object in Section 1.3.6.7. Clearly in (46) the noun *object* does not denote the purpose of the rivalry, rather the entity towards which the rivalry is directed.

(46) There they were, all wrapped up in their rivalry, never guessing that **the object of it all** was sitting right in front of them. [G3G 2243]

1.3.6.16 Agent

Finally, we have a single example where the *of*-PP displays not a theme-like, but rather a more agent-like role with respect to the event denoted by the head noun. This example (47) involves the noun *consent*.

(47) Someone in possession with **the consent of them both** can be said to be in possession 'with consent of the owner.' [HH7 1233]

This more agent-like relation is again one which, like kinship, might be expected to be a preferred domain of the *s*-genitive. Note of course that we have here a universal personal pronoun, *them both*, which has no genitive counterpart.

1.4 *Of*-PPs and the Genitive Alternation

Although there might be quibbles about individual classifications, the corpus shows that the variety of semantic relations which *of*-PPs exhibit with respect to their head nouns is quite extensive. Not surprisingly, some of these relations are those known to be restricted to *of*-PPs and not to be available to the *s*-genitive construction (see Payne and Huddleston 2002: 477). The most frequent relation of all in our data, quantity, is systematically excluded from the *s*-genitive, and an *of*-PP is the only available option. For example, in comparison with *the lot of them*, *the rest of them*, and *the majority of them*, we do not have **their lot*, **their rest*, or **their majority*. Further relations of this kind are subset (partitive), collection, container, and content.

Nevertheless, except where somewhat formulaic or fossilised expressions are involved, a large number of the semantic relations observed in our data do participate, at least in principle, in the genitive alternation. There may be particular reasons why an *s*-genitive alternate is not available in particular cases. The alternation is, as we have already observed, only available when the determiner in the *of*-PP is the definite article, and excluded otherwise. Also, as examples with universal personal pronouns reveal, the *of*-PP construction may be the only variant because of the formal reason that such pronouns have no genitive counterparts.

The theme relation, which is the second most frequent relation in our data, systematically permits the genitive alternation. Compare for example *the evaluation of it ~ its evaluation*, *the interpretation of it ~ its interpretation*, *the portrait of you ~ your portrait*, *the clatter of it ~ its clatter*. So does property, the fifth most frequent relation. Compare *the colour of it ~ its colour, the beauty of it ~ its beauty, the absurdity of it ~ its absurdity*. Some other, less frequent relations also participate quite regularly, for example aspect (*the practical aspects of it ~ its practical aspects*), member (*the members of it ~ its members*), and result (*the outcome of it ~ its outcome*).

In some cases, the possibility of the genitive alternation seems more restricted. For example, with location, the third most frequent category in our data (largely due to the fossilised form *in front of*), the possibility of a genitive variant seems largely to be excluded because of the varying degrees of fossilisation. With some of the less fossilised expressions, a genitive variant seems entirely feasible: *by the side of me ~ by my side, to the left of them ~ to their left*, and *in the way of it ~ in its way*. Part-whole, the fourth most frequent category, also seems largely to participate, compare for example *the parts of it ~ its parts, the centre of it ~ its centre*.

In Table 1.1, we categorise the relations found in the corpus into three groups: (a) semantic relations which do not participate in the genitive alternation,[1] (b) semantic relations which do participate in the genitive alternation, and (c) semantic relations in which *of*-PPs occur but are strongly disfavoured. In group (c), the examples contain at least one factor which counterbalances the bias towards the *s*-genitive, e.g. indefiniteness of the whole NP, as in the interpersonal relation example (*friends of him*), or the use of a universal pronoun.

Qualitatively, the results confirm the claim made in Payne and Huddleston (2002), Payne *et al.* (2013), and Payne and Berlage (2014) that the set of semantic relations available to the *of*-PP construction is a superset of those available to the *s*-genitive. In particular, *of*-PPs are not excluded even when the relation is one prototypical of the *s*-genitive. Quantitatively, as observed in the introduction, the restriction to pronominal dependents gives us a new insight into the relations which are available to the *of*-PP construction. Those which occur with higher frequency are quantity, theme, location, part-whole, and property (these are allocated separate sections in Section 1.3 and appear with italicised capitalisation in Table 1.1). Important differences can be noted in comparison to the quantitative analysis of *of*-PPs following anaphoric *one* in Payne *et al.*

---

[1] The hash symbol in COLLECTION and SIMILITUDE in the table indicates that an example is unacceptable with the intended meaning. For example, *their gang* does not have the collection interpretation attributable to *the gang of them*.

Table 1.1 Of-*PPs* and the genitive alternation

of-PP only	*of*-PP/*s*-genitive alternation	*of*-PP possible, but strongly disfavoured
QUANTITY the rest of you/*your rest	THEME the evaluation of it/its evaluation	KIN the father of them all/their father
SUBSET the hottest of them/*their hottest	LOCATION by the side of me/by my side	INTERPERSONAL friends of him/his friends
COLLECTION the gang of them/#their gang	PART-WHOLE the centre of it/its centre	AGENT the consent of them all/their consent
CONTAINER the dishes of it/*its dishes	PROPERTY the colour of them/their colour	
CONTENT the idea of it/*its idea	ASPECT the practical aspects of it/its practical aspects	
	SOURCE the memory of her/her memory	
	MEMBER the officers of it/its officers	
LOCATION (fossilised) in front of me/*in my front	TIME the end of it/its end	
SIMILITUDE (fossilised) the likes of them/#their likes/(sg only) their like	PURPOSE the point of it/its point	
DOUBT (fossilised) no doubt of it/*its no doubt	RESULT the outcome of it/its outcome	
	FOCUS the object of it/its object	
	COMPONENT the fabric of it/its fabric	

(2013). Quantity (aka amount) is represented by just a single example following *one*, while the subset (aka partitive) and content relations, which figure very sparsely in this corpus, represent the vast majority of *of*-PP examples in the anaphoric *one* corpus. As intimated in the introduction, the fact that the head is restricted to this pronominal in the anaphoric *one* corpus evidently skews the overall picture of the relative frequency of semantic relations available to the *of*-PP construction. On the other hand, the corpus here equally evidently underestimates the frequency of the subset relation, which most typically, although not exclusively, leaves the head noun unexpressed (e.g. *three of them*). The corpus search carried out would only have found the rarer examples where the head noun is expressed.

1.5 A Single *Of*-PP Construction?

Given the diversity of the semantic relations it exhibits, a question that immediately arises is whether it makes sense to think of the *of*-PP construction as a single construction, with a unified semantics. One possibility to make this work would be to have all the semantic relations permitted to the construction cluster around a single core. As noted in the introduction, Stefanowitsch (2003: 431) makes a proposal along these lines, with the part-whole relation as the suggested core. While, however, the part-whole relation indeed turns out, on the basis of the data here, to be one of the most frequent relations associated with *of*-PPs, it is not the most frequent. It also seems that many of the relations identified in our survey (and indeed in Payne *et al.* 2013) have little genuine similarity to part-whole. Just taking our most frequent relations, while it might be feasible to assimilate the property relation to part-whole (e.g. in *the colour of X*, its colour might be considered part of X), at the very least it would be necessary to separate off distinct quantity and theme relations, and within the less frequent relations several more. And if instead of one core relation we had two, or three, or more, there would still be the difficulty of assigning some of the less frequent relations to a particular one of these. It is also important that some of the less frequent relations available to the *of*-PP construction are those which are prototypical of the *s*-genitive (e.g. kin and interpersonal relations, agent). These, as well as those more favourable to the *of*-PP construction, must be incorporated in any full account.

As noted in the introduction, an alternative conception deriving ultimately from the formal semantics literature of the 1980s is that the preposition *of* in *of*-PPs might be taken to be essentially meaningless. The semantic relation between the head and dependent in the construction would in this case be driven exclusively by the lexical semantics of the head noun itself. Proposals along these lines, e.g. Vikner and Jensen (2002), largely suggest that there is then a distinction to be made between relational nouns, which incorporate a specific relation with their dependent within their semantics, and non-relational nouns, where the relation derives from the context. It is not relevant here to establish a dividing line between relational and non-relational nouns (for arguments that this is ultimately a futile distinction to make see Keizer 2004, 2011 and Payne *et al.* 2013). The main objection is simply that a conception which regards *of* as meaningless fails to correctly delimit the full set of semantic relations which the *of*-PP construction subsumes. There are clearly semantic relations between a head noun and its nominal dependents which the *of*-PP construction cannot express, but which are available to compounds. For example, an A-line dress is a dress which resembles the letter 'A' in shape. But we could hardly express this relation as an *of*-PP (*dress of A-line). It might be argued that the shape of a dress is not something which is inherent to the concept 'dress'. But why then is the composition of a dress, arguably equally non-inherent, something which can be expressed as an *of*-PP (as in *silk dress/ dress of silk*)?

A further alternative might be that each semantic relation constitutes a separate construction with its own independent semantics and morphosyntactic idiosyncracies. The oblique genitive construction is clearly something which is formally as well as semantically distinct (for arguments see Payne and Berlage 2014), so we would naturally think of this as separate. It is also possible that the subset relation forms a separate partitive construction, as proposed by Barker (1998). However, we leave the status of the partitive as an open question: the fact that it sometimes occurs with overt head nouns at least suggests that the subset relation might have been subsumed within a general *of*-PP construction. With these provisos, however, the position we incline towards is that a greater overall perspective is achieved by recognising a single *of*-PP construction which expresses a closed set of possible semantic relations between head noun and dependent. The reason that this might be preferable is precisely the competition between the *of*-PP and *s*-genitive constructions. Firstly, a speaker's knowledge must include the knowledge that the relationship between the set of relations expressed by the *of*-PP and the set of relations expressed by the *s*-genitive is a superset relationship. And speakers must also be able to compare these semantic relations according to their ability to predispose towards one construction or the other.

1.6 The Status of Pronouns

In conclusion, we return to the observation which provided the impetus for this study, namely the intuitive judgement by Lyons (1986) that personal pronouns are ungrammatical or at least questionable as dependents in the *of*-PP construction. We have seen, on the contrary, that the occurrence of pronominal *of*-PPs is not restricted to isolated examples, and is found across a wide spectrum of semantic relations, including those in principle open to the genitive alternation. The isolated examples which have previously been cited in the literature are just the tip of the iceberg.

It should not be surprising that the most frequent semantic relation observed in our data is one where the *s*-genitive is systematically excluded, namely quantity. Where the genitive alternation is in principle available, the theme and part-whole relations figure prominently: these are not prototypical of the *s*-genitive, although they can clearly be expressed by it. What is important to note, however, is that our data include some of the semantic relations which predispose quite strongly towards the *s*-genitive. These include the kinship and interpersonal relations, as well as the agent relation, where a pronominal variant would hardly be expected. Nevertheless, when there are factors which force or predispose towards the *of*-PP variant, this is the one which is chosen, even in these cases. We have observed that such factors can be the indefiniteness of the whole NP, the use of universal pronouns, and the addition of supplements.

Perhaps it is still striking that there is not a single example of a pronominal *of*-PP being used for the semantic relation of possession, one relation in which the *s*-genitive has particular predominance. Nevertheless, this is probably due to the size of the thinned corpus. We would predict that these also exist in principle: a possible instance in the wider BNC is *the blood-groups of us all* [JYo 2991].

The behaviour of personal pronouns in *of*-PPs thus does not look special. It is somewhat as might be predicted given the general properties of the *of*-PP construction, its role in the genitive alternation, and the status of personal pronouns as short, one-word items with highly accessible reference properties.

CHAPTER 2

What For?

Bas Aarts

2.1 Introduction[*]

The lexical item *for* is treated in the literature either as a preposition (*We bought it for you*) or as a subordinator/complementiser (*I preferred for him to take the exam*). In this chapter I will argue that there are good grounds for regarding *for* exclusively as a preposition which can license a noun phrase or clause as complement. In what follows I first take a closer look in Section 2.2 at constructions in which *for* appears. In Section 2.3 I then discuss the now prevalent analysis of *for* as a complementiser after certain classes of verbs, and in Section 2.4 I present an account in which *for* is treated exclusively as a preposition. This analysis has a number of advantages, principally the fact that it allows for a simplification of the lexicon and grammar of English.

2.2 The Guises of *For*

2.2.1 For *as a Preposition:* [For + NP]

In the simplest cases *for* is a preposition which takes a noun phrase as its complement. The resulting prepositional phrases can carry a wide array of meanings (the *Oxford English Dictionary* lists thirty-one with dozens of sub-meanings), and can function in a number of ways, e.g. as complement – see (1) and (2) – or as adjunct – see (3) and (4).

(1)   He went **for a job** yesterday as a London Tourist Board information giver.   (S1A-005 202)[1]

---

[*] Earlier versions of this chapter were presented at the universities of Zürich, Oxford, and Essex. I thank the audiences there, as well as the editors of this volume, for their valuable feedback.
[1] Examples with these codes are taken from the British component of the *International Corpus of English* (ICE-GB). 'S' texts are spoken, 'W' texts are written.

(2) You can't blame her **for that** really, can you? (S1A-007 017)

(3) Hold it **for a moment**. (S1A-002 127)

(4) I love talking, but if I talk **for three days flat** without a longish period of solitude I begin to feel ill. (S1B-046 020)

2.2.2 For + *Finite Clause*

When followed by a finite clause, *for* is often analysed as a subordinating conjunction (see e.g. Quirk *et al.* 1985: 1104). Used in this way *for* is rather formal, and carries the meaning 'because', as in examples (5)–(8).

(5) 'I'm afraid I've always been bad at names', she told him **for she'd no recollection of him**. (W2F-020 203)

(6) So when Alice and I go round we always you know borrow a book **for it's like our own library really**. (S1A-025 326)

(7) If you're seeking to attract me to say anything about Douglas that is ungracious you will fail, **for I have the highest possible respect for Douglas as a close friend and as a very experienced colleague**. (S1B-043 85)

(8) Translated into at least thirty-four languages, his work raises important questions about the mobility of literary texts and invites a new theoretical approach, **for to read Nooteboom straightforwardly as a Dutch author would be to do him an injustice**.
(www.ucl.ac.uk/selcs/departments/dutch/dutch_news_publication/nomadic)

The analysis of *for* as a subordinator in finite subordinate clauses (5)–(8) is not universally accepted. Thus Palmer (1987: 97) notes that whereas in sentences containing *although* and *because* the order of the clauses can be reversed, this is not possible with *but* and *for*, as a comparison between (9) and (10) shows.

(9) a. John came, although/but Mary stayed at home.
     b. John laughed, because/for he was a fool.

(10) a. Although (*But) Mary stayed at home, John came.
     b. Because (*For) he was a fool, John laughed.

This is sufficient evidence for Palmer to deny that *for* is a subordinator in these constructions. He offers the following semantic explanation:

> Provided the subordination of the clause is indicated, information of a concessive or causal nature can precede the main clause because its semantic relationship is signalled. If there is no such mark of subordination, information of a concessive or causal nature (or any kind of 'satellite') must simply follow normal rules of discourse – and such comments must follow the statement of the information to which they relate. Subordination and sequence are then related devices. (Palmer 1987: 97)

It is not clear what analysis of *for* Palmer proposes, if this element is not a 'mark of subordination'.

Huddleston and Pullum *et al.* (2002: 1321–2) also mention the issue of clause order and the inability of *for*-clauses to co-ordinate (see also Quirk *et al.* 1985: 927). They see *for* (along with *only* and resultative *so+that*) in this construction as falling 'at the boundary between coordinators and prepositions'. Also: 'They lack the more positive features of each, so that their classification remains problematic'. However, on balance they prefer to analyse *for* as a preposition in the sentences above, taking a finite clause as complement. This entails the analysis in (11) for the *for*-string in (6).

(11)   [PP [P for] [clause it's like our own library really]]

In a slightly different usage *for* has the meaning 'because of' in the following example (12), where it is followed by a noun phrase.

(12)   'In London generally, you can't move **for dead people connected to Dickens, fictional and real**,' she says.
(*Islington Tribune*, 22 November 2013)

This use is also found in similar set expressions such as *for fear (of), for lack (of), for want (of)*, etc. I will not be discussing these uses further in this chapter.

2.2.3   *[For [NP to VP]]*

In this section I will discuss the pattern [*for* [NP *to* VP]] which occurs in various positions: as a subject or subject predicative, as the complement or modifier of a head (typically a verb, adjective, or noun), or as the focus element in a pseudocleft construction. Here are some examples in which the pattern occurs, with the function of the italicised portions indicated in bold – see (13)–(24).

(13) subject:
For the roles to be reversed would be a tragedy for many Conservative MPs and voters. (W2E-004 064)

(14) extraposed subject:
It's also important **for management to provide an environment in which people and ideas can develop.** (S2A-037 69)

(15) subject predicative:
The idea was **for me to see the material.** (S1A-060 12)[2]

(16) verb complement:
But the role calls **for her to do some moving.** (S1A-083 106)

(17) extraposed complement of verb:
His face becomes dusky, because the muscle spasm makes it impossible **for him to breathe.** (W2B-023 46)

(18) adjective complement:
What's hard **for us to understand in retrospect** is how anyone could have thought otherwise. (S2B-029 15)

(19) adjective postmodifier:
As a medium-sized contractor, HTV would be too large **for any independent to try to bite off.** (W2C-017 71)

(20) noun complement:
I was surprised to see more of them here than in NY, maybe as many as in London but the only place where settlements have been made is outside City Hall where the Mayor has given permission **for them to sleep.** (W1B-011 53)

(21) noun postmodifier:
Alice left a message **for him to call her urgently**, but she knew she wouldn't hear from him until the next day. (W2F-009 4)

---

[2] It could be argued that in fact the *for*-clause is the subject here, which would then have been inverted with the NP *the idea* functioning as subject predicative. The reading would then be the same as in the uninverted version *For me to see the material was the idea*, with *the idea* ascribing a property to the subject clause. Huddleston and Pullum *et al.* (2002: 1385) call this *subject-dependent inversion* (as opposed to *subject-auxiliary inversion*). However, because we can say *Was the idea for me to send the material?*, which displays subject-verb inversion, and because subject-dependent inversion is only possible with ascriptive *be*, but not with specifying *be*, which we have here (cf. Huddleston and Pullum *et al.* 2002: 1385, fn. 8), I have analysed *the idea* as the subject.

(22) extraposed postmodifier in NP:
And this really left the way open **for Webster to pull away from his pursuers**. (S2A-012 20)

(23) complement of a preposition:
Your judgment seems so compromised, it is hard to advise you about a specific course of action, other than **for you to take a long look in the mirror and make a promise to yourself to act in your son's best interests from here on out**. (*Washington Post*, 10 July 2014)

(24) in the focus position of a pseudocleft construction:
What I want is **for it to continue the way it is at the moment**. (*The Guardian*, 8 May 2013)

The syntactic status of *for* in structures like those above has long been debated in the literature. Stoffel (1894) and Zeitlin (1908) use the term 'inorganic *for*', as do Zandvoort (1949) and Visser (1963–1973). According to Fischer (1988: 85, n. 2), '[i]n the older literature, a distinction is made between "organic" and "inorganic" *for*. *For* is organic when used purely as a dative marker; it is inorganic when used as a complementiser.'[3]

With regard to the development of the construction some linguists have argued that at some point in time there was a reanalysis of structures containing *for* such that ' ... [*for* + NP] [*to* ...]' becomes ' ... [*for* NP *to* ...]'. We find this analysis in Jespersen:

> The prepositional group is gradually disconnected from the word or words with which it was originally closely connected; it comes to be used in places and in combinations in which the original meaning of the preposition is excluded: *for* becomes **the mere grammatical sign** of the subject (S) of the infinitival nexus. (Jespersen 1940: 308; emphasis added)

Here's an example given by Jespersen (1940: 308):

(25)

It is good [PP **for** a man] [not to touch a woman]
↓
It is good [[? **for**] a man not to touch a woman]

---

[3] This may be a general tendency, but it is not invariably true, because at least Zeitlin (1908: 137–8) seems to treat inorganic *for* as a preposition.

Some constructions are what Jespersen calls 'double-barrelled', i.e. ambiguous between a reading in which *for* belongs to the higher clause and a reading in which it belongs to the lower clause, as in (26).

(26) It is no slight matter **for** a man of my character to be thus injuriously treated.

For other instances the new analysis is the only option (Jespersen 1940: 310) – see (27).

(27) [I]t is a rare thing [**for** a night to pass without one or other of us having to trudge off].

In Lexical-Functional Grammar (LFG) Jespersen has been influential, as the following citation from a textbook (Falk 2001) makes clear, though note that Jespersen does not seem to have claimed that *for* is a preposition.

> The generative tradition has considered *for* to be a complementizer, and researchers in LFG have generally followed this tradition. If *to* is a complementizer, however, it is not clear that *for* would also be a complementizer. If it were, *for* infinitives would have two complementizers. What *for* actually seems to be is a marker for the SUBJ of the infinitive, since it is present when the SUBJ is represented in c-structure and absent when it is not. This is the position taken by Jespersen (1940: 308). The c-structure of the infinitival would then be:

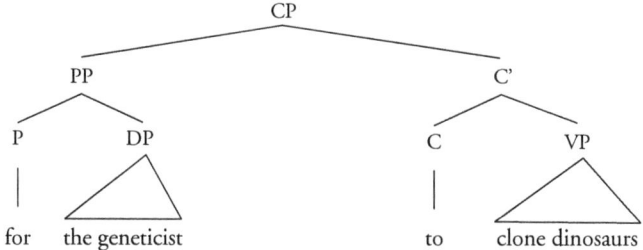

> The ID rule for CP has to license a SUBJ in specifier position for an infinitive, and specify that it be PCASE-marked with *for*.
>
> (Falk 2001: 146–7)[4]

Visser's (1963–1973) account is similar to Jespersen's:

---

[4] Diagram tree as originally presented in Falk (2001: 147), here reproduced with kind permission from CSLI Publications. ID rule = Immediate Dominance rule.

In the majority of the subjoined instances *for* is 'organic', that is to say, it is quite natural as an introduction to a complement to the verb, noun or adjective in the preceding *it*-phrase (it is good for, it is lawful for, etc.), so that the syntactical unit in which it occurs can be apprehended as 'it is good for him, to go', and not as 'it is good, for him to go.' Among the later instances, however, there are a few in which it is possible that 'for him to go' is a close unit in which *him* is pre-eminently realized as the subject of the infinitive, and *for* is 'inorganic.' (Visser 1963–1973: 968)

What is notable in the passages cited above is that the authors do not use the label 'subordinator', or an equivalent term, for *for*, but instead describe this word vaguely as a 'mere grammatical sign', or as being 'inorganic'. While one could argue that such locutions come close to labelling *for* as a subordinator, that step is not quite made by these authors. Uncertainty regarding the labelling of *for* persists to the present day. For example, although Quirk *et al.* (1985: 1004) do regard *for* as a subordinator, at the same time they note that '[s]ince *for* may be combined with the subordinator *in order to*, it seems to be **a device for introducing the subject** rather than to be a true subordinator' (emphasis added; see also 1985: 1186, 1193).⁵ It is not clear exactly what kind of device they have in mind. No doubt influenced by Quirk *et al.*, Mair (1990: 40) discusses the sentence in (28).

(28) It will be necessary **for me to simultaneously admit her husband to one of my beds**, as there is unlikely to be anyone else to look after him. (W.7.12.76)

Noting the two possible syntactic analyses we can assign to this 'double barrelled' sentence, Mair observes that with regard to the reading under which *for* belongs to a subordinate clause the string *for me* 'could be described as a complex subject noun phrase, consisting of the subject-introducing particle *for* and the subject proper ("me" in the above example)'. This raises the question of what is meant by 'subject-introducing particle', and how a string introduced by it can be regarded as a noun phrase constituent functioning as subject. This question is very pertinent especially in the light of the passive version of (28), also discussed by Mair, which clearly shows that *for* does not enter into construction with the following noun phrase (29).

---

⁵ In view of the text that precedes this passage, the authors must have intended to write 'the subordinator *in order*', not 'the subordinator *in order to*'.

(29) It will be necessary **for her husband to be admitted to one of my beds simultaneously**.

We find a similar analysis to Mair's and Falk's in De Smet (2013), who speaks of 'reinforcing *for*', which introduces the subject of the subordinate clause. De Smet writes:

> By *for* ... *to* infinitive is understood here the kind of structure illustrated in [(i)], in which a noun phrase introduced by *for* (henceforth a *for*-NP) functions as the subject of a following *to*-infinitive, with which it forms a single clausal constituent. [...]
>
> (i) a. It was neither my intention or aim *for* this *to happen*.
>   b. We do not *seek for* all *to be* totally convinced.
>
> (De Smet 2013: 73)

A question that is left unanswered by Jespersen, Falk, Mair, De Smet, and to some extent Quirk *et al.*, is this: What is the exact syntactic status of *for* and the '*for*-NP'?

In work subsequent to Jespersen and Visser the reanalysis account has become the standard one for the development of this construction;[6] see e.g. Bresnan (1972: 29), Fischer (1988: 79ff., 2007: 15ff.), Harris and Campbell (1995: 62), Haspelmath (1998: 324), and Fischer *et al.* (2000: 214ff.).

In generative theoretical work, the treatment of *for* as a complementiser dates back to early Transformational Grammar, specifically Rosenbaum (1967: 24ff.). In this work the construction was analysed as involving the paired complementisers (or *complementising morphemes*) *for* and *to*, referred to as the '*for-to*' *complementiser* or the *infinitive complementiser for ... to* (Jacobs and Rosenbaum 1968: 164). It was never quite clear in the early analysis how discontinuous complementisers such as *for ... to* (and poss-*ing*) fitted into the theory and how they were split up in actual syntactic structures.

Another account from the early transformational period worth mentioning is presented in Emonds (1976: 195ff.). To explain the contrast in grammaticality between the sentences in (30) and (31), whereby the former allows for lexical material to be interposed between the subordinator and the clause that follows, but the latter does not, he assumes a local transformation called 'For *Phrase Formation*' that essentially operates in the reverse way from the process proposed by Jespersen, discussed in Section 2.2.3, as shown in (32).

---

[6] More recently, though, it has been criticised in De Smet (2009).

(30) He doesn't intend that, in these circumstances, we be rehired.

(31) *He doesn't intend for, in these circumstances, us to be rehired.

(32)

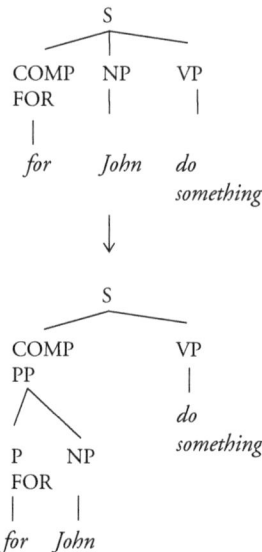

This analysis is modified in Emonds (1985: 295–6), but in essence it remains the same, in that *for* is regarded as being in construction with the following NP at surface level. Lightfoot (1979: 195) also regards *for* as a preposition:

> I shall argue that it has been a preposition throughout its history as a clause-introducer. This is not to deny that it also constituted an optional part of the infinitival morphology during M[iddle] E[nglish], re-inforcing the newly established *to* form. In fact, its ability to occur as an infinitival marker seems to be a function of its prepositional status.

With a small modification Lightfoot then adopts the analysis proposed in Emonds (1976), shown in (32). This analysis faces a similar problem to the analyses discussed earlier that treat *for* as some kind of device that marks the NP subject. In Emonds' and Lightfoot's case, as in the LFG account, it is not made clear how the subject of the clause can be conceptualised as the complement of a preposition. I will argue below that *for* is not in construction with the NP that follows it.

Bresnan (1972: 9ff.) refers to complementisers as *conjunctive particles* and discusses the possibility of deriving sentences with *for . . . to* by means of a *for-to* insertion transformation.[7] In her account the sentence in (33) is derived as in (34):

(33) It may distress John for Mary to see his relatives.

(34) [NP It [S Mary sees his relatives]] [M may] [VP distress John]
↓
[NP It [S for-to [S Mary sees his relatives]]] [M may] [VP distress John]
↓
[NP It] [M may] [VP distress John] [S for-to [S Mary sees his relatives]]

Here *for-to* is adjoined by a transformation (called 'R'; triggered by a set of verbs marked [+R] in the lexicon) to the 'S' *Mary sees his relatives*, and the resulting complex is then moved rightwards.

However, Bresnan rejects this transformational account in favour of what she calls the *phrase structure hypothesis* (1972: 13), under which complementisers are inserted under a node labelled 'COMP' in deep structure and there is no transformation 'R'. The feature [+R] is no longer needed, and verbs now subcategorise for certain types of complements. The deep structure from which *It may distress John for Mary to see his relatives* is derived is as shown in (35).

(35) [NP It [S' [COMP for] [S Mary see his relatives]]] [M may] [VP distress John]

Bresnan's account was very influential in proposing that COMP and S together form an S-bar constituent (indicated as S' in (35)). However, it is not clear how *to* is accommodated in the clause labelled 'S'. This analysis was adopted in later Government and Binding Theory in which *for* was no longer regarded as being coupled with *to*, but as a single element, although it was recognised that '[t]here are evidently relations between COMP and INFL (*that*-tense, *for-to*)' (Chomsky 1981: 54). In more recent work this 'single complementiser analysis' has become the standard analysis in Chomskyan grammar, but also in other generative frameworks, such as HPSG (Head-driven Phrase Structure Grammar). For example, in Sag (1997: 458ff.) *for* is also treated as a complementiser – see (36).[8]

---

[7] In Bresnan (1970) this is called the 'transformational hypothesis'.
[8] Diagram reproduced here (see following page) with kind permission from Cambridge University Press.

(36)

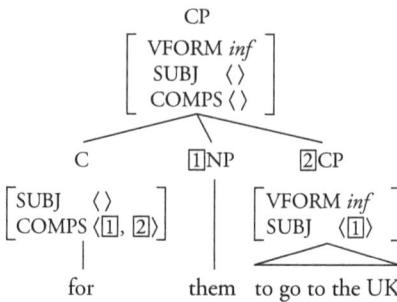

Here *for* is regarded as an 'object-raising element'. What this means is that the NP complement of *for* (*them*) is also the subject of the infinitival CP complement (*to go to the UK*), as indicated by the shared indices, and can hence be seen as having been raised out of the CP. See also Green (2011: 31).

In the next section I will take a closer look at the analysis of *for* as a marker of subordination, as inspired by early generative theory.

2.3   *For* as a Subordinator in the Pattern [*for* [NP *to* VP]]

Huddleston and Pullum *et al.* (2002: 1181ff.) and Radford (2004: 54ff.) discuss the categorial status of *for* as a preposition and as a subordinator, and opt for the latter label in the pattern shown above. In the next two sections I will discuss the arguments put forward by these authors in favour of analysing *for* as a subordinator, but I will argue that their reasoning is not convincing. I will claim instead that *for* in the construction under discussion is a preposition that takes a clausal complement. Specifically, I will argue that verbal, adjectival, and nominal heads license prepositional phrases headed by *for* taking a clausal complement, as is shown in the tree below (37) for the bold part of (16).

(37)   But the role calls . . .

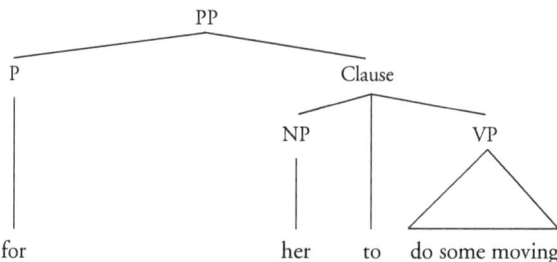

In Section 2.4 I will discuss this analysis further.

2.3.1 Huddleston and Pullum et al.'s Arguments

In their grammar Huddleston and Pullum *et al.* (2002: 1181ff.) explore the possibility of analysing *for* as a preposition. They give three reasons why one might wish to do so for constructions like those in (13)–(24) in Section 2.2.3.

- When the noun phrase following *for* is a pronoun, it takes accusative case:[9]

(38) He arranged for **her**/***she** to be interviewed first.

- Nothing may intervene between *for* and what follows:

(39) It's important **for you** to read the first one immediately.

(40) *It's important **for** the first one **you** to read immediately.

- PPs introduced by *for* and clauses introduced by *for* have a similar distribution:

(41) the need **for peace**/the need **for us to cooperate**

(42) too cold **for a swim**/too cold **for us to go out**

(43) *I'm thinking of **for a holiday**./*I'm thinking of **for us to leave**.

Despite the considerations above, they argue that *for* is a subordinator, and they analyse the sentence *It's mad for you to lend him the money* as in the tree diagram (44) (Huddleston and Pullum *et al.* 2002: 1187).[10]

(44)
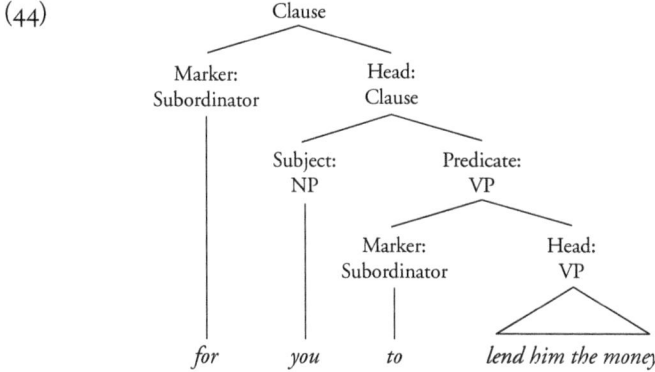

---

[9] Examples in the text that follows are taken from Huddleston and Pullum *et al.* (2002).
[10] Note that this tree contains information about both form and function, and *for* is analysed as a subordinator that functions as a 'marker'. Diagram reproduced here with kind permission from Cambridge University Press.

Huddleston and Pullum *et al.* then give a number of reasons for regarding *for* as a subordinator. Before looking at these reasons it is important to be aware of the fact that the main point that these authors are arguing for is that '[t]he item *for* that appears with *to*-infinitivals differs in important ways from the one that takes NP complements' (2002: 1182), and that *to*-infinitivals (other than interrogative ones) can only occur as complements of prepositions 'under very restrictive conditions' (2002: 1262), and only after *in order* and *as if/though*. They thus rule out *to*-infinitivals as complements of *for*. Let us first take a closer look at Huddleston and Pullum *et al.*'s arguments for their claims.

- Clauses introduced by *for* can occur in positions where 'regular' PPs cannot normally occur:

(45) **For you to give up now** would be tragic. [subject]

(46) It's rare **for the bus to be so late**. [extraposed subject]

(47) This made **it** necessary **for the meeting to be postponed**. [extraposed object]

(48) I can't afford **for them to see me like this**. [complement of *afford*]

- 'Except for the matter of accusative case' (2002: 1182), the subjects after *for* are the same as those that occur in finite clauses, including e.g. *there*:

(49) It's essential **for there to be no misunderstanding on this point**.

(50) He called **for close tabs to be kept on the new recruits**.

- The string *for* + NP + VP is a constituent and 'there is no reason to say that the NP combines directly with *for*' (2002: 1183).

- The subordinator *for* is very similar to the subordinator *that* in that it can only be placed at the beginning of a clause (see also Quirk *et al.* 1985: 927), and is meaningless. Furthermore, the syntactic roles of *for* and *that* are 'closely parallel' and there is 'functional similarity' between them (Huddleston and Pullum *et al.* 2002: 1183), as examples (51)–(56) purport to show.

(51) It is important **that detailed records be kept**.

(52) It is important **for detailed records to be kept**.

(53) That's the best course **that you can take**.

(54) That's the best course **for you to take**.

(55) In order **that the bill may be passed** major amendments were made.

(56) In order **for the bill to be passed** major amendments were made.

The arguments arguing in favour of *for* as a preposition are quite strong, especially the ones based on case, as in (38), and on distribution, as in (41)–(43).[11] However, the arguments in favour of *for* as a subordinator are much less convincing, as I will now show.

First, it is not true that PPs cannot occur in subject position, and this is presumably the reason for the insertion of the hedge *normally* in Huddleston and Pullum *et al.*'s claim that PPs cannot occur in this position. Examples of PP subjects are cited in Quirk *et al.* (1985: 658) and in Jaworska (1986: 355ff.). These mostly involve PPs that express a spatial or temporal meaning, as in the following examples (57) and (58).

(57) **Under the tree** is a shady spot.

(58) **Between 9 and 10** is a good time to meet.

Whether or not extraposition is possible is less clear. However, the following sound fine to my ears:

(59) It's a shady spot **under the tree**.

(60) It's a good time to meet **between 9 and 10**.

With regard to (47) and (48), it is true that structures like (61) and (62) are dubious for regular PPs.[12]

(61) ?The heat made **it** very desirable **under the trees**. [extraposed PP]

(62) *I can't afford **in the spa**. [PP as complement of *afford*]

However, the explanation for these judgements is likely to be a semantic one, in that the argument for *make ... necessary*, *make ... desirable*, etc. should involve a proposition, as in (47), or a noun phrase that expresses dynamic meaning, as in (63).

(63) His actions rendered **his efforts to improve education** useless./His actions rendered useless **his efforts to improve education**.

---

[11] The second argument, involving examples (39) and (40), is arguably a variant of the first argument, since the ungrammaticality of (40) is due to the fact that, in Chomskyan terms, the NP *you* is not adjacent to its case assigner *for*. See also Emonds (1976) and Sag (1997).

[12] To the extent that (61) is possible, we are probably dealing with ambient *it*.

In (61) this is not the case, because a PP such as *under the trees* cannot express such meanings.

And with regard to (62) the meaning of the verb *afford* is such that it requires a noun phrase complement (*can't afford a holiday*), or a constituent that expresses a proposition (as in (48)). Again, 'regular' PPs involving a P+NP sequence cannot express such meanings.

Turning now to the next two bullet points in their discussion, Huddleston and Pullum *et al.* observe that the subjects after *for* are the same as those in finite clauses. Notice that this is not actually an argument in favour of analysing *for* as a subordinator. What it amounts to is arguing *against* an analysis in which *for* forms a PP constituent with the NP that immediately follows it. But this is only one possible alternative analysis. One could also argue, as I will be doing, that in (49) and (50) *for* is a preposition that licenses clauses with *there* and *close tabs* as subjects. There would then indeed be 'no reason to say that the NP combines directly with *for*' (Huddleston and Pullum *et al.* 2002: 1183).

Regarding the last bullet point about the placement of *for* and *that*, I would draw attention to the fact that the same restriction applies whether we analyse *for* as a subordinator or as a preposition. In both cases it can only be placed before the complement it licenses, and with which it forms a constituent. For Huddleston and Pullum *et al.*, in (51)–(56) the italicised strings are clauses introduced by a subordinator. I will argue that they are PPs and that the complement of *for* is a clause.

Turning now to the perceived 'close parallelism' between *for* and *that*, the first point to note about this claim is that an important difference between these lexical items is completely ignored, namely the fact that *for* governs accusative case. No other subordinator in English assigns case. This was an issue that linguists working in the Government and Binding framework grappled with. They dealt with the problem by referring to *for* as a *prepositional complementiser* (see e.g. Chomsky 1981: 66). The use of this label is quite remarkable, because it amounts to admitting that *for* exhibits hybrid categorical behaviour. Such dual categorisations of formatives are highly unusual in theoretical frameworks like Chomsky's, since they constitute a violation of the Aristotelian principle of categorisation, which holds that in the same linguistic context an element cannot belong to two word classes at the same time (see Aarts 2007: 11ff. for discussion). Related to this is the difference in behaviour between *that* and *for* noted in Emonds (1976: 196, 1985: 297), Sag (1997: 460), and Culicover (1999: 60), namely that *that* can be followed by an adjunct, but *for* cannot, as (30) and (31), repeated here as (64) and (65), show.

(64) He doesn't intend that, in these circumstances, we be rehired.

(65) *He doesn't intend for, in these circumstances, us to be rehired.

These data are a problem if we regard *for* and *that* as being functionally identical, but unproblematic if we assume that *for* and the NP that it assigns case to must be adjacent. Having said all this, there does appear to be a neat correspondence between the sets of sentences in (51)–(56) which we need to account for. I believe that we can easily do so by observing that the correspondence is not so much between a subordinator *that* and a subordinator *for*, but the fact that the *that*-strings and the *for*-strings are licensed in each case as complements of a higher head. In other words, the parallelism is not lost if we analyse the *that*-string as a clause and the *for*-string as a PP, as has been proposed here.

At this point it is also worth looking at further parallelisms, this time between *for* used in [*for* + NP] and [*for* [NP *to* VP]] structures, as observed by Culicover (1999: 59) (see (66)–(72), bold added).

(66) a. **For Terry**, I bought this book.
b. **For Terry to learn French**, I bought this book.

(67) a. I bought **for Terry** the book that I had seen.
b. I bought **for Terry to read** [the book that I had seen].

(68) a. I bought this book yesterday **for Terry**.
b. I bought this book yesterday **for Terry to read**.

(69) a. This book is **for Terry**.
b. This book is **for Terry to read**.

(70) a. What this book is for is **for Terry**.
b. What this book is for is **for Terry to read**.

(71) a. ***For Terry** is the purpose of this book.
b. ***For Terry to read** is the purpose of this book.

(72) a. *I bought this book for _ yesterday [a person that I wanted to impress].
b. *I bought this book for _ to read [a person that I wanted to impress].

Despite these parallels, Culicover argues on the basis of (73a)–(73c) that the *for*-strings cannot be PPs, because the position in which they occur are not PP positions, as (74a) and (74b) show (and cf. (45)

above, which Huddleston and Pullum *et al.* (2002) cite to make the same point).

(73) a. **For you to call me at 1 a.m.** would irritate my parents.
 b. It was a great thrill for us **for Rodney to discover himself standing in front of such a huge crowd.**
 c. It is important **for there to be some consistency here.**

(74) a. *__For you__ would irritate my parents.
 b. *It was a great thrill for us **for Rodney**.

According to Culicover, *for* also cannot be regarded as a complementiser in view of the data in (64) and (65), and his own examples in (75). Here the complementiser *that* can be followed by an adjunct, but *for* cannot.

(75) a. It was a great thrill for us that at 1 a.m. Elvis suddenly called.
 b. It was a great thrill for us for Elvis to suddenly call at 1 a.m.
 c. *It was a great thrill for us for at 1 a.m. Elvis to suddenly call.

For Culicover '[t]here is a single element *for* that is neither a preposition nor a complementizer, but a *sui generis* category that shares properties with both prepositions and complementizers' (1999: 57), and semantic interpretation determines the distribution of *for*-strings. I already dealt with the putative counterevidence in (74) above, when I showed that PPs are not excluded from subject position. As for the data in (75), we have already seen that we can explain the ungrammaticality of (75c) by appealing to the notion of case: a (pronominal) NP occurring in the position of *Elvis* in (75c) can only receive accusative case if it is adjacent to *for*. We can conclude that the distributional facts in (66)–(74) and (75c) constitute strong evidence in favour of an analysis of *for* as a preposition.

I conclude that on balance the evidence in favour of analysing *for* as a preposition outweighs the evidence in favour of analysing it as a subordinator.

2.3.2 *Radford's Arguments*

Radford (2004: 54ff.) also discusses the differences between the preposition *for* and the complementiser *for*.[13]

---

[13] Examples in the text that follows are taken from Radford (2004).

- Prepositional *for* can 'in some but not all of its uses' be intensified by *straight* or *right*, whereas *for* as a complementiser cannot be modified in this way:

(76) He headed *straight/right* **for** the pub. [*for* = preposition]

(77) *He was anxious *straight/right* **for** nobody to leave. [*for* = complementiser]

- Clauses introduced by *for* can be the subject of *would cause chaos*; PPs headed by *for* cannot:

(78) **For him to resign** would cause chaos. [= *for*-clause]

(79) *****For him** would cause chaos. [= *for*-phrase]

- Prepositions are typically not followed by infinitival complements, but by *-ing* clauses.

- *For*-phrases can be preposed, or *for* can be stranded (cf. (80) and (81); clauses introduced by *for* cannot (cf. (82) and (83)):

(80) **For** *which senator* will you vote in the primaries?

(81) *Which senator* will you vote **for** in the primaries?

(82) *****For** *which senator* were they anxious to keep his cool?

(83) **Which senator* were they anxious **for** to keep his cool?

- A clause introduced by *for* can be replaced by a string introduced by *that* (cf. (84) and (85)); this is not the case for PPs (cf. (86) and (87)).

(84) Is it really necessary **for there to be a showdown**?

(85) Is it really necessary **that there (should) be a showdown**?

(86) We are heading **for a general strike**.

(87) *We are heading **that there (will) be a general strike**.

In the same way as I have done with regard to Huddleston and Pullum *et al.*'s arguments, I will now look at each of Radford's bullet points in turn.

The first bullet point concerns the modification of prepositional phrases by *for*. While many PPs, involving both transitive and intransitive prepositions as heads, can indeed be specified by *straight* or *right*, these are principally PPs headed by prepositions expressing spatial or temporal meanings, as in (88)–(92).

(88) straight back   (S1A-045 033)

(89) straight through   (S2A-018 255)

(90) straight into the next day   (S1A-005 152)

(91) straight after the Dean's sermon   (S1A-020 167)

(92) straight over the top   (S2A-002 073)

However, if a phrasal constituent cannot be modified by *straight* or *right*, this cannot be taken as evidence that the unit in question is *not* a prepositional phrase. Examples (93)–(98) all involve phrases headed by *for*, which most linguists would analyse as prepositional phrases, and yet in none of these cases can *for* be preceded by *straight* or *right*.

(93) The concern **for most people** is the danger of terrorist activities breaking out on the British mainland. (W2C-012 7)

(94) It will do wonders **for the team's morale**. (W2C-014 20)

(95) He stays at school **for lunch**. (W2F-020 194)

(96) Oh, you have to pay **for these**. (S1A-030 50)

(97) They went off to a restaurant **for a meal**. (S1A-039 75)

(98) Here's a quick look at London's weather **for today**. (S2B-016 26)

This is just a random dip in the results generated by the search software ICECUP retrieving examples of the string *for* + NP from the ICE-GB corpus. I have not checked all examples, but it appears that the majority of phrases headed by *for* cannot in fact be specified by *straight* or *right*. I conclude that Radford's *straight/for* argument carries no weight.

Radford's second bullet point is similar to Huddleston and Pullum *et al.*'s claim that PPs cannot function as subject. However, we have already seen that this is not correct. Radford takes the analysis of the *for . . . to* string as a clause introduced by the complementiser *for* to be *a priori* correct. But if we allow PPs as subjects then his example (78) would simply be another instance of a PP subject.

Next, Radford claims that prepositions are typically not followed by infinitival complements, but by *-ing* clauses. As it stands, this (hedged) claim is simply an *assertion* that *for* in *for . . . to* strings is not a preposition.

It is not a reasoned argument, and as such it can be discounted. I will return to *-ing* clauses in Section 2.4.

In Radford's fourth bullet point the strandability of *for* is tested in constructions involving straightforward PPs and in constructions involving *for . . . to*. While the patterns in (80) involve straightforward *for*-NP displacements in an interrogative structure and a stranding structure, respectively, the ungrammaticality of (82) and (83) can be explained by noting that the string *for which senator* in (82) is not a constituent. In other words, *for* is not in construction with the NP *which senator*. Similarly, the ungrammaticality of (83) can be explained if we assume an analysis in which *which senator* is not in construction with *for*, as I have suggested.

Radford's last bullet point concerning (84)–(87) is the same as Huddleston and Pullum *et al.*'s point about the close parallelism in the use of *for* and *that*. I have already dealt with this above.

2.4 *For* as a Preposition in the Pattern [V/Adj/N [*for* [NP *to* VP]]]

The analysis of *for* as a subordinator/complementiser in the pattern shown in the heading of this section has become commonplace, and is rarely questioned. Having considered the data and arguments presented by Huddleston and Pullum *et al.* and Radford, the conclusion ought to be that synchronically *for* is on balance best regarded as a preposition. As noted in Section 2.3, I propose to analyse (16) as in (37), repeated here as (99).

(99) But the role calls . . .

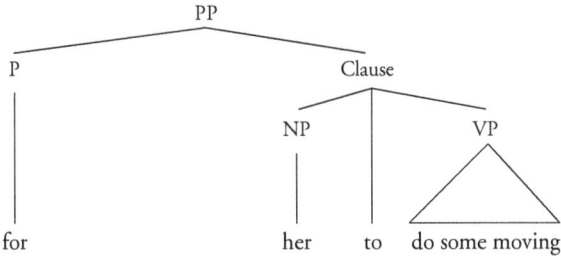

In the remainder of this section I will discuss the strengths of this analysis.

The first advantage of regarding *for* as a preposition is that it allows for a straightforward and elegant account of a large number of parallel structures like those in (41) and (42), noted in Huddleston and Pullum *et al.* (2002: 1182), repeated below as (100) and (101), and like those in (66)–(72), noted in Culicover (1999), repeated below as (102)–(108).

(100) the need **for peace**/the need **for us to cooperate**

(101) too cold **for a swim**/too cold **for us to go out**

(102) a. **For Terry**, I bought this book.
b. **For Terry to learn French**, I bought this book.

(103) a. I bought **for Terry** the book that I had seen.
b. I bought **for Terry to read** [the book that I had seen].

(104) a. I bought this book yesterday **for Terry**.
b. I bought this book yesterday **for Terry to read**.

(105) a. This book is **for Terry**.
b. This book is **for Terry to read**.

(106) a. What this book is for is **for Terry**.
b. What this book is for is **for Terry to read**.

(107) a. ***For Terry** is the purpose of this book.
b. ***For Terry to read** is the purpose of this book.

(108) a. *I bought this book for _ yesterday [a person that I wanted to impress].
b. *I bought this book for _ to read [a person that I wanted to impress].

Another advantage of the proposed analysis is that it will allow us to treat [*for* [NP *to* VP]] and [*for* [(NP) V-*ing*]] constructions on a par. To see why, consider first [*for* [(NP) V-*ing*]] clauses that function as the complement of a preposition. These have not received a great deal of attention in contemporary grammars of English, perhaps because they are relatively rare. Although Huddleston and Pullum *et al.* (2002: 641, 1262) mention what they call *gerund-participials*, with and without a subject, as complements of prepositions, they do so only briefly, giving (109)–(113) as examples.

(109) They're talking **about moving to New York**.

(110) I'm looking forward **to you/your returning home**.

(111) **On hearing the news** she immediately telephoned her father.

(112) She was reported **as saying that she would appeal against the ruling**.

(113) **Although claiming to have a Ph.D.**, he didn't in fact have any degree at all.

As we have seen, for Huddleston and Pullum *et al.*, *to*-infinitivals do not normally occur as complements of prepositions, but *-ing* participle clauses can function in this way because '[s]uch clauses are like NPs' (2002: 333). See also Quirk *et al.* (1985: 1231). Here are some further examples of *-ing* participle clauses, this time as complements of *for*, in which the *for* ... *-ing* clauses perform a variety of functions: noun complement in (114) and (115), with and without a subject, adjective complement in (116) and (117), again with and without a subject, and adjunct in (118) and (119).[14]

(114) I often feel this way, especially in the early rounds of a tournament, and the truth is that while he deserves credit for so many good things in my career, he also deserves blame **for me being more insecure than I ought to be**.   (*Daily Telegraph*, 18 August 2011)

(115) Many thanks for your additional investment of £8,000 gross, £6,000 net, and please accept my apologies **for not acknowledging this sooner**.   (W1B-022 078)

(116) Sven said scandals at the FA were responsible **for him being given the boot and heading back to Sweden**.
        (*Daily Mirror*, 3 November 2013)

(117) Wasn't he famous **for being an amazing conversationalist**?
        (S1A-084 010)

(118) She hated herself **for allowing the policeman to intimidate her**.
        (W2F-009 100)

(119) What we do understand better **for having read this book** is that a stubborn blindness to immediate danger and an eerie prescience of disaster existed concomitantly in European Jewish communities.
        (*Times Higher Education*, 27 March 2014)

---

[14] *For* ... *-ing* clauses are excluded from subject or object position.

The question now arises on what grounds Huddleston and Pullum *et al.* and other grammarians would wish to distinguish *for* ... *to* from *for* ... *-ing* constructions. If we allow *for* to be analysed as a preposition in (114)–(119), I can see no reason why we cannot also do so for structures in which *for* is followed by a *to*-infinitive. Consider the parallel examples in (120) and (121).

(120) It's essential **for there to be no misunderstanding on this point**. (= (49))

(121) I see Warren got a lot of stick **for there being 10 Welshmen in the starting XV**. (*Daily Telegraph*, 8 July 2013)

For Huddleston and Pullum *et al.*, example (120) involves *for* as a subordinator, as we have seen, but in (121) *for* would be regarded as a preposition (2002: 1262). The analysis presented here allows for a parsimonious and elegant parallel way of treating these constructions, including also the *for* + finite clause constructions discussed in Section 2.2.2.

In short, the analysis shown in (99) permits *for* always to be classified as a preposition in the lexicon, either taking an ordinary NP as complement or a clause. The latter can be finite, as in (5)–(8), or non-finite, as with the *for* ... *to* examples discussed in Section 2.3 and the *for* ... *-ing* examples in (114)–(119). As a result, the grammar of English is simplified in treating *for* ... *to*, *for* ... *-ing*, and *for* + finite clause constructions in a parallel fashion, and the lexical entries for verbs involving these constructions will be less complex. An added bonus is that we can do away with the overly complicated historical account in which *for* ceases to be a preposition and becomes a subordinator.

Let's look at a few examples of verbs whose lexical entries are simplified by regarding *for* as a preposition, beginning with *long*. This verb can occur in the following patterns:[15]

(122) On the other hand I **long** to travel, to get out of London, to go to America or just to see wide open unspoilt spaces. (W1B-006 85)

(123) She **longed** for his dismissal.

(124) She **longed** for him to be dismissed.

We can account for these constructions straightforwardly by assuming a lexical entry for *long* as in (125).

---

[15] Examples (123) and (124) are from Huddleston and Pullum *et al.* (2002: 1230).

(125)

$$\textit{long (v.)}: \left[-, \left\{ \begin{array}{l} [_{\text{clause}} \textit{to}\text{-infinitive}] \\ [_{\text{PP}} \textit{for} \left\{ \begin{array}{l} \text{NP} \\ [_{\text{clause}} \text{ NP } \textit{to}\text{-infinitive}] \end{array} \right\}] \end{array} \right\} \right]$$

The entry in (125) shows that *long* licenses either a *to*-infinitive clause without a subject, or a prepositional phrase headed by *for* which in turn licenses an NP or a *to*-infinitive clause with a subject. The analysis proposed here is also adopted in Quirk *et al.* (1985: 1193–4), who regard *long (for)* as a prepositional verb (i.e. a verb taking a PP as complement, along with e.g. *arrange (for)*, *ask (for)*, *burn (for)*, *clamour (for)*, *hope (for)*, *prepare (for)*, etc.). However, for Huddleston and Pullum *et al.* (2002: 1203, 1230), *long* licenses a clause in what they call the '*for*-complex construction'. This necessitates the more complicated lexical entry in (126) in which *for* is either a preposition or a subordinator.[16]

(126)

$$\textit{long (v.)}: \left[-, \left\{ \begin{array}{l} [_{\text{clause}} \textit{to}\text{-infinitive}] \\ [_{\text{PP}} \textit{for } \text{NP}] \\ [_{\text{clause}} \textit{for } \text{NP } \textit{to}\text{-infinitive}] \end{array} \right\} \right]$$

The verb *prefer* occurs in the constructions in (127)–(131). The element *for* in *to*-infinitival constructions is usually omitted in British English.

(127) People **prefer** numbers ending with zeros. (S1B-004 246)

(128) I'd **prefer** to have everything. (S1A-050 97)

(129) Would you call into the station or would you **prefer** him to come to your house? (W2F-009 112)

(130) As before, Hutch sensed that Starsky would **prefer** for him to hurry rather than worrying about being gentle.
(www.starskyhutcharchive.com/starskyhutchslash/HAS4/sink1.htm)

(131) That questions continue to be asked of unpaid internships does not baffle me. I would **prefer** that it did.
(*Daily Telegraph*, 20 March 2014)

---

[16] For Huddleston and Pullum *et al.* (2002: 1230), the following verbs also occur in this construction: *ache, agree, aim, apply, arrange, be dying, burn, burst, can afford, care, clamour, hope, itch, long, opt, pine, say, wait, yearn*. As we saw immediately above, many of these are regarded as prepositional verbs in Quirk *et al.* (1985: 1194).

For *prefer* I suggest that the lexical entry is as in (132).

(132)

$$prefer\,(\text{v.}): \left[-, \left\{\begin{array}{l}\text{NP}\\ [_{\text{clause}}(\text{NP})\,\textit{to}\text{-infinitive}]\\ [_{\text{PP}}\textit{for}\,[_{\text{clause}}\,\text{NP}\,\textit{to}\text{-infinitive}]]\\ [_{\text{clause}}\,\textit{that}\ldots]\end{array}\right\}\right]$$

This entry indicates that *prefer* can license a simple NP complement, a *to*-infinitive clause with or without a subject, a PP introduced by *for* which in turn licenses a clause, or a clause introduced by *that*. An advantage of this analysis is that the syntactic analysis matches the semantic analysis in that the NP *him* in both (129) and (130) is regarded as a subject. Quirk *et al.* (1985: 1193) have the entry in (133) for *prefer*.

(133)

$$prefer\,(\text{v.}): \left[-, \left\{\begin{array}{l}\text{NP}\\ [_{\text{clause}}\,(\text{NP})\,\textit{to}\text{-infinitive}]\\ [_{\text{clause}}\,\textit{for}\,\text{NP}\,\textit{to}\text{-infinitive}]\\ [_{\text{clause}}\,\textit{that}\ldots]\end{array}\right\}\right]$$

For these authors, in (133) the NP is either a straightforward direct object, or it is a subject, just as in (132). However, a difference between (132) and (133) is the categorical status of *for*: it is a preposition in (132), but a subordinator in (133).[17] Huddleston and Pullum *et al.* (2002: 1230) have a lexical entry that differs again, as shown in (134).

(134)

$$prefer\,(\text{v.}): \left[-, \left\{\begin{array}{l}\text{NP}\\ (\text{NP})\,[_{\text{clause}}\,\textit{to}\text{-infinitive}]\\ [_{\text{clause}}\,\textit{for}\,\text{NP}\,\textit{to}\text{-infinitive}]\\ [_{\text{clause}}\,\textit{that}\ldots]\end{array}\right\}\right]$$

For these authors the NP is a 'raised object' in the infinitival constructions when *for* is not present, but a subject when it is.[18] Thus the

---

[17] Quirk *et al.* refer to *for* as a 'peripheral subordinator' (1985: 90, 927–8), but, as we have already seen, they often prefer to avoid the label 'subordinator', and instead refer to *for* as a 'marker of the construction as a nonfinite clause' (1985: 1186), or as the marker of a subject of an infinitive clause (1985: 1193).

[18] Raised objects are the grammatical objects of verbs that license them, despite not having a semantic relationship with those verbs. Thus, even though *prefer* in (129) does not assign a semantic role to

NP immediately following *prefer* in (129) is a raised object, but in (130) the NP following *for* is the subject of the subordinate clause.¹⁹ In the analysis of (129) the syntactic and semantic analyses do not match: syntactically *him* is an object, but semantically it is not.

We end up with several different analyses for constructions in which *prefer* occurs. For the reasons discussed earlier in this section, and on the grounds of simplicity and elegance, the analysis in which *for* is analysed as a preposition, as in (132), is to be preferred.

2.5 Conclusion: *For* is Always a Preposition

In this chapter I have argued that the long-standing analysis of *for* in *for ... to* constructions as a subordinator/complementiser is not supported by the syntactic facts. I have argued instead that *for* is always a preposition. I briefly alluded to this possibility in Aarts (2007: 222). While others have also proposed that *for* is always a preposition (Emonds 1976, 1985; Lightfoot 1979), for these authors *for* is in construction with the following noun phrase. In the present account *for* is in construction with the following clause. This account has a number of advantages. First, it explains the parallelism that obtains between a number of structures in which *for* behaves in the same way (see (51)–(56)). Secondly, this account permits us to treat [*for* [NP *to* VP]] and [*for* [(NP) V-*ing*]] constructions in the same way, as involving a clausal complement of *for*. Thirdly, the

---

him, this NP is still the object of that verb. Surprisingly, Huddleston and Pullum *et al.* do not list *prefer* in the class of verbs that occur in the *for*-complex construction (class 2Aiii; 2002: 1230). They only mention it in a footnote:

> We have noted that the subordinator *for* is like *that* in marking clause boundaries very clearly, so that the *for*-complex construction provides the same kind of evidence for a raising analysis with the few verbs that enter into both plain- and *for*-complex constructions. Compare, then, *I'd prefer Liz to do it herself* and *I'd prefer for Liz to do it herself*; there is no perceptible difference in meaning and the lack of a direct semantic relation between *prefer* and *Liz* is transparent in the *for* construction. (Huddleston and Pullum *et al.* 2002: 1201–2, fn. 20)

The wording here is somewhat misleading, in that it would seem to suggest that both (129) and (130) involve a raised object of *prefer*, whereas in Huddleston and Pullum *et al.*'s (2002) analysis this is only the case for (129).

[19] For discussion, see also Postal (1974: 176ff.), who regards *prefer* as a W-verb, along with *expect, hate, intend, like, mean, need, want,* and *wish*.

account makes for simplified lexicon entries for a number of verbs. And finally, the analysis proposed here leads to a simpler historical account of *for* ... *to* constructions without the need for the kind of category shift proposed by Jespersen (1940) and Visser (1963–1973), adopted widely in the literature.

CHAPTER 3

Whatever Happened to Whatever?

Dan McColm and Graeme Trousdale

3.1 Introduction[*]

The research presented below focuses on aspects of the contemporary forms and uses of *whatever* in Present-day English, along with some discussion of recent diachronic variation which has given rise to these contemporary forms and uses. The research is partly quantitative and partly qualitative in nature; the quantification of variants is an attempt to complement the work of Brinton (2017), whose research on *whatever* is primarily qualitative, and we extend her qualitative analysis by considering additional data from a web corpus. For purposes of comparability with Brinton (2017), we restrict our discussion to variation in the modern period of the history of English, particularly the late Modern period onwards. We use the synchronic and diachronic variation in *whatever* to explore aspects of the nature of directionality in language change, and to consider what we refer to as *bolstering*. Bolstering is a term intended to capture the idea that, while one construction may be the most likely source of a new form-meaning pairing, other constructions serve to strengthen the representation of the new pattern; while these other constructions may not be the primary source, they bolster the new pattern via a formal or a functional alignment (or both). Our notion of bolstering has affinities with both Malkiel's view of pluricausality (Malkiel 1967) and Pijpops and Van de Velde's notion of constructional contamination (Pijpops and Van de Velde 2016), though our focus is predominantly on how bolstering relates to chunking and entrenchment, both of which are concerned with the

---

[*] We are grateful to an anonymous reviewer, to Willem B. Hollmann, and to audiences at the *Gradience and Constructional Change* workshop at the University of Edinburgh, and at a meeting of the Grupo de Estudos Discurso & Gramática UFF in Niterói, in November and December 2017, for helpful comments on some of the material presented here. All shortcomings are our own.

development of a unit-like status that language users ascribe to a given phonetic sequence.

The chapter is structured as follows. In Section 3.2, we outline some of the main ways in which the various forms and functions of *whatever* have developed over time, with a particular focus on recent change. In this section we also consider how those formal and functional changes may be related. This leads to Section 3.3, in which we discuss the methods used to collect and analyse the relevant data. As noted above, in order to complement aspects of the recent corpus work carried out by Brinton (2017), we have included data from a contemporary web-based corpus, but we provide a quantitative analysis based on data from other corpora, including a historical corpus. Section 3.4 is the results section, in which both quantitative and qualitative analyses of the corpus data are related to aspects of the discussion in Brinton (2017). Section 3.5 is the main discussion section, which relates the principles of change to the data presented in Section 3.4. Section 3.6 provides a brief conclusion.

3.2 The Forms and Functions of *Whatever* in Contemporary English

Huddleston and Pullum *et al.* (2002) observe a number of possible functions for *whatever* in standard English, as exemplified in (1).[1]

(1) a. They will not like it, **whatever** you decide. [open interrogative in exhaustive conditional]
 b. They will not like **whatever** you decide. [relative determinative in fused relative]
 c. **Whatever** made you rush out of the office like that? [interrogative determinative]
 d. I see no reason **whatever** for not agreeing to the plan. [negatively-oriented polarity-sensitive item, or NPI]

The relative determinative function has a range of subtypes, some of which are restricted to particular syntactic niches, as illustrated by the examples in (2).

(2) a. He can eat **whatever** he likes. [the 'free choice' construction]
 b. He wants to be a film star or a rock guitarist or **whatever** all of his friends want to do. [head of final element in a co-ordinated NP]

---

[1] We borrow the classificatory terminology from Huddleston and Pullum *et al.* (2002), but the examples are our own unless otherwise stated.

c. He wants to be a film star or **whatever**. [subtype of (2b), where *whatever* has no complement]

By syntactic niche, we mean that there appears to be some constraint on some aspect of the distribution of *whatever* with this particular function, above and beyond other members of the class of relative determinatives. For instance, in relation to the 'free choice' construction (2a), Huddleston and Pullum *et al.* (2002: 1075) observe that '[t]he verb in this construction belongs to a small class consisting primarily of *choose, like, please, want, wish,* and is interpreted as if it had a clausal complement'.

More generally, however, Huddleston and Pullum *et al.* (2002) observe that *whatever* (as opposed to *whichever*) is non-selective. Selectivity is a property of both interrogative and relative determinatives. In connection with the use of interrogative *which*, Huddleston and Pullum *et al.* (2002: 902) state that selectivity 'implies that the value which an answer substitutes for the question variable is to be selected from some definite set'. In (3), for instance, the set is specified by the prepositional phrase that follows the interrogative:

(3) Which of the cakes did you bake?

and the ungrammaticality of (4) suggests that not all interrogatives are selective:

(4) *What of the cakes did you bake?

Huddleston and Pullum *et al.* (2002) recognise, however, that in particular cases where the interrogative is a determiner to a nominal head, both *which* and *what* may be used, but sometimes with a slight difference in meaning, to do with the extent to which a set may be said to be identifiable. The example they provide is given in (5).

(5) Which/What approach to the problem would you recommend?

They suggest that *which* is typically used when a set of approaches has already been identified previously in the discourse; where there is no such clearly defined set from which an approach can be selected, *what* is preferred. This distinction is also a feature of the relative determinative uses of *whichever* and *whatever*: in (6a), the set of books is more clearly identifiable than the set of benefits is in (6b).

(6) a. Buy **whichever** books you want to take on holiday.
     b. He lost **whatever** benefits he'd gained through years of practice.

A further and more general issue concerns the relationship between *what*, *whatever*, and *whatsoever* in the functions that Huddleston and Pullum *et al.* (2002) identify. In many cases, both *what* and *whatever* may be used with a similar function, as illustrated in (7).

(7) a. **What(ever)** made you rush out of the office like that?
    b. He can eat **what(ever)** he likes.

As NPIs, only *whatsoever* and *whatever* are acceptable, while as the last item of a co-ordinated sequence, neither *what* nor *whatsoever* are acceptable, as illustrated by (8a) and (8b) respectively.

(8) a. I see no reason **whatsoever/whatever/*what** for not agreeing to the plan.
    b. He wants to be a film star or **whatever/*what/*whatsoever**.[2]

In cases such as (7b), Huddleston and Pullum *et al.* (2002: 1075) suggest that there is 'no detectable difference in meaning between the *-ever* and simple forms'; we suggest, however, there may well be a formality difference between *whatsoever* and *whatever* in cases where both are permissible.

An additional use of *whatever*, not discussed by Huddleston and Pullum *et al.* (2002), is as a pragmatic or discourse marker, and it is this function that we will be primarily focusing on in the remainder of the chapter. An instance of this use, taken from the *Corpus of Contemporary American English* (COCA), is given in (9).

(9) All right. **Whatever**. I'll let Rush speak for millions and myself.
                                                              (COCA, 2012)

We classify this use as an interjection, following the *Oxford English Dictionary* (*OED*) draft entry dated May 2001 (and see further Brinton 2017). The *OED* definition specifies that the function of the interjection is typically to mark a dismissive, ignorant, and/or unengaged stance on the part of the speaker, often in response to a prior comment made by an interlocutor (see also von Fintel 2000). Brinton (2017: 271), in a discussion of online dictionaries and usage blogs, observes that some users claim that *whatever* may have a more ameliorated meaning, suggesting that it 'may

---

[2] In some cases *or what* appears to be acceptable (e.g. *I don't know whether that was a genuine answer or what*), but such cases seem to us to be canonically associated with clauses which are complements of mental predicates such as *know*, *recall*, and *remember*.

express amenability, that is, acceptance of or acquiescence to the interlocutor's point of view'.

This brief survey of the uses of *whatever* in contemporary English suggests the following:

- *whatever* enters into a partially paradigmatic relationship with *what* and *whatsoever*; not all forms can be used for each function;
- some functions of *whatever* are restricted to a particular syntactic niche (e.g. the use of the form as a relative determinative in the 'free choice' construction);
- there is a sense of indeterminacy which links the fused relative function of *whatever* and the function of *whatever* as an interjection – the first relates to the set from which the value is selected, the second to the stance of the speaker.

3.2.1 Some Non-Standard Forms

Of the little research that has been conducted in this area, most has focused on the form *whatever*. Liberman (2007) and Brinton (2017) suggest that the interjection use of *whatever* tolerates some formal variation, namely a set of abbreviated forms. Such forms include *whatev(s)* and *wevs*, which are considered clippings, along with other types of abbreviation, some of which, by virtue of their orthographic properties, are restricted to the written medium (e.g. *w/ev*, *w'ever*).

That certain uses of *whatever* should be manifest in phonologically and orthographically shorter forms suggests some parallels with a formal change in grammaticalisation (i.e. phonetic reduction); by contrast, on the functional side, the fact that *whatever* – and the reduced forms – in some of their uses come to encode a 'speaker's attitude to the hearer' (Aijmer 1997: 2) suggests some parallels with a functional change in either grammaticalisation, pragmaticalisation, or semantic change more generally (i.e. subjectification). The rest of this section provides a brief summary of the most detailed account of the historical development of the pragmatic marker, i.e. Brinton (2017: 268–83).[3]

In terms of the dating of the change, Brinton (2017) observes that the use of exclamatory *whatever* appears to be a late twentieth-century phenomenon, and suggests two potential syntactic origins for the

---

[3] For information regarding the corpora used by Brinton in her study of the development of English pragmatic markers, see Brinton (2017: 298–9).

pragmatic function: the co-ordinate structure (i.e. *or whatever*), which Brinton refers to as a type of general extender (Overstreet 1999, 2014; Cheshire 2007) and a clause of the type *whatever you say/think*, where *whatever* is followed by a second-person subject and a verb of cognition, volition, or speaking.

Brinton (2017: 272–82) notes that the use of *or whatever* as a type of general extender has a late Modern English (lModE) origin, citing examples from the *Corpus of Historical American English* (COHA) from 1877 onwards. Drawing on Pichler and Levey (2011) and Traugott (2016a), she observes that a development typical of general extenders, namely a shift from the marking of set membership to topic closer or hedge, occurs in the case of *or whatever* in the mid-twentieth century. At a further historical remove, Brinton (2017) sees the use of *or whatever* as a co-ordinator (i.e. as a precursor to the general extender use) as originating from the truncation of parentheticals of the type *or whatever it may be*, in the early Modern English period. The second source that Brinton (2017) identifies is also attested from the lModE period onwards. As in the case with the general extender instances, Brinton observes a certain kind of speaker/writer stance, often associated with irritability or exasperation associated with the interlocutor, as illustrated by (10) (from Brinton 2017: 279).

(10) '**Whatever you please**, M. de Pavannes,' the Italian retorted contemptuously. 'Explain it for yourself!'
[1890 Weyman, *The House of the Wolf*, CEN]

In terms of general frequencies, Tagliamonte (2016: 201), in her corpus of data from the speech of teenagers across different English dialect areas, finds the general extender to be the most frequent function of *whatever*, with the discourse marker function (i.e. the use of *whatever* as a stand-alone expression or conversational turn) accounting for nearly a third of tokens.

A final point to be made is that Brinton does not consider other *whatever*-constructions as likely sources because of the nature of their syntactic embedding; the free choice construction, for instance, involves the phrase headed by *whatever* functioning as a verbal argument, and such cases 'would not lead to the rise of independent *whatever* by any simple process of ellipsis' (Brinton 2017: 279, fn. 27). We return to this in the discussion in Section 3.5.

The question then naturally presents itself as to which of the two sources is the most likely, given that more than one route to the present-day patterns may be traced. Brinton's position is that the *whatever you say*-type is the more likely source than the general extender type, and this position is reached on the grounds of the specific discourse contexts in which the constructions are found. In particular, Brinton sees the *whatever you say*-type as 'always uttered either explicitly in response to a suggestion or wish of an interlocutor or when a possible claim by the interlocutor is presumed or imagined. This is the same context in which we find *whatever*' (Brinton 2017: 282).

In the remainder of this chapter, we consider the following research questions, in light of the research context presented in this section:

- RQ1: To what extent is a quantitative analysis of data from a lModE corpus consistent with the qualitative analysis of the development of *whatever* presented by Brinton (2017)?
- RQ2: Based on a qualitative analysis of a contemporary web corpus, what are the functions of the reduced, non-standard forms, and how does this link up to the historical development of the non-reduced form?
- RQ3: What do these developments suggest about the nature of change from a constructional perspective?

In the following section, we provide an outline of the methods we used to extract and analyse our data.

3.3 Method

The following sections outline the method of the study, describing the corpora used and the process by which the data were collected. The method section also discusses the advantages and disadvantages of using these corpora, as well as the benefits of using variability-based neighbour clustering (VNC) on our dataset.

3.3.1 The Corpora and Token Extraction

The following corpora were used in our study: the *Corpus of Historical American English*, COHA (c. 400 million words), for tokens of *whatever* from 1810 to 2009; the *Corpus of Contemporary American English*, COCA (c. 560 million words), covering the period from 1990 to 2017; and part of the ENCOW16A subcorpus of the COW (*Corpora from the Web*) group of corpora, a 1.6 billion word corpus containing data retrieved from the web between 2012 and 2014 (Schäfer and Bildhauer 2012; Schäfer 2015).

Using this combination of corpora has several advantages. For example, these corpora are balanced in terms of genre, ranging from fiction, newspapers, and magazines to very informal web-based data. A further advantage is that it allows us to explore from a more quantitative perspective some of the principles of constructionalisation and constructional change as outlined by Traugott and Trousdale (2013). While online discourse has been noted as a site of innovation and change, particularly where changes progress at a rapid rate (see e.g. Crystal 2001), using the ENCOW16A corpus presented something of a problem, as information on the year of publication of a given text may either be missing or difficult to find. Nevertheless, it can be inferred from the nature of the corpus that the texts are highly likely to be informal web-based publications such as blog and forum posts published within the last fifteen years. A further problem arose with the corpus in that some of the texts contained typographical errors (sometimes minor, sometimes rendering the text unintelligible). Problematic data such as these were not counted for the purposes of the analysis.

Following Brinton (2017), all three corpora were searched for *whatever* and the following variants: *wev, whatev(s), w/e, w/ever, w/lev, wever, w'ever, (t)evs*. In addition, we searched the corpus for *whatevers*, to test the hypothesis that a new form of *whatever* might have emerged as a result of analogy with *whatev > whatevs*. Searching the corpora for *whatevers* returned some irrelevant results, such as *whatevers* being used in place of *whatever's* (as in *Whatever's the matter?*). These examples were manually excluded.

The COHA and COCA corpora contain 58,668 and 65,657 tokens of *whatever* respectively. To facilitate analysis, we took a random sample of 125 tokens from each of the twenty decades in the COHA corpus. A further problem arose when collecting the COCA examples; it is not possible to take a random sample from each decade of this corpus. A total of 2,500 tokens was initially taken from COCA; after removing data which involved false starts, duplicates, and the like, 2,393 tokens remained, with the distribution across each decade as indicated in Table 3.1.

Each token of *whatever* was coded as belonging to one of the following categories: (i) exhaustive conditional (as in example (11)), (ii) relative determinative (12), (iii) interrogative determinative (13), (iv) discourse marker (14), (v) general extender at the end of a list (15), (vi) negatively oriented polarity item (NPI) (16), (vii) replacement (17), (viii) reduced discourse marker (18), and (ix) component of a chunk (19), which we considered as a routinised frequent collocation (see further Beckner and Bybee 2009; Bybee 2011). No reduced discourse markers were found in the COCA or COHA data, suggesting that reduction in this function is a very recent phenomenon. As a result, not all of the categories listed in (i) to (ix) appear in every table and figure in this chapter. We classified the following as

Table 3.1 *Distribution of* whatever *in the COCA corpus per decade*

Decade	Tokens
1990s	468
2000s	431
2010s	1,494
Total	2,393

chunks in our data, on the grounds that they are idiomatic to some degree: *for whatever reason*; *whatever* S V patterns of the kind *whatever you think*; *whatever else*; *or whatever*; *whatever floats your boat*; and *whatever* PRO *name is*. Some tokens of *whatever* were underdetermined; for the purposes of our analysis, these tokens were treated as a separate category, and will be discussed in more detail in the qualitative analysis in Section 3.5.

(11) **Whatever** was the purpose of his visit, it was not long continued (COHA, 1824)

(12) I will partake of **whatever** you have for supper (COHA, 1824)

(13) Why Billy, **whatever** is the matter? (COHA, 1909)

(14) Yep, that's us. '**Whatever**.' (COHA, 2002)

(15) Imagine you're on the center court at Wimbledon, hitting that ball, left hand, right hand, forehand, backhand, **whatever**. (COCA, 2007)

(16) in no respect **whatever** have I bred disturbance among the people (COHA, 1824)

(17) Right. The Universal Theory of **Whatever**. (COCA, 2012)

(18) No one ever made the argument you just summarized there, so **whatevs**. (ENCOW16A, 2004)

(19) And for **whatever** reason, she cares about you. She loves you. (COCA, 2000)

Tokens were excluded if they fell into one of the following three categories:

A. Where the speaker or writer made a 'false start', e.g. as in (20).

(20) I always like to say therapy is like a – **whatever** works for you works. (COCA, 2012)

B. Where the expression is incomplete in some way, as in (21).

(21) And secondly, you know, I'll do **whatever** the – you know, I – there – you know, I – I (COCA, 2012)

C. Where *whatever* or its reduced variants represented part of a book or film title, as in (22).

(22) Although *The Will to* **Whatevs** is comedy, is there some aspect of it that would actually help someone? (ENCOW16A, 2012)

Furthermore, duplicates in the corpora were also excluded.

3.3.2 Periodisation and Variability-Based Neighbour Clustering (VNC)

Periodisation in historical linguistics is a complex issue: pre-defined periods such as decades or half-centuries may not be particularly meaningful for the development of the particular linguistic item under investigation and may in fact provide misleading conclusions (Gries and Hilpert 2012: 134–5). For this reason, we decided to apply a VNC analysis to our COHA dataset. We did not apply a VNC analysis to our COCA dataset, because COCA covers a very small time period and therefore does not require further periodisation. In order to perform the VNC analysis, we used the script published on the companion website to Gries and Hilpert (2012).[4] This script generates a dendrogram, from which we can infer the most informative way of dividing the dataset into clusters. We return to this in Section 3.4.1 immediately below.

3.4 Results

In this section we present the results of the corpus investigation. We begin with the historical corpus COHA in Section 3.4.1. In Section 3.4.2, we present the findings from COCA, and compare these with the COHA data from Section 3.4.1. In Section 3.4.3 some data from ENCOW16A is given.

---

[4] See http://global.oup.com/us/companion.websites/fdscontent/uscompanion/us/static/companion.websites/nevalainen/Gries-Hilpert_web_final/vnc.individual.html.

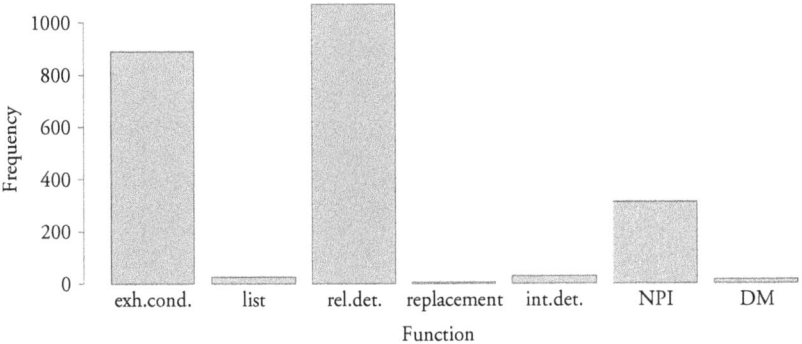

Figure 3.1 Distribution of *whatever* by function in COHA

3.4.1 COHA

Of the 2,500 tokens from COHA we initially sampled, three were removed due to duplication and similar reasons as mentioned in Section 3.3.1, and fifty-three were underdetermined as to their function, meaning that 2,444 tokens were available for quantitative analysis. The distribution of *whatever* in functions (i)–(vii) outlined above is shown in Figure 3.1. Note that the fifty-three tokens which were underdetermined are not represented in this figure.

We also found forty-seven tokens of *whatever* in chunks, function (ix) above. The distribution of these chunks is shown in Figure 3.2.

As discussed in Section 3.3 above, in order to efficiently periodise the COHA data in an informative manner, a VNC analysis was performed. The dendrogram which resulted is shown in Figure 3.3.

This dendrogram suggests that the COHA data can be divided into three clusters: one cluster covering the period 1815–1915, one covering the period 1920–1990, and one covering the period 1990–2000. The tokens sampled in these periods were grouped together and a normalised frequency per one million words was calculated for each cluster. As some of these clusters begin and end in the middle of a decade, and COHA only provides word counts for periods of whole decades, it was assumed that the word count for the second half of a decade is equal to the total word count for that decade divided by two. Table 3.2 shows the distribution of *whatever* by function in COHA per million words. No instances of *whatever* functioning as a replacement were found in COHA.

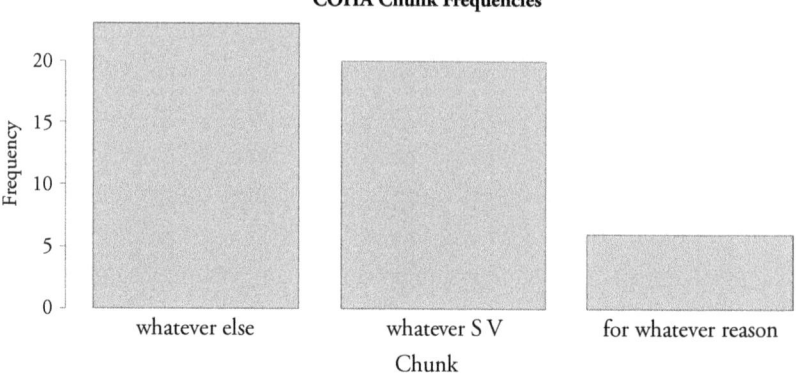

Figure 3.2 Distribution of *whatever* in chunks in COHA

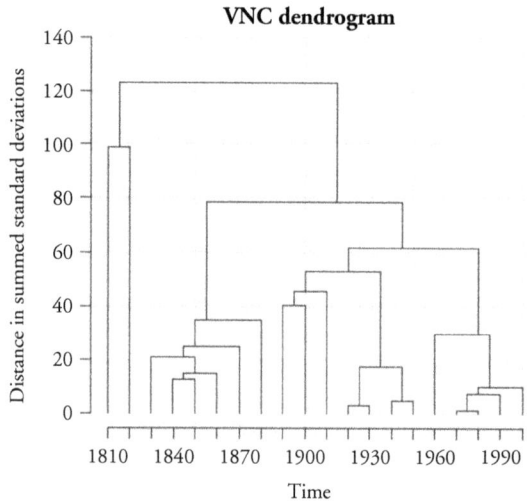

Figure 3.3 COHA VNC dendrogram

As Table 3.2 shows, the exhaustive conditional and NPI functions of *whatever* are sharply decreasing in frequency while the list and discourse marker functions are increasing in frequency, albeit only slightly. Further, the frequency of the relative determinative function underwent a sharp decline between 1915 and 1990, but has now increased to almost the same frequency as between 1815 and 1915.

Table 3.2 *Distribution of* whatever *in COHA per million words*

	Cluster		
Function	1815–1915	1920–1990	1990–2000
exhaustive conditional	9.390	7.168	4.144
relative determinative	2.762	1.816	4.596
NPI	2.406	1.111	0.301
interrogative determinative	0.045	0.251	0.000
general extender at the end of a list	0.000	0.179	0.301
discourse marker	0.011	0.048	0.829

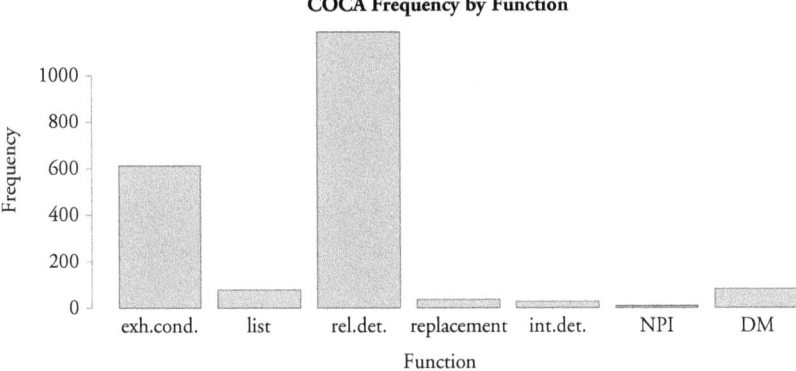

Figure 3.4 Distribution of *whatever* by function in COCA

3.4.2 COCA

In total, we investigated 2,353 tokens of *whatever* in COCA. The distribution of *whatever* across each function is shown in Figure 3.4. Note that as was the case with the COHA data, tokens which appeared in chunks and underdetermined tokens of *whatever* are not shown in this figure. In addition, 117 chunks were found in the COCA data. The distribution of these is shown in Figure 3.5.

Although we did not apply a VNC analysis to the COCA data, we nonetheless calculated normalised frequencies per million words in each decade of the COCA data. This was done because the data in the COCA corpus is not equally distributed across each decade. Table 3.3 shows the normalised distribution of tokens of *whatever* across each decade per million words.

Table 3.3 *Distribution of* whatever *in COCA per million words*

Function	Cluster		
	1990s	2000s	2010s
exhaustive conditional	1.020	1.033	4.795
interrogative determinative	0.039	0.015	0.111
discourse marker	0.098	0.099	0.556
general extender at the end of a list	0.172	0.149	0.750
NPI	0.015	0.015	0.028
relative determinative	0.917	0.785	3.697
replacement	0.005	0.010	0.160

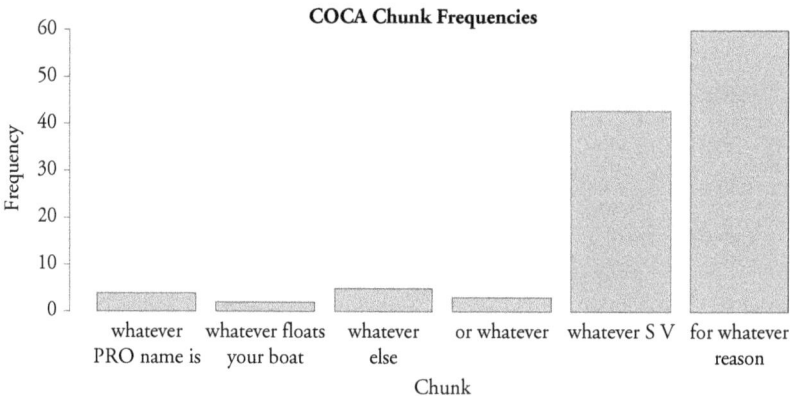

Figure 3.5 Distribution of *whatever* in chunks in COCA

The results of the VNC analysis of the COHA data suggested that the period spanning 1990 to 2000 constituted a coherent period of analysis; this period overlaps partly with the COCA data. The low token frequency of the interrogative determinative and NPI uses in COCA may be a formality issue, with such uses becoming restricted to a more formal register. Formality might also explain the absence of the replacement function from the COHA data.

3.4.3 ENCOW16A

In order to extend the qualitative analysis provided by Brinton (2017), we provide a discussion of some data from the ENCOW16A corpus. As mentioned in Section 3.3, the ENCOW16A corpus contains highly informal web-based data, and as such, we used this corpus to search for shortened variants of *whatever*. *Whatev* and *whatevs* were both attested in the discourse marker function. In addition, we found *whoevs*, *howev*, *whenev*, and *wherev* functioning as discourse markers, which may be bolstering discourse marker functions of *whatev(s)*. Some examples of these tokens are given in (23)–(25).

(23) [...] God or David Attenborough or **whoevs**. (ENCOW16A)

(24) have to tell u one thing Al-qaudah (or **howev** u spell it) arent muslims. (ENCOW16A)

(25) a hairstylist willing to jet off **whenev wherev**. (ENCOW16A)

We initially hypothesised that reduced variants of *whatever* would only be associated with the discourse marker function. However, we also found some instances where reduced variants of *whatever* functioned as a replacement (26), an exhaustive conditional (27), or interrogative determinative (28).

(26) You lying son of a **whatev**. (ENCOW16A)

(27) **Whatevs** you do, check the middle of the chicken to see if it's cooked through (ENCOW16A)

(28) LOOOOL **whatev** happened to the HiSTORIC Obysmal GOTV effort? (ENCOW16A)

3.5 Discussion

The overall picture from the quantitative data in Section 3.4 may be summarised as follows:

- Some functions of *whatever* reduce in token frequency (e.g. *whatever* as NPI, interrogative determinative, and exhaustive conditional).
- Some functions of *whatever* remain frequent (e.g. *whatever* as a relative determinative).
- Some functions of *whatever* increase in frequency (e.g. *whatever* and – especially in the twenty-first century – the reduced forms as a discourse marker).

Our discussion centres around the three questions posed at the end of Section 3.2, which are repeated here for convenience. We deal with each of these questions in Sections 3.5.1 to 3.5.3, respectively.

- RQ1: To what extent is a quantitative analysis of data from a lModE corpus consistent with the qualitative analysis of the development of *whatever* presented by Brinton (2017)?
- RQ2: Based on a qualitative analysis of a contemporary web corpus, what are the functions of the reduced, non-standard forms, and how does this link up to the historical development of the non-reduced form?
- RQ3: What do these developments suggest about the nature of change from a constructional perspective?

3.5.1 Quantitative and Qualitative Analyses

Our results provide quantitative evidence for the various grammatical and semantic developments affecting the history of *whatever* in the lModE period, to complement the work of Brinton (2017). In this section, we consider the extent to which 'multiple sources' may be said to play a role in the development of *whatever* as a discourse marker, following up suggestions from Brinton's research. We begin with a more detailed discussion of our findings based on the COHA data. Quantitative data (see Figure 3.1) suggest that exhaustive conditional and relative determinative functions of *whatever* dominate. These are illustrated in (29) and (30).

(29) Your language, sirrah, **whatever** you may be, is ruffianly and insolent (COHA, 1831)

(30) they are fearless Englishmen who will do what they say, and say **whatever** their landlord shall please to require of them (COHA, 1835)

While the relative determinative function involves a form that is more embedded within the matrix clause than is the case with the exhaustive conditional, in both cases there is a pragmatic inference that the variable element concerns a list of possible but ultimately irrelevant options that the speaker chooses not to enumerate. In (29) the inference is that the addressee may be any one of a number of possible things, but that the speaker does not wish to list them; similarly, in (30) the list of things that the Englishmen could possibly say is not important enough for the speaker to provide details. In other words, for both of the dominant types in the COHA data (in terms of token frequency), there is a salient pragmatic inference that the variable concerns an irrelevant but exhaustive list.

This listing is more explicit in some of the less frequently attested uses of *whatever*. Another early nineteenth-century example is provided in (31).

(31) The squaws seized clubs, axes, or **whatever** weapon of offense first offered itself to their hands (COHA, 1826)

Here *whatever* introduces the general category from which the specific instances in the list are taken (i.e. clubs and axes are both types of offensive weapon). Again there is the inference that it is unnecessary for the speaker to be any more detailed in listing particular instances of the general category.

A similar situation arises with examples of *whatever* being used as a general extender. This case is like that of the list example in (31), with one significant difference: the more general category is not verbalised. We consider this to be an instance of formal reduction. An example of this from COHA is provided in (32).

(32) forage of any kind, meat of any kind, vegetables, corn-meal, or **whatever** is needed by the command (COHA, 1875)

Such instances also serve to code a certain attitude or stance on the part of the speaker, particularly one which appears to be dismissive to the addressee, as illustrated in (33).

(33) Well, Willoughby Pastures, – or **whatever** your name is, – you'll get yourself into the papers this time (COHA, 1877)

Particular 'chunked' examples (e.g. *whatever you call it*) are also attested in the COHA data with a similar inference, i.e. that it is unnecessary for the speaker to be any more detailed than they already have been in an earlier part of the discourse. However, in some cases, the sense that the speaker is being dismissive does not seem to be present, as in (34).

(34) The central object, the globe, air-ship, or **whatever you may be pleased to call it**, is your own conception (COHA, 1898)

Rather than being dismissive, the speaker/writer pays attention to the hearer/reader's face in order to mitigate the effects of a potentially face-threatening act. Indeed, whether the use of *whatever* is face-protecting or face-threatening is not as important as the fact that the utterance is clearly involved in some sort of face-work. This is an important step in the development of *whatever* as an entire conversational turn in the twentieth century. As Brinton (2017) observes, there is a long history of *whatever* being used with chunks involving the second-person pronoun and a verb (i.e. *whatever you* V). She cites the following example from Henry Fielding's *Tom Jones* (1749):

(35) 'Very well, madam,' quoth Western, '**whatever you please**'

And later examples from COHA seem rather to confirm that such chunks may indicate a deferential attitude of the speaker towards the hearer, as in (36) and (37).

(36) **whatever you think best**, mother (COHA, 1943)

(37) **Whatever you say**, honey (COHA, 1950)

The quantitative analysis of the COHA data therefore supports the qualitative analysis provided by Brinton (2017) and elaborates on it in the following ways:

- While the exhaustive conditional and relative determinative functions both have high token frequency in the COHA sample, there are clear instances in which there is a pragmatic inference that the variable element in both constructions consists of a list of things which the speaker appears to consider trivial or unworthy of verbalisation in some way.
- This inference becomes more salient in cases where some items of the list are mentioned, and *whatever* is appended to the end of the list, sometimes with a following nominal or clausal complement, and sometimes without. These latter cases constitute the general extender function; the former may involve chunking of various kinds (e.g. *or whatever your name is*; *or whatever you want*).
- The general extender use, along with the chunks, come to serve as means of engaging in face-work. This face-work may show deference to the speaker (*whatever you say, dear*), or the expression may constitute a dismissive, face-threatening act (*A: You really annoyed me last night. B: Whatever.*).

Brinton (2017) raises the interesting question of whether the general extender function or the second-person chunk (e.g. *whatever you say*) is the most likely source of the stand-alone discourse marker, suggesting that the latter is likely to be the source, with the general extender facilitating (or in our terms, bolstering) the development. Her explanation focuses on the dialogic context of use associated with the chunked forms, which is not the case for the general extender uses. Our analysis has foregrounded the 'trivialisation' effect of many of the uses of *whatever* (pragmatically in the case of some exhaustive conditional and relative determiner uses, perhaps semantically in the case of general extenders and the discourse markers). We would therefore support the idea of multiple sources (see Van de Velde et al. 2013 for an overview of multiple sources in a theory of language change) for the development of the discourse marker form, in which developments in the (dialogic) chunks reinforce developments in the (monologic) general extenders, and vice versa. This reciprocity is further manifest in the use of formally reduced forms with functions typically associated with the full forms (i.e. the use of *whatevs* as a relative determinative) in the contemporary data from ENCOW16A. Just as there is a tendency for the dialogic contexts to promote the discourse marker function of *whatever*, so there is a tendency for the non-reduced forms of *whatever* to fulfil the older functions; and just as monologic contexts may atypically bolster the development of the discourse marker, so atypically the reduced forms may appear in exhaustive conditionals. We address this issue in detail in the next section.

3.5.2 *Reduction and Expansion in the Contemporary Language*

We noted above that general extender uses involve some degree of formal reduction (by virtue of not specifying the more general category to which listed members belong). Even more salient reductions are attested in the contemporary corpus, where the word *whatever* is reduced to *whatevs* or *whatev*. Typically, but not exclusively, the function of these reduced forms is as a general extender or stance marker (see example (27) above for a case where *whatevs* is used as a marker of an exhaustive conditional).

The developments of *whatever* > *whatev(s)* is paralleled by a further change, *whatever* > *whatevers*. These changes are interesting in several ways. In both cases, the original *whatever* has undergone expansions (Himmelmann 2004), coming to encode new functions beyond its original uses in exhaustive conditionals and as a relative determinative. In the first case, the form has undergone phonological attrition, and while it is most commonly used as a discourse marker, in some cases it has been 'recycled' in the original functions of *whatever* as seen in (24) and (25) above. The case of *whatevers* is rather different – there has been no phonological attrition (quite the reverse, in fact), but there have been syntactic and semantic expansions. Some tokens of *whatevers* in the ENCOW16A corpus appear to be plural nouns (see examples (38) and (39) below); in such cases the *-s* might thus be categorised as the plural inflection.

(38) collecting 20 **whatevers** in your standard fantasy RPG

(ENCOW16A)

(39) Most of the big innovative **whatevers** have been largely disappointing (ENCOW16A)

Interestingly, whenever *whatevers* is used as a general extender at the end of a list, the speaker/writer appears to be indicating that he cannot remember or is indifferent to other items which could be listed (as is the case with the general extender *whatever*), but *whatevers* seems to be used in this function when the list preceding the general extender contains plural nouns.

Most notably, however, *whatevers* was also attested as a stand-alone discourse marker. In such cases, the *-s* suffix cannot be categorised as the plural marker; in other words, there has been a further neoanalysis, motivated by analogical thinking (see the discussion in Traugott and Trousdale 2013). We hypothesise that *whatevers* as an interjection arose by analogy with *whatev* > *whatevs* or indeed *wev* > *wevs* or *tev* > *tevs* (though the latter two pairs of reduced variants were not attested in our historical data). The development of *whatever* > *whatevers* is consistent with other linguistic items which contain an *-s* marker encoding speaker familiarity or informality, e.g. *totally* > *totes*, *obviously* > *obvs*, and *awkward* > *awks* (see Spradlin 2016). While this pattern typically involves a suffixed clipping, clearly the analogical pull has applied to the full form too: further research in this area might consider developments like *whenevs* and *wherevers*, to see how other *-ever* forms are changing. This not only supports the idea that analogical thinking is key to constructional changes in the network; it also shows how formal and functional reduction and expansion are intertwined: it is usually the case that the reduced form is associated with an expanded function, but this is not always so. While there are instances of the 'reduced form, older function' combinations, as in example (27), frequently it is the non-reduced form that is used with the expanded function, as in (40).

(40) Mama frowned at her mother-in-law. '**Whatever**.' Grandma sighed. (COCA, 2012)

How does this relate to general patterns of grammatical change? Traugott and Trousdale (2010), in their discussion of the relationship between gradience, gradualness, and grammaticalisation, observe that diachronic gradualness may be understood as a sequence of (micro-)stepwise changes affecting both the structural properties of a sign and its use. Changes to the structural properties of *whatever* are more salient in the very recent history of English (i.e. the phonologically reduced forms *whatevs* and *whatev*), but it is also possible to include in this the development of the general extender (*or whatever*) and the chunks like *whatever you say* and *whatever you think*. These involve reduction in terms of fixing, the development of collocational bonding, and more generally, idiomaticisation. Changes in use are typically more long term, and involve the general shift from *whatever* as a marker of an expression involving an undetermined list, through to the general extender and stance functions discussed above.

Traugott and Trousdale (2010) are also concerned with the nature of synchronic gradience and its relation to gradualness. In the case of *whatever*, the synchronic gradience may be found in the mismatch between the 'typical' form and the 'typical' function. In other words, the reduced forms are typically associated with a discourse marker function, while the full form has a range of different uses (including as a discourse marker).

3.5.3 On Constructions and Change

Our last question concerns the role of constructions in change. We have not presented the research using an explicit construction grammar formalism, but much of our findings tallies with some of the general ideas regarding constructional change laid out by Traugott and Trousdale (2013). We consider the following to be particularly relevant, and possible avenues for further research: chunking; schemas with slots; and directionality as the constructional network changes.

In a discussion of chunking, Bybee (2013: 54) observes that '[m]emory storage of complex units such as idiomatic phrases or constructions requires links of various sorts. First, there is the sequential linking that comes about through repetition of sequences of units'. This is clearly relevant for the development of the patterns of the type *whatever you* V, where V is a slot filled by a verb of speaking or reasoning (Brinton 2017), but it also holds for the development of general extenders of the kind [CONJ *whatever*], where CONJ is a slot for conjunctions of various kinds (most typically *or*). Thus the chunking is relevant both in dialogic and in monologic contexts. Furthermore, such chunking often leads to reductions of various kinds (see the discussion in Traugott and Trousdale 2013: 122–4), which might explain both the creation of discourse marker *whatever* in dialogic contexts (loss of the *you* V sequence) and in monologic ones (loss of the conjunction at the end of the list, leading to an ambiguous context where *whatever* could be considered either as a general extender or as a stance/discourse marker).

As observed in Section 3.5.2 above, reduction and expansion are very closely entwined in the development of *whatever*, and expansion in constructional terms may usefully be considered as the creation of schemas with slots (see e.g. Hilpert 2014, among others). The kind of expansions that Himmelmann (2004) observes in relation to grammaticalisation often involves a broadening of the slot in such a pattern. For instance, as *be going to* V as a future marker undergoes a collocational shift from purely non-stative verbs to both stative and non-statives, the range of verbs that can fill the slot in *be going to* V increases, entailing an increase both in type frequency and potentially token frequency (see the discussion in Traugott and Trousdale 2013: 114–18, and references therein). A similar situation arises in the case of *whatever*. The typical pattern for *whatever* as a general extender is illustrated in (41).

(41) That guy Bobby Klein came up as somebody who had worked in that world of psychotherapy or drug management **or whatever**.

(COCA, 2017)

Here *whatever* is preceded by a sequence of noun phrases, and immediately preceded by the conjunction *or*. However, neither of these is obligatory, as examples (42) and (43) illustrate.

(42) You may try to explode it, blow it up, **whatever**, depending on what you want to do with it (COCA, 2006)

(43) he didn't care whether they were young, old, female, male **whatever**

(COCA, 2001)

The relaxation of this constraint, i.e. that the general extender function needs to consist of a schema whose formal pole may be represented as [NP CONJ *whatever*], has a number of effects. First, the form of the new schema, i.e. [XP (CONJ) *whatever*], involves expansion since the items that constitute the list are not required to be noun phrases. Second, the fact that the conjunction becomes optional aligns this monologic context with that of the dialogic context, which further facilitates the development of the discourse marker. In other words, the general extenders and the reduced chunks become structurally more similar, consisting of a phrase whose category is not specified followed by *whatever*. Once this level of generality is reached, it is easy to see how *whatever* could come to be interpreted as a stance marker.

Our final point concerns directionality. We have argued that processes involving reduction and expansion are closely linked in the development of *whatever*. Following Traugott and Trousdale (2013), we do not see this as contradictory. Certain parts of the schema – i.e. the 'fixed' part – have undergone reduction, particularly in the very recent history of English, as the data from the ENCOW16A corpus show. Here we see traditional patterns of reduction, including a weakening of the phonetic signal (i.e. attrition) in the development of *whatever* > *whatev* (and the further attested reduced form *tev*). The expansions occur in the three types of context that Himmelmann (2004) identifies: host-class, syntactic, and semantic-pragmatic, as we have shown. This suggests that the developments surrounding *whatever*-constructions constitute grammatical constructionalisations in the terminology of Traugott and Trousdale (2013). We do not suggest that the reductions in *whatever*-constructions constitute an increase in dependency, as is typically the case for the development of case or tense markers in grammatical constructionalisations. Rather, because this change involves the development of a discourse marker, we see a decrease in syntactic dependency (Brinton and Traugott 2005: 99; Traugott and Trousdale 2013: 108). Indeed, we see the development of the discourse marker *whatever*, from both dialogic and monologic contexts, as fitting nicely with parts of the following description of the development of discourse markers provided by Traugott and Trousdale (2013: 109):

> there is often a change in meaning from contentful to procedural (sometimes involving reduced segments and bonding), followed by recruitment to clause periphery position as a pragmatic marker (expansion of syntactic scope). One of these functions may be to mark the speaker's metatextual evaluation of the relationship of the upcoming clause to what has been said before.

The key feature of *whatever* as a right periphery discourse marker is that what is 'upcoming' is often silence on the part of the speaker: *whatever* can function as a stand-alone turn that signals not only the speaker's view on what has been said before, but also the view that the discourse should come to an end.

While we have not couched our discussion in explicitly constructional terms, we see clear overlaps between this quantitative study and the kind of qualitative analysis regarding constructional changes that Traugott and Trousdale (2013) set out. The development of *whatever* as a discourse marker clearly involves chunking of various kinds, and demonstrates the interrelatedness of reduction and expansion in language change. It also suggests that a network based approach (which allows for alignment between related constructional types) is well-suited to explain patterns of language change.

3.6 Conclusion

Our aim in this chapter has been to investigate the development of *whatever* in recent and contemporary English, as a complement to the recent work by Brinton (2017). In particular, we sought to extend the discussion by investigating some of the patterns from a quantitative perspective. The summary answers to our research questions presented at the end of Section 3.2 are as follows:

- RQ1: To what extent is a quantitative analysis of data from a lModE corpus consistent with the qualitative analysis of the development of *whatever* presented by Brinton (2017)?
  We concur with Brinton that certain chunks (such as *whatever you* V) have a significant role to play in the development of the discourse marker *whatever*, which typically serves as a distinct conversational turn. In addition, our results suggest that a similar (but not identical) path may be traced in monologic contexts.

- RQ2: Based on a qualitative analysis of a contemporary web corpus, what are the functions of the reduced, non-standard forms, and how does this link up to the historical development of the non-reduced form?
  While reduced forms typically have more procedural functions, it is not the case that they exclusively function in this way. Data from the ENCOW16A corpus (such as the use of the reduced form *whatev* in the exhaustive conditional construction) raise interesting questions about directionality of change in a network model of language.

- RQ3: What do these developments suggest about the nature of change from a constructional perspective?
  Our study lends weight to an approach to grammatical change which privileges a view of language as a conceptual network of constructions at various levels of generality, and change as a change to the links between nodes in that network. In focusing on understanding grammatical change as change to the structure and function of schemas in a network, we are able to see similarities between what appear to be fairly diverse structures, and illustrate how changes in one part of the network may bolster change in another, related or linked part, a property which seems to be characteristic of changes involving multiple inheritance.

CHAPTER 4

Are Comparative Modals Converging or Diverging in English? Different Answers from the Perspectives of Grammaticalisation and Constructionalisation

Elizabeth Closs Traugott

4.1 Introduction[*]

In the last few years several papers have appeared on the synchrony and diachrony of the 'comparative modal' *(had/'d) better*, inspired by Denison and Cort (2010), which pays particular attention to the rise of 'bare' *better*, as in *You better go*. Van der Auwera *et al.* (2013) provide extensive statistical analysis of British and American usage of *'d better* and its variants. Van der Auwera and De Wit (2010) investigate another comparative *had/'d rather* as well in the Brown family of corpora. A third comparative modal *had/'d sooner* is mentioned in these papers. Van linden (2015) investigates all three in the history of American English as represented in the *Corpus of Historical American English* (COHA), from the perspective of grammaticalisation. Likewise, Traugott (2016b) investigates all three, but in the context of the role of semantic modal maps in a constructional approach to change. Earlier works include van der Gaaf (1904, 1912).

Fairly recent examples from the *British National Corpus* (BYU-BNC) of the three comparative modals are presented in (1a)–(1d).

(1) a. he never turned up so about nine o'clock I says, **I'd better** phone the police.

(1985–1994 *Oral History Project*
[BYU-BNC: GYT S_interview_oral_history])

b. I suppose I **had better** make a move to get some clothes on you think? (1991 *Conversations* [BYU-BNC: KB7 S_conv])

---

[*] Many thanks to Willem B. Hollmann and an anonymous reviewer for helpful comments on an earlier draft.

c. I mean don't hesitate to come back, because at the end of the day I**'d rather** you know too much than not enough

(1991 *Conversations* [BYU-BNC: KB7 S_conv])

d. He wanted twelve shillings. I said we**'d sooner** sleep under the hedges.

(1978 Macdonald, *The Rich Are With You Always* [BYU-BNC: HPo W_fict_prose])

The purpose of the present chapter is to complement Van linden's (2015) study of developments in the history of American English with an investigation of BETTER, RATHER, and SOONER in the history of British English through the end of the nineteenth century, from the perspective of constructionalisation. Following Denison and Cort (2010) and the other authors cited here, I use the forms BETTER, RATHER, and SOONER to generalise over the various morphological forms such as *had/'d better*, *would/'d/had rather*, and *would/'d/had sooner* and to distinguish them from the adverbs *better, rather, sooner*.

Van linden (2015) focuses on grammaticalisation as evidenced in COHA by reduction in morphophonological form of the auxiliaries *had* and *would*, and of the standard of comparison *than*. She concludes that the three comparative modals 'are overall developing in the same direction' (2015: 221), despite heterogeneity in structure and meaning. She also establishes a grammaticalisation cline BETTER > SOONER > RATHER (2015: 223), based on the fact that in her data BETTER shows the highest erosion of auxiliaries, SOONER the second highest, and RATHER the least. My perspective is that of Construction Grammar (e.g. Croft 2001; Goldberg 2006) and constructionalisation and constructional changes (Traugott and Trousdale 2013). Since the basic architecture of Construction Grammar consists of form-meaning pairings, I consider meaning as well as form. Comparison of the grammaticalisation and constructionalisation approaches shows that they lead to different perspectives on directionality. Since BETTER, RATHER, and SOONER have variously been said to form a 'set', 'group', or 'class', I assess whether they are best viewed as forming a single subschema of modality, or as members of different subschemas. In this case I conclude with Van linden (2015) that RATHER and SOONER form a set distinct from BETTER (see also Traugott 2016b: 119).

The structure of this chapter is as follows. In Section 4.2, I introduce elements of the constructional model that are key to the argument. Data and methodology are outlined in Section 4.3. Section 4.4 introduces the main characteristics of the comparative modals in Present-day English (PDE) and the similarities and differences identified in earlier work. Section 4.5 outlines the main historical morphosyntactic and semantic developments of the constructions BETTER, RATHER, and SOONER until the eighteenth century. Section 4.6 details the uses of the three modals from the beginning of the eighteenth century to the turn of the twentieth as evidenced by the *Old Bailey Corpus* (OBC). Section 4.7 addresses the question of how the three micro-constructions were organised in late Modern English (lModE). Section 4.8 compares the grammaticalisation and constructionalisation approaches, especially with respect to directionality, and Section 4.9 concludes.

4.2 Data and Method

Whereas Van linden (2015) cites early examples from van der Gaaf (1904), I explore evidence for early developments in the electronic version of the *Middle English Dictionary* (*MED*) and from a number of electronic databases that reflect relatively informal early Modern English (Culpeper and Kytö 2010), including *A Corpus of English Dialogues 1560–1760* (CED) and the *Corpus of Early English Correspondence Sampler* (CEECS). The main analysis is based on the *Old Bailey Corpus* (OBC). OBC is a balanced subset of 13.9 million words for the years 1720–1913 of the 113 million word *Proceedings of the Old Bailey* (OBPO, 1674–1913) selected to provide evidence of spoken language of the time: '[s]ince the proceedings were taken down in shorthand by scribes in the courtroom, the verbatim passages are arguably as near as we can get to the spoken word of the period' (OBC website: 'About the project').

Searches were conducted for *better, rather, sooner* preceded by an auxiliary, not only those that have been attested in other works (*'d, had, might, should, would*), but also *can, could, may, must, shall,* and *will*. Further searches targeted particular uses, such as that of *have V-en* for 'past tense', or a complement clause immediately following *better, rather, sooner*.[1] Data for most of the searches were sparse, so the study is necessarily largely qualitative. By contrast, Van linden's study is quantitative, based on the far larger database of COHA (400 million words).

Only examples in which *auxiliary + better/rather/sooner* is followed by *(not) V* (see (1a)), *different subject (not) V*, or complement clause were counted. 'Different subject' refers to a subject of V that is different from that of the

---

[1] As discussed in Section 4.4, *have V-en* is often counterfactual and modal rather than past tense.

auxiliary, as in *I'd rather you know* (1c). Coding was conducted manually, based on evidence of plausible paraphrases. The parameters coded for were: ± modal, if + modal, ± advisability; ± animate subject (of the auxiliary), if + animate, person and number. Examples with zero auxiliary and zero subject are covered at length in Van linden (2015) and are not included here.

4.3 A Constructional Approach

The main tenets of Construction Grammar models that are relevant to the present chapter are that a construction is a form-meaning pairing and that constructions are types that are hierarchised taxonomically (see e.g. Goldberg 1995, 2006; Croft 2001) in what has come to be known as a 'vertical network'. There is no fixed set of hierarchical levels. The set used here is: i) macro-schemas: the super-ordinate level of abstraction; ii) schemas: abstract sets with several members; iii) subschemas: groupings within a schema; and iv) micro-constructions: item-specific types like BETTER, RATHER, SOONER. Micro-constructions may have morphosyntactic alternations or allostructions ('variant structural realizations of a construction that is left partially underspecified', Cappelle 2006: 18). For present purposes, in the case of BETTER these allostructions are *had better*, *'d better*; in the case of RATHER *would rather*, *had rather*, *'d rather*, *should rather*, *will rather*; and in the case of SOONER *would sooner*, *had sooner*, *'d sooner*, *should sooner*, and *will sooner*.[2] Token utterances that are the data for hypothesising constructions are termed 'constructs'. (Sub)schemas in this vertical network may be enriched by 'horizontal' ones that capture the facts that schemas and subschemas 'may be partly motivated in relation to [their] neighbours' (Van de Velde 2014: 147) and that 'structurally different elements can fulfil the same function' (2014: 141).[3] The combined vertical and abstract network is modelled in Figure 4.1 (Cxn is short for construction; the horizontal line shows a horizontal relationship between subschemas).

The form-meaning pairing is a sign that consists of features: minimally, on the form side, syntax, morphology, phonology, and on the meaning side, semantics, pragmatics, and discourse function (Croft 2001), although not all are necessarily specified for all constructions. Historically, what we find is that features can change individually (see Hilpert 2013). Traugott

---

[2] Other auxiliaries like *might* and *must* were not attested in my data, and so are not cited among allostructions, but might be for other data.
[3] See also Traugott (2018).

Are Comparative Modals Converging or Diverging in English? 109

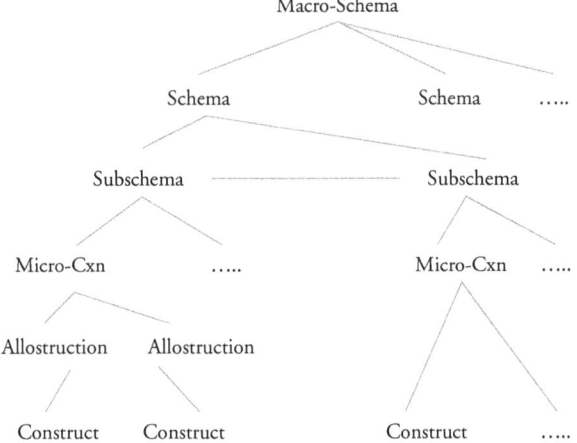

Figure 4.1 Model of a constructional hierarchy

and Trousdale (2013: 26) call changes to individual features 'constructional changes'. Accumulations of constructional changes may lead to constructionalisation, the development of a form$_{new}$-meaning$_{new}$ construction (Traugott and Trousdale 2013: 22).

Hüning and Booij (2014: 592–3) have suggested that:

> From a diachronic point of view, it is not the status of the 'grammaticalizing' element that is interesting (is it still a word or an affixoid or already an affix?); what is worthy of note is the emergence of a new construction, a new constructional (sub)schema, and its place within the network of constructions.

In this spirit, the questions addressed in this chapter are:

- RQ1 – What evidence is there of the emergence of the three micro-constructions under consideration?
- RQ2 – Do the three micro-constructions form one subschema in the 'vertical' hierarchy of modality or belong to different subschemas, as Van linden (2015) suggests, and have a 'horizontal' relationship?
- RQ3 – What does a constructional approach add to a grammaticalisation approach to the data?

4.4 BETTER, RATHER, and SOONER in PDE

Here I outline some of the main characteristics of the BETTER, RATHER, and SOONER micro-constructions in PDE to serve as points of comparison with the earlier data.

Among similarities, with respect to meaning, all three comparative modals are weakly deontic, i.e. relatively low on a scale of assessments about the desirability of states of affairs.[4] With respect to form, all three are adverbs ending in comparative *-er*. All three can occur with *had* or *'d* and exhibit the properties of auxiliaries (e.g. they do not occur with *do*) (Van linden 2015: 201). 'Past tense' of all three modal comparatives is formed with *have V-en*, as in the case of core modals (e.g. *I could/might/should have left yesterday*). Contemporary examples are rare, but include those like (2).

(2) a. 'Oh, Doctor,' threatened Fakrid, 'you**'d better** *have* come up with something. For your own sake.'
 (1993 Roberts, *The Highest Science* [BYU-BNC: FR0 W_fict_prose])

 b. Not that there haven't been mornings when he**'d rather** *have* stayed in bed.
 (1985–1994 *Central Television News* [BYU-BNC: K1V W_news_script])

 c. No groom she knew would ever have left his bride at the altar. He**'d sooner** *have* had a heart attack and died.
 (1996 Douglas, *The Southern Review* [COCA])

Denison (1998: 140) regards *have* in such constructs as 'a signal of unreality' and Van linden (2015: 206) argues that such uses are counterfactual rather than past tense. This analysis seems correct for (2b) and (2c), but not for (2a). The latter exemplifies past in the future (relative tense). This is perhaps because BETTER is future-oriented. A further similarity is that all can be used without an auxiliary or a subject (Van linden 2015).

Despite these similarities, there is a distinct asymmetry between BETTER and the other two. BETTER in (1a) and (1b) is an advice modal that can be paraphrased by *should/ought to/it would be advisable if*, but RATHER and SOONER in (1c) and (1d) are preference modals that can be paraphrased by *would prefer to/it would be preferable if*. In the case of BETTER, advice or at least suggestion of a better outcome is based in the speaker – see (3).

(3) You **had better** leave.

Van der Auwera and Plungian (1998: 80) call this 'participant-external necessity' – the speaker, not the subject *you*, suggests the action X is

---

[4] Whereas deontic modality is traditionally associated with obligation, I adopt Van linden and Verstraete's (2011) characterisation of deontic modality as involving desirability rather than obligation (see also Narrog's (2012) identification of deonticity with volition).

advisable. However, in the case of RATHER and SOONER, preference is based in the syntactic subject – see (4).

(4)   You **had rather/sooner** leave.

This is what van der Auwera and Plungian (1998: 80) call 'participant-internal necessity' – the subject *you* has a preference/wants one thing more than another. Although most works on modals mention desire and sometimes advisability, few mention preference. An exception is Narrog (2012), who includes preferential modality among subcategories of modality. Van der Auwera and De Wit (2010: 142) suggest the link between advisability and preference is volition and desire: 'preference can be understood as comparative volition: one wants one thing rather than another'.

BETTER is often used performatively, whereas the other two are not: *You'd better leave* can be a directive, whereas *You'd rather leave* cannot. This presumably is related to participant-external modality. Especially in contemporary English, BETTER is subjective in the sense of being based in the speaker's attitude or perspective (Traugott 2010: 32).[5] *You had better X* means 'I think you ought to X in the future (of speech time)'. The speaker, not the subject *you*, suggests the future action X. As Mitchell (2003: 143) points out, in using BETTER, the 'speaker is [...] deciding that the advice should be acted on'. Unlike BETTER, RATHER and SOONER are not directive. *You had rather X* is normally an assertion about what the speaker thinks or knows the addressee to prefer at the present regarding possible future states of affairs.

BETTER, RATHER, and SOONER are also different with respect to form and distribution. Given its meaning, in the case of BETTER the subject of *had* is also the subject of V, as in (1a). Different subject as in **I had better you stayed home* is unattested. However, both RATHER and SOONER allow a different subject as in (1c) and (5), and even occasionally a complement clause, at least in writing. In (5) note the different subject in the first complement clause:

(5)   They **would rather** *that you paid interest on your overdraft* than that they paid interest on theirs.
(1988 Buckland, *Debt Collection Made Easy*
[BYU-BNC: CD0 W_commerce])

A further distinction is that BETTER never occurs (and never has occurred) with *would*. But RATHER and SOONER occur with both *would* and *had*;

---

[5] Van der Auwera and De Wit (2010: 134–5), however, find that some examples of BETTER in the Brown family are non-subjective.

therefore reduced *'d* is potentially ambiguous. Finally, BETTER does not occur with a standard of comparison, but RATHER and SOONER do.

A striking development based on bare BETTER (without auxiliary) has been noted. Nothing comparable is based on bare RATHER and SOONER. It is the development of BETTER as an auxiliary that is partially aligned to the core modals, although the core modal category was established by the seventeenth century (Warner 1993), has not been added to since, and is well known to be in decline (see e.g. Krug 2000; Leech 2013; and elsewhere). This partial alignment involves use of BETTER with the negative *n't* clitic (cf. *shouldn't, wouldn't*), rather than *do*-support.[6] Denison and Cort quote an internet example that illustrates use of the tag *bettern't*:

(6) lol well you **better** start staying in then **betternt** you!!!!!! lol
(http://profile.myspace.com/index.cfm?fuseaction=user.viewprofile&frien did= 81374563, accessed 13 August 2007; Denison and Cort 2010: 380, fn. 13)

A search of *Google Books* reveals that it has been cited in the literature on language acquisition at least since 1887 – see (7).

(7) I recollect his beginning an interesting talk over early English, upon a child's saying to me, '**Bettern't** we go out now?'
(1887 Scott, *Life of William Barnes* [https://books.google.com/books?id=A CtXAAAAYAAJ&pg=PA204&dq=bettern't&hl=en&sa=X&ved=0ahUKE wjEi-r87-nLAhVS3WMKHSunD_s4HhDoAQgbMAA#v=onepage&q= bettern't&f=false]; accessed March 2016)

However, the occurrence of *bettern't* is sporadic. There is only one example in COHA (8), and it is in a fictional passage representing dialect.

(8) '[...] You stay here.' I shifted, uncomfortable in his eyes. '**Bettern't** you? I got some vinegar to rack off an' you kin help me mos' likely. [...]'
(1935 Barnes, *Edna His Wife* [COHA])

Despite differences in meaning and in distribution, the comparative modals BETTER, RATHER, and SOONER have been regarded as a set. Denison and Cort (2010: 350) refer to 'a group of phrasal items of similar shape', but acknowledge that *would* was preferred with *rather* and *sooner* from earliest times, so *had/'d* does not occur equally frequently with all of the comparative modals. Van der Auwera and De Wit (2010: 144) refer to

---

[6] However, some uses with *do*-support do occur, e.g. *You better don't go there without us* (van der Auwera *et al.* 2013: 143–5). Compare *You needn't go* and *You don't need to go*. This and other factors lead van der Auwera *et al.* to propose a different analysis from that of Denison and Cort (2010).

the comparative modals as a 'class' and passingly suggest that they form a '(marginal) paradigm' (2010: 128). Quirk *et al.* (1985: 141) suggest they belong to a larger category of 'modal idioms' that includes *had/'d better* and *would/'d rather*, along with *have got to* and *be to*. However, Van linden (2015: 221) regards them as members of two types, a BETTER modal and two preference modals, RATHER and SOONER, with differences linked to their earlier semantics and syntactic histories. Among the main theoretical questions raised by Construction Grammar for the historical linguist is how to conceptualise the ways in which constructions come into being (see Hilpert 2013), and whether at the level of the micro-construction or of the schema (Traugott and Trousdale 2013). As indicated above, whether or not the comparative modals can usefully be considered a schema from the perspective of Construction Grammar is one of the topics of the present chapter.

4.5 The Rise of Modals BETTER, RATHER, and SOONER

As Denison and Cort (2010) and Van linden (2015) point out, from the beginning the three comparative modal constructions under discussion have had rather different distributions. BETTER was the last to develop. I therefore start with brief comments on precursors of RATHER and SOONER. Both were adverbs in Old English (OE) and both could collocate with *would*.[7]

4.5.1 The Origins of Comparative Modal RATHER

In OE the precursor of RATHER was the comparative of temporal *hræþe* 'quickly, straightaway' and was used with the meaning 'sooner (in time), instead'. By ME it had come to be used mainly with the meaning 'on the contrary, instead'. It could also mean 'indeed, actually', and, in the context of a modal, 'preferably' (*MED rathere*). In eModE it also appears as an intensifier, e.g. *rather clever*.[8] All but the temporal meanings are currently still in use.

Early entries for *rather* in the sense 'preferably' appear with *will* (9a), *would* (9b), and *should* (9c). *Had* appears only in very late ME (9d). In all cases, the preference originates in the syntactic subject. It is therefore a 'participant-internal' modal. *MED* cites eleven examples, of which

---

[7] Periods in the history of English are roughly Old English (OE, 650–1100), Middle English (ME, 1100–1500), early Modern English (eModE, 1500–1700), late Modern English (lModE, 1700–1970), Present-day English (PDE, 1970–).
[8] For the history of intensifier *rather*, see Rissanen (2008).

none has an explicit standard of comparison. The standard is, however, pragmatically inferable from prior context, and might be present in a fuller citation – see examples in (9).[9]

(9) a. þe   ӡeongere   ӡeaf   soch   answere,
       the   younger   gave   such   answer
       '**Raþir** ich   **wolle** þe   slean   mid   mine   spere.'
       rather   I   will   thee   slay   with   my   spear
       'The younger man gave an answer like this: "I would rather kill you with my spear."'
       (c1300 Lay. *Brut* (Otho C 13) 1967 [*MED rathere* adv. comp. 2b])

   b. I nam   no þef   To breke mi treuþe   oӡain   mi lord;
      I NEG-am   no thief to break my troth   against my lord
      Raþer ich **wald**   hing bi a cord.
      rather   I   would   hang by a rope
      'I am no thief who would break my trust against my lord. I would rather hang by a rope.'
      (c1330(?a1300) *Arth. & M.* (Auch) 2324 [*MED rathere* adv. comp. 2b])

   c. Ich **sholde raþere** sterue:
      I   should rather   die
      'I would rather die.'
      (c1400(?a1387) *PPl.C* (Hnt HM 137) 7.290 [*MED rathere* adv. comp. 2b])

   d. Thovght vnkyndnes haith kyllyd me . . .
      though unkindness has killed me
      Yett **haid** I **rether** dye for his sake.
      yet had   I rather die for his sake
      'Though his unkindness has killed me, yet I would rather die for his sake.'
      (?c1500 *Grevus Ys* (Sln 1584) 87 [*MED rathere* adv. comp. 2b])

RATHER was well established as a modal by the end of the sixteenth century (with both *would* and *had*), in so far as paraphrases such as *would prefer/it would be better if* seem appropriate for examples like (10).

(10) I **would rather** be torn with wild Horses, than forsake my Religion.
                               (1571 CED: D1TNORFO [Traugott 2016b: 115])

---

[9] In BYU-EEBO, which became available after this chapter was written, the majority of examples with RATHER in the 1470s have a standard of comparison.

While there is only one example of *had better V* in Shakespeare, there are sixty of *had rather V*, mostly with first-person pronoun subjects, but some second- and third-person pronouns and full NP subjects appear as well. This suggests RATHER was constructionalised as a modal by Shakespeare's time, the very end of the sixteenth century and very beginning of the seventeenth.

As the examples in (9) above show, modal RATHER is often used with negative semantic prosody (Stubbs 1995). In other words, it is often preferred with a semantically negative verb such as *die* and *tear*. This is still a characteristic of RATHER in PDE, but not as strongly so.

4.5.2 The Origins of Comparative Modal SOONER

Like RATHER, SOONER has temporal origins. The precursor of SOONER was ME *soner* 'sooner'. Unlike in the case of RATHER, the temporal semantics is still transparent to contemporary speakers, which sometimes leads to ambiguity even in PDE. As in the case of RATHER, temporal *soner* came in ME to be used in a way that implies preference (at least to a present-day reader) in the context of a human subject, modal *would*, *should*, or *had*, and a standard of comparison. As with RATHER, the modality is based in the subject's perspective and is participant-internal, the preference is oriented to the time of the current state of affairs, and *would* is preferred over *had*.

MED (*sone* adv.) cites six examples, none of which appear with *had*, and four of which include a nominal or adjectival standard of comparison. Example (11a) exemplifies comparison of NPs ('poor people', 'hypocrites') and (11b) clausal comparison.

(11) a. For god wole **sonere** here many pore ri3tfully
 for god will sooner hear many poor rightfully
 criynge vengaunce þan a lord &   many ypocritis.
 crying vengeance than a lord and many hypocrites
 'For God would sooner hear many poor people crying vengeance than hear a lord and many hypocrites.'
 (?c1430(c1400) *Wycl. Serv. & L.* (Corp-C 296) 240
 [*MED sone* adv.comp. 5d])

 b. He [...] **sonner   wolde**   suche thre [...] Hafe youe
 he   sooner   would   such   three   have given
 than so forgone that euydence.
 than so forgone that evidence

'He would have preferred that three people like this had given rather than refrained in that way from giving that evidence.'

(?1457 Hardyng *Chron. A* (Lnsd 204) p. 743
[*MED sone* adv. comp. 5d])

Examples of *Aux. sooner V* appear in sixteenth-century texts, suggesting it was established as a modal by that time. Like RATHER, it tends to be used with negative semantics – see (12).

(12) Nay I meane to follow yee: I will **sooner** leese my life, then fight of you till this dinner be done.
'No, I intend to follow you: I would sooner lose my life than fight you till the end of this dinner.' (1595 CED: D1CWARNE)

4.5.3 The Origins of Comparative Modal BETTER

According to Denison and Cort (2010: 351–3), the source for comparative modal BETTER is the ME adjective *betere* 'better' in a subjunctive impersonal copula construction that can be characterised as NP$_{oblique}$ BE$_{subjunctive}$ Adjective + clause. An example is (13), which is a comment about what the narrator assesses would be literally and objectively 'better' for a father, given Christian tradition and contemporary mores.

(13) A   mon   **were**   **betere** for   is   sunne be[o] sori   and
     a   man   would-be   better   for   his   son   be   sorry   and
     vnssriue þanne   issriue   wiþoute   sorinesse.
     unshriven than   shriven   without   sorriness
     'It would be better for a man if his son were sorry and not receive the sacrament than to receive the sacrament without being sorry.'

(a1325 *SLeg.* (Corp-C 145) 131/91 [*MED unshriven* ppl. a;
Denison and Cort 2010: 352])

This example is similar in its impersonal structure to the Latin proverb that accompanies (9c) in *MED*: *Melius est mori quam male uiuere* 'It is better to die than to live badly'. The English version of (9c), however, has a first-person subject in a RATHER construction. It appears that in the fourteenth century, if they were used with modal meaning, *rather*, *sooner*, and *better* were all preference modals. Their morphosyntax is, however, very different, as highlighted by the difference between first-person subject, auxiliary *should*, and adverb *rapere* in (9c), but impersonal copula with adjective *betere* in (13).

During the ME period a systemic change occurred: the loss of impersonal constructions (Allen 1995). Constructs like (13) came to be expressed with different syntax, such as *It were/would be better for a man's son to be sorry*, as in (14).

(14) I am myself indifferent honest, but yet I could accuse me of such things that **it were better** my mother had not borne me.
'I myself am not particularly honest, yet I could accuse myself of such things that it would have been better if my mother had not given birth to me.' (Shakespeare, *Hamlet* III.i.1814 [OSS])[10]

By the fifteenth century a new form *had better* with adverb *better* had begun to be used, but it is rare through the seventeenth century. There are no examples of *had better V* in CED period 1 (1560–1599), only one in Shakespeare (in *Henry VIII*, 1613 [OSS]), and only two in CEECS (1418–1680), e.g. (15). Meaning still indicates preference modality. In (15), as in (13), the preference is still presented as based in general mores rather than the personal opinion of the speaker/writer, and the subject is third person.

(15) A man **had better** take upon him to perswade twenty learned men that are not 'propositi defensores', then one suche.
'A man would do better to try to persuade twenty learned men that are not "defenders of the proposition", than a person like this.'
(1600 Whitgift, *Letter to Hutton*
[CEECS: HUTTON; Traugott 2016b: 112])

Semantic similarities between examples like (13) and (9c) show that modal expressions with *better* were at first semantically similar to those with RATHER and SOONER. The difference was mainly structural. Since the form has changed, but there has been no significant change in meaning, the shift to personal subject illustrated by (15) is a constructional change. Discussing the structural shift from impersonal copula with adjective *better* to personal *had* with adverb *better*, van der Gaaf (1904: 52, cited in Van linden 2015: 196) proposes that BETTER might have been analogised to *I had lever* 'I would prefer'. On the other hand, Denison and Cort (2010: 353–4) suggest BETTER might have been analogised to RATHER. Analogy may have been a partial factor where the shift from adjective to adverb is concerned, enabled by use of the same form for adjective and adverb. But it

---

[10] Since OSS, the online Shakespeare, numbers lines sequentially from Act 1.i on, I have added act, scene, and line number from SHC (Craig 1951).

does not appear to have been so with respect to the auxiliary, since *would* does not collocate with *better*. Van der Gaaf's hypothesis seems better supported by the data.[11]

By the beginning of the eighteenth century, however, *had better* appears slightly more frequently (six examples in CED period 4 (1680–1719), five of them with personal subjects). There is evidence of semantic divergence: speakers began to use *had better* in ways that can be understood as advisability rather than (or as well as) preference, as in (16).

(16) a. Pray, Gentlewoman be pleased to wear your Mask, till we're got out of this Road of Foppery; I **had better** have gone Ten Miles about.
(1696 Manley, *The Lost Lover* [CED: D4MANLE];
'I would have preferred to/I would have been better advised to')

b. I ordered my Husband to come and fetch me Home at such an Hour, but he never came; but he **had better** have come: For I made him Court me a whole Week afterwards, before I'd let him come to Bed to me.
(1714 Ward, *Whole Pleasures of Matrimony* [CED: D4FWARD];
'he would have been better advised to/he would have preferred to')

Denison and Cort (2010: 366) suggest that in the copula contexts 'the action sought is beneficial to the subject and is also wished for by the speaker'. One would not mention that one thinks it is better for the subject that they should do/have done something unless one wished them to do/have done it. Over time the invited inference of the speaker's wish/desire became semanticised (Denison and Cort 2010: 367). This is reasonable. But examples like those in (16), which are ambiguous, suggest that the advisability reading arose in the context of *had better* as well as of the copula construction.

Had better was firmly entrenched as a modal expression by the early eighteenth century. This change is a constructionalisation, since the new form is now linked to a new meaning. It is used not only to express advisability, but to direct others' behaviour and announce decisions

---

[11] Indeed, van der Gaaf's hypothesis appears to be supported by BYU-EEBO. There are 196 hits for *I had leuer* and four for *I had lever* prior to 1600. However, a careful analysis is needed to argue for analogy since many examples introduce a complementation rather than *V*, e.g.:

(i) **i had leuer** that my wyf and chyldren shold suffre moche hurte
'I had rather that my wife and children should suffer much hurt'
(1481 Caxton, *Reynart the Foxe* [BYU-EEBO])

(ii) **i had leuer** to deye presently than to lyue without to be aduenged on them
'I had rather die immediately than live without being avenged on them'
(1481 Caxton, *Eracles* and *Godefrey of Boloyne* [BYU-EEBO])

about one's own (Mitchell 2003: 143). Recently it has been extended to express hope (van der Auwera *et al.* 2013: 124; Van linden 2015: 194).

Despite the fact that it was used as a modal later than RATHER and SOONER, BETTER rapidly came to be the dominant 'semi-modal'. It is not only far more frequent from the eighteenth century on, in PDE it is more reduced in that use of the standard of comparison has been almost completely lost. This is a counterexample to the hypothesis that older forms are likely to be more grammatical than younger forms (see e.g. Bybee *et al.* 1991).

The changes discussed in this section precede in time those that Van linden (2015) investigates: the various kinds of reduction that are typical of repeated use and frequency effects (e.g. Bybee 2003). While they are excellent examples of grammaticalisation as form reduction, they can also be thought of as constructional changes affecting the form of the constructions.

4.5.4 Summary of the Changes Discussed in This Section

To summarise the developments discussed so far, RATHER and SOONER emerged as preference modals by the sixteenth century. Although there were impersonal copula constructions with the adjective *better* and preference readings during this period, modal BETTER with *had* did not become entrenched until the eighteenth century, when it became highly productive and rapidly came to be used more frequently than the older comparative modals and as an advice modal.

I now turn to a small study of the development of the three modals in the period 1720–1913, the period of greatest growth, as represented in OBC.

4.6 BETTER, RATHER, and SOONER in OBC

The most striking fact about the use of BETTER, RATHER, and SOONER in OBC is that there are no instances of *'d* with *better* or *rather*, and only two with *sooner*. Given that *'d* outnumbers the full forms in lModE and British PDE (van der Auwera and De Wit 2010; van der Auwera *et al.* 2013), one might expect evidence of gradual cliticisation such as is found in the *Corpus of Late Modern English Texts (Extended Version)* (CLMETEV). For example, van der Auwera *et al.* (2013: 128) find two examples of *'d better* in CLMETEV period I (1710–1780), thirty in period II (1780–1850), and 120 in period III (1850–1920). The absence of *'d* forms in OBC is noteworthy because certain scribes of the *Proceedings of the Old Bailey*, especially during the eighteenth century, represented the phonological contraction *n't*

Table 4.1 *Occurrence of auxiliaries with* BETTER, RATHER, *and* SOONER *in OBC*

	had	'd	would	should	will	TOTAL
BETTER	975	0	0	0	0	975
RATHER	69	0	137	3	1	210
SOONER	2	2	53	1(?)	2	59
TOTAL	1,046	2	190	3	3	1,244

(Huber 2007). There are ten examples of *n't* with auxiliaries in OBC, the last in 1898, but the first nine all occur in the period 1726–1739. In OBC past tense and past participle *-ed* are variably represented as cliticised (e.g. *hang'd* in (24b) below; also *clapp'd* and *cry'd* in the same trial (t17400903-6)),[12] and cliticised *is* in *there's* and *it* in *'tis*. We may conclude that cliticisation of *had* and *would* in the early period was not a factor about which the scribes were conscious, perhaps because it did not occur often in the trial setting, or perhaps because it had no perceived social value. Absence of the clitic in the later OBC is probably related to increased editorial control and formality in the later period (Huber 2007). Table 4.1 summarises the findings in OBC with respect to combinations of auxiliaries with BETTER, RATHER, and SOONER.[13]

4.6.1 BETTER *in OBC*

The 975 instances of *had better* … *V* in OBC all have advisory meaning. Evidence is paraphrasability by *should/ought to/it would be advisable if*. In a few nineteenth-century examples *had better* is in fact paraphrased by participants in the trial with *should* and *should recommend*, e.g. (17).

(17) to prevent all further dispute and trouble between you, you **had better** leave; I **should recommend** you to do so   (t18570615-709)

Although deonticity is generally fairly weak, in some instances, especially when *had better* is followed by *or*, it can be interpreted as a threat, and therefore relatively high on the scale of deonticity – see (18).

---

[12] Trials in OBC are identified by a reference number consisting of 't' (trial), year, month, day, and, after a hyphen, the line number in the transcribed text. So this reference should be read as 'trial, 1740, September 3, line 6'.
[13] SOONER may be temporal in the one example with *should* (see (28b) in Section 4.6.3 below), and is thus not included in the totals of this table.

(18) there was some conversation, in which he said I **had better** give him the money, **or** he would take action in Chancery, (t18701212-92)

In the first ten years of the trials (1720–1730), there are six examples of modal *had better*. Of these, two have first-person subjects, e.g. (19a), and three have second-person subjects, e.g. (19b). There is one example of a third-person subject (19c), but this is in an indirect speech report of an original second-person utterance.

(19) a. we struck a Bargain, and went to a Gin Shop, and I thought I **had better** do so than wander about the Street all Night, (t17260114-5)
b. Tis a long way, (says she) and you **had better** drink before you go any further, for fear you should faint upon the Road. (t17241204-68)
c. I said, if there was any danger, he **had better** go out of the way, (t17261012-7)

In these examples the advice given is based on the speaker's point of view, not general mores, and is therefore subjective. In (19b) the speaker expresses the opinion that the addressee should drink and in (19c) the speaker reports giving his opinion that the addressee should go out of the way.

The examples in (19) are representative of the corpus as a whole, as overt animate pronoun subjects are preferred (946 out of the 975 examples of *had better*). Second-person pronouns predominate (430 examples). That this is not due to the trial context is suggested by comparable figures for the use of second-person subjects in COHA (Van linden 2015: 208–9). There are 221 first-person examples (155 singular *I*, sixty-six plural *we*). Third person ranks in between with a total of 295 examples. The sole example with subject *it* does not occur until 1872 (see (20)). Here *it* refers to the clause *whether this would amount to larceny*.

(20) Mr. Justice Lush [. . .] has rather grave doubts whether this would amount to larceny. He thinks it **had better** be left to the Jury, and take their opinion on the facts. (t18720923-675)

A search of OBC shows that no auxiliary other than *had* occurs with *better*. There is only one example of *better* without an auxiliary (21).

(21) 'Very well, then, **you better** stop a little bit;' (t18610408-369)

Use of an overt standard of comparison with BETTER ceases to be attested in OBC in the 1850s. The last example of the structure BETTER *V than Clause* is (22).

(22) I thought I **had better** make sure of one **than** lose both,
(t18530103-193)

The very last example in the corpus with a standard of comparison is dated 1854 and compares two NPs. Loss of an explicit standard of comparison by the mid-nineteenth century is consistent with Denison and Cort's (2010: 355) finding based on different data that a standard of comparison has not been used since the nineteenth century in British English. The COHA data suggest that in American English it had been all but lost by the early part of the nineteenth century (Van linden 2015: 215–16).

In sum, over the course of the trials, BETTER comes to be used in OBC much the same way as it is in PDE. The main exception is absence of examples with reduced *'d*.

4.6.2 Rather *in OBC*

In OBC there are ninety-five hits of *had rather*. In one example *rather* means 'instead', in twenty-five others it is a degree modifier (e.g. *had rather too much to drink*) or quantifies an indefinite noun (e.g. *had rather a suspicion*), so only sixty-nine exemplify comparative modal uses. Of these, five have a different subject, e.g. (23c).

(23) a. Upon which he said he **had rather** have given 100 l. than I should have said any such Thing of his Sister. (t17251208-55)
b. Wells answered, he did not value dying, for he **had rather** die, than live and starve, but for the Disgrace. (t17400116-46)
c. but his Mother said, She **had rather** *he* should die quietly than go thro' that barbarous Operation. (t17320906-25)

In OBC *would rather (X) V* is twice as frequent as *had rather (X) V* (137 compared to sixty-nine instances). Examples (24a)–(24c) are typical examples. A fourth, with clausal complement (24d), is less typical.

(24) a. I **would rather** have given 500 l. than this Thing should have happened; (t17431012-31)
b. No; he would not tell, he **would rather** die than tell, – he **would rather** chuse to be hang'd: (t17400903-6)
c. the prosecutor said at the station he **would rather** take them into the back yard than charge them. (t19020210-190)
d. I **would rather** *that the House should fall down, and knock his Brains out*, than he should be hanged. (t17431012-37)

Are Comparative Modals Converging or Diverging in English? 123

Note how similar examples (23a) and (23b) are to (24a) and (24b) with respect to content and form. This suggests that *would rather* and *had rather* were in variation.

Even though historically *would* was preferred with *rather* over *had* (see Section 4.5.1 above), the earlier trials evidence a modest preference for *had*. This is followed by a shift from *had* to *would* over time. RATHER occurs occasionally with additional auxiliaries. There is one instance with *will* (25a), and three with *should* (25b). In (25b) note the person switch changing the perspective from the speaker's evaluation of *you* to vocalise the addressee.

(25) a. No, I know myself innocent; and **will rather** go over the herring-pond than offer to make it up; (t18270712-192)

b. Said I, if you have murdered your Children it is a crying Sin; it is a Sin against the Holy Ghost, and if that is your Case. I **should rather** die than live. (t17431012-29)

With respect to an explicit standard of comparison, this continues to be used with RATHER throughout OBC, as the examples above attest.

Many examples of RATHER demonstrate negative prosody, particularly the collocation with *die* (see (23b), (24b), (25b)). In this it is different from BETTER (there are no occurrences of *had better die*). RATHER is also relatively more strongly associated with morphological negation than BETTER. In OBC only 49/975 (5 per cent) examples of *had better* are followed by *not*, compared to 16/69 (23.1 per cent) of *had rather*, and 25/137 (18.2 per cent) of *would rather*. Example (26) is an example with *had*.

(26) I told her I **had rather** *not* have any thing to do with her, (t17750111-23)

On the whole, uses with *not* occur later than those with negative prosody. In OBC the first example of *had rather not* is dated 1767, and of *would rather not* 1812, whereas those with negative prosody are attested from the 1730s on.

4.6.3 SOONER in OBC

Throughout its history, modal SOONER occurs less frequently than RATHER. In OBC there are only two examples of *had sooner*, the second a repetition of the first. However, there are fifty-three examples with *would*, e.g. (27a) from the same trial as (24b) above. Seven of these collocate with past tense/counterfactual *have*, e.g. (27c).

(27) a. He said he did not take it himself, but that a Woman gave it him; and he **would sooner** die than discover ['reveal'] who the Woman was. (t17400903-6)

b. I said I considered the mare worth a great deal more money, and I **would sooner** give him the 135*l*. and keep the mare (t18610408-286)

c. My mother **would sooner** *have* given him £20 than he should have done this; (t19020909-669)

There are two examples with *will* (28a) and one with *should* (28b), which is possibly a temporal use.

(28) a. but you know a man **will sooner** spend 50 l. than pay 18 d. wrongfully; (t17870418-118)

b. I do not know any man I **should sooner** put confidence in, (t17750531-1)

As mentioned in the introduction to Section 4.6, SOONER is the only one of the three comparative modals under discussion that appears in OBC with reduced *'d*, and only in two examples. These are presented in (29).

(29) a. No says the Deceas'd, And if I had I**'d sooner** let you know it than serve it upon you. (t17350911-99)

b. he said, he**'d sooner** spend 50 l. rather than submit to a villain. (t17551022-31)

In the case of (29a), an earlier witness cites the deceased's words with the full auxiliary, so *'d* in (29a) must be understood as the reduced form of *would*, not *had*:

(30) The Deceased answered, No Sam, and if I had I **would sooner** let you know of it, than serve it upon ye. (t17350911-99)

Like RATHER, SOONER continues to be used with an overt standard of comparison throughout the corpus, e.g. (27a)–(27c), (28a), (29a)–(29b), and (30).

4.6.4 Summary of Similarities and Differences among the Comparative Modals in OBC

All three modals occur with auxiliary *had*. All three share weak deontic modality (desire). Nevertheless, the differences are quite significant, and

Table 4.2 *Differences between* BETTER *and* RATHER, SOONER *in OBC*

	BETTER	RATHER, SOONER
Options for Auxiliary	*had*	*would* (preferred), *had*
Options for X	Neg	Neg, DS, *Comp*-S
Standard of comparison	No	Optional
Participant-external	Yes	No
Subjective	Usually	No
Directive	Usually	No

group RATHER and SOONER together vis-à-vis BETTER. I summarise the differences in Table 4.2 (DS is short for 'different subject').

In the next section I discuss the implications of these similarities and differences for the question whether the comparative modals form a subschema of modals.

4.7 The Schematic Status of the Comparative Modals

It seems uncontroversial that each expression can be viewed as a micro-construction: each is an idiosyncratic form-meaning pairing, the meaning of which is not predictable from its parts. The question addressed in this section is whether or not the three micro-constructions are best regarded as singletons or as being organised hierarchically within the higher-level Deontic Modal construction from the eighteenth century on. As Hilpert (2013: 191) comments, whether to label a group of constructions that share similarities but also differences under one abstract form-meaning set or (sub)schema might seem 'like an open-ended exercise in lumping and splitting'. The overarching similarities in surface form favour a lumping approach. But RATHER and SOONER have always been distinct from BETTER in distribution, and, although there was initially some semantic overlap in terms of preference, by the beginning of the eighteenth century a distinct division of labour had occurred, which favours a splitting approach for lModE.

RATHER and SOONER continue from ME times to express preference; they scale the state of affairs preferred/desired by the syntactic subject, an internal participant. The principal speech act involved is assertion. In the case of BETTER, the source of advice continues from the impersonal copula precursor to be external to the subject (first Biblical advice, social mores,

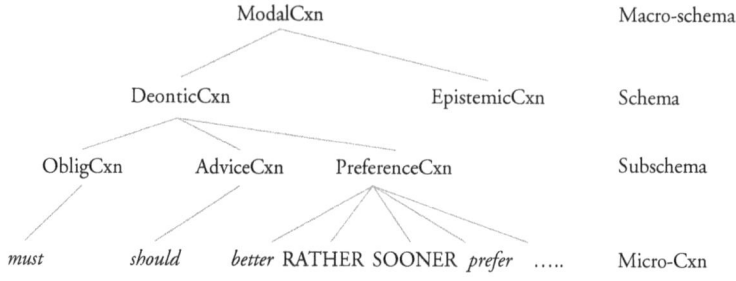

Figure 4.2 Partial constructional network of eModE comparative modals

later the speaker). To the extent that the speaker has come to be understood as the external advisor, BETTER has been subjectified. The principal speech act involved is directive. BETTER scales the speaker's advice (e.g. speaker strongly advises/desires that a certain action be taken).

The null hypothesis would be that each micro-construction is independent of the others, and simply happens to have similar form. This is implausible since speakers make generalisations across similarly structured expressions (Goldberg 2006). Given their closeness in distribution and meaning, RATHER and SOONER can be argued to form a subschema. It therefore seems best to postulate a small loosely related family of micro-constructions, the network relations of which have changed. Whereas in ME *better* was a contentful adjective in a copula construction, it came to be a procedural adverb with auxiliary *had* by the end of the seventeenth century, along with RATHER and SOONER. They have all become more similar with respect to formal reduction. They have, however, become distinct with respect to semantics. They originally all expressed preference semantics and were individual members of a weakly deontic external participant PreferenceCxn, as are *favour* and *prefer*, as represented in Figure 4.2. Note that *better* is not yet identified as the auxiliary, hence the lower case.

However, by the eighteenth century BETTER had come to be used as a member of the AdviceCxn subschema along with *should*, *might as well*, *recommend*, and *suggest*, but since advice implies preference and there are some overlaps between the subschemas, especially in the earlier stages, a horizontal link between the AdviceCxn and the PreferenceCxn can be postulated, as in Figure 4.3.

In addition, there are external network links that relate constructions to others at greater and lesser degrees of formal and contentful similarity (see Fried and Östman 2005). All three micro-constructions

Are Comparative Modals Converging or Diverging in English? 127

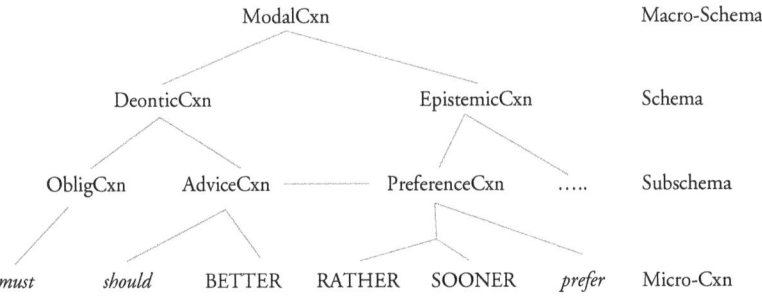

Figure 4.3 Partial constructional network of lModE comparative modals

are linked to positive scalars. This is especially clear in the case of RATHER, since the form *rather* is used as a degree modifier (*rather good*). In OBC there are twenty-five examples of *rather* with *should* that scale a verb of cognition or locution (e.g. *think, believe, suppose; say, swear, attribute*), as in (31).

(31) *Canwell.* Did not Davis take the Lace, and put it upon me.
Frances Coverley. I **should rather** think Davis took it; I had never seen her before, she looked like an ill Person.   (t17420909-29)

This appears to be a modalised variant of e.g. *I rather think* (ninety instances). Here the degree meaning ('somewhat, not completely') predominates. Given the difference in meaning and distribution from examples in Section 4.6.2, I have considered usages such as (31) to exemplify the degree rather than the modal meaning of *rather*, although degree converges with preference for the state of affairs expressed by the proposition. Scales entail alternatives and therefore contrast. In the case of BETTER, alternatives are now weak implicatures, since use with comparative *than* has been lost. But in the case of RATHER and SOONER contrast is still often overt.

Especially in the nineteenth century, *better* with zero subject and zero auxiliary had links to the proverb register, and may in fact have originated there (Denison and Cort 2010: 360–3; van der Auwera *et al.* 2013: 141–2). With the decline of use of proverbs, this network link has become weak or even (for many speakers) non-existent.

4.8 Comparison of the Grammaticalisation and Constructional Approaches

Clearly, reduction and erosion affected all three constructions. This is what Van linden's (2015) grammaticalisation approach has highlighted. From the perspective of grammaticalisation defined as reduction, they are indeed all undergoing similar changes.

To understand the history of the three comparative modals in depth, however, it is important to recognise other kinds of change as well. One is the constructional schematic reorganisation whereby three basically similar modals were split into BETTER versus RATHER and SOONER. Another is the extent to which BETTER has changed. As mentioned in Section 4.5.3, the most recent comparative modal, BETTER, is the most productive and has undergone the greatest amount of change, i.e. it is the most entrenched (Barðdal 2008). It has been used in increasingly subjective ways, as measured by the extent to which it is used to express the speaker's opinion rather than to draw on a social norm. Speakers have explored the possibility of using it like a core modal (see examples (6)–(8) in Section 4.4). On the other hand, the older comparative modals, RATHER and SOONER, have coexisted stably since ME with little or no difference in meaning. SOONER has consistently been the less frequent of the two.

The high productivity of BETTER is in fact a problem for the grammaticalisation analysis. As Bybee *et al.* (1991) argued, normally 'older grams' are more frequent than newer ones. BETTER is newer (as a comparative modal) than RATHER and SOONER, and far more frequent. Another problem is that there is no clear 'coevolution of meaning and form' (Bybee *et al.* 1994: 20): the meaning of RATHER and SOONER remains stable despite reduction of the *would/had* auxiliary, occasional use with a zero subject, and gradual decline in use of the standard of comparison.

As mentioned in Section 4.1, Van linden (2015) posits a cline of grammaticalisation: BETTER > SOONER > RATHER. This is on the grounds that SOONER shows the greatest reduction of auxiliaries *would* and *had*. But in terms of productivity, understood as generality, it has always been and continues to be the least productive and most likely to be ambiguous with the original temporal. From this perspective, even on a grammaticalisation analysis, it is not only the least frequent but it is also the least bleached. On a constructional analysis it is less highly constructionalised as a modal (however marginal) than RATHER and both less so than BETTER. Therefore from a constructional perspective RATHER is closer to BETTER than SOONER.

4.9 Conclusion

The three comparative modals are currently marginal members of the procedural modal system in several respects. Advice modality is marginal within the deontic system and preference more so. The three micro-constructions are procedural, but have a complex morphosyntactic structure unlike that of other procedural modals in English. Despite the smallness and marginality of the micro-constructions, they are instructive for historical linguistics.

In answer to RQ1, posed in Section 4.3, What evidence is there of the emergence of the three micro-constructions under consideration?, there is clear evidence of the rise of new meaning-form pairings consisting of an original comparative and an auxiliary, *had* in the case of BETTER (eighteenth century), *would, had,* and *should* in the case of RATHER (fourteenth century), and *would, will,* and *had* in that of SOONER (sixteenth century).

In answer to RQ2 in Section 4.3, Do the three micro-constructions form one subschema in the 'vertical' hierarchy of modality or belong to different subschemas, as Van linden suggests, and have a 'horizontal' relationship?, I have argued that although they originally all had preference semantics, post-constructionalisation, BETTER diverged and belongs to a different advice subschema. They are, however, 'partly motivated in relation to [their] neighbours' (Van de Velde 2014: 147), and so can be analysed as having a horizontal relationship.

With regard to RQ3 in Section 4.3, What does a constructional approach add to a grammaticalisation approach to the data?, it is essentially a semantic analysis in addition to the formal one. Focusing on grammaticalisation and phonetic erosion of the auxiliaries and of *than*, Van linden (2015: 221) concludes that the three comparative modals are converging and 'overall developing in the same direction', more rapidly in American than in British English. On the other hand, from a constructionalisation perspective, in which both form and meaning are of equal importance, the division of labour that emerged in the eighteenth century appears to be increasing and leading to greater divergence. Although constructionalisation has to account for the erosion of auxiliaries and loss of *than*, the various other factors that have led to contemporary uses of the three modals need to be accounted for as well. Once they have come into being, constructions are subject to grammaticalisation understood as reduction of form (Trousdale 2010), and to other factors as well, such as semantic constructional changes.

CHAPTER 5

The Definite Article in Old English: Evidence from Ælfric's Grammar

Cynthia L. Allen

5.1 The Controversy over the Definite Article in Old English

This chapter provides evidence bearing on the question of whether Old English (OE) had what can be called a 'definite article'. The status of SE, the cover term I use for the lexeme that includes *se*, *seo*, and *þæt* as well as the other forms in this paradigm, remains a matter of lively debate. Studies that take the point of view that OE had no definite article, or at least that definiteness marking was not obligatory, include Ackles (1997), Watanabe (2009), and Sommerer (2015), among others. In contrast, Christophersen (1939: 83) concluded that English already had a real definite article by King Alfred's time, and a small number of recent studies have argued for a similar conclusion.

Mitchell (1985: §328) comments that modern scholars have created an 'unreal problem' for themselves in their concerns about whether OE had a definite article. From a linguist's perspective, however, the problem is a real one, because OE must fit into the typology of human languages. What is right about Mitchell's observation is that we must not attempt to impose Present-day English (PDE) categories on OE. Denison (2006), in a welcome re-examination of the similarities and differences in OE between adjectives, pronouns, and what are usually called determiners, both analyses OE on its own terms and raises questions about how the history of the category D (Determiner) in English can increase our understanding of syntactic and morphological change more broadly.

Denison argues that the boundaries between the categories D, pronoun, and adjective are not clear-cut in OE, but became increasingly more so in Middle English through a process of incremental change, rather than sudden reanalysis. He notes that '[t]he development of articles is generally dated to the ME (Middle English) period' (2006: 289). Since he takes the articles to provide the strongest justification for a category D, this fact calls into question the existence of a category D in OE.

In what follows, I will focus on the question of whether OE SE sometimes should be analysed as a definite article. This is a sensible question to ask if we define what properties characterise a 'definite article' and then investigate whether SE had those properties. The problem is then to decide what those properties are, and here there is considerable disagreement.

In what Denison refers to as 'mainstream syntax', it is widely assumed that demonstratives in PDE are in the specifier position of the category DP (Determiner Phrase). The major alternative to this analysis of SE in its demonstrative function in OE is that it was an adjective. Denison (2006) demonstrates that OE SE showed more affinities with pronouns than with adjectives. Wood (2007), who also argues against the adjectival analysis, follows Giusti (1997) in assuming that an article is the D head of DP.[1] She treats the emergence of the modern definite article in English as the sort of sudden reanalysis that Denison (2006) correctly presents as the typical mainstream syntax treatment of category change: when the determiner became invariant *þe*, it was reanalysed as D, rather than the specifier of DP.[2] This general approach of reanalysis from specifier to head can be taken as the standard generative analysis of the birth of the definite article in English, as exemplified in Watanabe (2009).[3] I will adopt the assumption that the definite article is located in D, but reject the idea of reanalysis in the early Middle English (eME) period. I will add to the evidence provided by Crisma (2011) that this definite article was well established in OE, a time when English did not yet have a 'dedicated' article, but was like Modern German in having a form serving as both a demonstrative and an 'article-like' element. I will take the position that SE could be a demonstrative, in the specifier of DP, or an article, in the head D, although it is often unclear whether it should be regarded as an article or a demonstrative in a specific instance. I will use the term 'definite determiner' to refer to SE when I am not specifically arguing that it is an article.

---

[1] Pronouns still have properties in common with determiners, as pointed out in a transformational grammar framework by Postal (1969), who argued that pronouns should be treated as articles. The assumption that pronouns, like articles, occupy D, the head of DP, has gained acceptance in much current generative work, e.g. Bresnan *et al.* (2016: 102ff.). This general approach is also adopted in Allen (2007), where an analysis of the order possessive + adjective + determiner is offered.

[2] For Wood (2007), this means that D was usually null in OE. However, she also concludes that although SE was usually in the specifier position, this element could already sometimes be in D.

[3] More recently, Ringe and Taylor (2014: 449) adopt the same general approach but note that there is some evidence that the reanalysis had already happened in OE. Space does not permit further discussion here.

It is easy to show that OE did not have an element that was the same in its behaviour as the PDE definite article. That does not mean that it did not have a definite article – it is also easy to show that definite articles do not behave the same way in all languages that are usually agreed to have them. One major advance by Crisma's (2011) contribution is the application of cross-linguistic findings about the behaviour of articles in different syntactic positions. Specifically, Crisma notes that in deciding whether OE had a definite article, we need to be aware that even in languages that are usually assumed to have a definite article, there is variation concerning where one is needed. Of particular importance is the fact that the objects of prepositions (PObjs) are quite variable regarding the use of the definite determiner – even in different varieties of PDE. The use of SE in OE was variable with PObjs in a way that it was not with subjects and objects, as will be demonstrated in Section 5.3.2. Crisma also discusses the fact that non-arguments, including predicative noun phrases, can often lack an article in languages in which articles are necessary for arguments. Stowell (1989) explores the possibility that while arguments are required to be DPs, non-arguments can be NPs, lacking a determiner. Crisma notes that this proposal is not without problems, but the asymmetry between arguments and non-arguments in the use of a definite article is a well-established one, however it is to be accounted for formally. Examples like (1) are therefore not convincing evidence that OE lacked a definite article.

(1) Iohannes is geendung þære ealdan æ: &   angin   þære niwan.
    John   is ending   the old   law   and beginning the   new
    'John is the end of the old law and the beginning of the new'
    (cocathom1,ÆCHom_I,_25:382.80.4865)

Other situations not needing a determiner include 'special nouns', such as proper nouns, identifiable without any marking, and prenominal genitives, which confer definiteness. Crisma concludes that the definite article is needed only when the definite and indefinite readings are not disambiguated by other means, that is, that OE had a definite article because it fulfilled Criterion 1 discussed below (Section 5.1.1), i.e. that a nominal argument was not ambiguous in its interpretation as definite or indefinite.

Crisma's decision to limit her study to subjects and objects in OE enabled her to show that in these functions, SE occurred very regularly in OE prose from the late ninth century onwards, and that nearly all exceptions fell into classes that are familiar from other languages.

Another significant advance by Crisma is her separation of prose and poetry. Her demonstration that poetry was different from prose in its use of the definite determiner is important, because illustrations of the differences between OE and PDE in this regard typically rely heavily on examples from poetry. For example, Ackles' (1997: 31) examples of OE sentences lacking a determiner where PDE would require a definite article are drawn entirely from poetry, with the exception of one debatable example that will be discussed in Section 5.3.1.

Crisma concludes that the use of SE in the poetry indicates a grammar without a definite article, while the grammar producing the language of the prose had a definite article. As Crisma notes, one problem we face in investigating the syntax of OE poetry is that we are uncertain of the time of composition of most of it. However, given the clear difference that is evident between OE poetry and prose generally in respect of SE, it is reasonable to assume that the poetry reflects an earlier stage of the language in the area of determiners at least.[4]

5.1.1 What Is a 'Definite Article'?

A preliminary to investigating whether a language has a definite article is to define what we mean by this. Crisma (2011) follows Greenberg (1978) in considering that a discourse deictic becomes an article when it has become compulsory and means 'identified in general'. Crisma offers two criteria that a language must meet in order to be said to have a definite article. The criterion I will be concerned with here is Crisma's Requirement 1, which states that in a language with a definite article, a nominal argument must not be ambiguous in its interpretation as definite or indefinite. Definiteness may sometimes be marked by other means, but the language will always have some minimal morpheme that has no other interpretive function than to mark definiteness (although it may also mark other features, such as agreement features).

To evaluate this requirement for any language, we need to define what we mean by 'definite', a notoriously difficult matter. Lyons (1999) argues that we need to distinguish pragmatic/semantic definiteness from definiteness as a grammatical category because no pragmatic/semantic approach to defining definiteness is sufficient to account for definiteness marking in languages that have it. Languages that do not mark definiteness

---

[4] If we find that this presumably older grammar is also reflected in poetry known to be of late composition, that is not problematic; it could be treated as an instance of the poet drawing on conventions of traditional poetry. The study of OE poetic syntax is certainly made more difficult by the fact that the language may be a mixture of the old and the new. The most important thing is to be careful to distinguish between poetry and prose.

grammatically may make use of what Lyons calls 'semantic/pragmatic definiteness' to organise discourse, such as by requiring a fronted noun phrase, in topic position, to be interpreted as definite. In this sense, 'definite' means identifiable to the addressee by virtue of being established by the discourse or otherwise familiar. In languages that mark definiteness grammatically, however, definiteness is a grammatical category. This grammaticalisation is likely to extend beyond the semantic core of the category, i.e. familiarity, to include other uses such as inclusiveness. It follows that definiteness marking, although it will have semantic/pragmatic definiteness at its core, will not work the same way in all languages for which definiteness marking is obligatory. In particular, we cannot conclude that OE did not have obligatory definiteness marking on the basis that such marking is not used in exactly the same way as in later English. What is crucial is that there must be some sort of marking to show that a referent is definite in the semantic/pragmatic sense just defined.

In this chapter, I present evidence that the marking of definiteness was obligatory for subjects and objects in OE prose, at least by the late OE period, based on an examination of the use of SE in some of the works of Ælfric. On the other hand, the optionality of the definite article with PObjs went beyond the limits of what is possible in PDE. This evidence comes mainly from what seems at first an unlikely source, Ælfric's *Grammar* of Latin.

The remainder of this chapter is organised as follows. The next section briefly introduces Ælfric's *Grammar* of Latin. In Section 5.3 I argue that a study of Ælfric's use of SE with subject and object singular count nouns in the translations of determinerless Latin examples provides the sort of negative evidence that is usually lacking from corpus studies. That is, it gives us evidence of what Ælfric considered to be unacceptable English by the deviations he allows from the Latin. I argue that while his use of SE in these roles is consistent with his use in his other works, his practice in prepositional phrases is strikingly different. My conclusions and some directions for further research are summarised in Section 5.4.

5.2 Ælfric's *Grammar*

5.2.1 *What Can the* Grammar *Teach Us about OE?*

Ælfric's *Grammar* is a grammar of Latin, not English, and it is unsurprising that its main use in the study of OE has been in the area of vocabulary. However, as Menzer (2004: 107) points out, Ælfric's prefaces to his

Grammar mention as one of his goals his pupils' better understanding of their own language. Ælfric regarded English as having a grammar that could be discussed in a way similar to Latin grammar.

It is not Ælfric's direct comments on English that I will look at here, but the more indirect evidence offered by his use of SE in his translations of his Latin sentences that lacked a determiner. Ælfric's renderings of the Latin into English in his *Grammar* are by no means slavish, giving us clues to when he considered a determiner to be essential in English. Before looking at this question, a brief introduction to the *Grammar* is in order.

5.2.2   The Grammar *and the* Excerptiones

Ælfric based his *Grammar* on the *Excerptiones de Prisciano*. As Porter's (2002) introduction to the *Excerptiones* indicates, the authorship of this collection of excerpts from Priscian's treatise on Latin grammar is uncertain. Porter's own opinion is that Ælfric himself was the most likely author of the all-Latin *Excerptiones* (2002: 24).[5] Whatever the authorship of the *Excerptiones*, what is clear is that Ælfric adapted it for the boys learning Latin in his school, sometime between 992 and 1002 (2002: 1). Although based on the *Excerptiones*, the *Grammar* is quite different, with fuller paradigms, more examples, and additional explanations for English speakers.

A complete copy of the *Grammar* is found in St. John's College, Oxford MS 154, item 362 in Ker (1957). Ker assigns the date xi in. (i.e. beginning of the eleventh century) to the manuscript. This manuscript is therefore not far removed from the time of composition of the *Grammar* and can be assumed to reflect Ælfric's original well. Ker indicates that one scribe penned the bulk of the manuscript (folios 1–116ᵛ/3 out of 160 folios, or about 72.5 per cent). As will be discussed in Section 5.3.2, there is no evidence that the scribes differed in their use of the determiner.

This manuscript was edited by Zupitza (1880). A digital image of the manuscript is available online,[6] which I have used to double-check examples that seemed surprising to me. In what follows, I cite examples by reference to page and line number in Zupitza's edition, rather than to the manuscript folio. Note that in my presentation of these examples, I do not

---

[5] This conclusion is not universally accepted; see for example Godden (2003), who is sceptical on a number of grounds.
[6] http://image.ox.ac.uk/show?=stj&manuscript=ms154.

reproduce the circumflexes that Zupitza added to the manuscript readings to indicate vowel length.

5.3 The Study

The reason why the *Grammar* provides a sort of negative evidence about the marking of definiteness in OE is that Latin had no definite (or indefinite) article. It did have what Hale and Buck (1966) call 'determinative-descriptive pronouns', including ILLE 'that, such', IS 'this, such', ISTE 'that, such', and HIC 'this, such'. In their determinative (as opposed to pronominal) uses, Ælfric consistently translated these with an appropriate demonstrative determiner, e.g. *ab illo homine* 'fram þam men' ('from that man', Zupitza 10.17), *haec amans femina* 'þis lufjende wif' ('this loving wife', Zupitza 10.6), etc.[7] The question I investigated was Ælfric's use of SE in translating Latin phrases that lacked any determiner. If Ælfric felt no need to distinguish a definite from an indefinite interpretation, there would seem to be no need to supply a determiner. By his addition of SE when the Latin lacked a determiner, however, Ælfric leaves us a clue to places where an ambiguity between a definite and an indefinite reading was simply not acceptable English to him.

A Latin noun used without a determiner is ambiguously definite or indefinite in interpretation out of context. In the *Grammar*, the context necessary to make an inference of definiteness is usually lacking; phrases and sentences are mostly used in isolation, although Ælfric provides a few short dialogues such as (2).

(2) gif ðu befrinst: *quis equitat in ciuitatem?* hwa rit into ðam port?, ðonne cweð he:
rex et episcopus se cyningc and se bisceop.
'If you ask, *quis equitat in ciuitatem?* Who rides into the town? Then he says
Rex et episcopus The king and the bishop'

(Zupitza 10.10–12)

Note Ælfric's use of SE in three places where there is no determiner in the Latin. It was apparently natural to him to use this determiner in a situation in which 'king' and 'bishop' were new information but would be identifiable, as there would normally only be one king and one bishop familiar to

---

[7] No distinction is made in the manuscript between the presentation of the Latin and the English, but I follow Zupitza's edition in using italics for the Latin and Roman font for the OE.

a given person. This dialogue illustrates the marking of definiteness established on the basis of pragmatics and suggests the grammaticalisation of such marking.

Without further investigation, we might suppose that Ælfric would only add SE when the context established definiteness, as in (2). This is not so, however: most of the examples in the *Grammar* are not used in context, but Ælfric's addition of SE is very frequent. A notable exception is in citation forms such as *rex* 'cyning' and *episcopus* 'bisceop' (Zupitza 8.11), where the English equivalent of a Latin noun not in a larger phrase or sentence is being translated. These citation forms regularly lacked a determiner, and are not included in my data.[8] The data discussed in Section 5.3.1 suggest that while Ælfric was content not to mark definiteness with PObjs, he regularly marked it with what I will call 'direct arguments', i.e. subjects and objects, where the lack of SE probably meant that Ælfric intended his readers to understand an indefinite interpretation.

Of course, it is impossible to be certain that such an absence of a determiner with direct arguments was meant to convey an indefinite reading. However, an examination of the use of SE in translations of direct arguments without a determiner in the Latin is very suggestive of this conclusion. Let us now turn to this examination, before moving on to a consideration of PObjs.

5.3.1 Direct Arguments

I collected all instances of singular count nouns playing the role of subject or object of a sentence and translating a determinerless Latin noun.[9] The restriction to singular count nouns is not only to keep the investigation simple, but also because the behaviour of determiners with different types of nouns can be expected to follow different rules, and we get a clearer picture starting with one type and then studying further types.

It turns out that in a substantial majority of the instances where Ælfric used such a Latin noun, he supplied SE in his English translation, as shown in Table 5.1.

---

[8] A determiner is used in some instances, however, as when the citation form is for a unique noun, as in the superlative 'se mæsta' ('the largest') used to translate *maximus* (Zupitza 15.19).

[9] In a few of these examples, the sentence is not complete, but elliptical, as in the answer in (2). I have counted these. I have excluded examples in which the English translation has a (determinerless) noun but there is no noun in the Latin, e.g. 'ic sadelige hors' ('I saddle (a) horse'), which Ælfric gives as one of a number of possible translations for *sterno* (Zupitza 165.9–10). Here, an indefinite reading is guaranteed.

Table 5.1 SE *with direct arguments*

	SUBJ		OBJ		Totals	
SE	19	73%	8	73%	27	73%
Null	7	27%	3	27%	10	27%
% SE	26	100%	11	100%	37	100%

Table 5.2 Cyning *as a subject in Ælfric's* Grammar

Latin	OE	PDE	Zupitza
rex equitat	se cyningc rit	'the king rides'	128.2–3
ecce, uenit rex	efne nu, her cymð se cyning	'lo, here comes the king'	231.7–8
in ciuitatem equitauit rex	in to ðære ceastre rad se cyning	'into the city rode the king'	273.15–16
rex et episcopus	se cyningc and se bisceop	'the king and the bishop'	10.12
qualis est rex?	hwylc ys se cyning?	'which is the king?'	116.11
nescio, qualis est rex	nat ic, hwylc se cyning is	'I do not know which is the king'	116.13

With this small a number, it is possible to scrutinise all exceptions to the rule. We have seven subjects without SE. The example *ortus est sol* 'sunne is upp agan' ('the sun has risen', Zupitza 197.15) can be counted as containing a 'special noun', since *sunne* is inherently definite – although it is worth noting that Ælfric normally uses the determiner with it in his English works. In the remaining six determinerless examples, the subject is an animal and the verb the noise typical of that animal, e.g. *canis latrat* 'hund byrcð' (Zupitza 129.1). Here, a translation 'the dog barks' is not out of the question; the Latin could certainly have that interpretation. However, a generic interpretation 'a dog barks' is more probable here. The context of this list of animal noises is that Ælfric is explaining the role of person in the grammar. He remarks that one could use the first or second person with these verbs, but it would be *swiðe dyslic* 'very foolish' (Zupitza 129.6) that a person should bark or bleat. These can be treated as generics, to be rendered in PDE as 'a dog barks', 'a horse neighs', etc. In contrast, we find the noun *rex* 'king' used as a subject six times, and in each instance, SE is added (see Table 5.2).

In the last three of these examples, one of which is from the dialogue of (2), the definiteness of the Latin is without doubt. In the first three examples, a PDE translation 'a king' is not impossible, but is not nearly as likely as a definite interpretation. Similarly, *episcopus* 'bishop' can be indefinite, for example in discussions of the qualities that a bishop should have. The examples of *episcopus* in the *Grammar*, however, are not of this sort; in general, readers would only be familiar with one bishop, and so Ælfric's use of SE in all four examples of translating this noun in the subject role is unsurprising if he always marked definiteness of the subject.[10] Not all the subject nouns are so likely to favour a definite interpretation, but it appears that Ælfric favoured the use of the definite interpretation unless an indefinite one was more likely.

Turning to objects, subject to the exclusions already mentioned, I only found three examples where a determinerless Latin noun gets no determiner in the translation. The most complex of these is presented in (3).

(3)   rihtwisne   mannan,   gewislice,   ic   herige
      righteous   man   truly   I   praise
      Latin: hominem uidelicet iustum laudo
      'I truly praise a/the righteous man'

(Zupitza 262.1)

The (masculine accusative) adjective *rihtwisne* is declined strong, as expected of an adjective not preceded by a determiner or a possessive/genitive. Although it is not certain why Ælfric has abandoned his usual preference for definite noun phrases where possible here, it may have to do with the effect of *uidelicet* 'plainly, to be sure', which may be emphasising the clear righteousness of the man being praised rather than the fact that a/the man is being praised. It could also have to do with the fronted position of the object, which might suggest a contrastive reading if a determiner was added.[11] At any rate, an indefinite interpretation is certainly not difficult here. In the remaining two examples, an indefinite interpretation is unproblematic: *loquor uerbum* 'ic sprece word' ('I say a/the word', Zupitza 250.5–6) and *huic homini do equum* 'ðisum men ic forgyfe hors' ('I give this man a/the horse', Zupitza 22.17–18).[12] We cannot prove that Ælfric's audiences could only have given these determinerless nominals an indefinite interpretation, but I think that the striking difference between the non-use of a determiner and the high frequency of SE makes such a conclusion the most reasonable one, although I have given the

---

[10] Neither of these nouns appears as an object in the *Grammar*.
[11] An anonymous reviewer suggests the further possibility that this could be interpreted as a generic.
[12] As in his homilies, Ælfric occasionally specifically marks indefiniteness, e.g. *lego librum* 'ic ræde ane boc' (Zupitza 249.6–7).

definite interpretation as a possible one in my translations. One thing that is clear is that in none of the examples does SE fail to appear when a definite interpretation would be the most likely one.

To summarise, Ælfric's use of SE in his translations of determinerless Latin singular count nouns as direct arguments provides evidence that he was not willing to follow the Latin in leaving the definite/indefinite distinction unmarked. It follows from Crisma's (2011) study that in this respect, Ælfric's practice in the *Grammar* mirrors his use with direct arguments in his homilies, since these homilies were in the corpus she studied.

Crisma's (2011) study, in order to keep her data manageable, looked only at words beginning with the letter <h>. As she shows, this is a valid approach because the frequency of the definite determiner with nouns beginning with this letter is similar to its frequency in the larger corpus from which this sub-corpus was drawn, the *York-Toronto-Helsinki Parsed Corpus of Old English Prose* (YCOE). However, an examination of a different sub-corpus makes a useful check on Crisma's results and can be expected to throw up some more examples that help test the explanations she proposed for the apparent exceptions she found. I accordingly carried out a limited investigation of three of Ælfric's homilies, homilies 19, 25, and 40 of his First Series of *Catholic Homilies*, looking for non-marking of definite singular count noun subjects only.[13] Within the limitations of the study, I found ninety-eight instances of SE in subjects. In contrast, I found only one example where Ælfric did not use a definite determiner (or some other definiteness marking, such as a proximal determiner) but we would need *the* (see (4)).

(4)   On   frymðe   wæs   word.
        in   beginning   was   word
        'In the beginning was the Word'
        (cocathom1,ÆCHom_I,_25:384.142.4907)

---

[13] I chose these homilies, all written by the same scribe, as representing one homily each from the beginning, middle, and end parts of the manuscript. I excluded from my study nominal phrases beginning with premodifiers like *eall* 'all' and also the noun *deofol* 'devil', which Ælfric sometimes used without a determiner, parallel to the proper noun *God*. I excluded *heofon* 'heaven' and *eorþe* 'earth' on the basis that these sometimes act like place names, especially when contrasted with each other. On the other hand, I included *hælend* 'Saviour', which Ælfric usually used with a determiner. I also excluded *God fæder* 'God the Father'. Mitchell (1985: §335) mentions this expression as an instance where we must use a definite determiner in PDE. This is true, but we have the usual OE pattern of name + title here. In the homilies under investigation at least, when *fæder* 'Father' was used to refer to God without the preceding word *God*, we always find *se*. This makes an interesting contrast to prepositional phrases, where we frequently find *mid fæder* 'with the Father' (but *mid þam ælmightigan fæder* 'with the Almighty Father') as part of the closing formula in Ælfric's homilies.

This sentence is the opening sentence of the Gospel according to Saint John, and is found in essentially the same form in the *West Saxon Gospels*. The *West Saxon Gospel* version of the sentence is the sole prose example that Ackles (1997: 31) uses to illustrate the lack of a definite determiner in OE where PDE cannot leave it out. Although this example certainly illustrates a difference with PDE, it is not a convincing example of ambiguity in a definite or indefinite interpretation. For one thing, it is possible that it should be considered a 'special noun' that was unique. This is made less likely by the fact that having introduced *word*, Ælfric then uses the determiner with it (see (5)).

(5) & þæt word wæs mid Gode.
    and the word was with God
    'and the Word was with God'
                                    (cocathom1,ÆCHom_I,_25:384.142.4908)

There are always a number of possible explanations for a single example. It could be that OE translators of this passage were really treating *word* as indefinite in (4), where it is introduced for the first time, for the sake of an audience that contained lay members not well versed in Christian theology. Ælfric is careful to explain that this is no ordinary *word*. The overall pattern of obligatory marking of a definite singular subject count noun is apparent, however we treat this example.

5.3.2 PObjs

It seems clear that Ælfric's use of SE in translations of subjects in his *Grammar* faithfully mirrors his usage in his English homilies. I did not systematically study objects in Ælfric's homilies and so can make no direct comparison. However, my study of subjects serves as a test of Crisma's methodology and conclusions, and given that Crisma's study covered all the homilies that I studied and the fact that my study of subjects uncovered only one example in which a definite determiner is not used when we might expect one in PDE, it seems very likely that a further study of objects beyond the letter <h> would find that the use of the definite article with objects in Ælfric's homilies would also be found to mirror his use of them in his *Grammar*.

When we turn to PObjs, we also find a sort of mirror, but in this case the mirror seems to give a rather distorted image. Ælfric's use of the definite determiner with a PObj was variable in his writings generally, but even more variable in the *Grammar*. Unlike direct arguments, PObjs appear very frequently without a determiner in the *Grammar*, as in *in aula sedeo* 'on healle ic sitte' (Zupitza 274.2–3), where a PDE translation 'in the hall I sit' seems more likely than 'in a hall I sit'.

It is difficult to make a meaningful comparison of Ælfric's overall use of SE with PObjs in the *Grammar* and his other works because there are so many variables involved, including the combination of preposition and noun and the combination of the verb and the preposition. In Ælfric's own prose, a PObj might also be followed by a relative clause, not usual in the *Grammar*. All of these may affect the choice to use a determiner. Furthermore, a given noun may have more than one meaning, particularly in combination with different prepositions, and Ælfric might be more inclined to use a definite determiner with one of these meanings than another. The difficulties can be demonstrated briefly with the noun *ende*, which has a number of senses in OE. Ælfric frequently uses it without a determiner, especially in the phrase *oþ ende* 'forever'. It is no surprise to find Ælfric translating Latin *finetenus* as *oð ende* in his *Grammar*, given that we find similar use in his homilies (see (6)).

(6) heo leofode hire lif oð ende æfter Iohannes slege.
    she lived   her   life until end after John's   killing
    'she lived her life until the end after the killing of John'
                        (cocathom1,ÆCHom_I,_32:456.153.6477)

The non-use of a determiner with *ende* as PObj is very common in Ælfric's works, but we occasionally find him using the determiner (7). Here, we have not only a different sense of *ende* but also a following relative clause.

(7) on ðam ende þæs eardes ðe   þæt Godes   folc   on eardode.
    in the part the land   that the God's   people in dwelled
    'in the part of the country that the people of God dwelled in'
                        (cocathom2,ÆCHom_II,_12.1:111.57.2417)

Because of the complexities involved in making a meaningful comparison of the *Grammar* and Ælfric's other works in the use of SE with PObjs in general, I restricted my systematic investigation to a noun where it really is surprising not to find a determiner, namely *cyning*. The reason why I have chosen this particular noun for further scrutiny is that the *Grammar* contains examples that struck me as quite unusual for Ælfric. As noted above, *cyning* has a definite interpretation as the most likely one in all instances in the *Grammar*, not only for its use in subject function, but also as PObj. All the examples of *cyning* as PObj in the *Grammar* are presented in Table 5.3.

Table 5.3 Cyning *as the object of a preposition in Ælfric's* Grammar

	Latin	OE	PDE	Zupitza
No Det	cum rege est	mid cynincge he is	'with the/a king he is'	271.15–16
	a rege ueni	fram cyninge ic com	'from the/a king I came'	23.13–14
	ad regem equito	ic ride to cyninge	'I ride to the/a king'	10.19–20
	ad regem equito	to cyninge ic ride	'to the/a king I ride'	269.1
SE	ante regem stat	ætforan ðam cyninge he stent	'before the king he stands'	269.4–5
	de rege loquitur episcopus	be ðam cyncge sprecð se bisceop	'about the king speaks the bishop'	272.4–5
	apud regem sum	ic eom mid ðam cyninge	'I am with the king'	10.18–19

While the number of examples is hardly large, it is enough to show that the determiner was not obligatory with this noun as PObj in the *Grammar*, even though a definite reading is the most likely one in all examples. It is not clear why a definite determiner is added after *mid* translating *apud regem sum* but not with *cum rege est*, for example. Since this copy of the *Grammar* was written by two scribes, I considered the possibility of a correlation between the omission of SE and scribal hand. This does not appear to be the case, however. The two examples *ic ride to cyninge* and *to cyninge ic ride* in Table 5.3, both lacking a determiner with the same combination of verb, preposition, and object of preposition, were each written by a different scribe. Even if Ælfric was following some sort of rule here in the *Grammar* about when to add a determiner, the determinerless examples are surprising when we look at his other writings.

To test my impression that they did not follow his usual practice, I made a systematic investigation of *cyning* as PObj in the works of Ælfric contained in the YCOE. Excluded from this investigation were plurals, examples in which *cyning* received definiteness marking by means other than SE (such as by a proximal determiner or prenominal genitive/possessive), and examples where *cyning* had an indefinite interpretation, e.g. in expressions meaning 'choose as king', as in (8).

(8) þa   ða   he   wæs   to   cyninge   gecoren.
    then when he   was   to   king   chosen
    'when he was chosen as king'
                    (cocathom1,ÆCHom_I,_10:263.156.1943)

The results confirm that it was not Ælfric's normal practice to leave definite 'king' unmarked: I found fifty-three relevant examples of *cyning* used with a definite determiner as PObj in the Ælfric texts I studied, but no examples of it lacking a determiner as PObj. None of the examples exactly parallel the determinerless *Grammar* examples in the use of verb and preposition. However, some of the examples do use the same prepositions found in the *Grammar* and seem very close in meaning (see (9) and (10)).

(9) ac   hi   ealle ut   eodon ansunde to   ðam cynincge.
    but   they all   out   went   sound   to   the king
    'but they all went out, uninjured, to the king'
    (coaelive,ÆLS_[Memory_of_Saints]:71.3371)

(10) forðam   þe   se   bisceop wæs bysig mid   þam cynincge,
     because   that the bishop   was busy   with the king
     'because the bishop was busy with the king'
     (coaelive,ÆLS_[Swithun]:230.4371)

It seems clear that Ælfric's use of SE in prepositional phrases with *cyning* in the *Grammar* was different from his practice in his other writings. It is not clear exactly why this should be. The general difference between prepositional arguments and direct arguments can easily be explained as a translation effect of the sort studied by Taylor (2008). That is, when OE allowed for two possibilities and Latin only allowed for one, translations of Latin can be expected to favour the Latin pattern. Thus we find that with direct arguments, there is no translation effect because only one possibility, to use a definite determiner with a definite referent, was possible in OE, but since the non-use of an article was generally possible with PObjs, we get a higher frequency of non-use of the determiner than in original compositions in OE. But the non-use of the definite article does not seem to have been a possibility with the noun *cyning* even as a PObj for Ælfric in his own writings, and so a translation effect with this particular word seems surprising. We might speculate that although Ælfric always used a determiner with definite *cyning*, he was aware that other people did not. I have not found much support for this idea in the texts. Space does not allow a full discussion of my investigations, but I can note here that I have collected sixty-seven examples of the target type, i.e. definite and singular *cyning* as the object of a preposition and preceded either by SE or no determiner. In only eight of these is the determiner absent.[14] What is important here is not to explain the

---

[14] Further discussion of the exceptional examples is not possible except to mention that six of them come from legal documents, suggesting that the non-use of a determiner might be a feature of the genre.

exceptions (as interesting as that is) but to see that the definiteness marking of *cyning* was apparently nearly universal at a time when such marking was certainly more variable with other nouns as PObj. This suggests that the situation in later English, where the non-marking of definite PObjs became exceptional and limited to particular combinations of prepositions and nouns, was achieved by an increase in this marking with particular nouns or constructions, rather than by some sudden change to the use of the definite determiner more generally.

5.4 Conclusion

I have used investigations of more than one type to argue that late OE had a category of definite article. All of these investigations were limited to singular count nouns. In my investigations of a selection of Ælfric's homilies, I have established that SE is not simply optional for subjects, and it is used where no demonstrative meaning can be detected. In contrast, it is easy to establish that no definite article was necessary in Ælfric's homilies for PObjs. These findings alone show the importance of methodological decisions in collecting empirical data and support Crisma's (2011) decision to exclude PObjs from her study. It is simply no longer defensible to treat all grammatical relations the same in studying the development of the definite article in English. The present study also adds to the evidence given by Crisma that English had what we can call a definite article prior to the eME stage that is most commonly accepted as the period when this category emerged, even though the rules concerning the use of this article were different and complications arise from the fact that it also had other functions, as a demonstrative and a pronoun, and also its different behaviour with NPs bearing grammatical relations other than subject and object.

Data from Ælfric's OE translations of Latin in his *Grammar* show how fairly close but idiomatic translations of this sort can provide a sort of negative data generally lacking from a corpus. The difference in frequency of SE with direct arguments versus PObjs in translations where no determiner is found in the Latin is striking and hardly likely to be due to chance. It is not possible to prove beyond doubt that in the small number of examples of a definite singular count noun serving as subject or object in his Latin *Grammar* and lacking SE, Ælfric intended an indefinite interpretation. However, this seems a more plausible explanation than the alternative, that a determiner was simply optional in Ælfric's grammar. The asymmetry between Ælfric's very high frequency of SE with direct arguments versus a much lower frequency with PObjs is most easily explained by assuming that leaving the determiner out in a subject or object when a definite reading was intended would be a real violation of the rules of his grammar. In contrast, Ælfric was willing to dispense with the determiner in prepositional phrases more frequently than was his usual practice in his homilies, as is evident in the categorical use of a determiner with *cyning* as PObj in the homilies as opposed to its variable use in the *Grammar*.

A reasonable interpretation of the comparatively high frequency of the non-use of a determiner with a PObj in the *Grammar* is that translation effects came into play here, where there was no grammatical prohibition against leaving out the determiner. It remains a bit of a puzzle why Ælfric was comfortable with leaving the determiner out sometimes in his translations when *cyning* played the role of PObj but added it in a few examples. What is clear, however, is that the determiner was pretty much essential with some definite count nouns used as PObjs at an early stage in English prose, while not with others. Impressionistically, it seems that some nouns could occur in this role without a determiner more easily with some prepositions than with others. It also seems likely that not only the combination of preposition + noun, but the larger combination of verb + preposition + noun, played a role in whether a determiner was needed. Case studies of the use of the determiner in different combinations will help us to understand under just what circumstances the marking of definiteness was still not necessary in OE.

This study supports Denison's (2006) contention that the accretion of the properties that make the PDE determiner easily identifiable as a category was a gradual, rather than sudden, process. If we make the usual generative assumption that articles are in the head D of DP, we need to assume that this D position emerged sometime before the period of substantial prose records. This emergence would have been sudden, but we can still maintain a sort of gradience. First, we have ambiguity in whether a particular instance of SE is in D or the specifier of DP. Many examples are unclear in this respect to the modern linguist, and we have no way of knowing whether OE speakers/writers had a clear-cut distinction in mind. Second, we can assume gradience in whether D was required to be filled or not. That is, at an early stage definiteness was required to be marked for subjects and objects, with some identifiable classes of exceptions, while such marking gradually became essential with non-arguments and most PObjs. Further study of the use or not of the definite article in specific constructions in OE and eME is a promising avenue of research into how the article system of later English developed.

PART II

Approaches to Constructions and Constructional Change

CHAPTER 6

How Patterns Spread: The To-Infinitival Complement as a Case of Diffusional Change, or 'To-Infinitives, and Beyond!'

Bettelou Los

6.1 Introduction[*]

This chapter revisits my earlier work on *to*-infinitives (Los 1999, 2005) in the light of the new insights about the spread of complementation patterns provided by De Smet (2013) and Rudanko (2015). Their investigations into the spread of the gerund as a verb complement benefited from the fact that the gerund came into existence relatively recently, which made it possible not only to construct a scenario of how it spread through the system of verbal complementation, but also to date the various stages. Although the spread of the *to*-infinitive took place too early for us to do the same, the distribution of the *to*-infinitive in Old English (OE) did allow me to identify the niche in which it first arose, and to suggest a scenario of its spread. De Smet's concepts of broad and narrow paradigmatic analogy make it possible to construct a more fine-grained scenario for the rise of *to*-infinitives, as they also take into account semantic groups; this means that the original semantics of the individual groups of verbs, as reflected in their etymologies, may provide additional data. That etymologies of individual verbs can be very useful for such a purpose has been demonstrated by Lau (2015).

Testing the trajectory of the spread of the *to*-infinitive against De Smet's (2013) scenario has the advantage of checking whether reconstructing that spread solely on the basis of the synchronic distribution of the *to*-infinitive in OE is valid. Cuyckens (1999) in his investigation of the pathway from 'proximity' *by* to 'passive' *by* noted that there is an

---

[*] I would like to thank Hendrik De Smet and an anonymous reviewer for their very helpful comments. The final words of the subtitle of this chapter are a tribute to David Denison, who, as the external examiner for my PhD, made them the end of his speech at my after-viva party.

uneasy relationship between the concept of synchronic family resemblance networks and actual historical reality: important transitional meanings may vanish at a later stage, and need not always be synchronically present. In the case of the development of the *to*-infinitive, however, we lack the historical data to back up the historical pathway of change suggested by the synchronic distribution of the *to*-infinitive in OE. We can see that the proposed pathway is in line with the distribution of the *du*-infinitive in Gothic, but that is about as far as we can get. We will see that tracking broad and narrow paradigmatic analogies between semantic groups confirms the trajectory hypothesised on the basis of synchronic OE data, and may even account for the rise of the *to*-infinitival Exceptional Case-Marking (ECM) construction, the most recent development in the trajectory, as we will see in the final section of this chapter.

6.2 Paths of Diffusion: De Smet (2013)

Hendrik De Smet's (2013) study about diffusional change in the English system of complementation contains a detailed account of the spread of the gerund as verb complement in early Modern English (eModE). The first gerunds that appear as verb complements are bare gerunds as in (1); they derive from the OE *-ungl-ing* suffix that builds nouns from verbal stems. These early gerunds do not have any modifiers or complements (De Smet calls them 'bare gerunds'), and hence do not show clear signs of their category, whether nominal or already verbal.

(1) and halde þe   in chastite, and iuil langingis do away; luue **fasting**
     and hold yourself in chastity and evil longings do away love fasting
     'and keep yourself chaste, and get rid of evil desires; love fasting'
                                              (PPCME2, a1425; De Smet 2013: 162)

Luue 'love' in (1) is one of the first verbs attested with a gerund complement. This verb and the other early gerund-taking verbs share another complement besides the gerund: the abstract noun. Typical examples of such nouns are the vices listed in (2).

(2) Jake loves lechery, foul language, war, theft, whoredom, and drunkenness.

Present-day English (PDE) examples of bare gerunds after verbs like *love* usually force subject control, but this is not what we find with these early bare gerunds. They denote generic rather than specific acts, events, or situations, and like the bare abstract nouns in (2), the control relations depend on the context. It is probably for the same reason that gerunds do not at first appear in a passive construction with *be* (as in *Jake fears being captured*); instead, we get gerunds that are active in form but passive in sense (*Jake fears capturing*), by analogy of *Jake fears capture*. It is from this tiny niche of bare abstract nouns that the gerund takes off. De Smet calls this first stage of the diffusion of the gerund complement *narrow paradigmatic analogy*.

The second stage involves *semantic analogy*, in which verbs of Emotion, Avoidance, Necessity, and Endurance start to occur with the gerund. The model here is still the bare abstract noun, although indefinite nouns with a generic interpretation are also found, as in (3a); the gerund is still voice-neutral, as shown in (3b).

(3) a. Jake avoids/escapes/fears/risks capture/punishment/shipwreck.
    b. [He] escaped drowning verye narrowely.
       (*OED*, 1560; De Smet 2013: 174)

Endurance verbs are found with bare gerunds in a construction with *cannot* or *could not*; note that the conditional in (4b) implies a negative: '. . . but it could not bear recapitulating'.

(4) a. He cannot endure/bear criticism/banishment.
    b. I would summ up the Particulars of this Second Head, if the Examiner's Performance could bear recapitulating.
       (*OED*, 1699; De Smet 2013: 195)

Some kind of threshold appears to be reached at this stage: so many verbs appear with gerund complements that users have started to identify coherent groups that share the same semantics, and the bare gerund is gradually extended to verbs that did not themselves collocate with a bare abstract noun, but had similar meanings to these established gerund 'families'. Verbs of negative implication, which share a meaning component with the endurance verbs in the previous section but did not (and still do not) take bare abstract nouns, now start to appear with gerund complements. The gerund is being extended beyond its original model. A typical PDE example is (5).

(5) I could not help laughing.

Only one verb of this group provides a link with bare abstract noun complements: the now obsolete verb *forbear* 'refrain from', illustrated in (6).

(6)   Quen þaim biheld þat kinges here, was nan þat lahuter miht
      when they beheld the king's army was none that laughter might
      forbere
      forbear
      'When they beheld the king's army, none of them could abstain from
      laughter'   (*MED*, a1400; De Smet 2013: 173)

Note that (6) shows that the trajectory of the gerund cannot be recaptured on the basis of synchronic data alone – as a general rule, important transitional meanings are not always synchronically present, as we noted in Section 6.1, and in this particular case it is quite likely that some original action noun uses have been replaced by the gerund.

The extension to new groups of verbs has consequences for the gerund complement itself. Another member of this new group, *defer*, did not collocate with bare abstract or indefinite nouns but with 'definite' nouns – *the search, the journey, the visit* – probably because of its basic meaning of 'postpone'; what gets postponed is usually a plan that was made earlier and is hence identifiable (De Smet 2013: 186). The remaining members of this group – *decline, help, omit* – do not collocate with abstract nouns, but appear with gerund complements in eModE on the basis of their meaning only. *Help* is a relative newcomer to this group as it did not have the relevant meaning of negative implication when the group was first formed.

Stage III finds Retrospective and Proposal verbs taking gerund complements. These groups do not include a single member that ever collocated with bare abstract nouns, and the gerund did not appear here on the strength of their meanings either, so these verbs represent a significant departure from the original model. They emerged with non-bare gerunds, as in (7a) and (7b); the subjectless gerund, as in (7c), is a secondary development from the non-bare gerund rather than the original model (as it was for the verbs in Stages I and II), a process De Smet (2013: 197–8) terms *indirect paradigmatic analogy*.

(7)   a. I remember his turning off his chief ecuyer for merely whispering
         in the street with a maquignon, who was bringing him a horse for
         sale.   (*OED*, 1834 G. P. R. James *John Marston Hall* x)
      b. I remember/recollect/recall his mother asking him that.
      c. I remember/recollect/recall asking him that.

Proposal verbs, which take definite NPs, as in (8a), now also start to appear with gerunds, as in (8b) and (8c). Note the definite article in (8b), and the use of *of* in (8c). Note that the subjectless gerund in (8d) is a secondary development (from the definite NP stage) rather than a direct link to the earlier stage of *narrow paradigmatic analogy*.

(8) a. he was the man that did propose the removal of the Chancellor.
(CEMET, 1667; De Smet 2013: 203)
b. I to the office, whither Creed come by my desire, and he and I to my wife, to whom I now propose the going to Chetham.
(CEMET, 1667 *The Diary of Samuel Pepys*; De Smet 2013: 201)
c. Mr Warren proposed my getting of £100 to get him a protection for a ship to go out, which I think I shall do.
(CEMET, 1665 *The Diary of Samuel Pepys*; De Smet 2013: 201)
d. I am so sick of it all, that if we are victorious or not, I propose leaving England in the spring.
(CLMETEV, 1741; De Smet 2013: 200)

There is at this stage a broad association between gerund complements and noun phrases in general, not just between bare gerunds and bare abstract nouns: *broad paradigmatic analogy* (Stage IV). Note that the gerunds at this stage have achieved functional equivalence with a finite clause expressing e.g. propositions.

Although the *to*-infinitive developed much earlier than the gerund so that we lack synchronic data, the story of the *to*-infinitive is likely to have been a similar tale of gradual diffusion, including abrupt gearshifts where entirely new classes of verbs start to appear with this complement. This will be explored in the remainder of this chapter.

6.3 Origin and Development of *To*-Infinitives

To in the *to*-infinitive is a grammaticalised development from the preposition *to*. The formal similarity of the *to*-infinitive to a *to*-PP, as well as the etymological facts of the *to*-infinitive, gives us a niche from which the *to*-infinitive started its rise, analogous to the bare abstract noun in (2), (3a), and (4a), which provided a niche for the gerund to emerge as complement of a small number of verbs. The *to*-infinitive also seems to have arisen in a very local niche: a PP with *to* in which the preposition *to* does not refer to distance-in-space but distance-in-time, the future.

There were two infinitives in OE, the bare infinitive and the *to*-infinitive; they are given in (9).

(9) a. bare infinitive: *beran* 'bear'
    b. *to*-infinitive: *to berenne* 'to bear'

The etymology of the *to*-infinitive is often given as a bare infinitive in the complement of a preposition *to*, but this leaves the gemination ('doubling') of the *-n-* in the *to*-infinitive unexplained (Grimm 1837: 105, cited in Jolly 1873: 150–4). The gemination points to the presence of an earlier *-j-*, probably part of a nominalising suffix (Dirk Boutkan, personal communication). This parallels the origin of the gerund, which also started out as a verbal stem with a derivational suffix *-ung* that made it into a noun, capable of nominal behaviour such as having plural forms and case endings, like *herungum* 'praises', a dative plural, in (10).

(10) Hi wurdon þa ealle þurh þa wundra onbryrde, and on godes
     they became then all through the miracles excited and in God-GEN
     herungum hi sylfe gebysgodon
     praises-DAT they themselves busied
     'They then all became excited because of the miracles and busied themselves in God's praises'
     <ÆLS (Sebastian) 148>[1]

This etymology is provided in (11):[2]

(11) to (preposition) + ber- (verbal stem) + -anja (derivational suffix) + -i (dative sg) → Common Germanic *to beranjōi, OE: *to berenne*, ME: *to beren/bere*, PDE: *to bear*

The etymology of the bare infinitive is usually given as (12) (e.g. Szemerényi 1996: 325):

(12) PIE: *bher-o-no-m
     bher- (verb root) + -o- (thematic vowel) -no- (nominalising, derivational affix) + -m (nom/acc neuter)
     → OE form *beran*

Although the etymology in (12) is ambiguous as to the case of the form that was fossilised in place, an accusative makes sense as the case originally used

---

[1] The reference to an OE text enclosed in < > follows the system of short titles as employed in Healey and Venezky (1980) (in turn based on the system of Mitchell *et al.* 1975, 1979). It is identical to the TEI reference in the Toronto *Dictionary of Old English Corpus* (DOEC), which means that line numbers refer to the beginning of the sentence rather than the line in which the relevant structure occurs.

[2] I am indebted to the late Dirk Boutkan, then – 1995 – at the Department of Comparative Linguistics of Leiden University, for the etymology in (11).

as a purpose expression after a verb of motion (GOALS are apparently expressed by accusatives in earlier stages of Indo-European languages, cf. Latin *Romam* (acc) *ire* 'go to Rome'). This is interesting in view of the fact that the niche from which the *to*-infinitive sprang was also an expression of purpose, the *to*-PP. This means that the bare infinitive may well have traversed the same developmental path as the *to*-infinitive, only at a much earlier time.

There is no evidence of any other prepositions taking an infinitive as complement apart from *to*, or of an infinitive without *to* being used as subject or object in OE. The earliest function of the *to*-infinitive appears to have been as purpose adjunct, as in (13), where it is conjoined with a *to*-PP, also expressing purpose. Neither the *to*-PP nor the *to*-infinitive (both in bold in (13)) are arguments of the higher verb *undon* 'undo', whose arguments are *he* 'he' and *his muð* 'his mouth'. (The -*anne* in *wurðianne* in (13) is a common variant of -*enne*.)

(13) þæt he [...] mihte [...] undon his muð **to wisdomes**
that he might undo his mouth to wisdom's
spræcum, (*to*-PP) and **to wurðianne**
speeches and to praise
God (*to*-infinitive)
God
'so that he [...] could [...] open his mouth for words of wisdom, and to praise God'

<ÆHom 16, 184>

The counterpart of the *to*-infinitive in Gothic, the *du*-infinitive, is only attested in the function of purpose adjunct (Köhler 1867). The fact that the *to*-PPs expressing purpose adjuncts in OE invariably contain nominalisations of action nouns – *spræc* 'speech' in (13) is related to *sprecan* 'speak' – supports the hypothesis that the form that gave rise to the *to*-infinitive did so, too. The *to*-infinitive was, at first, a *to*-PP which contained an action noun created by the derivational suffix -*anja*. Just like -*ung*/-*ing* of the gerund, -*anja* was reanalysed at some point as inflection. As inflection is not category-changing, the verbal stem remains verbal, and the form becomes part of the paradigm of the verb. All non-finite forms in Germanic ultimately derive from formations that contained derivational suffixes and only came to be considered part of the verbal paradigm at a later stage (see e.g. Ringe 2006).

The *to*-PP, then, is the niche in which the *to*-infinitive first appeared. The preposition *to* governs the dative, and this is the case of the NP inside the *to*-PP *to wisdomes spræcum* in (13), and of the fossilised inflection of the *to*-infinitive. That the case-ending is fossilised is clear from the behaviour of the *to*-infinitive in OE, and the behaviour of the *du*-infinitive in Gothic. Verbal stems inside nominalisations cannot assign accusative case to their objects; their objects have genitive rather than accusative case, like *wisdomes* in (13) and *godes* in (10).

The *to*-infinitive is a clause by the time of OE. The *to*-infinitive in (14a) has a stranded preposition *mid* 'with', while the *to*-PP in another version of the same passage, in (14b), does not.

(14) eall swa hwæt swa mihton beon gesewene lustfullice …
all so what so might be seen desirable
'whatever might appear desirable … '

    a. þone lichaman mid to gereordianne
       the-ACC body-ACC with to nourish
       'to nourish the body with'
                                                                                                                                   <GD (2) C 13.128.35>

    b. to þæs lichaman gereordunge
       to the-GEN body-GEN nourishment-DAT
       'for the body's nourishment'
                                                                                                                                  <GD 2 (H) 13.128.32>

Stranding can only take place in clauses, not in phrases, so that the *to*-infinitival constituent must be a clause, and the *to*-infinitive itself a verb.

Both gerund and *to*-infinitive, then, appear to have developed out of nominalisations to become clauses. Unlike the bare abstract noun as in (1), which constituted the initial niche for the gerund, the *to*-infinitive did not start out as a complement to verbs but as an adjunct, so before we reach the stage that we can chart the *to*-infinitive's progress through De Smet's stages of *narrow paradigmatic analogy*, *semantic analogy*, and *indirect paradigmatic analogy*, we will need to discuss the jump from adjunct to argument.

6.4 From Adjunct to Verb Complement

There are a number of other historical examples of adjuncts being reanalysed as arguments, i.e. complements, of verbs. One example is provided by De Smet (2013) in his discussion of another form in *-ing*, the present participle. Example (15) is an adverbial clause from eModE.

(15) Up, and to the office betimes, and there all the morning very busy, **causing papers to be entered and sorted**, to put the office in order against the Parliament.

(PPCEME, 1666 *The Diary of Samuel Pepys*; De Smet 2013: 115)

After some verbs and adjectives, this adverbial clause was reinterpreted as a complement, i.e. as a constituent that expressed an argument of the higher predicate, as in (16).

(16) He was busy sorting a sheaf of letters.

Busy in (15) is complete; its single argument is catered for (by the implicit first person of the diarist), and the clause after the comma can be deleted without affecting the sense of *busy*. The *ing*-clause in (16), however, is a complement – an integral part of the clause which cannot be deleted without affecting the sense of *busy*.

Although being busy, happy, or tired is complete in themselves as descriptions of certain states people may be in, there is an additional semantic role lurking in the background: the reason (or SOURCE) why they are busy, happy, or tired. The present participle clause originally described the circumstances in which the state arose. These circumstances need not be the SOURCE, but the implication must often have been that they were, and in time this led to the reinterpretation that the participle clause was a complement (De Smet 2013: 121).

Another example of an adjunct being reinterpreted as a complement in a similar process of pragmatic implicature is provided by López-Couso (2007), who charts the development of the conjunction *lest* (OE *þy læs* (*þe*), ME (Middle English) *the lesse the, thi les the, lest*). This connective originally meant 'so that not', and introduced clauses of negative purpose. It was often used with verbs meaning 'fear, dread', and, as with *busy*, the inference that the clause following such verbs would explain what people were afraid of meant that *lest*-clauses started to be used interchangeably with *that*-clauses after such verbs (López-Couso 2007: 21). See (17) below, and for an overview of the phenomenon, see López-Couso and Méndez-Naya (2015).

(17) but bycause this texte of sayncte Paule is in latyn, and husbandes commonely can but lyttell laten, I fere **leaste** they can-not vnderstande it. (Cf.: *I fear that they cannot understand it.*)

(HC, 1534 Fitzherbert, *The Book of Husbandry*, 99; López-Couso 2007: 14)

Such a change in status of the infinitive, from adverbial clause to complement clause, can be put to the test, as there are syntactic operations that only work if a constituent is an argument of the verb, i.e. a complement, and not if it is an adjunct. In (18), a constituent – in bold – has been moved out of a *to*-infinitive, to make a *wh*-question (see Los 2005: 14).

(18) **On hwilcum godum** tihst þu   us to gelyfenne?
     in   which   gods   urge you us to believe
     'In which gods do you urge us to believe?'

<ÆLS (George) 148>

On hwilcum godum 'in which gods' cannot be an argument of the higher verb *tihst* 'urge' in (18), as this verb is not attested with *on*-PPs; it does, however, fit the complementation pattern of the verb *gelyfan* 'believe' ('believe in something'), which suggests that *on hwilcum godum* has been fronted out of the *to*-infinitive *to gelyfenne*. This indicates that *to gelyfenne* is a complement, an argument of the verb *tihst* 'urge' and not a purpose adjunct.

Tihst in (18) is from *tyhtan* 'urge', a member of a set of verbs in OE with meanings of 'persuade, urge'. Some thirty-nine OE verbs of Persuading and Urging can be found with the subcategorisation frames in (19).

(19) Semantic roles: AGENT, THEME, GOAL
     Subcategorisation frames: NPACC (THEME), *to*-PP (GOAL)
                                NPACC (THEME), *to*-infinitive (GOAL)
                                NPACC (THEME), subjunctive clause (GOAL)

Note that the GOAL-argument in (19) takes the same three forms as the purpose adjunct in OE (and in Gothic; Köhler 1867: 451), i.e. *to*-PP, *to*-infinitive, and subjunctive clause, showing that these GOAL-arguments derive from purpose adjuncts.

We have now arrived at the point in which the *to*-infinitive has established itself as a possible verb complement. The next section reviews the scenario of its subsequent spread as proposed in Los (2005) against the background of the four stages De Smet identifies for the gerund.

6.5 The Spread of the *To*-Infinitive as Verb Complement

6.5.1 Stage I, Narrow Paradigmatic Analogy: Verbs of Spatial Manipulation

Many of the verbs of Persuading and Urging derive etymologically from verbs of spatial manipulation, and have basic meanings like PDE *force* in *They forced the ship to the shore*; this probably explains the accusative case of the THEME, as the deepest meaning is that of some inanimate object being

How Patterns Spread

pushed into a certain direction. This inanimate object was extended to human beings, as is also possible with PDE *force* (which has an *into*-PP in PDE rather than the *to*-PP of OE) – see (20) and (21).

(20) German Says Hypnotist Forced Him Into Crime.
(New York Times headline, 27 February 1947)

(21) A freak injury forced him into retirement.

Note that the *into*-PPs in these PDE examples contain action nouns, like the *to*-PP frame in OE in (19) (see the discussion of example (13) above). As in the OE *to*-PP frame, the implication is that it is the human object that is forced to be the AGENT of these actions. Note that these *into*-PPs can be rephrased as *to*-infinitives: (20') *The hypnotist forced him to commit a crime*, (21') *A freak injury forced him to retire*. *Into*-PPs play an important role in the competition between *to*-infinitive and gerund, from eModE to the present day (Rudanko 2015).

The *to*-infinitive developed into a verbal expression as a special case of the *to*-PP in this subcategorisation frame, much like the gerund emerged as a verbal expression as a special case of the bare abstract noun after verbs like *love, like, hate* (see (1)–(2)). This is De Smet's stage of *narrow paradigmatic analogy*.

6.5.2 Stage II, Semantic Analogy: Verbs of Firing Up

Apart from spatial manipulation verbs, the thirty-nine OE verbs of Persuading and Urging also contain a second coherent 'family' of verbs. Their etymology indicates core meanings like 'fire up, set fire to, inflame'; examples are *onælan* and *ontendan*. It is unlikely that they could take *to*-PPs in these meanings, and they probably acquired the frames in (19) only after they had extended their meanings metaphorically to 'fire someone up, inspire someone to do something'.

Both the *to*-PP and the *to*-infinitive must have appeared as complements with these verbs on the basis of these new metaphorically-extended directive meanings. This is entirely parallel to *semantic analogy*, Stage II of the spread of the gerund.

6.5.3 Stage III, Indirect Paradigmatic Analogy: Verbs of Commanding and Permitting

The *to*-infinitive may then have spread to groups of verbs that are also not attested with a *to*-PP in OE, but have a similar directive meaning – the verbs of Commanding and Permitting. These verbs derive from core meanings of 'give' – the RECIPIENT receives a permission or an order, cf. PDE examples (22a) and (22b).

(22) a. Toy libraries and other sharing schemes allow [NPchildren] [NPaccess to a large variety of toys].

(*OED*, 1990 *Lifestyle* Summer 28/2)

b. That reminded him to order [NPHeathcliff] [NPa flogging], and [NPCatherine] [NPa fast from dinner or supper].

(1847 Emily Brontë, *Wuthering Heights*, Penguin 87)

The three-place subcategorisation frames in OE of these verbs are as in (23).

(23) Semantic roles: AGENT, RECIPIENT, THEME
    Subcategorisation frames: NPDAT (RECIPIENT), NPACC (THEME)
                              NPDAT (RECIPIENT), *to*-infinitive (THEME)
                              NPDAT (RECIPIENT), subjunctive clause (THEME)

A minority of the verbs of Permitting and Commanding are also found with two-place frames, one of which is an Accusative and Infinitive (AcI) construction with a bare infinitive. There is a semantic difference between the role of the NPs in such an AcI-construction and in an NPDAT+*to*-infinitive construction: the RECIPIENT of the permission or command has greater freedom of action in the latter construction in that he or she may choose not to carry out the action expressed in the infinitival complement. Another difference is that the AcI-construction does not entail that any communicative act took place between the issuer of the command or permission and its executor; the accusative does not denote a RECIPIENT or ADDRESSEE, but an executor of the command. The AcI-construction, then, is much more akin to the complement of causatives, and this is a natural development for predicates with meanings of commanding and permitting, as noted by Royster (1918):

> Causation may be euphemistically concealed in permission: it is represented by the allowing-causing verb that a desire to do something arises in the consciousness of the secondary actor, and that someone who has authority over him grants him permission to do the thing he wants to do; as a matter of fact, the desire to have something done originates with the one who has power over the will and act of the performer. The performer's attitude toward the act is, in reality, as vague and uncertain as it is represented to be by the causative verb; but it is formally and politely represented as being desirous of bringing about the act.   (Royster 1918: 88)

These politeness mechanisms may at least partially explain why some verbs of Commanding and Permitting occur with both two-place and three-place constructions. *Lætan* 'let', which is not found with a *to*-infinitive but with a bare infinitive in an AcI-construction, derives from a form that must have meant 'let go, neglect, allow to happen', rather than an explicit granting of permission requiring a RECIPIENT, but acquired strong causative connotations by the time of OE. For the other causative verb, *don* 'do', I argued in my PhD dissertation that the AcI-construction in OE after this verb typically expresses the more causative end of the scale, the 'peremptory command' rather than a request or suggestion (Los 1999: 187–92). Royster notes that the use of the AcI-construction after such verbs often, although not invariably, implies an entailment relation that the act expressed by the infinitival complement will be performed, unlike the ditransitive NPDAT+*to*-infinitive construction or NPDAT+*that*-clause complement. This co-existence of three- and two-place argument structures can be compared to the three- and two-place uses of verbs like *allow, permit,* and *order* in PDE, as in (24a) and (24b).

(24) a. The general ordered his soldiers to blow up the bridge.
    b. The general ordered the bridge to be blown up.

(Cf. Postal 1974: 318)

If causatives are a natural development from verbs of Commanding and Permitting, these verbs are themselves also the outcome of semantic shifts. I argued in Los (1999: 172) that the semantic shift that made them into verbs of Commanding is the result of Politeness mechanisms. Commands are potential Face-Threatening Acts (Brown and Levinson 1987); hence often create cycles in which there is a continual search for new euphemisms to express obligation or commands. Direct directives perform the command baldly, without considering the addressee's Face, while indirect directives satisfy the addressee's negative Face wants, i.e. the addressee's desire to be unimpeded in his freedom of action (Brown and Levinson 1987). Such indirect directives often take the form of requests or suggestions, which will be felt – at least initially – to be more polite, in that the felicity conditions originally attached to them allow the addressee (the RECIPIENT) greater freedom to reject or ignore the obligation. In a survey of the origins of directive verbs in English, Lau (2015: 8) notes that the felicity conditions of requests and commands overlap, as both Speech Acts have the following conditions: (i) The requested act is a future act of the hearer/addressee (H); (ii) H is able to do the act and the speaker (S) believes so; (iii) S sincerely wants the act to be done by H; (iv) S has the intention to attempt to get H to do the act (Austin 1962; Searle 1969: 66). The only difference is that commands have an additional felicity condition, which is that S is in a position of authority over H. If used frequently, the assumptions underlying expressions for requests will in time become those of commands (Traugott 1972: 100), and new euphemisms will have to be found.

Requesting is one of the typical meanings from which verbs of Commanding develop. Of the other typical meanings identified by Lau (2015), *pushing* takes us back to the verbs of spatial manipulation that gave rise to some of the verbs of Persuading and Urging, while *calling* (cf. OE *hatan*) represents the outcome of a pragmaticalisation: calling somebody to come over is usually done for the purpose of directing that person to do something, and this purpose seems to become an entailment. The other meanings – *giving* or *offering, desiring, being aware, causing others to be aware, expecting* – all seem to stem from addressing the felicity conditions of a directive speech act, which is a favourite strategy for creating indirect directives (cf. the famous 'request' *Can you pass the salt?*, which addresses the felicity condition that H needs to have the ability to perform the act). In OE, the meanings of giving or telling are much to the fore, which explains the ditransitive frame NP𝐷𝐴𝑇 (RECIPIENT), NP𝐴𝐶𝐶 (THEME) of (23). The reconstructed ancestor of the core lexeme underlying *bebeodan, beodan* 'command', and *forbeodan* 'forbid', Proto-Germanic *beuð-, is connected to a Proto-Indo-European lexeme that must have meant 'observe' and acquires meanings of 'point out, warn' in Germanic and Celtic, and then 'order' (Lehmann 1986: 30); but note that 'offer' is one of the meanings given for *bebeodan* and *beodan* in Bosworth and Toller (1882–1898, 1908–1921), as well as in the *Dictionary of Old English* (*DOE*), for both verbs given as the C-meaning, and is still the core meaning of cognates *bieten* in Modern German and *bieden* in Modern Dutch. *Dihtan* 'direct' is a loan from Latin *dictāt*-, a past participial stem of *dictare*, itself a frequentative of *dicere* 'say, tell' (*OED, dight*). *Wissian* 'direct' is formed on the adjective that developed into PDE *wise* (*OED, wis*) as a causative formation 'make wise', hence 'tell'.

The etymologies of verbs of Permission show various semantic origins (*OED*) but do not appear to address felicity conditions. *Aliefan, liefan*, and *lofian* are all derived from a root meaning 'leave, permission' (and, at an earlier stage, 'approval', cf. the meaning of the related PDE noun *love*); *sellan* 'give, grant' similarly derives from a root meaning 'gift, delivery'. The etymologies of *tiðian* and *ðafian*, both meaning 'grant', are unknown.

There are some twenty OE verbs with meanings of 'command, permit' that appear with the frames in (23), but not with purposive *to*-PPs, so that the appearance of the *to*-infinitive here represents an extension into new territory, beyond the distribution of its earliest model. What appears to have happened is that the new non-finite expression has moved into the realm of the 'dependent desires': expressions of potential, non-actuated, irrealis complements after verbs with meanings of commanding, allowing, promising, intending, hoping, trying, and the like. This represented a major gearshift for the distribution of the *to*-infinitive to a whole raft of new verbs: extension through *indirect paradigmatic analogy*. Like the gerund extending to verb groups that did not include a single member that ever collocated with bare abstract nouns, the *to*-infinitive moves to verbs that were never found with a *to*-PP, and did not share the same meaning as the original set of verbs of Persuading and Urging.

6.5.4 Stage IV, Broad Paradigmatic Analogy: To-*Infinitives as the Expression of 'Dependent Desires'*

The original sense of direction of the preposition *to* allowed the action noun within a *to*-PP to refer to actions and events that are in the future, which was a good fit with the purpose adjunct, as such adjuncts referred to future GOALS. The GOALS of verbs of spatial manipulation when applied to people rather than to inanimate objects are more in the nature of directives: pressure is brought to bear on people to perform an act. GOALS of directives can still be described as being in the future, but the focus is probably more on the fact that they are as yet unrealised. This is the meaning that takes both the *to*-PP and the *to*-infinitive to the irrealis domain of the subjunctive – finite clauses that are the complement of verbs with meanings of fearing, promising, ordering, hoping, expecting, or insisting. All of these verbs share a meaning component of desire (on the part of some AGENT in the higher clause), which is why Ogawa (1989) refers to these complements as 'dependent desires'.

In PDE, the preferred expression of 'dependent desires' is a *to*-infinitive, but in OE it is a subjunctive clause; the *to*-infinitive was found after the same verbs but with a low frequency. It is in ME that these frequencies flip (Los 2005; see also Rohdenburg 1995 for data on eModE). Adjectival predicates of the type *be crucial/important/vital* and the like see similar shifts, but somewhat later than the verbal predicates (Van linden 2010).

The diffusion of the *to*-infinitive from verbs of Persuading and Urging, where its model was the *to*-PP, to verbs of Commanding and Permitting, where this model was not available, allowed the *to*-infinitive to acquire a more abstract meaning, very similar to that of the subjunctive clause. The subjunctive clause may have provided a new model, so that the *to*-infinitive started to appear with verbs that not only had no *to*-PP but also no directive meaning: they were verbs of intention with meanings of intending, hoping, trying, promising – some seventy-five verbs in all, of which only a handful have survived the large-scale replacement of native words by French loans in ME (i.e. *a/on-drædan* 'dread', *ceosan* 'choose', *deman* 'condemn', *earnian* 'deserve, earn', *forsacan* 'refuse', *giernan* 'yearn', *leornian* 'learn', *onscunian* 'shun', *secan* 'seek', *swerian* 'swear', *ðencan* 'think, intend', and *understandan* 'understand, manage'). This is parallel to De Smet's stage of *broad paradigmatic analogy* in that there is a broad association between *to*-infinitives and subjunctive clauses rather than between *to*-infinitives and *to*-PPs. Like gerunds at this stage, *to*-infinitives have achieved functional equivalence with clauses.

That this stage was reached already in OE is clear from a comparison between manuscript C of the ninth-century OE translation of *Gregory's Dialogues* and manuscript H, a late tenth-/early eleventh-century revision (see Yerkes 1982). H systematically replaces subjunctive clauses expressing 'dependent desires', as in (25), with *to*-infinitival clauses, as in (26). More detail can be found in Los (2005: 179–89).

(25) [...] Dauid, þe gewunade, þæt he hæfde witedomes
David who was-wont that he had-SUBJ of-prophecy
gast in him
spirit in him
'[...] David, who was wont, that he had the spirit of prophecy in him'
<GD 1 (C) 4.40.24>

(26) [...] Dauid, þe gewunode to hæbbenne witedomes gast
David who was-wont to have of-prophecy spirit
on him
in him
'[...] David, who was wont to have the spirit of prophecy in him'
<GD 1 (H) 4.40.22>

6.6 The Replacement of Native Directive Verbs by French Loans

The wholesale replacement of the English lexicon by French loans in the wake of the Norman Conquest is particularly evident in the directive verbs; of the thirty-nine verbs of Urging and Persuading in OE presented in Los (1999: 154–6), only *bid* and *set* make it into PDE, although *biegan* 'cause to bend, compel', *drefan* 'excite', *gremian* 'provoke', *halsian* 'entreat, adjure', *hatan* 'order', *læran* 'teach', *laðian* 'summon, invite', and *niedan* 'urge' persist for a while as *bey*, *dreve*, *greme*, *halse*, *hight*, *lere*, *lathe*, and *nede* (*OED*), respectively; and native *driven* 'drive', *spurren* 'spur', *steren* 'stir, move', and *warnen* 'warn' start to occur with the NPACC (THEME) + *to*-infinitive (GOAL) frame in ME. Ultimately, the great majority of these lexemes are ousted by French loans like *encourage, force, incite, persuade, provoke*, and *urge* as verbs of Persuading and Urging.

Of the sixteen OE verbs of Commanding and Permitting in Los (1999: 171),[3] only *do, forbid, let, sell,* and *teach* have survived, although not all of them with their OE directive meanings. *Liefan* and *aliefan*, both meaning 'allow', *dihtan* and *reccan*, both meaning 'direct', *tiðian* and *ðafian*, both meaning 'grant', persist for a while as *leve, dight, rech, tithe,* and *thave*. Native *polien/thole* (OE *polian* 'bear, suffer') comes to mean 'allow' in early ME and as such occurs with the NPDAT (RECIPIENT), *to*-infinitive (THEME) frame, while native *maken* comes to be used as a causative, with an AcI-construction.[4] The French loanwords *allow, command, order, permit,* and *suffer* take over as the favourite verbs of Commanding and Permitting in the course of ME.

The influx of borrowings does not disturb the original arrangement of two sets of verbs, each with their own sets of subcategorisation frames, and, even more remarkably in the face of the loss of case-marking, the basic distinction between the two groups survives up to the present day. Even though a verb like *persuade* is a French loan, it takes the same three expressions as GOAL argument as its OE counterpart *tyhtan*: finite clauses, purposive PPs (although with *into* rather than *to*), and *to*-infinitives. Like *tyhtan*, it does not have a two-place variant (*He persuaded the Town Hall to be demolished*). Its purposive *into*+gerund complements in fact become a new arena for competition, as part of what has been called the Great Complement Shift (Rohdenburg 2006a; Vosberg 2006; Rudanko 2012). *Into*+gerund complements are particular favourites with newer verbs of Persuading and Urging, like *bully* and *coax*; see particularly Rudanko (2015: 83ff.). The *into*+gerund complement is not found with verbs of Commanding and Permitting; and these verbs continue to have two- and three-place variants, although the two-place variants are Small Clauses (*He ordered them pardoned*) or *to*-infinitival complements (Exceptional Case-Marking (ECM) construction: *He ordered them to be pardoned*), rather than bare-infinitival AcI-constructions.

---

[3] Subtracting the four verbs that have dual membership (exhibiting both argument structures of (19) and (23)), i.e. *biddan, hatan, læran,* and *wissian*; see Los (1999: 195–203).
[4] This verb takes a *to*-infinitive in PDE when passivised, on the model of the causative two-place variants of the verbs of Commanding and Permitting that develop in ME; the most likely reason is that the accusative NP in an AcI-construction does not allow passivisation (cf. *I let him get away/*He was let get away; I saw him cross the road/*He was seen cross the road*).

6.7 Stage V: Verbs of Thinking and Declaring

Towards the end of the ME period, the *to*-infinitive starts to appear with a subject of its own instead of a PRO subject controlled by the subject or object of the higher predicate, the ECM-construction, as in (27).

(27) 49 per cent of women and a surprising 32 per cent of men reported that they were virgins at marriage. In spite of this, 79 per cent of [the] ... men believed [$_{subclause}$**their wives** to have been virgins when they married]. *(MicroConcord Corpus)*

Their wives in (27) receives a semantic role from the predicate 'be virgins' rather than from *believe*. The verbs that allow this construction constitute a distinct group, with meanings of 'thinking or declaring something to be the case'; the *to*-infinitival clause expresses a proposition rather than a dependent desire.

The rise of the *to*-infinitival ECM-construction has been discussed extensively in the literature, e.g. Zeitlin (1908), Bock (1931), Jespersen (1940), Warner (1982), Fischer (1989, 1990, 1992), primarily around the question of it being due to Latin influence, or a native construction, i.e. an extension of the two-place variant that may appear with verbs of Commanding and Persuading, as in (24b), which may itself be the product of another extension, i.e. of the Small Clause (*He ordered them (to be) pardoned*). Although assuming Latin influence offers a solution to the question why the construction appears after verbs of Thinking and Declaring, it is at odds with the fact that the first examples of the construction with these verbs do not occur in translations from Latin (Dreschler 2015: 160–9). Drawing on Warner's concept of minimal alterations, Dreschler (2015: 169) suggests that the passive ECM represents only a minimal alteration from another existing construction, the *to*-infinitival postmodification of past participles (see (28)).

(28) & wes **iwunet**   ofte to cumen wið him to his in
 and was accustomed[5] often to come with him to his lodgings
 & iseon his dohter
 and see his daughter
 'and was often in the habit of coming with him to his lodgings to see his daughter'
 (c1225(?c1200), cmjulia,96.12; Dreschler 2015: 176)

---

[5] Dreschler glosses *iwunet* as 'wont', which is of course its PDE reflex; I have changed it to 'accustomed' to highlight the fact that *iwunet* is actually a past participle, whereas PDE *wont* is usually labelled an adjective (as for instance in the *OED*).

Although Dreschler calls this a 'fixed adjectival construction' (2015: 176), in which such passive participles appear 'to have lexicalized into a fixed construction where the status of the passive participle as verbal is no longer clear' (2015: 176), she still thinks they are relevant because they provide a template for the emerging ECM, because of their frequency. This would mean that we should not be looking at reanalysis as the only source of the construction, but also at constructions as in (28), where the paradigmatic analogy is with past participles rather than with verbal constructions. Past participles make sense of a striking feature of the ECM with verbs of Thinking and Declaring: from its earliest emergence, passives are much more frequently attested than actives (Warner 1982; Fischer 1994a). Some verbs, like *say*, *repute*, and *rumour*, can only occur in the passive and not in the active at all (Noël 2001: 257–9). Paradigmatic extension from the adjectival construction finds some support in suggestions to take the passive construction as primary (Noël 2008), as a constructional template with a meaning of its own (cf. Wierzbicka 1988: 47–8; Visconti 2004), as a dedicated information-packaging construction (Ward *et al.* 2002: 1365), and as derived paradigmatically on the model of another construction, rather than transformationally (as in Quirk 1965, who suggests the model is *he is known to be careful*).

The fact that the ECM represents a break in the diffusion from one class of verbs to the next is supported by a break in the semantics: the earlier *to*-infinitival complements expressed 'dependent desires', i.e. included an element of volition, but this is not true of the ECM-construction; even Wierzbicka (1988: 98) has to concede that there are *to*-infinitival complements that do not encode 'wanting' but 'awareness', and her attempt to find a unifying semantics for the two (Wierzbicka 1988: 105–6) is not persuasive (see also Palmer 1990: 230–1).

The remaining question is why the adjectival construction was paradigmatically extended to this particular set of verbs in only English, and not in its West-Germanic cousins, which have analogues of (24a) and (28), but not of (24b) or (27). Mair (1990: 180) suggests that the relevant point of the passive ECM is that it helps textual coherence, as it allows the link to the preceding discourse to be expressed by a subject. This led me to propose (Los 1999: 324–7) that its rise might be connected to the loss of V2; V2 allows links to the preceding discourse, like *this herb* in the OE example in (29), to be expressed as clause-initial adjuncts.

(29) Be   ðysse wyrte ys   sæd   þæt   se   hara,   ðonne he
     about this   herb   is   said   that   the   hare   when   he
     on   sumura for   swiðlicre hætan   geteorud byþ,
     in   summer because-of great   heat   faint   becomes
     mid   þysse wyrte hyne sylfne   gelacnað
     with this   plant him -self   medicates
     'About this herb it is said that the hare, when he becomes faint in
     summer because of the great heat, medicates himself with this herb'
     <Lch I, 114>

PDE might well prefer to fashion *this herb* into a subject: *This herb is said to be used by hares as self-medication*. This preference for expressing discourse links by means of subjects is a new development in English. The quantified study by Dreschler (2015) shows that the emergence of the ECM-passives cannot be linked to the loss of V2, although its later spread, by paradigmatic analogy, can.

6.8 Conclusion

Revisiting the rise and spread of the *to*-infinitive against De Smet's (2013) account of the rise of the gerund, then, has thrown up remarkable parallels in the progression of the distinct stages in which the expression fanned out from its original niche as a purposive *to*-PP. Of particular interest is the gearshift at Stage IV, *broad paradigmatic analogy*, where so many verbs have started to take the *to*-infinitive as complement that its semantics generalises from encoding a directive complement – an action that someone is urged or commanded to do – to an action that is as yet a non-actuated possibility. This could imply that its semantic bleaching was the result, rather than the cause, of lexical diffusion. These more general semantics, in turn, allow it to appear with an even greater range of verbs, including subject control verbs with meanings of trying, intending, hoping, and the like. It is this matching of the perceived semantics of the complement with the semantics of the higher predicate that gives diffusional change its diffusional character, and explains why a new pattern does not arise in different environments simultaneously but in perceptible stages and gearshifts.

The odd one out in this scenario is the extension of the *to*-infinitival ECM construction to include verbs of Thinking and Declaring. This extension cannot be made part of any natural progression from the previous stages; the model for extension by paradigmatic analogy seems to be an adjectival/participial rather than a verbal construction. Its spread in eModE can be argued to be a response to a syntactic change, the loss of V2, which had compromised the syntactic options available to encode links to the previous discourse. The passive ECM-construction after verbs of Thinking and Declaring has since become recognised as an information-packaging construction, a non-canonical word order pattern whose primary function is to facilitate the information flow in the clause (Ward *et al.* 2002).

CHAPTER 7

Me Liketh/Lotheth *but* I Loue/Hate:
Impersonal/Non-Impersonal Boundaries in Old and Middle English

Ayumi Miura

7.1 Introduction[*]

Impersonal constructions form one of the most extensively researched topics in English historical syntax, with dedicated publications ranging over a century (e.g. van der Gaaf 1904; Elmer 1981; Allen 1995; Möhlig-Falke 2012). These constructions are commonly distinguished by three morphosyntactic features: (i) a nominative subject is missing; (ii) what is commonly labelled as 'Experiencer' – the human argument involved in the action of the verb – bears objective case; and (iii) the verb is in the third-person singular form. This chapter addresses semantic distinctions between some of the verbs which occurred in impersonal constructions and those which are not known to have done so. Compare the following pairs of examples (all taken from the *Middle English Dictionary* (hereafter *MED*)), where (1a) and (2a) illustrate impersonal constructions and (1b) and (2b) show personal constructions.

(1) a. Me   **liketh**   nat   to lye.
       me-OBJ pleases   not   to lie
       'I do not like to lie.'
                          (c1425(a1420) Lydg. *TB* (Aug A.4) 4.1815)

  b. I   **loue** well to make mery.
       I-NOM   love   well to make merry
       'I love much to make merry.'
                          (c1475 *Mankind* (Folg V.a.354) 266)

---

[*] I am sincerely obliged to Linda van Bergen and two anonymous reviewers who generously devoted their time and effort into providing helpful feedback for this chapter.

(2) a. Of oure liffe vs **lothis**; we leve to lange.
    of   our   life   us-OBJ   loathes   we live too   long
    'We loathe our life; we live too long.'
                                          (a1450 *Yk.Pl.* (Add 35290) 448/8)

    b. For he schold lese his lemman, his liif þan he **hated**.
       for he should lose his lover   his life then   he-NOM   hated
       'For he should lose his lover, he then hated his life.'
                                            (a1375 *WPal.* (KC 13) 1484)

Verbs such as *like* and *loathe*, which are attested in impersonal constructions, are conventionally called 'impersonal verbs', and verbs like *love* and *hate*, which regularly select a nominative Experiencer, are referred to as 'non-impersonal verbs' in Fischer and van der Leek (1983: 357), Denison (1990: 133), and Fischer *et al.* (2000: 75). There is in fact one Middle English (ME) instance where *love* appears in an impersonal construction, but it is very likely to have been affected by the direct co-ordination with *list* 'please', which is one of the most common impersonal verbs of emotion – see (3).

(3) The Fader was first as a fust with o   fynger folden,
    the father was first as a fist with one finger folded
    Til hym   **lovede**   and   liste   to unlosen his fynger
    till him-OBJ loved   and   pleased to unloose his finger
    'The Father was first like a fist with one finger folded, until it pleased him to stretch forth his finger.'
                                (*Piers Plowman B-Text* XVII 139–40; Schmidt 1995)

As this exceptional example does not crucially alter the fact that *love* usually selected a nominative Experiencer, for the sake of convenience, the verb will be regarded as non-impersonal in this chapter.

    What made *love* and *hate* non-impersonal, while their apparent near-synonyms *like* and *loathe* were impersonal? This puzzling question on the semantic definition of impersonal verbs, especially in contrast to non-impersonal verbs, first received serious attention when Denison (1990) cited *lufian* 'to love' and *hatian* 'to hate' among examples of Old English (OE) non-impersonal verbs. Since then, *love* and *hate* have been the most frequently quoted non-impersonal verbs. One reason for this may be that, broadly speaking, they both express emotion or a psychological state, which is well known to feature in a large number of impersonal verbs in OE and ME (see e.g. Möhlig-Falke 2012: 113, 148). Allen (1995: 129, fn. 35) observed that, whilst non-impersonal verbs 'usually refer to quite a strong emotion' such as *love* and *hate*, there are 'enough exceptions',[1] acknowledging the difficulty of making an indisputable semantic generalisation about when a verb is impersonal or non-impersonal. More recently, Möhlig-Falke (2012: 67) noted that the different morphological realisation of the Experiencer for impersonal verbs (i.e. objective case) and non-impersonal verbs (i.e. nominative case) may be due to the double properties exhibited by Experiencers, namely 'the proto-agent property of sentience' and 'the proto-patient property of affectedness': Experiencers are animate and prototypically human and thus potentially capable of sentience, intention, and control, whereas they are also affected by undergoing a certain emotional experience.

For a long time, impersonal and non-impersonal verbs of emotion and other semantic fields have not been subject to any comprehensive analysis which directly contrasts their syntactic and semantic properties. However, as far as ME verbs of emotion are concerned, this gap in research was recently filled by Miura (2015), where it was demonstrated on the basis of data from the *MED* that a range of factors are behind the (non-)realisation of impersonal use of these verbs. This chapter will revisit the same topic in a corpus-based approach with special reference to *love*, *hate*, *like*, and *loathe* and will investigate whether the generalisations made in Miura (2015) could be extended to the OE period and the near-synonymous phrasal impersonals *be/have lief* and *be loath*. These phrasal impersonals tend to be neglected in studies of impersonal verbs and constructions, and they are not dealt with in Miura (2015) either. Yet, Denison (1990: 125) notes that, in OE, *be loath* is more common than its simplex *loathe*, suggesting that the exclusion of phrasal impersonals may lead to missing some important insights.

The next section will revisit the factors which were identified in Miura (2015) to be relevant to distinctions between *love* and *like*, on the one hand, and between *hate* and *loathe*, on the other. Section 7.3 will provide a corpus study of the said verbs in relation to those factors. *The York-Toronto-Helsinki Parsed Corpus of Old English Prose* (YCOE) and the second edition of the *Penn-Helsinki Parsed Corpus of Middle English* (PPCME2) will be used as the primary source of data, with examples sometimes supplied from the *Dictionary of Old English Web Corpus* (DOEC) and the *MED*. The chapter will finish with a summary and concluding remarks in Section 7.4.

[1] For example, verbs of anger such as *gramen* 'to make angry, infuriate' and verbs of fear which involve physical manifestation of fear such as *(a)grisen* 'to shudder with fear' start to occur in impersonal constructions in ME. The intensity of emotion is therefore not the most compelling factor for the absence of impersonal use in some verbs of emotion.

7.2 Four Factors Which Distinguish *Love* and *Hate* from *Like* and *Loathe* in ME

7.2.1 Causation

Love and *hate* are distinguished very clearly from *like* and *loathe* by the notion of causation. As impersonal verbs, *like* and *loathe* are Experiencer-object verbs, which are cross-linguistically agreed to be lexical causatives, while non-impersonal verbs *love* and *hate* are Experiencer-subject verbs, which are not causative (Croft 1993; Pesetsky 1995; Arad 1999). The impersonal verb *like* is usually glossed as 'please', and *please* is an Experiencer-object verb which can be paraphrased with *cause* or *make* ('make someone like somebody or something'), but *love* cannot be paraphrased in the same way. Furthermore, *love* and *hate* have apparently never been causative in their history. In contrast, *like* and *loathe* in ME could be causative and occur in the construction where the Cause argument (the argument which is not the Experiencer) is the nominative subject of the clause and the Experiencer is the object. This construction is called 'Cause-subject construction' in Fischer and van der Leek (1983), and it is illustrated in (4) and (5).

(4) ʒif us   oht   ilimpeð, we   him   þa   bet   **likieð**.
    if us   anything   happens we-NOM   him-OBJ   the better please
    'If anything happens to us, we please him the better.'
                                            (c1275(?a1200) Lay. *Brut* (Clg A.9) 26738)

(5) Sibbe he luuede;   unstronge   monnen   he   **leoðede**.[2]
    peace he loved   [non-strong men]-OBJ   he-NOM   displeased
    'He loved peace; he was unpleasing to non-strong men.'
                                            (c1275(?a1200) Lay. *Brut* (Clg A.9) 6097)

7.2.2 Transitivity

Möhlig-Falke (2012: 86, 195) observes that OE impersonal verbs in general are characteristically low in transitivity, with the two profiled participants not maximally opposed to each other because neither of them is highly agentive or physically highly affected. Impersonal constructions, in

---

[2] Allen (1995: 227) notes that *monnen* is 'the normal dative plural form', whereas it is 'apparently not used in the *Brut* as a nominative/accusative plural'.

Trousdale's (2008: 309) words, are prototypically 'atelic, non-volitional and often denote states rather than actions', and their transitivity is lower than that of prototypical transitive constructions, which are 'telic, volitional and denote action'. Low transitivity may look contradictory with causation because, according to Hopper and Thompson (1980: 264), causatives are high in transitivity. Nevertheless, Hopper and Thompson (1980: 254) also note that many two-participant sentences have very low transitivity. This is observed specifically in clauses with participants which do not quite count as patients, in that they do not receive any action. As a case in point, Hopper and Thompson quote the Present-day Spanish instance in (6).

(6) Me **gusta** la cerveza.
    me pleases the beer
    'I like beer.'

A Patient would be a prototypical semantic role for the object in a transitive construction, but the oblique pronoun *me* in (6) is an Experiencer. The sentence in (6) literally means 'The beer pleases me', which is a Cause-subject construction comparable to those recorded with *like* and *loathe*, as seen above in (4) and (5). *Like* and *loathe* may thus belong to a subtype of causatives which features low transitivity or at least lower transitivity than *love* and *hate*.

    Like and *loathe* in ME have two independent indications of lower transitivity than *love* and *hate*. First, the quotations in the *MED* entries for these verbs seem to imply that passivisation is more limited for the impersonal verbs *like* and *loathe* than for the non-impersonal verbs *love* and *hate*. The entry for *loathe*, with more than sixty citations, includes no example of passive use, and the entry for *like*, with more than 250 citations, has only one instance, but such an apparent restriction on passivisation is not seen with *love* and *hate*. In this respect, ME *like* is similar to Present-day English (PDE) *appeal to* rather than its common gloss *please*: *appeal to*, a 'genuinely unaccusative' Experiencer-object predicate, does not allow passivisation (**Mary wasn't appealed to by the play*), but the 'non-unaccusative' *please* does (*Mary wasn't pleased by the play*; Pesetsky 1995: 59–60). Pesetsky (1995: 50–3) considers *appeal to* and its Italian equivalent *piacere* as representative members of a group of unaccusative Experiencer-object verbs which select two internal arguments (discussed in Belletti and Rizzi 1988; see also Reinhart 2016: 52).[3] In having such atypical configuration, *appeal to* and *piacere* have low transitivity, while, as Experiencer-object predicates,

---

[3] I am grateful to one of the anonymous reviewers for directing me to these works by Pesetsky and Reinhart.

they can be causative. We could extend the argument to hypothesise that ME *like*, an Experiencer-object verb which bears close resemblance to *appeal to* and *piacere*, is less transitive than the Experiencer-subject verb *love*.

Another case of different transitivity is that *like* and *loathe* allow alternation between a direct object and a prepositional object (i.e. a transitive and an intransitive construction), as illustrated for *like* in the two examples given in (7), whereas *love* and *hate* are virtually restricted to the transitive construction.

(7) a. Þe whiche stroke   he **lyked** ful ille.
       [the which stroke]-OBJ he liked very badly
       'Which stroke he disliked very much.'
       (c1425(a1420) Lydg. *TB* (Aug A.4) 3.2847)

   b. Of this message   he **liked** yll.
      [of this message]-PP he liked badly
      'He disliked this message.'
      (a1450 *Gener.(1)* (Mrg M 876) 3124)

Hopper and Thompson (1980: 262–3) discuss this kind of alternation as having subtle differences in transitivity. Specifically, they regard partitive objects like the prepositional object in (7b) as 'universally associated with intransitive verbs, or at least with some signal of REDUCED Transitivity' (emphasis in original). In other words, *like* and *loathe*, which are attested in the intransitive variant as well as in the transitive variant, are capable of lower transitivity than *love* and *hate*.

7.2.3 *Duration of the Emotion*

Causation, which crucially distinguishes ME *like* and *loathe* from *love* and *hate*, is correlated with duration of the emotion. Croft (1993: 57) points out that causative psych-verbs are cross-linguistically 'quite punctual', and Pylkkänen (2000: 429) observes that *love*, *hate*, and Present-day Finnish equivalents (*rakastaa* and *vihata* respectively) do not become causative because they denote 'mental states that cannot easily be construed as episodic'.[4] In

---

[4] Incidentally, duration is an important concept in the psychological definition of emotion. For example, Paul Ekman, in a commentary in Darwin (1998: 83), notes that emotions are 'brief and episodic, lasting seconds or minutes', while love and hatred as well as jealousy and envy last much longer. Like Ekman, some psychologists have cast doubt on regarding love and hate as emotions. Among linguists, Tissari (2003: 162–3) similarly admits that seeing love as an emotion is not unproblematic. See Miura (2015: 238–43) for more discussion on the relation between the definition and classification of emotions and the (non-)occurrence of ME verbs of emotion in impersonal constructions.

short, causation (as an event) implies shorter duration than a state like *love* and *hate*. Similarly, Pishwa (1999: 133) assumes that love 'tends to be [an] analysable and eventually controllable long-term feeling', and liking 'is rather an immediate and unanalysed feeling for the experiencer and cannot therefore be controlled'. The *MED* provides textual evidence that *love* as well as *hate* can even express a lifelong feeling – see (8) and (9).

(8) If fader   saw his son þar ... Or frend   he   **lufd**   had al his lif.
     if father saw his son there   or friend he-NOM   loved   had all his life
     'If the father saw his son there ... or the friend he had loved all his life.'

(a1400 Cursor (Phys-E) 23336)

(9) Ichab   him **ated**   seþþe ic was boren.
     I-NOM have   him hated   since I was born
     'I have hated him since I was born.'

(c1400 St. Greg. (Cleo D.9) 116/726)

Like and *loathe*, in contrast, are not exemplified in sentences like (8) and (9), which may imply that their inherent semantics do not allow occurrence in these types of instances. Such absence of a strong link with long duration may have facilitated the occasional use of *like* and *loathe* in instances which show that the emotion arises as the direct result of some action – see (10) and (11). The feeling in these cases is only temporary.

(10) Wan he was war   of þe frenschemen, on h[ert] him
     when he was aware   of the Frenchmen   in heart   him-OBJ
     likid   ille.
     pleased   badly
     'When he became aware of the Frenchmen, he was displeased in his heart.'

(c1380 Firumb.(1) (Ashm 33) 76)

(11) Smit him se luðerliche þet him   **laði**   &   drede
     beat him so viciously   that him-OBJ   loathe   and dread
     to snecchen eft   toward te.
     to snatch   again   towards you
     'Beat him so viciously that he would be disgusted and afraid of snapping again at you.'

(c1230(?a1200) Ancr. (Corp-C 402) 167/3)

The quotations in (10) and (11) both illustrate impersonal constructions. Interestingly, duration of the emotion is implied in the semantic-pragmatic distinction between impersonal and personal constructions: Möhlig-Falke (2012: 160–2) notes that, for some OE impersonal verbs of emotion (e.g. *(ge/of)hrēowan* 'to feel sorrow', *(ā/ge/for)sceamian* 'to be ashamed', *(ge)twēogan/twēon* 'to doubt', *(ā)twēonian* 'to doubt'), the impersonal construction could be used to express that the emotion arises spontaneously or with less control on the part of the Experiencer, whereas the personal construction might involve the Experiencer's contemplation of the situation or more control over the emotion. Compare the impersonal construction in (12a) with the personal construction in (12b), both involving *twēonian*.

(12) a. ac þi læs þe þe **tweonige** þare spræce,
but unless you-ACC/DAT doubt [the speech]-GEN
Apollonium ic wille, minne lareow
Apollonius I want my teacher
'but in case you may doubt these words, Apollonius I want, my teacher'

(ApT [0231 (22.7)]; Möhlig-Falke 2012: 162)

b. se ðe mid ealle **twynað**. he is geleafleas
he-NOM who with all doubts he is faithless
'he who doubts everything, he is faithless'

(ÆCHom II, 28 [0118 (227.208)]; Möhlig-Falke 2012: 161)

There thus could be a parallel relationship between the meanings of verbs and those of constructions: verbs which can express a lifelong feeling such as *love* and *hate* are more compatible with personal constructions, which might involve the Experiencer's contemplation, while verbs which lack explicit reference to long duration such as *like* and *loathe* have more potential to appear in impersonal constructions, which can express immediate feelings.

7.2.4 *Animacy of the Target of Emotion*

Animacy of the target of emotion does not have any direct connection with causation, transitivity, or duration of the emotion, which were taken up in preceding subsections. Nevertheless, it is a noteworthy feature for OE and ME impersonal verbs of emotion. Its relevance goes back to the study by Allen (1986: 403–5; 1995: 144–9, 331–8), who discovered that one of the important differences between apparent synonyms *like* and *queem* in OE and ME lies in the animacy of Theme (or 'Target of Emotion' in her terminology). As can be seen in (13) and (14) below, the Target of Emotion of *like* was typically non-human, whereas that of *queem* was nearly always a human being, potentially volitional and bearing some measure of responsibility for the emotion.

(13) ac   gode   ne   **licode** na heora geleafleast,
     but   God-DAT   not   pleased   no their unbelief
     ne   heora ceorung,   ac asende him to fyr
     nor   their grumbling   but sent   them to fire
     'but God did not like their unbelief or their grumbling, but sent fire to them'

(ÆHom 21 [0014 (68)]; Allen 1995: 114–15)

(14) gif hig   gode   willan   rihtlice   **cweman**
     if   they-NOM   God-DAT   will   properly   please
     'if they wish to please God properly'
     * hig = þa þe þyssere þeode nu sceolan rædan 'those who must now advise these people'

(HomU 40 (Nap 50) [0021 (66)]; Allen 1995: 146)

Like was an impersonal verb in OE and ME, and *queem* did not become impersonal until the fourteenth century despite having existed since OE. This fact suggests that there is some correlation between impersonal use and the animacy of the Target of Emotion. Indeed, Möhlig-Falke (2012: 109) points out that the second participant for most OE impersonal verbs is 'typically inanimate'.

The link with inanimate Targets of Emotion is also seen in the *MED* entries for *like* and *loathe*. On the other hand, the *MED* quotations do not show any clear tendency for *hate*, and animate Targets seem to be more common for *love*. A notable feature for *love* is that it often targets God or Christ,[5] as in (15). Connections between love and God are explicitly mentioned in the *MED* entry for *love*, but not that for *like*, which chooses words for God as the Target of Emotion only sparingly.[6]

(15) Þa   gode menn þatt **lufenn** Crist.
     the good men   that love   Christ
     'Those good men who love Christ.'

(?c1200 *Orm.* (Jun 1) 3602)

---

[5] Strictly speaking, God may not be considered animate on a par with human beings, but I will classify God as animate on the strength that *he* is the conventionally used pronoun.

[6] Emotions aimed at or caused by God, who is perpetual, are more likely to be lasting dispositions than immediate or spontaneous feelings. This collocational difference between *love* and *like* could therefore be related to the difference in their duration.

7.3 Corpus Results

7.3.1 Overview

Based on Miura's (2015) study of the *MED* data, the previous section presented four factors which influenced the boundaries between ME impersonal verbs *like* and *loathe* and non-impersonal verbs *love* and *hate*: causation, transitivity, duration of the emotion, and animacy of the Target of Emotion. The rest of this chapter will revisit these factors with regard to the same four verbs in OE and their near-synonymous phrasal impersonals *be lief* and *be loath* by studying the data from YCOE. The analysis will also include ME in order to test some of the factors on the basis of corpus data from PPCME2 and to examine the relationship between the four verbs and the two phrases as well as *have lief*, which emerged in ME as a new phrasal impersonal. *Have lief* had been used with a nominative Experiencer since the beginning of the fourteenth century (*MED* s.v. *lef* 5a.) before it came to take an objective Experiencer too.

Table 7.1 and Table 7.2 summarise the tokens of the verbs and phrases in question in YCOE and PPCME2 respectively.[7] The tokens of unambiguous impersonal constructions are also indicated.[8] In both corpora *love* is by far

---

[7] The data from these two corpora have been extracted by means of CorpusSearch 2 (developed by Beth Randall; http://corpussearch.sourceforge.net/).

[8] The numbers given for unambiguous impersonal constructions exclude all instances of the types exemplified in (a) to (c) below. The Experiencer in (a) is not unambiguously in the objective case (*hir housbonde*), and there is a dummy nominative subject in (b). Except for two instances with *be loath* in YCOE, patterns like (b) are exclusive to *like* (seven tokens in YCOE, twenty-seven tokens in PPCME2). In (c) the Experiencer is in the objective case, but this is attributable to the impersonal verb *behoove*. Patterns like this are found only in PPCME2 (forty-three times with *love*, six times with *hate*).

   (a) Whanne dame Prudence, ful debonairly and with greet pacience, hadde herd al that hir
       when dame Prudence full courteously and with great patience had heard all that her
       housbonde **liked** for to seye, thanne axed she of hym licence for to speke,
       husband pleased for to say then asked she of him license for to speak
       'When dame Prudence heard with full courtesy and great patience all that her husband wished to say / all that pleased her husband to say, then she asked him liberty to speak,'
       (CMCTMELI,220.C1.121)

   (b) And þere it **lykede** him to suffre many repreuynges and scornes for vs
       and there it-NOM pleased him-OBJ to suffer many reproachings and scorns for us
       'And there it pleased him to suffer many insults and scorns for us.'
       (CMMANDEV,1.4)

   (c) Alswa þe behoves **luf** God wysely;
       also you-OBJ needs love God wisely
       'You also need to love God wisely;'
       (CMROLLEP,112.856)

Table 7.1 *Tokens in YCOE*

	like	loathe	love	hate	be lief	be loath
total	280	7	1,109	113	146	52
unambiguously impersonal	91 (32.5%)	1 (14.3%)	0 (0%)	0 (0%)	65 (44.5%)	11 (21.2%)

Table 7.2 *Tokens in PPCME2*

	like	loathe	love	hate	be lief	have lief	be loath
total	180	15	1,315	210	68	31	58
unambiguously impersonal	49 (27.2%)	2 (13.3%)	0 (0%)	0 (0%)	23 (33.8%)	0 (0%)	11 (19.0%)

the most frequent, and *loathe* is the least frequent, with three of its seven occurrences in YCOE being variants of the same sentence.[9] *Have lief* in PPCME2 never appears in impersonal constructions, but the *MED* entry for *lief* quotes the earliest instance of the impersonal use from Chaucer, and the usage continues to be attested until the end of the fifteenth century.[10]

7.3.2 Analysis by Factors

7.3.2.1 Causation

Section 7.2.1 suggested that causation draws a sharp line between ME impersonal verbs *like* and *loathe* and non-impersonal verbs *love* and *hate*: only the former are attested in the Cause-subject construction with a nominative Cause and an objective Experiencer, as illustrated in (4) and (5) above. Table 7.3 shows the number of examples of unambiguous Cause-subject constructions in YCOE.[11] The figures in parentheses

---

[9] For the sake of comparison, Möhlig-Falke's (2012: 115) comprehensive investigation of DOEC shows that *loathe* has only nine instances, three of which are impersonal constructions, while *(ge/mis/of)lician* is impersonal in 24.8 per cent of its occurrences in the corpus.

[10] *Lief* in *be/have lief* frequently occurs in the comparative form (*be lief*: seventy tokens (47.9 per cent) in YCOE, twenty-eight tokens (41.2 per cent) in PPCME2; *have lief*: thirty tokens (96.8 per cent) in PPCME2). *Be/Have lief* may have been chosen instead of *like* when the author wanted to express preference from a comparative perspective. These examples involving comparative forms of *lief* are all included in the analysis in this chapter.

[11] Table 7.3 considers only the examples whose inflectional endings make it clear that the Cause is the nominative subject and the Experiencer is the object. A large number of instances are thus excluded

Table 7.3 *Unambiguous Cause-subject constructions in YCOE*

like	loathe	love	hate	be lief	be loath
80 (28.6%)	1 (14.3%)	0 (0%)	0 (0%)	40 (27.4%)	16 (30.8%)

Table 7.4 *Unambiguous Cause-subject constructions in PPCME2*

like	loathe	love	hate	be lief	have lief	be loath
7 (3.9%)	2 (13.3%)	0 (0%)	0 (0%)	7 (10.3%)	0 (0%)	9 (15.5%)

represent the proportion out of the total tokens of each verb or phrase indicated in Table 7.1. *Love* and *hate* do not have any instances of unambiguous Cause-subject constructions, but all the other four verbs and phrases, which could be used impersonally, have examples (see e.g. (16) and (17) for *be lief* and *be loath* respectively).

(16) He **wæs** his hlaforde swyþe **leof** ær þan,
he-NOM was [his lord]-DAT very dear before then
'He was very pleasing to his lord before then,'
(coaelive,ÆLS_[Swithun]:327.4422)

(17) forðan ðe seo ceorung **is** swyðe **lað** Gode,
because [the murmuring]-NOM is very loath God-DAT
'because the murmuring is very disgusting to God,'
(coaelive,ÆLS_[Pr_Moses]:230.2990)

Table 7.4 summarises the instances of unambiguous Cause-subject constructions in PPCME2.[12] The frequency is extremely low largely because a considerable number of examples involve a morphologically

---

because the Cause argument is morphologically ambiguous (e.g. indeclinable pronouns, nouns without any explicit ending), but the examples which show a plural concord between the verb and the Cause are included (e.g. *& manege para*-PL *þe me*-DAT *ne **licodon**-*PL *ic awearp mid minra witena geðeahte* 'and I rejected many of those that did not please me with the advice of my councillors' (colawafint, LawAfEl:49.9.140)).

[12] Table 7.4 excludes the instances where the Experiencer is realised as a prepositional object (e.g. *Lucan, my famylier, telleth that the victorious cause **likide** to the goddes,* 'Lucan, my friend, tells that the victorious cause pleased the gods,' (CMBOETH,453.C1.516)). This is seen only in PPCME2 and only with *like* (ten tokens) and *be lief* (three tokens).

ambiguous Cause. Nevertheless, *like, loathe,* and *be lief/loath* are still found in this use, whereas PPCME2 again does not show any evidence for this construction with *love* and *hate,* like YCOE. The correlation between causation and impersonal use seems to be tenable in ME too, except that *have lief,* a new phrasal impersonal in this period, is apparently not causative. At least as a single parameter for the impersonal use, appearance in Cause-subject constructions may not have been absolutely indispensable in late ME (lME). However, given that *love* and *hate,* which have been available since OE, are still neatly distinguished from *like* and *loathe* by the (non-)use in Cause-subject constructions, we could assume that verbs and phrases which emerged in lME were less subject to these conditioning factors than the verbs which already existed in OE.

7.3.2.2 Transitivity

Section 7.2.2 pointed to the possibility that, while being causative, ME *like* and *loathe* have lower transitivity than *love* and *hate.* In particular, *like,* in its apparent resistance to passivisation in ME, parallels PDE *appeal to* and Italian *piacere,* which are near-synonymous with *like* and unaccusative Experiencer-object (thus causative) predicates featuring low transitivity. This leads us to hypothesise that ME *like,* also an Experiencer-object verb, likewise has low transitivity or lower transitivity than the Experiencer-subject verb *love.*

YCOE and PPCME2 offer small pieces of data which are consistent with this hypothesis. In YCOE, only *love* is attested in passive use (thirteen tokens), as in (18).

(18) Fram cristenum   he   wæs swiþost   **gelufod** for þan þe
      from Christians   he-NOM   was most   loved   because
      he gehwilce eardas   namcuðlice   on gemynde hæfde.
      he all   countries   by name   in mind   had
      'He was most loved by Christians because he had all countries by name in his memory.'

(cocathom1,ÆCHom_I,_37:498.27.7337)

Like is found in passive use several times in DOEC (Möhlig-Falke 2012: 285, 291), but the frequencies are low, and all the examples are in fact from translations of Latin, most notably psalms. The passivisation of *like* in OE may appear to be more limited than that of *love,* but caution is required as the evidence for *love* is hardly abundant. Incidentally, *hate* and *loathe* do not reveal any differences in passivisation in OE, with no examples found for either of them in YCOE and apparently in DOEC too.[13] A difference emerges in ME, however: in PPCME2 only *love* and *hate* are attested in passive use (fifty-seven and five tokens respectively). Both in OE and ME *like* appears to resist passivisation, indicating that it is less transitive than *love*, whereas *loathe* may be less transitive than *hate* at least in ME.

The low transitivity of *like* in OE is also evidenced in its occurrence in the alternation between a direct object and a prepositional object (see (19)), which was already mentioned for ME in Section 7.2.2.

(19) a. and him   **gelicade**   hire þeawas,
       and him-DAT   pleased   [her virtues]-ACC
       'and he was pleased with her virtues,'
                              (cochronD,ChronD_[Classen-Harm]:1067.35.2283)

   b. and **gelicie**   þe   on urum lichaman,   þæt hi
      and please   you-DAT   [in our bodies]-PP that they
      ne   beon totwæmede,
      not be   divided
      'and take pleasure in our bodies so that they may not be divided,'
                                       (coeust,LS_8_[Eust]:441.462)

Loathe is not exemplified in either of these two variants. *Love* and *hate* are limited to the accusative variant like (19a), just as they are in ME. *Be lief* and *be loath* govern a prepositional phrase too, each once in YCOE, and such instances are also found in the *MED* entries for *lief* and *loath*. In PPCME2 *have lief* governs neither a noun phrase nor a prepositional phrase, but the *MED* entry for *lief* has several examples like (19a) with a direct object, as cited in (20) below, and none like (19b) with a prepositional phrase. As far as we can tell on the basis of the available evidence, *have lief* shares with *love* and *hate* the feature of apparently not allowing the option of reduced transitivity.

(20) Y   **hed leuer**   þe sight   of that than A Scarlet hure.
     I-NOM   had rather   [the sight]-OBJ of that than a scarlet cap
     'I preferred the sight of that to a scarlet cap.'
                                   (a1475 Russell *Bk.Nurt.* (Hrl 4011) 376)

---

[13] The one example of *loathe* in the 'passive verb form (*bēon* + past participle)' cited in Möhlig-Falke (2012: 278) actually illustrates a homograph *laðian* 'to invite'.

7.3.2.3 *Duration of the Emotion*

Section 7.2.3 referred to a correlation between causation and duration of the emotion: causative verbs of emotion are punctual, whereas non-causative verbs denote non-episodic states. As causative verbs, *like* and *loathe* can be assumed to express shorter duration than *love* and *hate*, which are non-causative. Indeed, as we saw in (8) and (9) above, *love* and *hate* in ME can last even one's lifetime.

A search regarding co-occurrence with temporal adverbs ('ADVP-TMP') presents a similar picture about *be lief*, *like*, and *love* in YCOE. The most frequent temporal adverb with *be lief* is *þonne* 'then' (five tokens), as in (21), followed by *þa* 'then' (four tokens), whereas *symle* 'always' is selected only twice. With *like*, *þa* is by far the most common choice (twenty-one tokens), as in (22), followed by *þonne* and *nu* 'now' (five tokens each). In contrast, *symle* is never selected, and its synonyms *a* (two tokens) and *æfre* (one token) are extremely rare. In short, *be lief* and *like* are found more often with adverbs of limited duration than those of long duration.

(21) Hwæt, him   þonne þæt **wære leofre** þonne eall middangeard
     what him-OBJ then that were dearer than all world
     mid þam gestreonum þe   heofon behwylfeð!
     with the treasure which heaven covers
     'Lo, that would then be dearer to them than all the world with its treasure which the heaven covers!'
                                         (coverhom,HomM_13_[ScraggVerc_21]:205.2764)

(22) Þa se biscop þæt þa   geseah, þe him big sæt, <u>þa</u>
     when the bishop that then saw   who him by sat then
     licode him   seo arfæste dæd þæs cyninges;
     pleased him-OBJ   the virtuous deed the king's
     'When the bishop, who sat next to him, saw that, the king's virtuous deed then pleased him;'
                                         (cobede,Bede_3:4.166.8.1593)

Love is also attested with *þonne* (fifteen tokens), *þa* (twelve tokens), and *nu* (nine tokens), but these are all outnumbered by *æfre* (eighteen tokens), as in (23), and *symle* (ten tokens) is not uncommon.

(23) Drihten leof, <u>æfre</u> ic   þe **lufode**,
     Lord   dear ever   I-NOM you loved
     'Dear Lord, I have always loved you,'
                                         (comargaC,LS_14_[MargaretCCCC_303]:5.16.63)

The evidence for *be loath*, *loathe*, and *hate* in YCOE is unfortunately limited. *Loathe* is not attested with any temporal adverbs at all. *Be loath* is never found with durative adverbs like *æfre* and *symle* in YCOE and instead co-occurs with *þa* and *ær* 'formerly', though only once for each. *Hate* in YCOE does not occur with any durative adverb, although instances with temporal adverbs in general are scarce (*þonne*: two tokens; *þa*: one token). Incidentally, DOEC has the following instance (24), which indicates that the Experiencer has held an unpleasant feeling for a long period of time:

(24) For þæm þu **hatodest** symle leornunga, and forwurpe min
because you-NOM hated always learning and rejected my
word symle under bæc fram þe.
word always backwards from you
'Because you always hated learning and always turned my word away from you.'

(PPs (prose) B8.2.1 [0745 (49.18)])

PPCME2 also lacks sufficient evidence for *be loath*, *loathe*, and *hate*. *Hate* takes a number of temporal adverbs in the corpus, including *ay* 'always' and *then*, but only once or twice for each. Similarly, *be loath* is found only once each with *æfre* and *nuðe* 'now', and *loathe* again does not occur with any temporal adverbs, although it is employed in a context where the Experiencer's feeling of displeasure is temporally limited to the situation described – see (25).

(25) and when þou feles joy in Criste lufe, þe wil **lathe** with þe
and when you feel joy in Christ's love you-OBJ will loathe with the
joy and þe comforth of þis worlde and erthly gamen.
joy and the comfort of this world and earthly joy
'And when you feel joy in Christ's love, you will be displeased with the joy and comfort of this world and earthly pleasure.'

(CMROLLEP,63.36)

As for verbs and phrases which involve pleasure, *be lief* is recorded exclusively with *eauer/æure* 'ever', but only twice, and *have lief* does not have any examples with temporal adverbs, though it is attested in the context which suggests temporary pleasure (*for sche thowt sche*-NOM **had leuar** *ben deed þan consentyn perto* 'for she thought she would rather be dead than consent to it' (CMKEMPE,14.277)). *Like* and *love*, on the other hand, present features which distinguish each other: *like* is restricted to

Table 7.5 *Animacy of the Target of Emotion in YCOE*

	like	loathe	love	hate	be lief	be loath
animate	72 [8] (38.5%)	1 (33.3%)	651 (61.0%)	87 (79.8%)	50 [1] (60.2%)	14 [1] (35.9%)
inanimate	115 [3] (61.5%)	2 (66.7%)	416 (39.0%)	22 (20.2%)	33 [1] (39.8%)	25 (64.1%)

adverbials of limited duration (e.g. *as ofte as* 'as often as', *sonner then* 'sooner than', *þan* 'then'),[14] and although *love* occasionally co-occurs with adverbs of the same kind, it is also found with adverbials of long duration such as *al-wei* 'always', *ay* 'always', *euyrmor* 'evermore', and *ever afftir* 'ever after'. Furthermore, unlike other verbs and phrases, *love* takes various expressions denoting long duration such as *all here lyvys tyme* 'all their lives' time', *ful longe* 'very long', *in al my lyf* 'in all my life', *lastandely* 'lastingly', *longe tyme* 'long time', *this seven yere* 'these seven years', *whyl sche leuyth* 'while she lives', and *wyth-owtyn ende* 'without end'.

7.3.2.4 Animacy of the Target of Emotion

Section 7.2.4 noted a connection between ME *like* and *loathe* and inanimate Targets of Emotion, whereas *love* appears to favour animate Targets, especially God. Table 7.5 shows the distribution of animate and inanimate Targets of Emotion in YCOE with the verbs and phrases under investigation.[15] The figures in square brackets refer to the occurrences in unambiguous impersonal constructions. On the one hand, we can see some ties between verbs and phrases which allow impersonal use and preference for inanimate Targets: *like* and *be loath* are found more often with inanimate Targets (and the same is true for *loathe*, but the numbers for this verb are very low), while the non-impersonal verbs *love* and *hate* tend to choose

---

[14] The *MED* entry for *like* has the following instance, which shows that liking can be long term, but the wording may have been affected by the Old French original:

Hyre holynesse	and hyre blysse,	long time	ich	me	**lykede**.
her holiness	and her bliss	long time	I-NOM	me-OBJ	liked

'For a long time I have been pleased with her holiness and bliss.'

(c1350 *Ayenb.App.* (Arun 57) 267/22)

[15] The figures in Table 7.5 concern only the cases where the Target of Emotion is expressed in the form of a (pro)noun or noun phrase, and infinitival and clausal complements are excluded. When the Target of Emotion is pronominal, I checked the context to identify the animacy of the referent. When it involves a combination of an animate being and an inanimate entity (e.g. *Ne þe, ne þinum godum ic næfre ne* **lufige** 'I shall never love you or your goods' (comargaC,LS_14_ [MargaretCCCC_303]:17.6.279)), the example is excluded from the table.

Table 7.6 *Animacy of the Target of Emotion (other than God) in YCOE*

	like	loathe	love	hate	be lief	be loath
animate (bar God)	70 [8] (37.8%)	1 (33.3%)	428 (50.7%)	81 (78.6%)	50 [1] (60.2%)	14 [1] (35.9%)
inanimate	115 [3] (62.2%)	2 (66.7%)	416 (49.3%)	22 (21.4%)	33 [1] (39.8%)	25 (64.1%)

Table 7.7 *Animacy of the Target of Emotion in PPCME2*

	like	loathe	love	hate	be lief	have lief	be loath
animate	20 [2] (20.6%)	4 (30.8%)	856 (70.1%)	102 (50.5%)	19 (44.2%)	0 (0%)	13 (38.2%)
inanimate	77 [0] (79.4%)	9 [1] (69.2%)	365 (29.9%)	100 (49.5%)	24 (55.8%)	0 (0%)	21 (61.8%)

animate Targets. On the other hand, *like* in unambiguous impersonal constructions shows an opposite tendency to that of its overall distribution, and the phrasal impersonal *be lief* shares the same preference as *love* and *hate*. The data for the impersonal use of *like* are too scarce to allow for any solid claim, and although one could hypothesise that phrasal impersonals did not always conform to the tendency of verbs, it is difficult to explain why this might be the case.

Incidentally, about one-third (223 examples) of animate Targets with *love* refer to God, whereas *be lief* never chooses God as the Target, and *like* does so only twice. *Hate* selects God as the Target only six times, and *loathe* and *be loath* never do so, possibly because it is unlikely in the OE literature that one hates God or God causes one a hateful feeling. Table 7.6 contrasts the examples of animate Targets other than God and inanimate Targets. While *like*, *loathe*, and *be loath* are still associated more strongly with inanimate Targets and *hate* with animate Targets, *love* is used with the two types of Targets almost equally. Its apparent preference for animate Targets thus owes much to its frequent co-occurrence with God.

The situation in ME is summarised in Table 7.7. *Have lief* is never found with (pro)nominal Targets of Emotion, instead taking either an infinitive or a finite clause. The *MED* entry for *lief* includes instances of *have lief* with both an animate Target and with an inanimate one, but it is hard to detect any tendency. As in YCOE, *like*, *loathe*, and *be loath* are found more frequently with inanimate Targets, while *love* has a definite preference for animate Targets, and *hate* is equally divided between animate and inanimate Targets. *Be lief*, which clearly prefers animate Targets in YCOE, has an opposite choice in PPCME2. Connection between impersonal verbs/phrases and inanimate Targets is therefore stronger in ME.

Ties between *love* and God are also a little stronger, with 315 examples (36.8 per cent) of animate Targets choosing God. In contrast, *like* and *be lief* are never recorded with God as the Target of Emotion. Unlike in YCOE, *love* is still inclined towards animate Targets even after examples of God are eliminated (59.7 per cent animate, 40.3 per cent inanimate). Although excluding instances of God makes inanimate Targets become slightly more common for *hate* (49.2 per cent animate, 50.8 per cent inanimate), *loathe* and *be loath*, which never select God as the Target of Emotion, still prefer inanimate Targets. In short, definite preference for inanimate Targets is observed only with impersonal verbs and phrases.

7.4 Concluding Remarks

The data from YCOE and PPCME2 have demonstrated that the four factors which are found in Miura (2015) to distinguish ME *love* and *hate* from *like* and *loathe* – causation, transitivity, duration of the emotion, and animacy of the Target of Emotion – have different effects on these verbs and near-synonymous phrases *be lief/loath* and *have lief* in OE and ME. Causation was found to be the most crucial: impersonal verbs *like* and *loathe* as well as phrasal impersonals *be lief/loath* are all attested in unambiguous Cause-subject constructions both in OE and ME, whereas non-impersonal verbs *love* and *hate* are not. The only exception to this impersonal/non-impersonal boundary is *have lief*, which developed impersonal use in lME and is not recorded in Cause-subject constructions. Animacy of the Target of Emotion is also generally relevant to the distinction between impersonal and non-impersonal predicates: *like*, *loathe*, and *be loath* prefer inanimate Targets both in OE and ME, and *be lief* does so in ME, but *love* and *hate* either co-occur more often with animate Targets or do not exhibit any definite tendency. Thus, impersonal predicates alone favour inanimate Targets, although *be lief* in OE prefers animate Targets and *have lief* in ME lacks evidence for any preference. The corpus data also provided some supporting evidence for the role of transitivity: passivisation is restricted to non-impersonal verbs, whereas governing a prepositional object is the option exclusive to impersonal verbs and phrases. This result suggests that non-impersonal verbs have higher transitivity than impersonal counterparts and that these impersonal verbs and phrases might, like *appeal to* and Italian *piacere*, represent causative predicates which feature low transitivity. Nevertheless, transitivity may well be a secondary factor given the limited frequency of *love* in passive constructions in OE, the apparent absence of the passive use of *hate* in OE, and the lack of evidence for *loathe* in OE and *have lief* in ME to govern a prepositional phrase. Duration of the emotion may also be regarded secondary since the corpus data fail to clearly distinguish *hate* from *loathe* and *be loathe*. Still, *be lief*, *like*, and *love* in OE as well as *like* and *love* in ME support the correlation with causation: impersonal and causative predicates are associated with shorter duration and do not particularly favour durative expressions which are observed with the non-impersonal and non-causative verb *love*.

Whilst the effects of the four factors are not remarkably different between OE and ME, they seem to work less for phrasal impersonals. Of the three phrases studied in this chapter, *have lief* in particular hardly shows the features shared among the other impersonal predicates. It does not appear in Cause-subject constructions, does not govern a prepositional phrase, and does not have any noticeable tendency in the animacy of the Target of Emotion. This may have something to do with the limited amount of data available in PPCME2, especially because the corpus lacks examples of the impersonal use of *have lief*. However, it is also possible that predicates which were originally non-impersonal and did not develop the impersonal use until lME were affected less by the contributing factors for this usage. The syntactic and semantic features of the verb *have* may also have prevented *have lief* from behaving in the same way as *like* and *be lief*. In the period when a number of verbs of emotion occurred in impersonal constructions apparently only once, analogy with *be lief* alone may have provided sufficient motivation for the impersonal use of *have lief*.

CHAPTER 8

That's Luck, If You Ask Me: *The Rise of an Intersubjective Comment Clause*

Laurel J. Brinton

8.1 Introduction

If you ask me is used in Present-day English (PDE hereafter) as a modalised comment on the following or preceding clause, as in these examples by linguists on the *American Dialect Society Listserve Archive*:

(1) a. Unlike 'truthiness', 'refudiate' wasn't coined to make a point [...] So it isn't a good word for a serious dictionary to lionize, **if you ask me.** (Ron Butters, ADS-listserve, 16 November 2010)
b. OED offers just one cite, from ca 1420. Pretty prescient, **if you ask me.** (Charles Doyle, ADS-listserve, 28 November 2006)
c. Actually, this is a pretty interesting question, **if you ask me.** Too bad we don't know more about bad language in the Civil War. (Jonathan Lighter, ADS-listserve, 17 July 2005)

If you ask me here is unusual in a number of respects. First, the verb *ask* typically takes both an indirect object (*me*) and a direct object (see Quirk et al. 1985: 1210), so *if you ask me* is elliptical or syntactically incomplete; it is missing its complement, whether a *wh*-interrogative clause, a noun phrase, or a *to*-infinitive:

if you ask me <u>why I say this</u>, ...
if you ask me <u>this question</u>, ...
if you ask me <u>to explain my statement</u>, ...

Second, *if you ask me* does not function in these contexts as a conditional protasis adjoined to a main clause apodosis. A *then*-clause cannot follow: e.g. **If you ask me, then this is a pretty interesting question*. We can contrast the examples in (1) with cases of actual conditionals ('direct conditions'):

(2) a. **If you ask me**, I'm required to give it.
 (2003 *Fantasy & Science Fiction* [COCA])
 b. **If you ask me**, I will choose to play with Yao 100 percent of the time. (2009 *Houston Chronicle* [COCA])
 c. **If you ask me**, I'd say to you, I think he's going to run,
 (2001 *USA Today* [COCA])

Here *then* would be possible in the apodosis: *If you ask me, then I'd say...* In contrast, there is no actual or hypothetical act of asking in the examples in (1), and *if you ask me* does not have its literal meaning. Rather, it functions as a kind of 'comment clause'. A comment clause is a parenthetical with clausal structure, such as *I suppose, as you see, you know*, or *what is more surprising*, which has procedural or pragmatic meaning; it typically expresses speaker attitude (epistemic, emotive) towards the content of the adjoined or 'host' clause or refers to the circumstances of the speech situation (see Quirk *et al.* 1985: 1112–18; Brinton 2008: 4–7).[1]

This chapter presents a diachronic study of the rise of *if you ask me*. It begins by discussing the form and function of *if you ask me* in PDE. Syntactically, *if you ask me* functions as an 'indirect condition', with similarities to insubordinated *if*-clauses (Section 8.2.1). Corpus evidence from Present-day American English shows the indirect use to be predominant (Section 8.2.2), with a range of pragmatic functions (Section 8.2.3). In order to account for the present-day form, Section 8.3 turns to the historical development of *if you ask me*, identifying its earliest uses as a procedural and tracing its semantic and syntactic development (Section 8.3.1). Its course of development is compared with the postulated development of insubordinated *if*-clauses (Section 8.3.2), and the rise of procedural and intersubjective meanings is discussed (Section 8.3.3). Section 8.4 concludes the chapter.

8.2 *If You Ask Me* in PDE

The *Oxford English Dictionary* (*OED* s.v. *ask*, v., Phrases P10) identifies *if you ask me* as a colloquial phrase meaning 'in my opinion'. Online dictionaries describe it variously as an informal phrase used 'when giving your opinion on something' (*Cambridge Dictionaries Online*) or 'to emphasize that a statement is one's personal opinion' (*Oxford Dictionaries*). While these definitions capture the basic meaning of the phrase, they do not

---

[1] Huddleston and Pullum *et al.* (2002: 1351 n.) propose the term 'anchor' for the clause to which a parenthetical is appended.

capture its full meaning and function. Closer to the mark is its description in *PhraseMix*, as a phrase used 'when you want to share your opinion, but no one has directly asked you what you think'. *PhraseMix* also notes that in initial position it may sound 'very bold' but in final position it 'doesn't sound quite as bold'.[2] In 'textese', *if you ask me* can be abbreviated IYAM (*InternetSlang.com*).[3]

Syntactically, *if you ask me* in (1) is parenthetical. It is structurally independent of the host clause, usually set off by commas, and presumably prosodically independent (see Dehé and Kavalova 2007: 1–22 and Brinton 2008: 7–14 on parentheticals). The host clause is complete (self-sufficient) without the *if*-clause. *If you ask me* has (limited) mobility, occurring in initial, final, and even medial position. In this case, the internal structure of the parenthetical is elliptical; the verb is missing an argument required by its valency. *If you ask me* can thus be classified as what Kaltenböck *et al.* (2011: 853) call 'conceptual theticals': these are syntactically independent, prosodically set off from the rest of the utterance, positionally mobile, and internally built upon the principles of sentence grammar, but elliptical.

8.2.1 Indirect Condition ~ Insubordinated Clause

In an example such as (1c) – *Actually, this is a pretty interesting question, if you ask me* – we cannot interpret 'if you ask me' as a condition on the question's being 'pretty interesting'. Rather, it is a condition on the implied speech act of telling ('if you ask me, then I will tell you'). Thus, *if you ask me* functions as what Quirk *et al.* (1985) term an 'indirect condition', which they define as 'dependent on the implicit speech act of the utterance' (1985: 1089, 1095).[4] They recognise a number of functions of indirect conditions. An indirect condition such as *if I may say so* 'makes the speaker's utterance seemingly dependent on the permission of the hearer' (1985: 1095), 'though the fulfilment of that condition is conventionally taken for granted' (1985: 1089).[5] An indirect condition may also point to the speaker's uncertainty about the correctness of the wording or his/her

---

[2] No mention is made of medial position, which turns out to be quite rare (see Table 8.2).
[3] Both its existence as a text abbreviation and notice of its existence by online sources might suggest increasing frequency in PDE. This is examined in Section 8.2.2.
[4] This meaning corresponds to what Kaltenböck *et al.* call the 'non-restrictive' meaning of conceptual theticals: they are not semantically part of the main clause but rather dependent 'upon the situation of discourse' (2011: 856, 861–3).
[5] Speaking of similar parentheticals (e.g. *if you like*), Claridge (2013: 162) notes that *you* does not function in a truly referential manner; i.e. it may not refer to an actual interlocutor but to the generic 'you'. This serves as further evidence of the indirect nature of such conditions.

uncertainty about the hearer's interpretation of the wording (1985: 1096). Thus, in their view, indirect conditions may serve as politeness forms or expressions of epistemic modality.[6] Quirk *et al.* (1985: 1097) conclude that '[f]or all [...] types the uncertainty of the condition provides a tentativeness which adds politeness to utterances'.

Because it does not depend on an overt apodosis, an indirect condition bears affinity to what has variously been called an 'isolated *if*-clause' (Stirling 1999), a 'free conditional' (Lombardi Vallauri 2004), an 'independent conditional clause' (Verstraete *et al.* 2012), or an 'insubordinated clause', which includes the '*conventionalized main clause use of what, on prima facie grounds, appear to be formally subordinate clauses*' (Evans 2007: 367; italics in the original). English examples include *If you'd like to get dressed now* or *If you could give me a couple of 39c stamps please*, as well as independent *as if*-clauses (*As if I cared!*) and *if only* constructions (*If only he would stop drinking!*) (Dancygier and Sweetser 2005: 217–19, 229). The most common function of insubordinated conditions is to express polite requests (Lombardi Vallauri 2004: 196; Evans 2007: 380, 387, 389–90) and wishes (Stirling 1999; Dancygier and Sweetser 2005: 217–19).[7] Scholars agree that what is characteristic of these independent *if*-clauses is their loss of conditional meaning. It has been argued that rather than being interpreted as an elliptical or truncated structure, these should be seen as a separate construction type that is 'pragmatically, semantically and intonationally complete and self-sufficient' (Lombardi Vallauri 2004: 204). Stirling (1999: 289ff.) argues for isolated *if*-clauses as a 'minor sentence type' because they are prosodically complete, constitute a separate illocutionary act, can be independent clauses in complex and compound sentences, and cannot be adequately explained by ellipsis. Of course, *if you ask me* differs from true insubordinated clauses in that it does not stand independently but is attached to a clause; for this reason, Heine *et al.* (2016: 57–8) would class *if you ask me*, like *if you will*, as a 'marginal formulaic IC [insubordinated clause]'.

---

[6] An indirect condition such as *if one may put it so* may also have a metalinguistic function, suggesting either 'that the wording is not quite precise or that it should not be misunderstood in some sense not intended by the speaker' (Quirk *et al.* 1985: 1095). Discussing the metalinguistic *If you don't mind the expression, he is a real bully*, Blakemore (2006: 1678) notes that the parenthetical no longer acts as a condition of the propositional content of the adjoined clause but rather on the act of saying itself. The consequent of the condition must be supplied through 'pragmatic enrichment' and integrated with the assumption schema *the speaker says that P*.

[7] The *if only* monoclause, as in *If only there was a camera that captured smells*, has lost its conditional meaning (Dancygier and Sweetser 2005: 217–19). It expresses a wish that the speaker knows to be impossible, yet desirable (thus speaker's positive emotional stance but negative epistemic stance). The wish sense can be interpreted as the 'sole conventional meaning' (2005: 218) of the construction, which functions as a performative (very close to *I wish there was a camera that captured smells*).

Table 8.1 *Complements of direct condition* if you ask me *in COCA (random sample of 200)*

Complement	N	%
Wh-clause	15	39.5
Infinitive	6	15.8
If/whether-clause	3	7.9
Direct question	4	10.5
NP	4	10.5
PP	2	5.3
Other	4	10.5
Total	38	100

8.2.2 Corpus Study of If You Ask Me *in Present-Day American English*

A search of the *Corpus of Contemporary American English* (COCA, 1990–2015) for *if you ask me* yielded 656 occurrences, or 1.41 per million (23 February 2015). Considering a random sample of 200 examples, I found that 80 per cent (162/200) were indirect conditions (as in examples in (1) above), and 19 per cent (38/200) were direct conditions. As an indirect condition, *if you ask me* is missing a complement and is not attached to an apodosis. As a direct condition, it is complemented by an interrogative *wh*-clause or *if*-clause (cf. (3a) and (3b)) or less often an infinitive or noun phrase (cf. (3c) and (3d)) and is adjoined to a *then*-clause (see Table 8.1). It may also be elliptical, as shown in (2) above. *Then* in the apodosis is possible, though rarely present (3b).

(3)   a.   **If you ask me** <u>what gets me mad</u>, it's the war issue,

(2008 *Washington Post* [COCA])

     b.   But **if you ask me** <u>if I mind</u>, then the answer is no.

(2009 Yardley, *Turning Japanese* [COCA])

     c.   And **if you ask me** <u>to explain that</u>, I'm going to have to demur,

(1998 *Texas Magazine* [COCA])

     d.   **If you ask me** <u>that question then</u>, I'll have a better answer.

(2004 *San Francisco Chronicle* [COCA])

Direct conditions invariably occur in initial position (or following an initial conjunction or pragmatic marker), but indirect conditions are found most

Table 8.2 *Position of indirect condition* if you ask me *in COCA (random sample of 200)*

Position	N	%
Initial	65	40.1
Medial	10	6.2
Final	83	51.2
Independent	4	2.5
Total	162	100

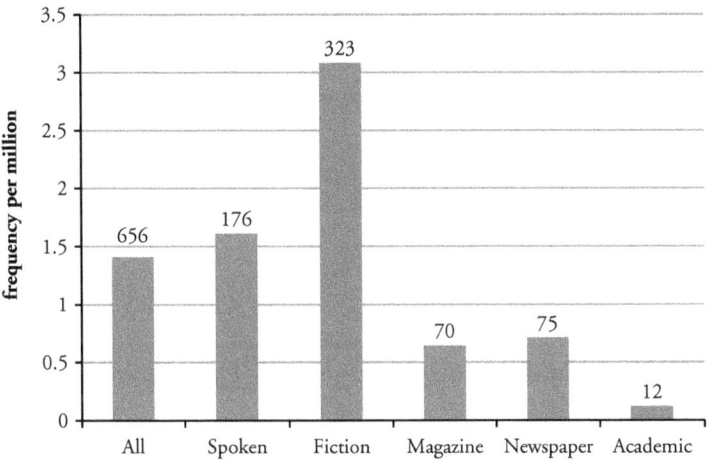

Figure 8.1 Distribution of *if you ask me* by genre in COCA (1990–2015)

often in final position (see Table 8.2). Punctuation is not always a clear indicator, but indirect condition *if you ask me* is typically set off as parenthetical.

Considering all instances of *if you ask me* (both direct and indirect conditions), we see (Figure 8.1) that the form is least common in the more formal, written Academic genre (0.12 per million) and most common in the more colloquial, oral genres, namely Spoken (1.61 per million) and Fiction (3.08 per million). As argued by Culpeper and Kytö (2010: 63), prose fiction – because of the high proportion of represented speech – can be considered 'speech-like'. The higher percentage of *if you ask me* in Fiction than in Spoken is not entirely explicable, however, given that

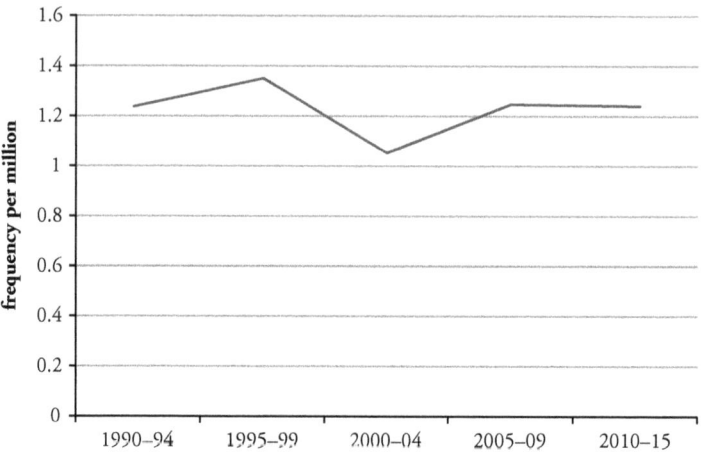

Figure 8.2 Distribution of *if you ask me* by period in COCA (1990–2015)

Fiction contains both narrative and represented speech.[8] Figure 8.2 also shows us that the form has remained relatively stable since 1990.

8.2.3 Function of Procedural If You Ask Me

Overwhelmingly, *if you ask me* is attached to a clause stating an opinion or making an evaluative comment (cf. Ford and Thompson 1986: 368), as in the examples in (4).

(4) a. It was all the mother's fault, **if you ask me**
(2005 Atwood, *Daedalus* [COCA])
b. All those people would make an ideal jury, **if you ask me**, for the O.J. Simpson case. (1994 Ind_Limbaugh [COCA])
c. **If you ask me**, a hospital is a scary place these days
(2003 Ruskin, 'Worry', *Canadian Medical Association Journal* [COCA])
d. 'It's just a waste of resources, **if you ask me**,' she said.
(2012 *Associated Press* [COCA])

---

[8] Interestingly, both the *British National Corpus* (BYU-BNC) and the *Strathy Corpus of Canadian English* show a much higher relative use of *if you ask me* in Fiction. In the BYU-BNC, it is 5.2 times more frequent in the Fiction corpus than in the Spoken corpus (compared to a ratio of 1.9 in COCA). However, here we must bear in mind the different ages of the corpora and the different types of spoken texts (scripted dialogue, for the most part, in COCA and natural conversation in the BYU-BNC). The *Strathy Corpus* has a relatively high frequency of 4.29 per million in Fiction and no examples at all in Spoken.

Note that there are often emotionally charged adjectives, such as *ideal* and *scary*, or nouns, such as *fault* and *waste*, in the adjoined sentence. *If you ask me* thus serves epistemic or hedging functions in 'softening' or undercutting to some degree the strength of the utterance ('this is just my personal opinion, it may not be universally accepted').[9] The *if*-clause no longer carries conditional meaning.

The epistemic function of *if you ask me* may be reinforced by an explicitly epistemic marker (*I think, would*, etc.), as in (5), or a pragmatic marker or other style disjunct expressing epistemic uncertainty, as in (6).

(5) a. **If you ask me,** I think you have commitment issues.
    (2007 Sparks, *The Choice* [COCA])
  b. **If you ask me,** there'd be a lot of ways to lobby
    (2005 PBS_Newshour [COCA])
  c. He seems rather savage **if you ask me.**
    (2007 Kelley, *Close Encounters of the Sexy Kind* [COCA])
  d. Looks a little light, **if you ask me**
    (1997 McManus, *The Maltese Fly* [COCA])

(6) a. You know, **if you ask me,** one of the best things about Bolcom and Morris, (1993 CBS_Sunday Morning [COCA])
  b. It's rather to the contrary, **if you ask me.** I mean, I've gone to these individuals for help (1991 CNN_King [COCA])
  c. Well, **if you ask me,** his name might as well be Mud for all the grief he causes (1991 *U.S. Catholic* [COCA])

In several different contexts, the epistemic quality of *if you ask me* lessens the threat to the interlocutor's face (see Brown and Levinson on 'hedging' opinions, 1987: 113–14, 162ff.), for instance, when correcting/contradicting an interlocutor's statement (7a), when anticipating a possibly different interpretation on the part of the interlocutor (7b), or when suggesting what point of view the interlocutor should take (7c).

---

[9] Whether there is a difference between the function of *if you ask me* in initial and final position (as noted by *PhraseMix*, Section 8.2) is difficult to determine. It was noted by a member of the audience at SHEL-7 (Bloomington, 2012) that *if you ask me* might sometimes function as an aggressive form, seeking to establish a contrast. It does seem that in initial position (which is rarer than final position, see Table 8.2), *if you ask me*, rather than acting as a softener, can act as a strong assertion of the speaker's right to express his or her point of view ('if you were to ask me, and you should, because my opinion is right'). The two uses seem to be intonationally different. I do not consider this assertive use of *if you ask me* in the remainder of the chapter.

(7) a. No, she looked half-starved **if you ask me**
(2011 *Iowa Review* [COCA])
b. **If you ask me**, I'd say she was writing a book
(2008 *Literary Review* [COCA])
c. **If you ask me**, you're the lucky one. You've got welfare.
(2012 *Iowa Review* [COCA])

In these instances *if you ask me* serves as a politeness marker. Suggesting that a contradictory opinion is proffered on the request of the hearer ('I'm only saying this because you asked me', 'If you hadn't asked me to express my opinion, I wouldn't have done so') mitigates the attack on negative (and positive) face.[10] Other markers of deference may occur in the context of *if you ask me*, as in (8).

(8) **If you ask me**, and with all due respect to you, it was never anything but an exercise in futility
(2007 *Analog Science Fiction & Fact* [COCA])

8.3 History of *If You Ask Me*

As *if you ask me* is a relatively low frequency item, in order to research its history, it was necessary to make use of a wide variety of databases and text collections. In addition to the quotation database of *OED* and *Google Books*, I used both American and British sources, as shown in Table 8.3.[11]

8.3.1 *Corpus Evidence for* If You Ask Me *in the History of English*

The clause *if you ask me* occurs as early as the mid-sixteenth century and becomes common in the seventeenth century.[12] In all cases (that I have identified; see (9)) it is a direct condition, typically complemented by a *wh*-interrogative clause, infrequently by an NP, as is still possible in PDE (see Table 8.1 and examples in (3) above).

---

[10] An opinion can threaten either negative face (because it may appear that I am trying to impose my opinion on you) or positive face (because it may appear that I do not share common ground with you).
[11] Unfortunately, as of early 2015, *The Modern English Collection, University of Virginia* (described as a 'heterogeneous collection contain[ing] fiction, non-fiction, poetry, drama, letters, newspapers, manuscripts and illustrations from 1500 to the present') is no longer available. It was formerly accessible online at: http://etext.lib.virginia.edu/modeng/modeng0.browse.html.
[12] BYU-EEBO contains 192 examples of *if you ask me*, all but four of which date from the 1640s onward.

Table 8.3 *Corpora and text collections used in this study*

	Corpus or text collection	Dates	Word count or size (where available)
British	*Early English Books Online* [BYU-EEBO]	1470s–1690s	755,000,000 words 25,368 texts
	Old Bailey Proceedings Online [OBPO]	1674–1913	197,000 trials c. 52,000,000 words
	The Corpus of Late Modern English Texts 3.0 [CLMET3.0]	1710–1920	34,386,225 words
	Corpus of English Novels [CEN]	1881–1922	26,227,428 words
American	*The Modern English Collection, University of Virginia* [UofV]	1500–present	–
	The Corpus of Historical American English [COHA]	1810–2009	400,000,000 words

(9) a. **if you ask me** how i prove it that infants can not believe, <u>i might answer</u> ... (1653 Fisher, *Baby-Baptism Meer Babism* [BYU-EEBO])
   b. **if you ask me** <u>the reason then of this their proceeding with him i can give you no other then what i have told you before</u>
      (1688 Prideaux, *The Validity of the Orders of the Church of England* [BYU-EEBO])
   c. **if you ask me** what shame is, i answer, [...]
      (1693 Ray, *Three Physico-Theological Discourses* [BYU-EEBO])

Elliptical structures without complements occur as early as the mid-eighteenth century (see (10)), but they still express direct conditional meaning (cf. PDE examples in (2) above).

(10) a. and the Spaniards have also a proverb That is (**If you ask me**, I'll tell you.)   (1764 Griffith, *The Triumvirate* [CLMET3.0])
      = if you ask me [to tell you] I'll tell you
   b. Is not a bag of feathers, a bundle? Q. **If you ask me** Mr. Impertinence, I tell you no
         (1794 Trial of David Humphies, t17940604-11 [OBPO])
      = if you ask me [to say if a bag of feathers is a bundle], I tell you no
   c. I don't think he can, **if you ask me**. But only think of their running such risk for the Major!
         (1848 *The Minor Drama: A Collection of the Most Popular Spring Comedies, Vaudevilles, Burlettas, Travesties, Etc* [https://books.google.ca/books?id=s19DAAAAYAAJ])
      = if you ask me [to say whether he can] I don't think he can

Note that the omitted complement in these cases refers to an act of communication, not to another kind of action, as it does in the examples in (11).

(11) a. 'I suppose you would let her wear that string of all coloured shells round her neck, would you not,' she asked, [...] **If you ask me** seriously, aunt, I certainly would, if she prefers it

(1827 Sedgwick, *Hope Leslie* [COHA])

= If you ask me seriously [to let her wear the string of shells], I certainly would.

b. 'Give me enough of this,' he added, as he tossed it down his hairy throat, 'and I'll do murder **if you ask me**'

(1839 Dickens, *Barnaby Rudge* [CLMET3.0])

= I'll do murder, if you ask me [to do murder].

Indirect conditions functioning as comment clauses do not appear until the nineteenth century. The earliest example in the *OED* quotation database dates from 1930. My examples date from the end of the nineteenth century (see (12b)–(12f)). One earlier example (12a) is an incomplete utterance and difficult to analyse.

(12) a. 'Nay, I am not critic,' said Churchill, confident in his habits of literary detection; 'but **if you ask me**,' said he, as he disdainfully flirted the leave back and forward (1834 Edgeworth, *Maria* [https://books.google.ca/books?id=mXxMAAAAcAAJ])

b. Well, it is the trick of the trade, **if you ask me**

(1883 Trial of George Bennett, t18831210-164 [OBPO])

c. A devilish pretty woman, **if you ask me**

(1885 Moore, *A Mummer's Wife* [CEN])

d. 'Well, he explains it pretty badly, **if you ask me**,' said Soulsby, with a droll, joking eye and a mock-serious voice

(1896 Frederic, *The Damnation of Theron Ware* [COHA])

e. your Bishop doesn't want you. Nobody wants you, **if you ask me**

(1897 Caine, *The Christian* [CEN])

f. it's not even thinkable, **if you ask me**.

(1909 Bierce, *The Shadow on the Dial and Other Essays* [COHA])

These are the earliest cases where there is no complement for *ask* and no performative main clause (i.e. one referring to an act of communication). The collected evidence does not point to either British or American English being in the vanguard of change.

Variant forms such as *if you ask my opinion/my views/my advice/the question* are contemporaneous, as illustrated in (13).

(13) a. You have made me a captain, and you are going to make me a colonel; but **if you ask me my opinion**, I am of DO [sic: no] use to you, nor have I any opinion of you   (1803 *Cobbett's Political Register* [https://books.google.ca/books?id=GQpbAAAAIAAJ])

b. But, **if you ask my opinion**, I am for proceeding immediately;
(1820–1822 Hunt, *Memoirs of Henry Hunt* [CLMET3.0])

c. For myself, ge'mmen, **if you ask my views** of liter-a-toor, I don't hesitate to say, in one sense o' the word, excuse the expression, it's nothin' but a powerful combination o' rags and brass;
(1843 Matthews, *Various Writings* [COHA])

d. 'Drapery, **if you ask me my opinion**', cried Mrs. Freke, 'drapery, whether wet or dry, is the most confoundedly indecent thing in the world'   (1850 Edgeworth, *Belinda* [https://books.google.ca/books?id=dvkpAAAAYAAJ])

e. which we did not think gentlemanly, **if you ask me the question**
(1857 Trial of William Pierce, James Burgess, William George Tester, t18570105-250 [OBPO])

f. **If you ask my advice**, Mrs. Ray, I should just tell her to be cautious   (1863 Trollope, *Rachel Ray* [UofV])

8.3.2 The Development of *If You Ask Me*

The indirect condition *if you ask me* is elliptical in two senses: first, it is missing the complement structure required by the verb's valency, and second, it is missing its main clause (the apodosis). If we were to consider that (3a), for example, derived from a full biclausal structure with verb complementation, we would postulate the development shown in Figure 8.3.

Does this postulated development correspond to either the synchronic or attested diachronic development of *if you ask me*? That is, is it possible to 'reconstruct' the ellipted elements?

8.3.2.1 *Reconstruction of the Complement Clause*

Synchronically, clauses without obligatory verbal complements are typically assumed to derive by ellipsis from fully formed clauses. For example, Huddleston and Pullum *et al.* (2002: 1529) describe 'special cases' of ellipsis

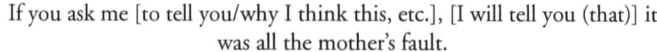

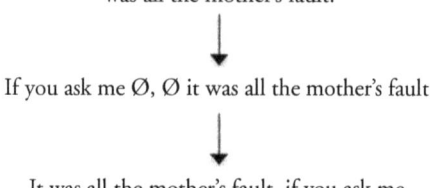

Figure 8.3 Postulated development of *if you ask me* from full biclausal structure

following verbs that normally do not permit it; one common case, they say, is in the complement of conditional *if*, citing *if you want, if you prefer, if you like, if you choose* (see Brinton 2014). They also list *ask* as a verb which permits ellipsis of its (interrogative) complement.

As discussed in Section 8.3.1, from its earliest appearance in the late sixteenth century through to the mid-eighteenth century, *if you ask me* always takes a complement, typically a *wh*-interrogative clause. Even in the nineteenth century, the majority of instances of *if you ask me* are followed by a *wh*-interrogative clause (14a), or much less often by a noun phrase (14b), or an infinitive (14c).

(14) a. **If you ask me** why I do not escape from my husband
(1849 Thompson, *City Crimes* [COHA])
b. **if you ask me** the reason   (1870 *Atlantic Monthly* [COHA])
c. **if you ask me** to explain seriously the allusion
(1883 *North American Review* [COHA])

Table 8.4 compares the syntax of *if you ask me* in the nineteenth century (1810–1899) in COHA with its syntax in the last forty-nine years (1960–2009).[13] In the earlier period *if you ask me* is followed by a complement in 71 per cent of the cases while in the later period it is followed by a complement in only 9.4 per cent of the cases. In PDE *if you ask me* occurs without a complement clause over 90 per cent of the time. Historically, then, there does indeed appear to be good evidence to suggest that *if you ask me* derives from a fully complemented structure, with subsequent deletion, or ellipsis, of the complement of *ask*.

[13] Regarding Ø complement, I am considering syntax only and not distinguishing between direct and indirect conditions. (See Section 8.2.2, where I found that over 80 per cent of the examples of *if you ask me* with Ø complementation in COCA were indirect conditions.)

Table 8.4 *Syntax of* if you ask me *over time in COHA*

	1810–1899		1960–2009	
	N	%	N	%
wh-clause complement	22	59.5	12	4.9
NP, PP, to V complement	4	10.8	11	4.5
Ø complement	11	29.7	221	90.6
Total	37	100	244	100

8.3.2.2   Reconstruction of the Apodosis (Main Clause)
Given its similarities with insubordinated *if*-clauses (see Section 8.2.1), one might assume that *if you ask me* develops from a direct *if*-condition, i.e. from a protasis adjoined to a main clause apodosis. This main clause apodosis would express the speaker's performative response (*I answer you, I tell you*, etc.) to the conditional request (*if you ask me*).

Evans (2007: 371–5, 430–1; Heine *et al.* 2016; cf. Brinton 2014) argues that insubordinated clauses begin as a subordinate construction with an overt main clause in a full biclausal structure. Ellipsis of the main clause ensues; the original subordinate clause is reanalysed as a main clause and assumes pragmatic meaning. In the early stages, it may still be possible to restore a grammatically compatible main clause (Evans 2007: 372, 430),[14] but as the insubordinated clause acquires greater semantic specificity, only a subset of ellipted main clauses can be restored: 'restoration of material is conventionalized to a subset of the grammatically tolerated possibilities', such as very general clauses like '*It would be nice/lovely if . . .* ' in the case of wishes (2007: 372–3). Finally, the main clause cannot be restored: the original subordinate clause is fully nativised as a main clause (2007: 374–5). Heine *et al.* (2016) argue that insubordinated clauses are 'elliptic', presumably derived from a full conditional construction; once a clause becomes insubordinated – by a process they call 'cooptation' – the ellipted apodosis (main clause) is recoverable from the context of discourse. Lombardi Vallauri (2004) likewise accounts for the development through ellipsis, which is brought about by shifts in discourse planning and dialogic interruption (perhaps interrupted because the conditional sense seems self-sufficient).

[14] For example, there may still be syntactic evidence for the underlying main clause, such as the presence of a negative polarity item like *ever* or *any* (e.g. *That I'll ever give you any money!*) which can be accounted for by the earlier presence of a negative matrix clause (*You don't believe*).

Both Evans and Heine *et al.* admit to certain difficulties in 'reconstruction' of the underlying main clauses of insubordinated clauses; '[e]xactly which main clause is restored is determined by processes of conversational inference' (Evans 2007: 371) and once constructionalisation has occurred it may not be possible to restore any ellipted material (2007: 374). For Heine *et al.* (2016: 45–6), reconstruction is 'hypothetical', since it is not possible to reconstruct the exact form of the ellipted matrix clause. Thus, *If you could give me a couple of 39c stamps please* might derive from either *I wonder [if you could give me a couple of 39c stamps please]* or *[If you could give me a couple of 39c stamps please] I'd be most grateful*. Importantly, there is only synchronic evidence for the reconstruction.[15]

In the historical development of *if you ask me*, we do find full structures with a performative main clause – see (15).

(15) a. But **if you ask me** the reason, <u>I know not what I shall answer</u>
(1651 Fioravanti, *Three Exact Pieces* [BYU-EEBO])

b. **if you ask me**, what these prescriptions are, <u>I must tell you</u>,
(1695 Horneck, *The Crucified Jesus* [BYU-EEBO])

c. **If you ask me**, my dear, how the caution befits me? <u>let me tell you</u>
(1748 Richardson, *Clarissa* [CLMET3.0])

d. **If you ask me** what these agreeable little citizens do for food in winter, <u>I answer</u>, they go without
(1832 *New England Magazine* [COHA])

e. <u>I think</u> – **if you ask me** – <u>that</u> one would not make you happy, in the long run (1852 Warner, *Hills of the Shatemuc* [COHA])

f. **If you ask me** whether a teacher has favorites, <u>I say that</u> he can not help having them (1864 Alger, *Frank's Campaign* [COHA])

g. <u>I don't think</u> those Boyd children look any too well cared for, **if you ask me** (1872 Simmen, *Gringos in Mexico: An Anthology* [https://books.google.ca/books?isbn=0875650295])

h. '**If you ask me**,' said Mrs Dosett, '<u>I think that</u> as Ayala has come to us she had better remain with us.
(1881 Trollope, *Ayala's Angel* [UofV])

i. And now **if you ask me** what is to be the great blessing to be sought, <u>my answer is</u> this (1893 Murray, *Jesus Himself* [COHA])

---

[15] Cf. Dancygier and Sweetser (2005: 218), who note that with monoclausal *if*-clauses, the apodosis is left 'to the hearer's contextually prompted construction'.

The exact form of the apodosis varies, from simple performatives, using different verbs (e.g. *I confess, answer, reply, say, advise, tell*, etc.) to modalised forms (e.g. *I must say, will tell, shall reply*) and more elaborate structures (e.g. *candour compels me to say*). Of the thirty-seven examples in COHA in the nineteenth century, thirty-one (or 83.8 per cent) are accompanied by an explicit performative main clause. In BYU-EEBO over 80 per cent of the instances contain an explicit performative verb (or equivalent) in the matrix clause.[16]

Therefore, it is likely that the development of insubordinated clauses from a full biclausal structure, which was postulated without diachronic data, holds in this case as well, though with an important difference. In the case of insubordinated clauses, the entire main clause is deleted, whereas here only the performative verb is deleted and the remainder of the main clause remains. In (15e'), for example, 'I think that' is deleted, but its complement 'one would not make you happy in the long run' remains.

(15e') I~~think~~ – **if you ask me** – ~~that~~ one would not make you happy, in the long run

When *if you ask me* is accompanied by a complement, arriving at the indirect form often involves more extensive reformulation, as both the complement of *ask* and the performative main verb must be deleted, with appropriate rearrangement of the pronominal and nominal forms. Thus for (15f'), 'he' must be replaced by 'a teacher' and 'them' by 'favorites':

(15f') **If you ask me** ~~whether a teacher has favorites, I say that he~~ [> a teacher] can not help [but have] ~~them~~ [> favorites]

Also, when negative raising has occurred, as in (15g'), it must be 'undone':

(15g') ~~I don't think~~ those Boyd children [don't] look any too well cared for, **if you ask me**

Note that these syntactic transformations are acceptable only in cases where an opinion is being expressed. Thus the transformations of (15d) (? *If you ask me, these agreeable little citizens go without food in winter*) or (15b) (*if you ask me, I must tell you what these prescriptions are*) are either semantically odd or must be interpreted literally.

---

[16] Equivalences include the abbreviation 'Answ' or 'Ans.' for 'answer', clauses such as 'it is', 'it is because', 'it followeth', 'I can give you', and 'the Prophet tells me', as well as instances of the reciprocal 'I ask you'.

The order in which the two types of ellipsis – ellipsis of the complement of *ask* and ellipsis of the apodosis main clause – occurs is difficult to determine. As discussed above, in the nineteenth-century examples of *if you ask* in COHA, 71 per cent are followed by a complement, and 84 per cent occur with an apodosis containing an explicit verb of answering. Uncomplemented *if you ask* occurs in the mid-eighteenth century, in either actional or communicative meaning (i.e. 'if you ask, I'll do it' or 'if you ask, I'll answer'), suggesting that deletion of the complement may occur first.

8.3.3   Semantic Change

8.3.3.1   From Content to Procedural Meaning

For *if you ask me*, the change from literal meaning (where the *if*-clause prefaces a response to an actual or hypothetical question) to purely pragmatic meaning (where no question has been posed or is hypothesised) is consistent with the multiple paths of semantic/pragmatic change discussed by Traugott and Dasher (2002: 40, 281). For instance, if we compare an example with literal meaning, where the speaker imagines a hypothetical question being posed, such as (2a) (*If you ask me, I'm required to give it*), with an example where no such question is imagined, such as (4c) (*If you ask me, a hospital is a scary place these days*), we see that in the first instance *if you ask me* is necessary for the truth-conditionality of the sentence, whereas in the second instance it can be deleted without affecting the truth-conditions of the sentence.

A second path of semantic change described by Traugott and Dasher (2002: 40, 281) is from content > procedural meaning. In its literal use (e.g. example (2a)), *if you ask me* encodes conceptual meaning, as it refers to the asking of a question. It serves as a conditional clause in relation to the consequent clause (*if P, then Q*). In contrast, in the use exemplified in (4c), *if you ask me* encodes procedural meaning. It does not refer to the (conditional) asking of a question, but rather serves to guide the hearer to the intended interpretation of the host clause. That is, the *if*-clause indicates that the host clause is to be interpreted merely as the opinion of the speaker, with suitable epistemic hedging ('It is merely my opinion – and you may not share this opinion – that a hospital is a scary place'). *If you ask me* indicates how the context in which it occurs is to be interpreted but does not itself add to the propositional meaning of the utterance.[17] As we

---

[17] The distinction between content and procedural meaning and their intersection with (non)-truth-conditionality have been widely discussed in the literature (see e.g. Bezuidenhout 2004).

saw, the procedural meaning most likely arises historically in contexts such as (15e) in which the host clause expresses an opinion of the speaker.

Despite its procedural function, the original (contentful) meaning of *if you ask me* persists (Hopper 1991). Throughout its history, the use of *if you ask me* has continued to risk the rejoinder 'But I didn't ask you', as in the following examples in (16).

(16) a. **if you ask me** – Mrs. Hunter interjects '<u>Which I don't</u>,' but Clara continues without paying any attention to the interruption. – I don't think Mr. Trotter is going to cry himself to sleep for your permission about anything!
(1894 Fitch, *The Climbers* [COHA])

b. we've had time to think it over, and **if you ask me** – '<u>I didn't ask you</u>,' said Jane, biting off a needleful of thread
(1902 Nesbit, *Five Children and It* [CLMET3.0])

c. **If you ask me**, I'll say – '<u>But nobody's askin' you</u>, Tom,' Mollie cut into his sentence sharply.
(1922 Raine, *The Fighting Edge* [COHA])

d. 'You've done pretty well, **if you ask me**!' '<u>Ask you! Why would anyone ever ask you anything?</u>
(1954 Stone, *Love is Eternal* [COHA])

e. the only one, **if you ask me** <u>(which he doesn't)</u> that we can really count on
(1966 Auchincloss, *The Embezzler* [COHA])

8.3.3.2 Intersubjectivity

A third correlated path of semantic change identified by Traugott and Dasher (2002: 40; also Traugott 2003: 135, 2010: 35) is

nonsubjective (or objective) > subjective > intersubjective

Intersubjectivity is understood as 'the explicit expression of the [speaker/writer]'s attention to the "self" of addressee/reader in both an epistemic sense (paying attention to their presumed attitudes to the content of what is said), and in a more social sense (paying attention to their "face" or "image needs" associated with social stance and identity' (Traugott 2003: 128).

In form, *if you ask me* seems highly intersubjective, containing both first- and second-person pronouns, and thus focusing on both the speaker and the addressee. It addresses what the hearer might do (i.e. ask for the proffered opinion). As it develops, however, *if you ask me* loses its literal conditional meaning (i.e. there is no presumption that a question is even imagined). Although this might be seen as a loss of intersubjectivity, since the speaker no longer is (or pretends to be) answering a question posed by the addressee, the new procedural meaning is now both strongly subjective and intersubjective. *If you ask me* is subjective in that it expresses the speaker's epistemic hedge on the content of the attached clause. As we saw above (Section 8.2.3), *if you ask me* often serves to soften or undercut the strength of the (possibly contradictory) opinion expressed ('this is just my personal view, it may not be universally accepted'). *If you ask me* is also highly intersubjective in that, by suggesting that the opinion is offered only at the request of the addressee, it mitigates the attack on negative (and positive) face that the expression of such an opinion might risk. The subjective and intersubjective (politeness) meanings become the sole conventionalised meaning of the clause. That is, the subjective/intersubjective meanings, which were previously only pragmatically inferrable, become the coded meaning (see Traugott 2010: 35, 54).

8.4 Conclusion

This chapter has examined the form, function, and history of *if you ask me*. In Present-day American English *if you ask me* is used over 80 per cent of the time not as a direct condition *if*-clause adjoined to an apodosis *then*-clause (*if P, then Q*), but as what has been termed an 'indirect condition' dependent upon an implicit act of communication: 'if you ask me', [understood, 'I will tell you'] X is the case. In this usage, it is typically attached to an expression of opinion or evaluation by the speaker and serves as an epistemic hedge ('this is just my opinion') and has politeness functions in addressing the addressee's face ('I'm only saying this because you asked me to'). It is a comment clause on the following or preceding clause. As a parenthetical, this type of *if*-clause bears similarity to so-called 'independent' or 'insubordinated' *if*-clauses (*If you could come in here. If only she could get a job!*), which have been postulated to derive from full biclausal structures. The historical data corroborate such a development for *if you ask me*. It seems to have originated in structures where *if you ask me* is followed by a clause with an explicit performative verb of communication (e.g. *I answer, I say*, etc.). Moreover, *if you ask me* originally contains the complement required by the valency of *ask* (typically a *wh*-interrogative clause or less often a *to*-infinitive or noun phrase). Thus, in the course of its development *if you ask me* undergoes two stages of deletion: deletion of the complement of *ask* and deletion of the performative main clause verb of communication.

If you ask me belongs to a larger class of indirect *if*-conditions in English which function as comment clauses, such as *if I may say so* (Brinton 2017), *if you choose/like/prefer/want/wish* (Brinton 2014), *if you will* (Brinton 2008), and others yet to be studied (*if you say (so)*, *if you will allow/permit me to say*, *if you don't mind my saying*). These show a range of pragmatic and procedural functions; for example, *if you choose/like/prefer/want/wish/will* are strongly metalinguistic. Not all can be traced back to full biclausal structures, however: the *if you choose* forms, for example, may originate in a 'Call it X [if you choose]' construction, whereas *if I may say so* appears fully formed in the sixteenth century. But the fact that indirect *if*-conditions arise repeatedly in the history of English, from the sixteenth century to the late nineteenth century, shows the viability and importance of the indirect *if*-condition, and calls for a better understanding of the construction in general.

CHAPTER 9

Misreading and Language Change: A Foray into Qualitative Historical Linguistics

Sylvia Adamson

9.1 Introduction: Doing Late Modern English Syntax 1998 and 2018[*]

David Denison's 'minigraph' contribution to volume IV of the *Cambridge History of the English Language* (Denison 1998, *CHEL IV*) is widely acknowledged as a landmark achievement in the study of late Modern English (lModE) syntax. Denison himself introduced it as a 'provisional' survey of relatively unexplored territory: 'syntactic change in late Modern English is only just beginning to get its share of serious scholarly attention' (1998: 92). The problems he saw facing lModE research at that time lay both in the 'elusive' nature of change in the period (which 'has more often been statistical' than 'categorical' and so 'can seem more a matter of stylistic than of syntactic' interest, 1998: 93) and also in the tools available to detect patterns in the data (there was 'little machine-readable corpus material dated between *c*. 1700 and *c*. 1960', 1998: 94). In the present century, the situation has changed dramatically. LModE research and digitised corpora have expanded exponentially and hand-in-hand. Where Denison was working with 'a preliminary and incomplete version' (1998: 95) of the ARCHER corpus, scholars now have at their disposal a plethora of machine-readable corpora, whose increase in number and size is matched by increasingly sophisticated methods of detecting diachronic trends via statistical analysis programs and tests of statistical significance.

As Kohnen and Mair point out (2012: 281), these technological developments 'have also drastically changed the way we do historical linguistics', allowing us to 'answer questions [...] about the frequency of usage of

---

[*] For comments and helpful discussions during the preparation of this chapter, grateful thanks to Andrew Ockwell, Nigel Vincent, John Woolford, Nuria Yáñez-Bouza, seminar audiences at the Universities of Cambridge and Sheffield, and an anonymous Cambridge University Press reviewer.

competing forms which [earlier generations of scholars] did not even ask'. But they enter some caveats: 'fewer and fewer historical linguists go back to the actual manuscripts or even read the texts they quote their examples from', and 'we should not forget that many important phenomena in the history of English [...] require qualitative analysis in addition to or even instead of quantification'. I believe these caveats have a particular applicability to historical work in lModE. Perhaps because the subject and its contemporary scholars have grown up in the digital era, research is typically conducted within a quantitative framework by automated procedures, which means that lModE as a period has largely missed out on what we might call the 'philological phase' of language history-writing with its detailed first-hand study of individual texts. Without disputing the value of the 'big data' revolution (Mayer-Schönberger and Cukier 2013) or the contribution of large-scale corpora to our understanding of lModE developments (Davies 2012), I want in this chapter to enter a plea for a complementary – or supplementary – qualitative approach, one that looks not only backwards to the text-and-context based methods of traditional philology but also sideways to recent developments in sociolinguistics.

In the late twentieth century, the great driver of the move to variationism and quantitative analysis in historical research was undoubtedly the influence of Labovian sociolinguistics. In the twenty-first century, Labov's successors are proposing a new agenda, which foregrounds the qualitative methods described by Barbara Johnstone (2000) and implemented in sub-disciplines such as interactional, constructionist, or 'third-wave' sociolinguistics (Gumperz 2001; Irwin 2010; Eckert 2012). What these approaches have in common is that they shift the object of research from 'common core' English (the prescribed target form for *CHEL IV* contributors) to the usage of more localised 'communities of practice', and from the linguistic variable (the 'countable' target of earlier sociolinguistic research) to the individual speaker, who deploys a specific repertoire of linguistic forms to project a persona or negotiate an identity within their own community. This shift in focus has brought sociolinguistics closer to forms of analysis and explanation previously practised in conversational analysis and in the literary exercise known as 'practical criticism', which involves a close encounter between a text and an interpreter who asks 'why these words in this order?'.

There are signs that historical linguistics is again following the sociolinguists' lead. The 'bigger trumps better' approach to data is being countered by a 'small is beautiful' backlash, even from those who were in the vanguard of quantitative work in lModE. For example, in separate collaborative studies with Marianne Hundt, Geoffrey Leech (doyen of the Brown family of corpora) argued in favour of 'small, carefully balanced reference corpora' because of 'the fine-grained analyses they allow us to achieve with respect to functional, regional, and genre variation' (Hundt and Leech 2012: 176) and, more radically, Denison (an early adopter and developer of the ARCHER corpus) explored the problems of retrieving relevant data from even a small, single register corpus of historical English (Hundt *et al.* 2012a, 2012b; Denison and Hundt 2013). These studies repeatedly found that engagement with the particularities of a text and its writer's overall intentions can be necessary to identify instances of a given construction and that in such cases the modern interpreter's *Sprachgefühl* 'can be used cautiously alongside other, more objective tests' (Denison and Hundt 2013: 135, 161).

In this chapter I will take their arguments a stage further and propose that understanding the changes in lModE grammar that Denison (1998) correctly described as 'elusive' may well require us to systematically rethink and readjust the balance between quantitative and qualitative approaches. In terms of method, I will evaluate the possibilities and limitations of the qualitative 'case-study' (epitomised by the use of misreading in Sections 9.3 and 9.4 and text-and-context analysis in Section 9.5); in terms of data, I will revisit (briefly in Section 9.2, more extensively in Sections 9.4 and 9.5) aspects of the specific historical issue – the relative construction – which engaged Hundt and Leech (2012) and Denison and Hundt (2013). The reliability of the modern *Sprachgefühl* will be a major question for Sections 9.3 to 9.5. And following the lead of Hundt *et al.* (2012b), I will begin by putting both method and data in the context of a larger problem affecting the study of diachronic change in lModE syntax – the role of prescriptive grammar.

9.2 Prescriptivism and the Cognitive Status of 'Rules of Grammar'

All historians of lModE find themselves working under the shadow of prescriptivism. This is the period in which 'the language was codified and the codifications disseminated' (Finegan 1998: 536). Hence most of our textual data – especially for the supra-regional variety described by *CHEL IV* as the 'common core' – is the product of speakers educated in national literacy programmes which were pervaded and shaped by prescriptive grammars. Until recently, the role of such grammars – whether as evidence of language change or as influences upon it – tended to be ignored or deplored or discounted. But the growth of lModE as a research area in the late twentieth century has forced scholars to acknowledge the existence of this elephant in the room, and the new millennium has witnessed a surge in studies of prescriptivism as a linguistic as well as a cultural phenomenon.[1]

This body of work puts in question – sometimes explicitly sometimes implicitly – one of the mainstream assumptions of twentieth-century linguistic thought, namely the belief that there is a categorical distinction between prescriptive and descriptive 'rules of grammar'. The orthodox binarism could be illustrated from any standard textbook, but since this chapter's focus is historical, I will borrow the formulation in Jean Aitchison's popular and influential introduction to the study of language change:

(1) A [prescriptive] grammar [...] lays down artificial rules in order to impose some arbitrary standard of 'correctness' [... which has] relatively little to do with what people really say.

For [descriptive] linguists, rules are [...] a codification of subconscious principles or conventions followed by the speakers of a language. (Aitchison 1981: 27)

Aitchison is typical in presenting the prescriptive-descriptive distinction as one both of kind and of value. Descriptive rules make explicit a cognitive reality – the 'subconscious principles or conventions' of 'the speakers of a language'; prescriptive rules, by contrast, are 'artificial', 'arbitrary', and without empirical foundation. In the more polemical language of Steven Pinker, 'prescriptive rules [...] are bits of folklore that originated for screwball reasons several hundred years ago' (Pinker 1994: 373).

By the time Aitchison and Pinker were writing, however, the foundations of this belief-system were already being undermined by the rise of sociolinguistics in the late twentieth century. The Milroys were among the earliest scholars to perceive the potential impact of the 'sociolinguistic turn' on traditional attitudes towards prescriptivism:

(2) When we view language as fundamentally a social phenomenon, we cannot then ignore prescription and its consequences.
(Milroy and Milroy 1985: 11)

But if 'prescription and its consequences' are not to be ignored by historical linguists, how are they to be dealt with? 'Not very easily' seems to be the

---

[1] Studies of the kind I have in mind include, in chronological order, Curzan (2003, 2014), Auer and González-Díaz (2005), Auer (2006), Hodson (2006), Tieken-Boon van Ostade (2006, 2011), Yáñez-Bouza (2007, 2016), Beal et al. (2008), Beal (2010).

answer. Thirty years on from the Milroys' manifesto, we find Curzan lamenting that 'institutionalized prescriptivism [...] has yet to be effectively integrated [...] into the broader study of "language change" in the history of English' (Curzan 2014: 9). Why is this so? Perhaps it is because the route to full integration would require historical linguists to overcome the deep-rooted dichotomy illustrated in (1) above, by reconciling descriptive and prescriptive rules of grammar. This is an ambitious goal, which in turn poses serious questions of evidence. How do we know when (or whether) an externally imposed rule has become internalised, or, in Aitchison's terms, an 'artificial rule' has turned into a 'subconscious principle or convention'?

As products of the digital era, most of the new prescriptivist studies addressing this question have adopted quantitative methods to answer it, aiming to discover whether the prescribing (or proscribing) of a particular linguistic construction is followed by an increase (or decrease) in its frequency of occurrence, either in the speech community or in the individual speaker. As Yáñez-Bouza (2016) notes in a recent survey of the field, the aim is to plait together the evidence provided by historical grammars on the one hand and historical text corpora on the other.

(3) A fundamental aim in the study of historical grammars is to assess the effect of linguistic thought on actual language usage.

(Yáñez-Bouza 2016: 168)

It is not always recognised, however, that there are problems with interpreting usage as evidence of belief or taking quantitative data as an index of cognitive states. I will illustrate with two cautionary tales of apparent change in linguistic behaviour.

My first example concerns the diffusion of the late nineteenth-century prescriptive rule: 'use *that* not *which* in restrictive relative clauses'. The most ardent and influential proponent of this rule was the American prescriptivist Alfred Ayres (1826–1902). In the lengthy Editor's Note on the subject with which he prefaced his 1883 edition of Cobbett's (1818) English grammar, he distinguishes between pairs such as (4a) and (4b) (Ayres 1883: 9).

(4) a. The house, *which* is built of brick, is very warm.
     b. The house *that* is built of brick is the warmest.

In the grammar itself, he systematically (if not always accurately) makes 'pronominal corrections' to Cobbett's original text 'in accordance with the fact that WHO *and* WHICH *are properly the* CO-ORDINATING *relative pronouns, and that* THAT *is properly the* RESTRICTIVE *relative pronoun*' (1883: 6; original emphasis).[2] One difficulty in assessing the influence of Ayres's edict on speakers' grammars is that his condemnation of restrictive *which* appears to have been adopted as house-style, first by US publishers and more recently by Microsoft's grammar checker. As a consequence, many speakers of non-American varieties of English (including myself) find their instinctive use of *which* changed by a copy editor's intervention between manuscript and print or challenged by an automatic machine objection to the text they have typed in. Gunnel Tottie reports such editorial interventions as the origin of her own interest in relativisation strategies (Tottie 1997: 84–5). In most cases (assuming that my response is typical), the author either does not notice the change or else lets it stand, simply because the substituted *that* is not 'incorrect' (even though 'not my dialect'), and because making verbal revisions at proof-reading stage runs the risk of knock-on consequences that might be more substantively damaging. The result can only be to skew the textual data by showing a steeper and more widespread decline in the use of restrictive *which* than is warranted by its status in internalised grammar.[3]

My second example concerns change of usage in an individual. Comparative data from two editions of *Listening to Spoken English* by Gillian Brown (1977, 1990) shows a quantitative shift away from the traditional prescription 'use generic *he* with generic nouns' [e.g. every *house-owner* worries about *his* mortgage] towards the post-1970s feminist proscription: 'do not use generic *he* (it is inherently sexist)'.[4] But does this shift in usage mark a cognitive change? In this case, we have the author's testimony that she (rather than her publisher) was responsible for the change; but, in addition, we have her introspective comment on its cause:

---

[2] Ayres's observation and terminology were anticipated by (and almost certainly borrowed from) Alexander Bain (1863: iv–v, 23–4, 88–91). Bain (1818–1903) was Professor of Logic (which presumably sharpened his eye for a distinction in scope) and both Bain (a Scot) and Ayres (an American) were native speakers of varieties of English which have been claimed to favour TH- over WH-relativisers (which presumably made Cobbett's usage – eighteenth-century southern English – perceptually salient to Ayres).

[3] Tottie's comments, like mine, on the effect of publishers' house-style are both anecdotal and speculative. Necessarily so. Even without the complication of a discrepancy between manuscript and edited text, quantifying change in restrictive relativisers has proved problematic because of the difficulties in identifying the restrictive/non-restrictive distinction, especially in large-scale diachronic corpora, where grammatical tagging needs to be automated and often relies on punctuation cues, which themselves vary chronologically (see Biber *et al.* 1999: 602ff.). More recently, these problems have been revisited and illuminated in Hundt *et al.* (2012a, 2012b) and Denison and Hundt (2013).

[4] For compact histories of generic *he*, see Wales (1996: 110–33) and Curzan (2003: 58–82).

(5) I remember holding the opinion when I wrote this book originally that the masculine third person pronoun was properly to be interpreted as neutral as between male and female where no question of different gender was involved. I find, somewhat to my surprise, that my feelings (note that I do not say 'my thoughts') have changed radically. I now find the insistence on the masculine pronoun dated and repetitive. You will be able to recognize those parts of the book which have been rewritten, by the elaborate lengths I go to to avoid using the singular pronoun.

(Brown, Introduction to the second edition (1990) of *Listening to Spoken English*, 1st edn. 1977)

This is a more complex and interesting case than my first example, in that the author recognises an internal change and one that she attributes not to 'opinion' or 'thoughts' but to 'feelings'. Yet she denies any shift in her *grammatical* intuitions, citing instead a conscious updating of her *style* (the 'masculine pronoun' appears 'dated and repetitive'). This example raises important questions both about the process by which an individual's idiolect changes over time and about the role played by style in the later evolution of a standardised language. The simpler point I want to emphasise here is that – as (5) shows – the task of inferring the cognitive status of a 'rule of grammar' from frequency of usage is by no means straightforward.[5]

Given these problems with quantitative evidence, I want to turn in Section 9.3 of this chapter to a form of qualitative evidence that may provide a window onto the 'subconscious principles or conventions followed by the speakers of a language' (see (1) above).

9.3 Some Types of Misreading

Errors in speech production and perception have long been used as evidence for cognitive hypotheses in psycholinguistics (e.g. Fromkin 1973, 1980; Levelt 2013), and communicative misfires of various sorts have held a similar place in the work of sociolinguists and ethnolinguists concerned with the unconscious conventions of social interaction (e.g. Gumperz 1982a, 1982b). In Adamson (1998), I cited an inter-generational misunderstanding as evidence of an ongoing historical change in English

---

[5] As with restrictive *which*, the aversion to generic *he* presents the preliminary difficulty of counting relevant instances of the variable. There is no clear-cut alternative to generic *he* and the more 'elaborate' avoidance strategies that Brown refers to are not easy to detect without access to both original and revised versions of the same text.

grammar, namely the expansion of the progressive construction. For earlier stages of the language, 'live' data of this kind is not available. But I want here to develop the suggestion (made in Adamson 2007) that an equivalent heuristic tool can be found in the textual records of inter-generational misreadings.

For the purposes of this chapter, *misreading* is defined to include:

- mistranscriptions of a written text
- misquotations (i.e. conscious or unconscious revisions to a text held in memory)
- editorial corrections of a text (where these can be shown to be erroneous or misguided)

The text-based discipline of literary studies provides two main models for the role of misreadings as a window on cognition. I will outline their use by literary scholars before going on to explore their possible applications to historical linguistics and in particular to the issues raised in Sections 9.1 and 9.2.

9.3.1 Misreading in Literary Criticism

Traditionally, the aim of literary criticism has been to interpret or evaluate literary texts and their authors. In this context, a misreading on the part of an author is often interpreted as a creative transformation of an earlier or precursor text.[6] The textual transformation is typically understood to be motivated and the motive to be, in some sense, psychological (whether aesthetic or neurotic in origin, conscious or unconscious in practice). In Bloom's work (1973, 1975), the motivation of authors is explicitly grounded in Freudian psychology, which is projected on to literary history as a way of explaining how literary influence works or how a literary tradition has developed. Bloom summarises his theory in (6a); in (6b) Said translates it into more general and less Oedipal terms.

(6) a. To live, the poet must *misinterpret* [his literary] father, by the crucial act of misprision, which is the re-writing of the father.
(Bloom 1975: 19)
b. every poem is the result of a critical act, by which another, earlier poem is deliberately misread, and hence re-written. (Said 1975)

---

[6] Variations on this stance include Eliot (1921), Bate (1971), Bloom (1973, 1975), and Ricks (2002).

This kind of misreading is not restricted to Oedipal competition between poets. Freud himself offers many accounts of textual misremembering as manifestations of the psychopathology of ordinary speakers. Among these 'faulty recollections', he includes Brill's detailed case-study of a patient who radically reworded Keats's *To Apollo* to express a traumatic event in her personal history (Freud 1914: 29–32). Here restrictions of space will confine me to a relatively brief and simple example from my own collection of literary misreadings.

The source text is an excerpt from William Thackeray's preface to the 1850 edition of his novel *Pendennis*, and it voices the frustration he had felt while writing that novel with the constraints on realism imposed by Victorian prudery:

(7) Since the author of 'Tom Jones' was buried, no writer of fiction among us has been permitted to depict to his utmost power a MAN. We must drape him, and give him a certain conventional simper.

(Thackeray 1850: xlviii)

Thackeray's discomfort was shared by many Victorian novelists and this passage is recalled with approval by Anthony Trollope nearly thirty years later in his study of Thackeray's achievement (1879: 108). But although Trollope quotes the first sentence verbatim, he misquotes the second, so that (8a) becomes (8b).

(8) a. We must **drape** him, and give him a certain conventional **simper**.

(Thackeray 1850)

b. We must **shape** him, and give him a certain conventional **temper**.

(Trollope 1879)

Some psycholinguists might class this as a simple error of lexical retrieval: each of the replacement terms converts a more specialised lexical item into one that is more generalised or more frequent. But we might well wonder why these items in particular? Or why this reader? Arguably it was Thackeray's choice of unusual keywords that made his complaint memorable and I have come across no other misreading of them in the many contexts in which it has been quoted.

One thing that a reader familiar with both writers might observe is that the difference between the two formulations directly reflects the different interests of the two novelists: Thackeray (who had studied as an artist, written as an art critic, and even used the name of Michael Angelo as part of an early pseudonym) opts for a visual analogy drawn from painting. And insofar as *drape/simper* are moral terms, they are socially orientated, referring to the outward signs of respectability (*drape*) and politeness (*simper*) that had long been the butt of his social satire.[7] The terms again coincide in his earlier critique of the affectations of those contemporary painters who offer their audience an escape from contemporary reality by creating images of medieval virgins invested with 'proper angular *draperies* [...] and the proper solemn *simper*' (Thackeray 1840: 51).

By contrast, Trollope's interests as a novelist are verbal rather than visual and his moral focus is insistently inward; the conscience and consciousness are his themes. Hence his narrative style makes far more extensive use of free indirect style than Thackeray's to represent the thoughts of his characters and even in his descriptive passages (conscientiously provided as a concession to the conventions of the time) 'the physical characteristics of his personages are rarely made clearly visible [...] It is their moral physiognomies that are sharply drawn' (Davies 1960: 14). His re-writing of Thackeray's text can thus be interpreted as a shift of perspective, from outer to inner, from surface to depth. The 'drape' (of clothing) gives way to the 'shape' of what lies beneath; the 'simper' of social self-projection gives way to the 'temper' of a moral interior (and Trollope's fiction – especially in the period around 1879 – abounds in the vagaries and extremes of human temper and temperament).

From this perspective, Trollope's 'faulty recollection' of the key terms in Thackeray's manifesto looks very like an unconscious 'critical act' of revision. The overt intention is simply to echo and endorse Thackeray's plea for 'the Natural in our Art' but, licensed by the phonetic clang (*drape/shape, simper/temper*), Trollope unconsciously translates it into terms more directly applicable to his own practice, and indeed to the general direction that realism was then taking in the work of his contemporaries, such as George Eliot and Henry James, and the mainstream novel of the following century.

A Bloomian analysis would take Trollope's motivation a stage further and argue that his misreading is evidence of his 'anxiety of influence' vis-à-vis his predecessor and patron; and the elements of an Oedipal drama are not hard to find in his memoir of Thackeray. But my concern here is to evaluate not Trollope but the type of analysis that I have just engaged in, which illustrates the analytical methods not only of psychoanalysis and literary criticism but also of some recent developments in sociolinguistics.

---

[7] Most explicitly in his *Punch* series, *The Snobs of England*, which did so much to shape our modern conception of snobbery.

It typifies the 'case-study' method, in which the linguistic behaviour of an individual speaker is subject to the interpretation of a (sufficiently well-informed) individual observer.

Following the rather acrimonious exchanges between Freud and Meringer at the turn of the twentieth century, the paths of psychoanalysis and psycholinguistics diverged, as did the methods of case-study and corpus collection. Relatively few psycholinguists have subsequently attempted to bridge the gap, although Fromkin, for example, always acknowledged that 'Freud's 1901 paper was seminal' in establishing the role of errors as 'windows into the mind' (Fromkin 1980: 2).[8] The case of Trollope reinforces Fromkin's point, by reminding us of what we all know from everyday experience as speakers or hearers – that 'Freudian slips' do occur and they occur precisely because sometimes people say what they mean rather than what they mean to say. Trollope's mis-quotation goes beyond what can be accounted for in terms of processing error and supports the hypothesis that at least some misreadings bypass conscious intentions to reveal more deep-seated cognitive states. At the same time, it illustrates the limitations of such case-studies as evidence. They readily turn into case-histories, often too complex, individuated, or context-dependent to be readily incorporated into general explanations. In addition – and this is the feature that most obviously makes the Freudian case-study ill-adapted to the present enquiry – Freudian slips are typically phonological-lexical in operation. They may well reveal the subconscious meanings of a speaker, but it is more specifically the forms of the speaker's *grammar* that we are concerned with here.

9.3.2 Misreading in Textual Criticism

Misreading plays a central role in another branch of literary studies, namely textual criticism. Traditionally, the aim of textual critics has been to establish authoritative texts for culturally authoritative works (originally the Bible and the Classics, more recently the works of canonical vernacular authors). This aim devolves on to a number of localised tasks. Where the original text is extant, the critic emends it to remove errors committed by a scribe or printer or even a careless author; where the original version of a text has been lost, the critic reconstructs it by choosing between the textual variants found in the surviving copies.

---

[8] See also Cutler and Fay (1978), Cutler (1979), Ellis (1980), Motley (1980), and Hinterhuber (2007).

From the perspective of textual reconstruction, a misreading is regarded not as creative transformation but as destructive deformation. Like literary critics, textual critics assume that the creative artist may produce language that is unique, deviant, or innovative; but they also assume that the average transcriber, when faced with the deviant or unexpected, is likely to simplify the text, usually by defaulting to a more conventional or familiar form of expression. This is the process known as *banalisation*. To avoid the danger of banalisation, an editor is advised to select the variant that is *prima facie* more problematic. From the renaissance humanists onwards, a key maxim of textual criticism has been *lectio difficilior potior* (or, in operational terms, 'prefer the less obvious reading'). But how do we know when this maxim applies?[9]

For a compact case-study of traditional principles in action, let's consider how modern editors have responded to a little local difficulty in Robert Browning's *Luria*. The excerpt in (9a) reproduces three lines from the first published edition of 1846; (9b) gives the final line of the group as emended by one of the leading twentieth-century editions of Browning.

(9) a. It is no novelty for innocence
      To be suspected, but a privilege:
      The after certain compensation comes.   (Browning 1846: 12)
    b. Then after certain compensation comes.   (Ohio 1973: 313)

The Ohio edition supports changing initial *the* to *then* with the argument that 'the sense requires a word other than an article' (Ohio 1973: 393). Presumably the editor is interpreting *after* as an adverb and so emends to give a reading approximating to 'then afterwards certain compensation comes'. By contrast, the Longman edition of the same lines rejects Ohio's emendation and reverts to the first edition text of (9a). Presumably parsing *after* as an adjective (with the sense of 'subsequent'), the editors argue that 'the sense here is: *the compensation comes that was sure to follow*' and cite a parallel collocation in Browning's *Sordello* iv. 475: 'to lay *the after* indignation' (Longman 1991: 414).

---

[9] Textual criticism has a long history and given the 'sacred' nature of its textual materials, its theory and practice have been more diverse and controversial than this summary implies. Since the 1980s, in particular, the traditional methodology I outline has been challenged by the rise of new historicism in literary theory (notably McGann 1983) and by the practical possibility of creating electronic hypertexts. An adequate bibliography would massively overfreight the needs of my argument in this chapter. But Patterson (1985) provides a useful snapshot of a 'traditional' edition viewed from a revisionist perspective.

Perhaps because they are literary critics rather than linguists, both sides in this debate argue from semantics rather than syntax and neither side appeals to evidence from the history of English. As a preliminary step towards setting the problem in its historical context, let's take data from the entry for *after* in the *Oxford English Dictionary* (henceforth *OED*). The quotations in (10) appear under the heading '*after* sense A. *adj.*' and illustrate the use of *after* as an attributive adjective.

(10) a. 1850 Tennyson *In Memoriam* cxv. 181 For fuller gain of after bliss.
    b. 1883 *Harper's New Monthly Mag.* May 947/2 Its [*sc.* painting's] creative character is an after and a higher development.
    c. 1930 A. Christie *Murder at Vicarage* iii. 25 I append a rough sketch here which will be useful in the light of after happenings.

Note that examples (10a) and (10b) are contemporary with Browning and (10a) is semantically as well as chronologically close to (9a) (compare *after bliss* with *after compensation*), while (10b) resembles the contested line syntactically, since *after* is directly preceded by an article and is part of a longer pre-modifying string (compare *the after certain* with *an after and a higher*). However, it is equally worth noting that the *OED* labels the adjectival use of *after* 'rare' or 'obsolete', and the 1930 quotation (10c) is the latest example listed under this heading. If we accept the *OED* data as a snapshot of historical usage, we might infer that sometime in the twentieth century, adjectival *after* was displaced by synonymous adjectives (such as *later* or *subsequent*), leaving *after* with the functions of adverb, conjunction, preposition, and prefix. Certainly all the post-2000 quotations in the *OED* are assigned to these functions, and recent uses of *after* in pre-modifying position (as in (11)) are classed as prefixes and usually selected so that the prefixal status is signalled in their orthography (as in (11b) and (11c)).

(11) a. 2004 R. A. Streett *Effective Invitation* (rev. ed.) 170 When practical circumstances call for it, Billy Graham will make use of the after meeting.
    b. 2007 R. Havard *Spanish Eye* iii. 61 The after-tremors of the French Revolution [. . .] were only unhappily resolved in 1814.
    c. 2008 *Five Lessons Bankers must Learn in minds eye* (Usenet newsgroup) 11 Aug. Their great respect for their forebears and concern for their afterbears.

A possible conclusion from this (necessarily limited) dataset is that the usage of Browning's contemporaries in (10) shows that the Ohio emendation is unnecessary, while the evidence of more recent data in (11) suggests that the Ohio editor is reading his nineteenth-century text through the lens of twentieth-century grammar and hence is guilty of banalisation. But even without judging between these editions or second guessing Browning's original intentions, we can see that the *lectio difficilior* maxim leads an editor to prefer the obsolete or rare construction while the banalising alternative leads an editor to make the line conform to the dominant norms of current usage.

What I want to propose here is that this conformity is of interest not only to textual critics but to historical linguists. If the *OED* evidence allows us to recognise Ohio's reading of Browning as anachronistic, a turn of the perspective allows us to argue that Ohio's misreading provides the speaker-based evidence required to support the decision of the *OED* linguists to categorise adjectival *after* as 'obsolete' and to analyse recent occurrences of pre-modifying *after* as a prefix, although, as they note, 'there is no absolute criterion distinguishing attributive uses [at the entry *after- adj.*] from those at *after- prefix*'. In this perspective, Ohio's banalisation is transformed from an editorial gaffe into a window on a particular historical *état de langue*.

9.4 Misreading in Historical Linguistics

The misreading of the texts of one generation by speakers of another chronolect has the same source as the perceptual errors of L2 language learners, described by Cutler in 'Listening to a second language through the ears of a first' (2000). In both cases, the forms of the language that speakers have internalised provide a coercive interpretive template for the forms of the language they encounter. Generalising from the individual case-study of Section 9.3.2 to its implications for historical method might lead us to a hypothesis such as (12):

(12) Banalisation is evidence that a grammatical change has become an internalised rule for the individual speaker.

It is this hypothesis that makes banalisation a potentially useful heuristic tool in historical linguistics. The hypothesis – it should be noted – applies to the internalisation of *any* historical language change, whether or not imposed by prescription. For instance, the shift of *after* from adjective to prefix, evidenced by the Ohio banalisation of Browning, is not a change sponsored by prescriptivists (as far as I know) and it would be accepted by most historical linguists as a straightforward example of grammaticalisation. But (12) has particular force and relevance to the questions raised in

Section 9.2 about the internalisation and integration of prescriptive rules of grammar.

For this reason, I will test the hypothesis of (12) by looking at the agreement rules for relative and third-person pronouns – two cases where prescriptive grammar has certainly had its say and where, as we saw in Section 9.2, the evidence of usage frequency can be misleading as an index of internalised grammar. For the sake of clarity and brevity, I will focus on the basic contrasts between *who/which* and anaphoric *he/she/it*. Quotation (13) gives the agreement norms for Present-day English (PDE) in the simplified form in which they are typically taught to native and non-native learners of English.

(13) [The English language] does have ways of distinguishing animate beings from inanimate entities, personal from nonpersonal beings, and male from female sexes. We simply observe which nouns and pronouns go together. (Crystal 1988: 106)

e.g. boy = *he/who*; girl = *she/who*; box = *it/which*; *a boy = *it/which*; *a box = *he/who*

In Crystal's terms, *boy* 'goes together' with *he/who*, *girl* with *she/who*, whereas *box* 'goes together' with *it/which*. A present-day pupil using the combinations marked with asterisks is likely to get bad marks in their SATS English exam.[10] But these agreement patterns have not always been so clear-cut. And the PDE norms that Crystal reports in (13) are essentially those promulgated by eighteenth-century grammarians and first inculcated through the eighteenth-century equivalent of SATS tests. The statements in (14) are typical of the period and formulated by its most influential spokesmen.

(14) a. For *it* the practice of ancient writers was to use *he*, and for *its*, *his* [...] *Who* is now used in relation to persons, and *which* in relation to things; but they were anciently confounded. At least it was common to say, the man *which*, though I remember no example of the thing *who*. (Johnson 1755: 44)

b. *Who* is appropriated to persons; [...] *which* is used of things only; [...] But formerly they were both indifferently used of persons: 'Our Father, *which* art in heaven.' *That* is used indifferently both of persons and things: but perhaps would be more properly confined to the latter. (Lowth 1762: 133–4)

---

[10] SATS = the national assessment tests of literacy in primary school pupils in the UK. For the evolution of methods of teaching and testing English grammar, the standard work remains Michael (1987).

c. The objects represented by '*who*,' are usually called '*persons*;' and those by '*which*,' '*things*.' (Ward 1765: 136)

For Samuel Johnson, Robert Lowth, and William Ward – as for most of their contemporaries – the most salient opposition expressed by pronoun agreement is between 'persons' and 'things': it is most directly encoded in the binary contrast between the relative pronouns *who* and *which* and mapped onto the third-person pronouns by aligning *he/she* together in opposition to *it*. Some eighteenth-century grammarians were conscious (though with varying degrees of historical accuracy and tolerance) that earlier writers had not always observed this opposition. In the mid-eighteenth-century writers of (14), the dividing line between prescription and description is rather blurred. Johnson's stance in (14a) is overtly descriptive but his phraseology ('is now used') recognises no variation in what he sees as current usage, unlike Ward's 'usually called' in (14c). Lowth slips from a descriptive stance in his historical remarks to a tentative prescriptivism when commenting on contemporary usage, especially in cases that fail to observe and signal the person/thing division. Hence the impropriety he finds in the use of *that* in relation to persons.

The variability of earlier usage noted by these mid-eighteenth-century grammarians is illustrated in the early Modern dataset below. In (15a) *who/which* are both used in relation to 'things' (i.e. *caskets*); in (15b) *which/who* both relate to 'persons' (i.e. *John of Gaunt* and *Henry V*); in (15c) *it/its/her* are used in the same text in relation to the same non-personal antecedent (i.e. *the English language*); similarly in (15d) *who/itself* have the same antecedent (i.e. *world*).[11]

(15) a. This first of gold, **who** this inscription bears ...
The second silver, **which** this promise carries ...
(Shakespeare, *Merchant of Venice*, 2.7.4–6)

b. John of Gaunt,/ **Which** did subdue the greatest part of Spain ...
Henry the Fifth,/ **Who** by his prowess conquerèd all France.
(Shakespeare, *3Henry VI*, 3.3.81–6)

c. [the English language] hath woords enou of **its** own, to expres any conceipt; besid's the stor' of borrowed woords, which by soom chang' **it** maketh **hir** own; (Butler 1634: *To the Reader*)

d. The world **who** of **itself** is peisèd well,
(Shakespeare, *King John*, 2.1.576)

---

[11] Shakespearean quotations in (15), (16), and (20) are adopted from Greenblatt *et al.* (1997).

It is not my aim here to examine the origins and extent of early Modern English (eModE) gender variability, which have been well documented and discussed by previous scholars.[12] Instead, I want to explore how variable agreement patterns of this kind are interpreted by readers who have been to differing degrees conditioned by eighteenth-century prescriptive rules. The example I will look at in detail is of the same type as (15d). In (16) we find *who/it* used in the same line of the same text for the antecedent *heart*.

(16)   Oft have I seen a timely-parted ghost
       Of ashy semblance, meagre, pale, and bloodless,
       Being all descended to the labouring **heart**;
       Who, in the conflict that **it** holds with death,
       Attracts the same for aidance 'gainst the enemy;
                               (Shakespeare, *2Henry VI* 3.2.161–5)

I have taken this text because it has attracted a series of interpreters, each linking it to pronoun agreement rules and each aware of a predecessor's comment. The first in my series is Dr Johnson, who uses it as the first illustrative quotation in his *Dictionary* (1755) entry for WHO. It strikes me as a distinctly odd choice, first because he has just defined WHO as 'a pronoun relative applied to persons', whereas in (16) the antecedent of *who* is the 'non-personal' noun *heart*; second, because it apparently contradicts his claim in (14a) that 'I remember no example of the thing *who*'; and third, because he makes no comment on either of these apparent anomalies. Does he expect the reader of this entry to remember what he said in the *Dictionary*'s preface (14a) and see the anaphoric sequence *heart ... who ... it* as an illustration of the inconsistency of 'ancient' practice? Or does he simply not notice that the text has violated his definition of the headword? In the latter case, we might suggest that he belongs to a generation that has not yet internalised its own prescriptions. We find a similar apparent self-blindness in (17), where Ward employs an agreement pattern (*writers which*) that he is in the very process of classifying as obsolete.

(17)   But in all the English writers, which flourished above a hundred years ago, '*which*' is applied both to persons and things.
                               (Ward 1765: 136)

---

[12] See particularly Mustanoja (1960: 45), Baron (1986), Nevalainen and Raumolin-Brunberg (1994), and Curzan (2003).

The anomaly could of course be intended as a humorous jolt to the reader's attention – but Ward's grammar has not been widely noted for this kind of pawky humour and it seems more likely that *writers which* reflects a more archaic (or provincial) internalised grammar than the one he is advocating.

Lowth, by contrast, makes both his intentions and his interpretation clear. In his 1762 grammar, he repairs Johnson's omission and implicitly criticises his practice. Quoting the same five lines as Johnson, he comments directly on the 'confusion of Genders' in its pronoun selection and provides two methods of resolving the confusion so as to make the anaphoric sequence both self-consistent and compliant with current best practice in observing a clear 'person' vs. 'thing' distinction:

(18) a. The Neuter Relative *which* would have made the sentence more strictly grammatical, but at the same time more prosaic [i.e. by giving the anaphoric sequence: *heart-which-it*].
b. If the Poet had said *he* instead of *it*, he would have avoided a confusion of Genders, and happily compleated the spirited and elegant Prosopopœia, begun by the Personal Relative *who* [i.e. by giving the anaphoric sequence *heart-who-he*].

(Lowth 1762: 35)

But the proposed textual emendations reveal not only Lowth's goals as grammarian but also his mind-set as reader. In expounding the problems of Shakespeare's syntax, he shows that he is reading the sequence *heart . . . who* as a personification rather than a vagary of 'ancient' grammar. The phrase 'the Prosopopœia begun by the Personal Relative *who*' is particularly significant. It suggests that for Lowth *who* ('a pronoun relative applied to persons') is in itself such a strong signal of *person*-hood that it triggers a retrospective metaphorisation of its antecedent, in this case shifting *heart* from the category 'thing' to the category of 'person'.[13] As Wales (1996: 134–65) has shown, the personifying force of anaphoric pronouns is still powerful in PDE, so in evaluating Lowth's interpretation, we need consciously to remind ourselves that neither he nor we have reason to suppose that Shakespeare intended to 'personify' a heart in (16) any more than a casket in (15a) or the world in (15d). In effect, Lowth is banalising Shakespeare's text by reading its use of *who* through the lens

---

[13] For some of Lowth's contemporaries, the personification trigger was also pulled by the use of *his* instead of *its* in eModE texts (by authors for whom *its* was historically not an available option) and even by the use of *whose* in contemporary texts (although there was and is no standard non-animate alternative).

of eighteenth-century agreement rules, rather than recognising it as an example of the eModE variability that he knows to have existed.

Two centuries later, the same interpretive crux is revisited in the *Dictionary of English Normative Grammar* (Sundby *et al.* 1991, hereafter *DENG*). In a note on p.118, the editors cite Lowth's discussion as an instance of normative response to 'gender conflict between coreferential personal and relative pronouns'. But although they agree with Lowth in their diagnosis of the problem, they differ in their reading of the text, as becomes apparent when they analyse it directly on p.108:

(19)   Nbigeneric
'Oft have I seen a timely-parted ghost [...] Who, in the conflict that it holds with death'

The way the passage has been truncated suggests that the *DENG* editors are assigning the role of antecedent to *ghost* rather than *heart*, and this is borne out by their classification of the antecedent as a 'bigeneric noun' (Nbigeneric). In other entries, an antecedent *heart* is classed as a 'non-personal noun' (Nnpers), as in the example of eModE 'gender confusion' that seems to have irked many eighteenth-century prescriptivists: *He that pricketh the heart maketh it to shew her knowledge* (*DENG*: 110).

But why have the *DENG* editors misread Lowth? Given that *heart* is the noun that immediately precedes *who* in the text Lowth quotes, whereas two lines of intervening material separate *ghost* from *who* and *it*, their decision is curious and seems to require explanation.

One explanation is that readers have been primed since the eighteenth century to read pronouns semantically rather than syntactically and so modern readers look for an antecedent noun that might plausibly prompt the gender conflict they perceive between *who* [+animate, +human] and *it* [-animate, -human]. The noun *ghost*, denoting a liminal entity hovering between the worlds of living and dead, of person and non-person, readily fits the bill and hence accounts for Shakespeare's apparent hesitation between *who* and *it*. By contrast, the sequence *heart-who-it*, though the easier reading syntactically, is the *lectio difficilior* semantically because for a modern reader a heart is a much less good representative of a bigeneric entity than a ghost. Hence banalisation takes over.

As in the case of the Ohio editors of Browning, I think we should regard *DENG*'s banalisation not as an error but as a diagnostic of diachronic change, either in the language system or in its speakers' interpretive strategies. Empirical support for this conclusion comes from my previous oral presentations of this data, where some members of my audience – native speakers of English – have agreed with *DENG*'s reading of the text and challenged my view that the antecedent of *who . . . it* is *heart* rather than *ghost*. This response suggests that, as predicted by Crystal in (13), semantic feature-matching of antecedent noun and anaphoric pronouns is the unmarked norm shaping the expectations of PDE readers.

9.5 Expanding the Data in Qualitative Analysis: Text-and-Context Method

What is meant by *qualitative evidence* in linguistics varies quite widely. At one extreme, it has the very restricted scope envisaged by Penke and Rosenbach (2007: 7), where it 'simply means that we use data to show that a certain form/construction is possible in a specific context'. This is contrasted with *quantitative evidence*, where 'we do not use data solely to show *that* a form/construction or effect exists but rather *how much* of it exists' and '[s]tatistical methods help to decide whether the differences found are meaningful (=significant) or random' or even 'to show whether a (categorical) rule exists' (2007: 9).[14] Traditional literary studies occupy the other end of the spectrum. Here the first court of appeal in disputes over the interpretation of a linguistic form is to enlarge the data laterally, by the text-and-context method. What sort of knowledge emerges from this form of procedure? Is it (like the Freudian case-history of Section 9.3.1) inevitably case-specific, or can it also contribute towards more general historical enquiry?

A test-case to hand is presented by the conclusion to Section 9.4. In asserting that *heart* and not *ghost* is the antecedent of *who . . . it* in (16), I am pitting my own *Sprachgefühl* against that of both fellow historical linguists (the *DENG* editors) and fellow native speakers (dissentient audience members). So it seems only right to pose the question: what is the evidence that *heart* was the antecedent that Shakespeare intended? I leave others to determine whether or how that question could be settled by quantitative methods. Since my aim in this chapter is to put the case for qualitative methods, this seems the moment to confess that I tested my interpretation of the construction by putting the excerpted text of (16) into a larger co-text, which in turn gives access to a wider cultural context. The five lines quoted by Johnson and Lowth (in bold below) are taken

---

[14] In the first phase of corpus-based linguistics, researchers were notably more inclined to propose a constant interplay between qualitative and quantitative approaches, e.g. (for relative constructions) Schmied (1993).

from a much longer speech by Warwick over the dead body of Humphrey, Duke of Gloucester (*2Henry VI* 3.2.160–78). Even the slight expansion of (20) clarifies the speech's pragmatic purpose and its syntax:

(20) See how the blood is settled in his face.
Oft have I seen a timely-parted ghost,
Of ashy semblance, meagre, pale, and bloodless,
Being all descended to the labouring <u>heart</u>,
<u>Who</u> in the conflict that <u>it</u> holds with death,
Attracts the same for aidance 'gainst the enemy,
Which with the heart there cools, and ne'er returneth,
To blush and beautify the cheek again.
But see, his face is black, and full of blood: [...]
It cannot be but he was murdered here.

(ll.160–8, 177)

Warwick is here trying to persuade his hearers that Gloucester has been murdered rather than dying a natural death. To do this, he draws on early Modern physiological theory, in which the heart, as the principal seat of life, 'attracts' the blood away from the face and other extremities as it labours to resist the onset of death. In an 'untimely' death – such as murder – the heart has no opportunity to do this, hence the dead person's face will be 'black and full of blood' (like Gloucester's), instead of 'pale and bloodless'. In this case, the forensic pragmatics of Warwick's argument prompts a statement of the contemporary belief-system that definitively identifies *heart* as the intended antecedent of the clause *who . . . attracts*.[15]

But the extended text of (20) does more than resolve a specific constructional relationship. It also throws light on some of the more general questions that this chapter has touched on.

Firstly, the punctuation of (20) follows the First Folio text, which marks off lines 2–8 as a constructional entity. It is a construction that well exemplifies the 'sentence length and complexity' noted by Hundt *et al.* (2012a) as causing difficulties for automated parsing. For a start, we need to extract the noun *blood* from the adjective *bloodless* before we can connect it with its postmodifiers, which unhelpfully take different constructional forms (the participial clause *being . . . descended* and the relative clause *which . . . cools*) and are separated from each other by two interpolated adnominal relatives *heart-who* and *conflict-that*. This kind of interlacing

---

[15] Similarly, in classifying relative clause types in eModE scientific texts, Denison and Hundt (2013) sometimes found that understanding the experimental scenario envisaged by the writer was an essential help in determining the intended scope of the adnominal relative.

structure – by no means uncommon in eModE texts – makes close reading not merely a desirable, but often an essential, adjunct to machine searching.[16]

Secondly, in the case of (20), extending the original text brings an additional bonus – or complication – by adding to our data on agreement patterns in adnominal relativisers. The central constructional sequence (lines 2–8) includes *blood-which* alongside *heart-who*. Why this distribution? Is it an instance of eModE free variation or an intentional contrast? Clearly it is not the same as the *person-who*, *thing-which* opposition prescribed by eighteenth-century grammarians and internalised as the unmarked option for PDE speakers. It looks more like the pronominal gender system, still found in some English dialects, which encodes a contrast between count nouns (e.g. *heart*) and non-count nouns (e.g. *blood*), or the distinction between individuated and non-individuated referents which, as Siemund (2008) has argued, provides the best generalisation for pronominal gender across dialectal and chronolectal varieties of English.

But the instances of Shakespeare's relativisers encountered elsewhere in this chapter suggest that something different is going on. A count-noncount hypothesis for *heart-who* vs. *blood-which* in (20) is challenged by counter-examples in (15), where *who/which* appears to be applied indifferently to caskets (15a) and princes (15b), both of which are individuated entities. However, taking all three examples together prompts another hypothesis. It is generally accepted that *who* is a late addition to the repertoire of relativisers and that it enters the system initially in construction with nouns denoting God, supplementing the earlier and more widely applicable *which* (Rydén 1983). It is possible then that for some speakers of eModE, the *who/which* contrast – especially if both relativisers occur in the same constructional space – might be used to signal distinctions not in animacy or individuation but in hierarchical rank, or what the sixteenth century called *worth*. Cultural history tells us that social rank was sufficiently salient in early Modern England to be made visible in legally prescribed dress codes; intellectual history tells us that social hierarchy was integrated into a universal hierarchy replicated in all categories of being, so that the gold [*who*] of (15a) ranks higher than the silver [*which*] just as Henry V [*who*] of (15b) ranks higher than John of Gaunt [*which*]. Similarly in the physiological scenario outlined in

---

[16] The larger theoretical question of 'what is a sentence in eModE?' is not easy to answer and too rarely asked. It is broached by Adamson (1999: 583–93) and Hundt *et al.* (2012b: 218–20).

Warwick's speech, the blood [*which*] is depicted as subservient to the heart [*who*].

To test this hypothesis about the role of the *who/which* contrast in Shakespeare's usage, or to relate it to more large-scale hypotheses about sixteenth-century relativisation patterns – such as the idiolect-based model of variation espoused by Görlach (1991: 125), or the differing dialectal norms identified by Nevalainen (2012) – we would need to extend the database further and hand the research baton over to quantitative analysis. Such an extension lies beyond the scope of this chapter, but is by no means alien to its aims.

9.6 Conclusion

This study offers no conclusive answers to the questions it addresses: the general difficulty of charting syntactic change in the post-prescriptive era and the particular complexities of the relative construction. Rather, these problems have provided the lens through which I have examined some of the advantages and limitations of using qualitative analysis as an adjunct/complement to the quantitative paradigm that now dominates English historical linguistics.

The digital revolution, like all revolutions, has been a heady affair and its ever-expanding possibilities of text mining on ever-grander scales have attracted the creative energies of many scholars into corpus creation and computer-supported quantitative research. The downside, as Matti Rissanen presciently predicted in 1989, has been 'the wane of philologically oriented language studies' (1989: 16) – a process accelerated by the development of corpus linguistics from an auxiliary tool to an autonomous discipline, whose evolving methodological traditions owe more to computation than to philology.

In this chapter, I have resuscitated some of the traditions of 'philologically orientated language studies': the psychological profiling of an individual author (Section 9.3.1), the procedures of textual reconstruction (Section 9.3.2 and Section 9.4), and finally (Section 9.5) the kind of contextualisation practised by literary critics, where *context* is defined not only as a longer text span, but as the pragmatic purposes a text expresses and the cultural ideologies it presupposes.

The conclusion that I hope readers will draw from this exercise is that some of these approaches have here shown their value, whether by throwing a new light on old data, or by confirming or challenging the results of previous quantitative accounts, or by suggesting new hypotheses for quantitative methods to test. The challenge for future researchers is to determine how far qualitative analysis can be methodised and how far its form of knowledge discovery must remain a matter of serendipity.

I suspect that the detection of misreadings may always fall into the latter category. So it seems appropriate to conclude with the serendipitous survival of a prequel to the chain of misreadings discussed in the last two sections. The 1623 Folio version of *The Second Part of Henry VI*, from which examples (16), (19), and (20) derive, was preceded by a Quarto playtext, printed in 1594 under the title *The First Part of the Contention betwixt the Two Famous Houses of Yorke and Lancaster*. Critical opinion is divided as to whether the 1594 version represents an actor's misremembering (and hence banalisation) of the lines Shakespeare wrote or whether it is Shakespeare's own first draft, which he later revised. One local difference between the versions suggests that this question may be of interest to historians of relativisation as well as Shakespearean scholars. The Folio speech of Warwick – successively cited by Johnson (1755), Lowth (1762), *DENG* (1991), and myself to illustrate the *who/which* distinction – appears in the 1594 text, but without any of our troublesome *wh*-relatives. Compare (20) with the corresponding lines in the First Quarto text of (21):

(21) Oft haue I seene a timely parted ghost,
      Of ashie semblance, pale and bloodlesse,
      But loe the blood is setled in his face,
      More better coloured then when he liu'd, [...]
      It cannot chuse but he was murthered.

                                            ([Shakespeare] 1594: E3r)

CHAPTER 10

The Conjunction and in Phrasal and Clausal Structures in the Old Bailey Corpus

Merja Kytö and Erik Smitterberg

10.1 Introductory Remarks*

10.1.1 Aim and Scope

Late Modern English (lModE) is characterised by comparatively few changes to the inventory of morphosyntactic variants (Denison 1998: 92–3). However, a great deal of linguistic change takes place in the period, as the frequencies and relative proportions of many linguistic features (e.g. the progressive and *be* vs. *have* as the perfect auxiliary with intransitive main verbs) change greatly between 1700 and 1900. Moreover, such changes are often constrained by linguistic as well as extralinguistic factors. One type of change that has been shown to occur is colloquialisation (see Mair 1997), whereby features that are frequent in spoken language become more frequent and/or accepted in (some) written genres (see, for instance, Smitterberg 2008).

However, an area that has so far received less attention is that of changes in the spoken medium itself; this is due in part to the lack of recorded speech for historical periods and the fact that methodologies such as historical pragmatics developed only recently. Although researchers are fortunate in having a comparatively rich written database to draw on for lModE data, our access to speech is heavily constrained. In the absence of authentic recordings, scholars rely on studying written, speech-like texts, which may be speech-purposed (e.g. plays) or speech-based (e.g. parliamentary debates) (Culpeper and Kytö 2010: 18). Using such texts, we can show whether writing appears to come closer to speech over time. However, the question also arises whether the speech of the period

---

* Warm thanks are due to Magnus Huber and Magnus Nissel for their help with the queries used to retrieve data from the *Old Bailey Corpus*.

remained stable or underwent similar – or different – changes compared with written language.

One feature that has been shown to exhibit different behaviour in spoken and written English is the co-ordinator *and*. In Present-day English (PDE), *and* tends to link clausal material more often than phrasal material in conversation, while the opposite holds true for written language. Moreover, written texts display considerable genre variation: formal, expository writing contains higher proportions of phrasal co-ordination than more speech-like texts such as fiction (Biber *et al.* 1999: 81; Chafe and Danielewicz 1987). These genre differences appear to have increased since early Modern English (eModE) (see Culpeper and Kytö 2010: 165 for evidence on cross-genre variation). As Smitterberg's (2014) study of newspaper language based on the *Corpus of Nineteenth-Century Newspaper English* (CNNE) has shown, nineteenth-century newspaper writing underwent linguistic change with regard to this feature: the percentage of clausal co-ordination rose during the 1800s. This raises the question of whether lModE speech exhibits similar tendencies, or whether newspaper writing gradually came closer to a stable spoken norm.

The aim of the present study is to chart the development of *and* in a speech-based genre to which we do have access for the lModE period, viz. trial proceedings. In addition, the study examines whether the proportions of clausal, phrasal, and possible other uses of *and* remain constant across two sociolinguistic parameters: gender and social class.[1] Both phrasal and clausal uses of *and* are part of the repertoire of 'oral' as well as 'literate' Standard English. Within this variety, however, there are differences in genre norms regarding the relative proportions of phrasal and clausal co-ordination; these genre norms are largely adhered to subconsciously when a grammatical feature like *and* is employed. If the genre norms for trial proceedings change in the direction of increased orality during the period studied, this may result in a higher percentage of clausal co-ordination, given the genre distribution in PDE (see Biber *et al.* 1999: 81). As it is probable that such a change would comprise change from below, women speakers are likely to be ahead of men in this development (Labov 2001: 292–3). Moreover, it is possible that access to higher education and frequent exposure to written English affected language users' spoken idiolects in the opposite direction: the written norm, with high proportions of phrasal co-ordination, may have influenced speech (see McIntosh

---

[1] We use the terms for these variables that were employed by the compilers of the *Old Bailey Corpus*, the data source on which this investigation is based.

1998 for developments within the written prose norm itself during the 1700s). If so, we would expect speakers from the higher echelons of lModE society to display higher percentages of *and* as a phrasal marker. In order to be able to isolate the factors of gender and social class, we focus on one single genre, trial proceedings, and on one category of participant in the trials, namely witnesses, where women and members of the lower echelons of lModE society are better represented than in other participant groups.

10.1.2 Previous Work

There are several indications that clausal and phrasal uses of *and* characterise spoken and written language, respectively, in PDE. Biber *et al.* (1999: 81) demonstrate that the proportions of clause-level *and* range from approximately 80 per cent in conversation to about 35 per cent in academic prose, with fiction and news language taking up intermediate positions on the cline. In addition, in Biber's (1988) factor analysis, clause-level co-ordination was an involved feature on Dimension 1, 'Involved vs. Informational Production', whereas phrasal co-ordination was associated with explicit reference on Dimension 3, 'Explicit vs. Situation-Dependent Reference'. As shown in Biber and Finegan (1997), both of these dimensions can be regarded as articulating an 'oral' vs. 'literate' distinction: clause-level *and* is then an oral feature on Dimension 1 and phrase-level *and* a literate feature on Dimension 3. This dichotomy is even clearer in Biber's (2003) new factor analysis of academic English, in which a single oral vs. literate dimension ('Oral vs. Literate Discourse') is identified. Here, clause co-ordination and phrasal co-ordination load as an oral and a literate feature, respectively. This difference between spoken and written English has also been identified for past centuries: Culpeper and Kytö (2010: 183) demonstrate that clause-level co-ordination is comparatively common in speech-related genres in their eModE material.

In Smitterberg (2014), this feature was also shown to undergo change in nineteenth-century newspaper English. There was a significant change towards more clausal co-ordination in the corpus examined, which can be interpreted as a sign of colloquialisation: as the readership of newspapers became bigger and more diversified, the language of this written genre approached spoken norms (as shown by Hundt and Mair 1999, newspaper English is a comparatively 'agile' genre in this regard in late twentieth-century English as well). However, the question arises whether spoken English itself underwent a similar change towards more clausal co-ordination, in which case the difference between speech and (some) writing may have remained constant. Biber's (1988, 2003) work shows that genre differences in the use of *and* persist in PDE, which means that written language has not reached spoken levels of clausal co-ordination and/or that speech itself also changed during the period. To examine this, we consider a genre that is based on actual speech produced in a formal setting: lModE courtroom discourse.

10.2 Method

10.2.1 Material

The present study draws for data on the extended version 1.0 of the *Old Bailey Corpus* (OBC), which is based on the *Proceedings of the Old Bailey* (OBPO) and covers the period 1720–1913. The off-line tool was used to retrieve the data from the corpus. The OBC is distributed with detailed extralinguistic classification of speakers, including their role in the trial, which made it an ideal source of data for our purposes (see Section 10.1.1; see also Huber 2007 for more information on the OBC).

As we were interested in change over time, we decided to sample two of the subperiods of the corpus defined by the compilers: 1753–1785 (period 1) and 1850–1881 (period 2). The two periods examined are thus approximately a century apart; in addition, the latter period is comparable to the coverage of the corpus used in Smitterberg's (2014) study of *and* in newspaper English (1830–1850 and 1875–1895). To ensure that the distribution of the different roles of trial participants (lawyer, judge, witness, etc.) would not affect results while keeping the scope of the study manageable, only language produced by witnesses was included in the study. One should of course keep in mind that records of witness statements were taken down by scribes and that this may have had an influence on the resulting texts. However, witness statements and other speech-related texts are still of great value both for the study of historical speech and 'as communicative manifestations in their own right' (Jacobs and Jucker 1995: 9).

The OBC includes sociolinguistic information on the speaker of each utterance in the corpus, where such information is available. The coding includes the parameters of gender and social class, which were of particular interest to us. Social class is assigned numerically based on the speaker's occupation. For the purposes of this exploratory study, we chose to work with only two categories in this regard. We used the predetermined categories 'higher' (class 1–5, including primarily non-manual occupations such as managers and professionals as well as clerical and sales personnel)

Table 10.1 *Categories of witnesses sampled*

Period	Years	Gender	Social class
1	1753–1785	Female	Higher
		Female	Lower
		Male	Higher
		Male	Lower
2	1850–1881	Female	Higher
		Female	Lower
		Male	Higher
		Male	Lower

and 'lower' (class 6–13, including mainly manual occupations, e.g. foremen, workers, farmers, fishermen, etc.).

This coding scheme resulted in a total of eight combinations of extralinguistic features, as shown in Table 10.1. As the results of the present study are based on the proportions of clausal vs. phrasal uses of *and* in random subsamples of data, word counts are not given here or below. Numbered examples from the OBC include the value 'm' or 'f' to indicate the gender of the speaker, the period span, and the value 'lower' or 'higher' to indicate the speaker's social class.

10.2.2 *Data Selection and Classification*

To retrieve our data, we used the OBC off-line tool. We adjusted the searches so that both <and> and <&> were covered. Owing to the impressive size of the OBC (the extended version of OBC 1.0, which was used for this study, contains more than seventeen million words), it was necessary to limit the amount of data analysed even when only witnesses from two time periods were considered. We used the random number that is assigned to every token in the output to limit the scope of the analysis. A total of 300 randomly selected tokens for each of the eight categories in Table 10.1 (Section 10.2.1) were included; the total number of tokens classified was thus 2,400. (A small number of extra tokens were included for each category to replace any tokens that had to be discarded after manual post-processing of the output; 2,668 tokens were thus given a classification, but only 2,400 of these tokens were actually used.)

In classifying the data we needed a set of selection criteria that would allow us to go through the data in a replicable way. We primarily wanted to distinguish clausal uses of *and* from phrasal uses; however, from a more data-driven perspective, we were also interested in whether there might be ambiguous or other instances that should not be included in either of those categories, e.g. conditional *and* (which, however, was not attested in our data). For our classification, we consulted previous literature, e.g. Quirk *et al.* (1985), Culpeper and Kytö (2010), and Smitterberg (2014). We will present our classification criteria below.

In what follows, we will use the term *conjoins* for the sets of overt linguistic material that are co-ordinated by *and*. To start from the category of clausal uses, our prototypical examples contain at least part of a verb phrase followed by one more clause element, as in example (1), where four predicates constitute the conjoins, and (2), in which two predicates are first co-ordinated, and the resulting main clause is then co-ordinated with another main clause.

(1) I ran after him for about 200 yards, came up to him, seized him, **and** knocked him down. (m, 1850–1881, lower)

(2) I spoke to him **and** went into my room, **and** he went out. (f, 1850–1881, higher)

As we were interested in the status of sentence-initial clausal *and*, the use of which in writing has been regarded as controversial, we coded such instances separately. However, the only sentence-initial token in our data proved to be (3).

(3) I told him. He found his substance cut to pieces and wasted; and miss'd things. **And** on making enquiry amongst us [there was a great noise about things being missing] we were obliged to tell. (f, 1753–1785, lower)

Example (3) was included as a clausal token, as it links two main clauses (in separate sentences). The proscription of sentence-initial *and* seems to have militated against its occurrence in writing in this genre: as Denison (1998: 256) notes, any increase in the frequency of this feature after the period studied here 'is probably more a change in written decorum and in punctuation practice than in syntax'. In other words, it is possible that, when the proceedings were published, tokens of *and* that could have been made sentence-initial were instead placed after semi-colons, as in (4), or commas, as in (5).

(4) The next day I was not very well; **and** on the Friday (I think the 31st) her husband came and told me she was dangerously bad indeed, and quite light-headed; [. . .] (f, 1753–1785, higher)

(5) [...] – the prisoner said some angry words, but I do not know what, **and** his father ordered him out – [...]   (m, 1850–1881, lower)

In examples such as (4) and (5), transcribers, publishers, etc. have some freedom in where to insert written sentence boundaries, and can thus avoid sentence-initial *and*. It is beyond the scope of the present study to examine the contexts where such choices may have been made, but such an investigation of speech-based material would clearly be of interest to scholars interested in the relationship between usage and precept.

Another category of clausal uses that were given a separate code comprised instances with two movement verbs conjoined by *and* in a set pattern that, in fact, could be understood to form one entity of action. These tokens constitute the separate category '*V and V*' in tables in Section 10.3. The pattern is illustrated in examples (6) and (7); (6) exemplifies the most frequent subpattern, where the first verb is a form of *to go*.

(6) I went **and** enquired in the places, the people would not trouble themselves about it.   (m, 1753–1785, lower)

(7) I ran **and** told my master.   (m, 1850–1881, lower)

As for the category of phrasal uses, the conjoins typically consist of items such as nouns, noun phrases, adjectives, adverbs, or prepositions; see examples (8), (9), and (10).

(8) I went down before them, and was standing by Mrs. Smith, at the stall, and while there I saw the prisoner **and** prosecutor speaking together at the door.   (f, 1850–1881, lower)

(9) I have not been present when she has addressed the prisoner in an angry **and** passionate manner.   (f, 1850–1881, lower)

(10) It is what is fastened to the rudder, for the rudder to swing backwards **and** forwards   (m, 1753–1785, higher)

The above examples illustrate the categories of clausal and phrasal uses of *and* that we will focus on in the present study. However, we also classified ambiguous uses such as those in (11) and (12) separately. In ambiguous tokens, more than one clause element is present in each conjoin – in (11), for instance, each conjoin contains a subject and an adverbial – but neither conjoin contains an overt verb phrase. We illustrate this by underlining the conjoins in (11); as the verb *went* is not repeated after *and*, it is considered to lie outside the conjoins and to be understood from the context. No more than seventy-nine instances were recorded for this category.

(11) My fellow servant went to dinner, **and** I to the barber's in the passage, (m, 1753–1785, higher)

(12) I found the pantry window wide open, **and** the pantry in great confusion. (f, 1850–1881, lower)

A small number of tokens (twenty-one) were excluded because they included conjoins that were not parallel constituents syntactically, as in (13).

(13) I saw his body agitated greatly, **and** move several times, that made me take particular notice of him; (m, 1753–1785, lower)

Finally, instances that incorporated parts of proper nouns (14), or appeared in scribal comments (15), were excluded from the data (altogether twenty-seven instances).

(14) I went into the Coach **and** Horses in Spur-street, Leicester-fields; (m, 1753–1785, lower)

(15) She gave in her name Ann Elliot. (Produced in court, **and** deposed to by the prosecutrix.) (m, 1753–1785, higher)

10.3 Results

10.3.1 Overall Results

Table 10.2 presents the diachronic development in the entire dataset taken together. The differences in Table 10.2 are statistically significant (d.f. = 3; χ^2 = 21.1; p < 0.001). The biggest difference in percentage points (6.2) between the early and late periods is the increase in the proportion of clausal co-ordination, while the proportions of phrasal, ambiguous, and *V and V*-type co-ordination go down. As mentioned in Section 10.1.2, clausal co-ordination is associated with oral communication in PDE, while phrasal co-ordination is characteristic of expository writing (Biber *et al.* 1999: 81). Against this background, the tendency towards increased clausal co-ordination, an indication of orality, in a spoken genre is interesting. It may indicate that the colloquialisation of written genres attested in lModE (see, for instance, Smitterberg 2008, 2014) is perhaps mirrored to

Table 10.2 *Co-ordination with* and *by period*

Period	Phrasal #	%	Ambiguous #	%	V and V #	%	Clausal #	%	Total
1	320	26.7	45	3.8	56	4.7	779	64.9	1,200
2	291	24.3	34	2.8	22	1.8	853	71.1	1,200
Total	611	25.5	79	3.3	78	3.3	1,632	68.0	2,400

some extent by a corresponding drift towards linguistic patterns characteristic of informal conversation in some spoken genres. Such trends may be especially likely if the genre analysed is not characterised by informal production circumstances. For instance, the relative formality of a courtroom setting may (consciously or subconsciously) cause language users to adapt their language in the direction of written patterns. It is also possible that the scribe changed aspects of the original speech event to make the language less speech-like (for a discussion of possible scribal influence on the incidence of the *V and V* pattern, see Section 10.4). It seems likely that the linguistic distance thus created between courtroom and everyday speech may then in turn decrease over time, partly in response to societal changes.

Alternatively, spoken English in general may have changed towards more clausal co-ordination, in which case courtroom language would merely be mirroring this general trend. In colloquialisation studies, informal spoken language is often implicitly treated as a constant to which writing becomes more similar over time. In reality, of course, speech is the locus of most language change (see, for instance, Milroy 1992: 75 for the importance of dialogic interaction in language change), and is thus very much a 'moving target' in this regard. More research on linguistic change in the OBC is necessary before conclusions can be drawn regarding whether the tendency towards more clausal co-ordination reflects changes in speech in general or is an independent development in this genre.

The other notable difference between the periods concerns the proportion of *V and V* constructions. This pattern clearly becomes less frequent over time. Although the difference is less than three percentage points, the proportion of all uses of *and* accounted for by *V and V* constructions in fact decreases by 60 per cent between the periods. This development would potentially lead witness statements in the opposite direction compared with the increase in clausal co-ordination; Biber *et al.* (1999: 1031–2) report

The Conjunction and in Phrasal and Clausal Structures 243

Table 10.3 *Co-ordination with* and *by gender*

Gender	Phrasal #	%	Ambiguous #	%	V and V #	%	Clausal #	%	Total
Female	286	23.8	36	3.0	47	3.9	831	69.3	1,200
Male	325	27.1	43	3.6	31	2.6	801	66.8	1,200
Total	611	25.5	79	3.3	78	3.3	1,632	68.0	2,400

that, in PDE, *V and V* binomial phrases are less frequent in news and academic prose than in fiction and conversation. These potentially contradictory patterns make it interesting to see whether any particular subsets of the data appear to be especially prone to change.

10.3.2 Gender

In the OBC, utterances are coded for gender with regard to the speaker. It is of course true that, in the absence of recording equipment, these speech events have been mediated through a scribal process, which means that the language we have access to is one step removed from the original speaker whose gender is used to classify the data. Nevertheless, a gender perspective may contribute to a better understanding of the social factors that influence the distribution of features such as *and*. The overall gender differences in the data are given in Table 10.3.

The gender differences in Table 10.3 indicate that, from a quantitative perspective, women witnesses use *and* in a slightly more 'oral' way than men do: the clausal and *V and V* categories, which are associated with orality, account for a higher proportion of all tokens in women's statements than in men's, while the opposite is the case for the more 'literate', phrasal category. However, as the differences in Table 10.3 only approach statistical significance (d.f. = 3; χ^2 = 6.94; p = 0.074), the results must be regarded as inconclusive in this respect. Nor do the gender differences in either period tested separately reach statistical significance (see Tables 10.9 and 10.10 in the Appendix).

In contrast, the use of *and* by both men and women changes significantly across the period covered by the study, as shown in Tables 10.4 and 10.5. Women's use of *and* becomes increasingly dominated by clausal coordination over time (d.f. = 3; χ^2 = 14.0; p = 0.003); almost three quarters of all tokens in the second period co-ordinate clausal material. This increase is

Table 10.4 *Co-ordination with* and *by period (female witnesses)*

	Phrasal		Ambiguous		V and V		Clausal		
Period	#	%	#	%	#	%	#	%	Total
1	154	25.7	22	3.7	33	5.5	391	65.2	600
2	132	22.0	14	2.3	14	2.3	440	73.3	600
Total	286	23.8	36	3.0	47	3.9	831	69.3	1,200

Table 10.5 *Co-ordination with* and *by period (male witnesses)*

	Phrasal		Ambiguous		V and V		Clausal		
Period	#	%	#	%	#	%	#	%	Total
1	166	27.7	23	3.8	23	3.8	388	64.7	600
2	159	26.5	20	3.3	8	1.3	413	68.8	600
Total	325	27.1	43	3.6	31	2.6	801	66.8	1,200

set against a decrease in the percentage accounted for by each of the other categories. Male witnesses also change significantly towards more clausal co-ordination at the expense of the other categories (d.f. = 3; χ^2 = 8.40; p = 0.038). However, the change is less conspicuous than for women in every category with the possible exception of *V and V* constructions: here the proportion of men's usage decreases by 2.5 percentage points as against 3.2 for women, but women's use of *V and V* decreases with 57.6 per cent while men display a decrease of 65.2 per cent.

Overall, the tendencies in the data are consistent with an interpretation of the increased tendency towards clausal co-ordination as a change from below; that is, speakers would not normally be conscious of their increased use of *and* as a clausal co-ordinator. According to Labov (2001: 292–3), women tend to be leaders in change from below as long as the norms for usage are not overtly prescribed (see also, for instance, Nevalainen and Raumolin-Brunberg 2017 for gender differences in historical periods). Women also appear to be in the vanguard of the change towards clausal co-ordination, although the fact that the gender differences do not reach statistical significance means that such a conclusion would need to be backed up by further research.

Table 10.6 *Co-ordination with* and *by social class*

Class	Phrasal #	%	Ambiguous #	%	V and V #	%	Clausal #	%	Total
Higher	301	25.1	36	3.0	37	3.1	826	68.8	1,200
Lower	310	25.8	43	3.6	41	3.4	806	67.2	1,200
Total	611	25.5	79	3.3	78	3.3	1,632	68.0	2,400

10.3.3 Social Class

As mentioned in Section 10.2.1, the sampling of the OBC was stratified for social class so that the higher classes (1–5) and the lower classes (6–13) were conflated into two categories. This enables a socioeconomic perspective on the results. It is possible, for instance, that the percentage of phrasal co-ordination will be proportional to education; speakers who had received more schooling might be more used to reading and producing written language with high proportions of phrasal co-ordination, and this difference may in turn affect their spoken usage. The overall differences between the two groups are presented in Table 10.6.

As Table 10.6 shows, class differences are of minor importance in the OBC data. For no parameter does the class difference reach two percentage points, and the differences taken together are not statistically significant (d.f. = 3; χ^2 = 1.20; p = 0.752). If witnesses from higher socioeconomic groups were more used to phrasal co-ordination, this seems not to have affected their spoken production even in a formal courtroom setting. Nor are there any tendencies towards class differences within each period sample (see Tables 10.11 and 10.12 in the Appendix).

However, the two socioeconomic groups behave differently with regard to the overall tendency towards more clausal and less *V and V* co-ordination over time in the data. The results are given in Tables 10.7 and 10.8. The diachronic tendencies are similar in the two datasets: the proportions of phrasal, ambiguous, and *V and V*-type co-ordination decrease, while the share of clausal co-ordination rises. However, the trends are somewhat more pronounced among higher-class witnesses, especially as regards the increase in clausal and the decrease in *V and V* co-ordination; as a result, the period differences for the higher classes are statistically significant (d.f. = 3; χ^2 = 14.4; p = 0.002). In contrast, the period differences among speakers from the lower classes only approach significance (d.f. = 3; χ^2 = 7.60; p = 0.055). The only aspect of these results that seems readily

Table 10.7 *Co-ordination with and by period (higher-class witnesses)*

	Phrasal		Ambiguous		V and V		Clausal		
Period	#	%	#	%	#	%	#	%	Total
1	158	26.3	22	3.7	28	4.7	392	65.3	600
2	143	23.8	14	2.3	9	1.5	434	72.3	600
Total	301	25.1	36	3.0	37	3.1	826	68.8	1,200

Table 10.8 *Co-ordination with and by period (lower-class witnesses)*

	Phrasal		Ambiguous		V and V		Clausal		
Period	#	%	#	%	#	%	#	%	Total
1	162	27.0	23	3.8	28	4.7	387	64.5	600
2	148	24.7	20	3.3	13	2.2	419	69.8	600
Total	310	25.8	43	3.6	41	3.4	806	67.2	1,200

amenable to an interpretation in terms of socioeconomic factors is the increased dispreference for *V and V* constructions among higher-class speakers. To the extent that these constructions were regarded as colloquial and/or proscribed, speakers who had received more schooling may have avoided using them frequently in formal speech. However, more research on the incidence and prescriptive evaluation of such binomial expressions is necessary before conclusions can be drawn in this regard.

10.3.4 Summary of Results

The investigation of the co-ordination patterns of *and* has revealed variation and change as well as stability in the OBC data. As regards change over time, the general trend in the data is towards a relatively clear increase in clausal co-ordination and decreasing proportions of the *V and V* type, with smaller decreases in phrasal and ambiguous co-ordination. These developments are present in all subsets of data considered, although, when lower-class witnesses only are included, the period differences do not reach statistical significance. There are some indications that women may be leading the trend towards clausal co-ordination and that higher-class witnesses are increasingly avoiding *V and V* constructions, which could potentially be linked to change from below and educated usage, respectively. (But the former connection is complicated by the fact that higher-class speakers also increase their use of clause-level *and* to a greater extent than lower-class speakers do.) Most differences between the different social categories of witnesses as regards change over time are too small to allow safe conclusions.

Synchronic differences with extralinguistic parameters are less pronounced than are patterns across time in the data. When the period samples are conflated, the differences between male and female witnesses approach statistical significance, and indicate that the 'oral' co-ordination patterns are possibly more prevalent in women's witness statements. However, neither period sample considered separately yields significant gender differences. As regards social class, there is no indication of different linguistic behaviour by higher-class and lower-class witnesses either in the total figures or in the period samples.

In sum, there is strong support in the data for change regarding the two patterns that seem characteristic of orality in PDE: clausal co-ordination becomes more frequent and *V and V* co-ordination less so. Weaker indications that higher-class speakers are in the vanguard of both types of change and that women are leaders in the linguistic change towards more clausal co-ordination can also be extracted from the data. No clear differences between genders or classes emerged when these parameters were considered synchronically.

10.4 Conclusion

Our investigation of the conjoins of the co-ordinator *and* has revealed two diachronic trends in the data. On the one hand, *and* is increasingly used as a clausal co-ordinator across time. This is likely to indicate 'genre drift': the relatively formal, speech-based genre of trial proceedings appears to become more 'oral' in this regard over time. This is potentially a very interesting finding: it implies that a change such as colloquialisation, which has hitherto been discussed chiefly in terms of spoken patterns having an effect on written usage (see, for instance, Mair 2006: 187), may need to be extended also to include some spoken (or, in historical terms, speech-related) genres changing to incorporate rising numbers of 'oral' features in diachrony.

On the other hand, the *V and V* pattern becomes less frequent across time. This change may reflect a decrease in spoken usage as a whole during the same period. However, it is also possible that such constructions were felt not to be suitable for a formal courtroom setting and thus increasingly avoided. Such avoidance may have taken place at the level of the speakers themselves, but also at the level of transcribers, publishers, etc. In (6), repeated here as (16), for instance, it would have been possible to omit *went and* in transcription with little change in meaning. Alternatively, the sentence could have been rewritten as, for example, *I went to enquire.*

(16) I went **and** enquired in the places, the people would not trouble themselves about it. (m, 1753–1785, lower)

The sociolinguistic parameters examined indicate that the language of most groups of speakers considered undergoes change in the same direction as indicated by the data as a whole; the main exception concerns lower-class speakers, where diachronic differences do not reach statistical significance. No significant differences with social class were found in the data, which also suggests relative sociolinguistic homogeneity in this regard. However, there are weak indications that women and higher-class witnesses are in the vanguard of the changes attested.

The results presented here invite further work from several perspectives. First, more research is needed on the *V and V* pattern and its development over time in speech-related genres, given that its share of all *and* usage clearly decreases in diachrony. A quick search in the *Corpus of Historical American English* (COHA) for the string *went/came and* followed by a verb in the past tense (*went* and *came* are by far the most frequent first verbs in our *V and V* data) indicates that the frequency of the pattern declines in American English after the late nineteenth century. Secondly, other extralinguistic parameters coded for in the OBC should be considered, such as witnesses vs. members of the legal profession and possible scribal influence. Our preliminary results do not indicate a great deal of variation between scribes as regards the distribution of clausal and phrasal *and*. However, one of the scribes, Thomas Gurney, is responsible for forty-five instances of the *V and V* pattern (58 per cent of all *V and V* tokens), while he only contributed 829 (35 per cent) of all tokens. This may indicate, for instance, that Gurney transferred a high proportion of spoken *V and V* tokens to writing, while other scribes omitted them by e.g. removing the first verb and the co-ordinator (e.g. *I went and asked what he wanted* > *I asked what he wanted*). Thirdly, the analysis as a whole should be extended to other lModE genres: the combination of a speech-based medium and a formal setting that characterises courtroom interaction may result in distributions that differ from those in other text categories. Fourthly, the present study should ideally be complemented by a multifactorial analysis that may show, for instance, whether time, gender, and/or class have an independent effect on the results. Finally, the occurrence – and, possibly, avoidance – of sentence-initial *and*, which was near-absent in our OBC material, should be studied in larger corpus samples, e.g. the OBC as a whole or COHA. Such an analysis should ideally include both sentence-initial instances of *and* and tokens which could have been sentence-initial, but which were instead placed after punctuation marks such as commas and semi-colons; in addition, contemporary prescriptive trends should be compared with actual usage. The versatility of *and* as a linker makes it an interesting feature to study from syntactic and sociolinguistic as well as pragmatic perspectives.

Appendix

Table 10.9 *Co-ordination with* and *by gender (period 1)*

	Phrasal		Ambiguous		V and V		Clausal		
Gender	#	%	#	%	#	%	#	%	Total
Female	154	25.7	22	3.7	33	5.5	391	65.2	600
Male	166	27.7	23	3.8	23	3.8	388	64.7	600
Total	320	26.7	45	3.8	56	4.7	779	64.9	1,200

d.f. = 3; χ^2 = 2.27; p = 0.518

Table 10.10 *Co-ordination with* and *by gender (period 2)*

	Phrasal		Ambiguous		V and V		Clausal		
Gender	#	%	#	%	#	%	#	%	Total
Female	132	22.0	14	2.3	14	2.3	440	73.3	600
Male	159	26.5	20	3.3	8	1.3	413	68.8	600
Total	291	24.3	34	2.8	22	1.8	853	71.1	1,200

d.f. = 3; χ^2 = 6.05; p = 0.109

Table 10.11 *Co-ordination with* and *by class (period 1)*

	Phrasal		Ambiguous		V and V		Clausal		
Class	#	%	#	%	#	%	#	%	Total
Higher	158	26.3	22	3.7	28	4.7	392	65.3	600
Lower	162	27.0	23	3.8	28	4.7	387	64.5	600
Total	320	26.7	45	3.8	56	4.7	779	64.9	1,200

d.f. = 3; χ^2 = 0.104; p = 0.991

Table 10.12 *Co-ordination* with *and* by class (period 2)

Class	Phrasal #	%	Ambiguous #	%	V and V #	%	Clausal #	%	Total
Higher	143	23.8	14	2.3	9	1.5	434	72.3	600
Lower	148	24.7	20	3.3	13	2.2	419	69.8	600
Total	291	24.3	34	2.8	22	1.8	853	71.1	1,200

d.f. = 3; χ^2 = 2.14; p = 0.545

PART III
Comparative and Typological Approaches

CHAPTER 11

The Role Played by Analogy in Processes of Language Change: The Case of English HAVE-to Compared to Spanish TENER-que

Olga Fischer and Hella Olbertz

11.1 Introduction[*]

In this chapter we will argue that the outcome of processes of grammaticalisation may be determined to a large extent by analogy, by the force of analogical relations that language users perceive to be present between constructions in their language,[1] on the basis of both concrete lexical as well as structural and functional resemblances (cf. earlier work by Fischer 2007, 2011, 2013 and De Smet 2009, 2012, 2013). We propose that the pathway of a particular grammaticalisation process can only be understood when we take into account not just the changes that take place on the historical language level but also when we consider the role of the speakers who are ultimately responsible for the change (cf. Fischer 2007: 116ff.). That is, we must look beyond the grammaticalisation process itself by considering both the contemporary grammatical system and the socio-cultural circumstances that speakers function in, which co-determine the way speakers process (and may change) their utterances. From this follows that there is nothing necessarily unidirectional about a grammaticalisation process (even though it frequently moves in one direction because it often involves processes of reduction in both meaning and form), that it is not necessarily steered by pragmatic-semantic factors only (see Section 11.2.1), and also that it is not a process that involves, as it were, some independent mechanism operating by itself. Our approach makes understandable why the process may turn one way in one language and another

---

[*] We would like to thank two anonymous reviewers and the editors for their careful reading of the manuscript and their most helpful suggestions.
[1] We understand by 'constructions' both lexically concrete structures and more abstract syntactic patterns which are defined by both their formal and pragmatic-semantic content, as is usual in Construction Grammar (cf. e.g. Goldberg 1995; Traugott and Trousdale 2013; Barðdal et al. 2015).

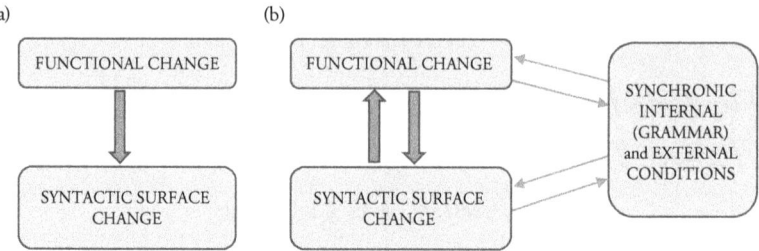

Figure 11.1 (a) The traditional scenario (b) Our scenario

way in another, i.e. it does not necessarily follow some universal pathway, as suggested for example in Haspelmath (1989) with reference to developments of infinitival markers in Germanic.[2]

In brief, we envisage the process of grammaticalisation to work as shown in Figure 11.1b, and not as shown in Figure 11.1a, which represents the traditional account.

Since the working of analogical processes is difficult to prove – especially where it concerns syntax, where there are so many constructions that in one way or another may resemble and thus influence each other – it would advance our knowledge of this area if we investigate whether the grammaticalisation of a particular construction follows a similar pathway in languages where the linguistic circumstances under which the new construction evolves are more or less similar. In the present case, we investigate a construction in English and Spanish involving a possessive verb that develops into a modal verb of obligation/necessity before an infinitive. We consider this against the background of the development of a similar construction in Dutch and German, where the linguistic circumstances are clearly different. This, we hope, will give a firmer foundation to our understanding of what shapes grammaticalisation, and also provide more insight into the way analogy operates in morphosyntax.

We will first briefly present some general background in Section 11.2, both on what has been written on the grammaticalisation process involving the possessive verb in English and the Romance languages (Section 11.2.1) and on the role played by analogy as an important cognitive principle present in language learning, which continues to play a role in the linguistic behaviour of adult speakers (Section 11.2.2). In Section 11.3, we will present

---

[2] For a counter-view to Haspelmath's 'universality' in the Germanic infinitival case, see Fischer (1997), who argues that the *to*-infinitive behaves differently in English, compared to German and Dutch, as a result of other changes involving infinitivals taking place in the history of English.

a summary of the circumstances under which the English possessive verb grammaticalised and what role analogy has played here, based on Fischer's (2015) study of this case. Section 11.4 provides information about the development of TENER-*que* in Spanish in relation to other constructions involving possessive verbs; here we also note the linguistic circumstances surrounding the grammaticalisation path of TENER-*que* and pay attention to the differences and similarities with the development of English HAVE-*to*. In Section 11.5, we will compare the situation in the two languages with developments in Dutch and German in order to establish whether the circumstances in English and Spanish were indeed similar enough to understand why the possessive verb developed into a modal of necessity in these languages and why it did not happen in Dutch and German, where the construction remained more or less the way it was in the earlier periods. Section 11.6 briefly concludes.

11.2 Some Background to Grammaticalisation and Analogy

11.2.1 The Traditional View of the Grammaticalisation of Possessive Verbs

It has usually been taken for granted that the development of English HAVE in the construction HAVE+*to*-infinitive represents a regular case of grammaticalisation, in line with similar developments involving a possessive verb like HAVE, where HAVE in combination with an infinitive (or a past participle) grammaticalised from a full verb into an auxiliary (and in some cases even into a suffix, as in the Romance future). Thus, van der Gaaf (1931), Visser (1963–1973: §1396ff.) – who do not yet use the term – Brinton (1991), Heine (1993: 42), Krug (2000), and Łęcki (2010) all more or less accept three developmental stages for the change in English from *I have [a book [to recommend]]* to *I [[have to recommend] a book]*. In their sketch of the putative development of HAVE-*to*, the grammaticalisation proceeds along a very gradual (almost invisible) path of pragmatic-semantic change with bleaching of possession first, followed by the development of obligative colouring later, while the word order change and the rebracketing are seen as the final stage of the development.

Also characteristic for the description of grammaticalisation processes is that usually only the construction that undergoes change is considered, as if it changes in isolation. Bybee (2010: 107), for instance, writes: 'grammaticalization involves the creation of a new construction *out of an existing construction*' (emphasis added). She also emphasises, as is traditional in grammaticalisation studies, the primary role of pragmatic inferencing in the process: '[s]emantic and pragmatic changes occur *as a result of the contexts* in which the emerging construction is used' (2010: 107; emphasis added). Similar gradual semantic pathways are considered for the development of the possessive verb into future and perfect markers in the Romance languages; see e.g. Fleischman (1982: 15 and *passim*), Heine (1993), Klausenburger (2000, 2008), Ledgeway (2012: 119ff.), and cf. also Heine and Kuteva (2002: 242–5) for the development of possessives to future and modal necessity meaning in non-European languages.

11.2.2 The Ubiquitous Presence of Analogy

Following Holyoak and Thagard (1995), Tomasello (2003), and other usage-based linguists, we believe that analogy plays a crucial role both in the way we learn language and in the way we keep using language as adults, causing changes to occur continuously in how we understand and produce utterances. Behrens (2009, 2017) stresses the strong role played by analogy in children's language acquisition, analogy of both a concrete lexical-semantic type (i.e. analogy caused by the use of the same lexical items in a construction) and also of a more abstract formal type (caused by the use of a similar syntactic pattern). She shows that it helps children to understand and formulate utterances (and, as a next step, learn the conventions of their language) when they can discern concrete similarities between lexical items per se and between structures containing such lexical items. In addition, she stresses that an *overlap* in semantic and syntactic information between two constructions strengthens the working of analogy. This analogical awareness always evolves from concrete to more and more abstract:

> children proceed from concrete to abstract representations. 'Concrete' here refers to the replication of strings of words or chunks without having analyzed their internal structure. [... The more abstract] schemas always start out with concrete similarities in the expression, as they are based on concrete usage events [...]. (Behrens 2017: 230)

Behrens refers also to Tomasello (1992), who showed that children learn syntactic structures verb by verb in the initial phase of syntax acquisition; that is, they do not yet generalise the argument structure of one specific verb to other verbs, nor do they spot any abstract relation between constructions in the early period. It is only later that children are able to 'generalize over the [concrete] form-function correspondences in the input' (Behrens 2017: 230). Behrens furthermore points to the ability of 'system-mapping', a notion familiar from cognitive science studies (e.g. Gentner and Namy 2006; Gentner 2010; Gentner et al. 2011; Gentner and Smith 2012). This concerns the ability to see functional relations between larger structures, which helps children to form abstract connections and enables them to make further analogically based inferences between the source and the target structure.

In what follows, we work from the presumption that the cognitive learning mechanisms in children as indicated above still operate in adults when they are using (and through it often changing) their language. Thus, the concrete and abstract patterns that speakers have conventionalised during acquisition (out of which their grammatical system emerges) will continue to influence neighbouring patterns when similar in lexical or syntactic form and/or function.[3] We also accept Deacon's (1997: 74) view that analogy works *by default*; i.e. it involves not so much the *perception of a similarity* between one form and another that causes the speaker to make one form/structure analogous to another, but rather the fact that the speaker does *not* see a difference between two forms (because they are much alike) and therefore, by *mis*perception as it were, makes the one form analogous to the other.[4] This unawareness would explain why such analogies (resulting in a reanalysis on a metalinguistic level) occur so easily in language use, language acquisition, and language change.[5] Analogies are constantly made by both children and adults. However, since children are still learning their language and hearing many new utterances every day, their analogies do not necessarily stick and may still be adjusted to what is seen as conventional during further learning. Similarly, not all analogies made by adults will cause change in language usage; it is only when the 'mistake' occurs *often enough* (which may well be due to other changes having taken place in the grammar system elsewhere) that such an analogical pattern may become the new norm (and hence become part of the

---

[3] Hofstadter (2001) and Hofstadter and Sander (2013) show how this analogical thinking pervades all that we do, all through our lifetime; not surprisingly the title of Hofstadter (2001) is 'Analogy as the core of cognition'.
[4] See also Day and Gentner (2007) and Weinert (2009), who show in different experimental studies (involving analogy-making in text comprehension with adults, and in implicit learning with children, respectively) that analogical inferencing processes occur without the participants being aware of it.
[5] Kahneman (2011), who makes a distinction between two ways of thinking (a 'fast' intuitive, emotional system and a 'slow' more deliberate, logical system), notes that it is 'ease of effort' that drives the fast system: a way of thinking that often leads to making the wrong inferences.

grammar system). Not surprisingly, frequency plays a crucial role in whether an analogical innovation will result in a change (for the importance of frequency in matters of change, see Paul 1909: Chapters 4 and 5; Bybee and Hopper 2001; Hopper and Traugott 2003: 126ff.).

Before we move on to the English and Spanish cases, it is necessary to say a few words on the way analogy is traditionally considered. The forms of analogy most widely recognised are those of analogical extension and levelling (and backformation to a lesser extent). These all involve what is usually called 'proportional analogy' (sometimes 'four-part analogy'), where the formation of a new word form is based on the morphological parallelism of three existing word forms, frequent in morphological paradigms. This view, however, involves a rather restrictive understanding of the working of analogy.[6] It should be mentioned that not only form is relevant but also meaning. When we widen the analogical schema to meaning as well as form, it is clear that metaphor is a similar example of analogical extension, but based on perceived similarities in meaning leading to an extension in use of an existing form. In syntax, the formal and semantic-pragmatic parallels may combine and strengthen the analogy as happens also in folk etymology (cf. Coates 1987). A good example of this is the change from Old English (OE) *brideguma* to modern *bride**groom***, where *guma* 'man' has been replaced by *groom* 'stable-boy'. What is interesting is that the extension of the form (*groom*) may take place even when the similarity on both the formal and the semantic level is not perfect. This 'looser', more fluid kind of analogy is what we also see in syntax. It can involve both a perceived similarity between the forms of the two constructions and a perceived similarity in their meaning as well, leading to one form being used for the other. This is what we also see happening in the syntactic cases discussed in Sections 11.3 and 11.4.

11.3 The Case of HAVE-*to* in English: Challenging the Traditional View

In Fischer (1994b), the traditional view described in Section 11.1 and Section 11.2.1 was challenged for the English development of HAVE-*to*.

---

[6] Cf. Hofstadter and Sander (2013: 15), who write '[t]here is no scarcity of people who believe that this [i.e. proportional analogy], no more and no less, is what the phenomenon of analogy is – namely, a template always involving exactly four lexical items (in fact, usually four words)'. They also mention that the term *proportional analogy* 'is itself based on an analogy between words and numbers – namely, the idea that an equation expressing the idea that one pair of numbers has the same ratio as another pair does ($A/B = C/D$) can be carried over directly to the world of words and concepts'.

Fischer argued on the basis of corpus evidence, which showed the frequencies of the various HAVE+infinitive constructions involved and the rather later emergence of the new grammaticalised form (later, in comparison to the traditional view) that in fact the word order change (whereby HAVE and the *to*-infinitive became adjacent) should be seen as a cause rather than a result of the grammaticalisation process. Fischer (2015), however, partially rejects her own earlier view, namely the idea that the word order change was the *only* cause for the changes seen in HAVE-*to*. She shows in her revised version of the process that in order to come to an understanding of what happened, we need to look not only at the construction itself undergoing change, but also at neighbouring constructions which show similarities in either form or meaning or both.[7]

Word order still remains an important element, related as it is to the fact that elsewhere verbs and infinitives came to be adjacent and fixed in position, thus providing a structural analogy for seeing HAVE+*to*-infinitive also as a unit. The word order change was especially relevant in cases where both HAVE and the *to*-infinitive *shared* an object, as in (1a) below.[8] Since in these cases the semantic relation between the object and the infinitive was often stronger than the one between (weak possessive) HAVE and this object, a strong tendency arose for the object to follow the infinitive when the word order in subordinate clauses (including non-finite ones) changed from OV to VO in the course of the Middle English (ME) period (cf. Fischer 1994b: 147–8). In addition, however, it is argued in Fischer (2015) that the new construction was supported analogically by other constructions, notably constructions involving the noun and verb *need* (see (1b)–(1e)), and the early existential use of HAVE, where it is used as an equivalent form of BE (see (2)).[9]

---

[7] The importance of multiple sources in the development of new constructions is also emphasised in the articles collected in De Smet *et al.* (2015).
[8] The examples in (1) are taken from the *Corpus of Middle English Prose and Verse* (CME), the corpus on which Fischer's (2015) data was based, and (2) is taken from the *Dictionary of Old English Web Corpus* (DOEC).
[9] This latter development in the grammaticalisation of possessives into existentials is also quite common world-wide. Evidence for this can be found in Heine and Kuteva (2002: 241–2). Heine (1997: 83ff.) discusses in detail the close relation between possessive and existential constructions when he shows the relations and possible developments between the 'Action Schema' of possession, which uses active possessive verbs like HAVE with a possessor as agent and the possessee as object, and the two schemas that function with an existential verb like BE (the 'Companion Schema' and the 'Goal Schema'), where the possessor is not agentive. On the evolution of possessive and existential constructions, see also Creissels (2013).

(1) a. By nyȝte, whanne   he hadde   no man to teche
       by night when   he had   no man to teach
       'By night, when there was no one that he could/should teach'
                                            (CME, Trevisa, *Polychronicon*)
    b. ȝif þei   **had   nede to ride** in þat   contrey
       if they   had   need to ride   in that country
       'if they had a need to ride in that country'
                                            (CME, *Three Kings of Cologne*)
    c. **To passe** þe se   **hastow**   no **nede**.
       to cross   the sea   hast-thou   no need
       'To cross the sea, you have no need.'
                                            (CME, *Guy of Warwick*)
    d. what **nede were the /   To selle** thi thrift   so hastely?
       what need were for thee to sell   thy prosperity   so hastily
       'what need would there be for you to sell your heritage so hastily?'
                                            (CME, *Altengl. Legenden*)
    e. **Me nedith**   not no lenger **doon**   diligence
       me needs   not no longer do   diligence
       'It is no longer necessary for me to do my best.'
                                            (CME, Chaucer, *Wife of Bath's Preamble*)

(2) And **her beoð**   swyþe   genihtsume   weolocas [...]   **Hit hafað**
    and here are   very   abundant   whelks   it   has
    eac þis   land   sealtseaþas, and hit   hafaþ   hat   wæter
    also this   land   salt-springs and it   has   hot   water
    'And there are plenty of whelks [...] The country also has (or: "there are also") salt springs and hot water.'
                                            (DOEC, c.900, Bede 1, 026.9)

These various neighbouring constructions all contributed to the 'necessity' meaning that HAVE-*to* acquired (rather than e.g. future meaning, another possibility), a development that the traditional gradual semantic-pragmatic grammaticalisation account cannot really explain. Fischer (2015) stresses the strong role played by analogy, analogy of a quite concrete type (i.e. the use of the same lexical items in a construction) as well as of a more abstract formal type (i.e. the use of a particular syntactic pattern). In a nutshell, the following abstract and (partially) concrete structures were seen to be important in and contribute to the development of modal HAVE-*to*:

i. The increasing structural adjacency of HAVE and the *to*-infinitive, due to increased SVO order (including a high frequency of preposed – topicalised or *wh*-moved – direct objects) (for quantitative details of these structures see Fischer 2015: 138)

ii. The increase in the adjacency of HAVE and the verb *to do*, next to the new use HAVE-*to-do* in the sense of 'have dealings with' (a construction without an object), which provided a further structural adjacency pattern (in the latter case the analogy was not functionally supported) (see Fischer 2015: 135, Table 2)

iii. The very high occurrence of the HAVE-*a-need-to*+infinitive construction, which provided a functional (i.e. a similar, necessity meaning) as well as a structural similarity (adjacency) pattern (especially when the object *need* was moved to the front of the clause; see also (i))

iv. The functional similarity between HAVE-*a-need-to* and constructions containing the impersonal verbs *neden*/BE-*nede* followed by a *to*-infinitive, all expressing external necessity

v. The loss of impersonal *neden*/BE-*nede* in late ME (a period in which most impersonal constructions were lost), creating a need for a new construction expressing external necessity (the new personal verb *neden* only expressed internal necessity)

vi. The functional and concrete similarity between the constructions MUST-*nedes*+infinitive and HAVE-*a-need-to*+infinitive, and the fact that *nedes* came to be left out after MUST creating the possibility for also leaving out *need* in the construction HAVE-*a-need-to*

vii. Due to (vi), the new role played by the subject in the HAVE-*to*+infinitive construction, which now (i.e. without the object *need*) resembles constructions with existential HAVE, which also show the use of a subject without a semantic role of 'agent' and no object. This makes HAVE-*to* a suitable replacement for the lost impersonal BE-*nede*/*neden* (see (v) and (1d)–(1e)) which also had no agentive subject.

The frequency and the importance of *nede* in connection with HAVE and the formal and semantic parallelism with MUST-*nedes* and the impersonal BE-*nede* (points (iii) and (iv) above) are shown in Table 11.1, adapted from Fischer (2015: 141): occurrences in CME of HAVE combined with the noun *nede* (usually) together with a *(for) to*-infinitive (the exceptions are subtypes (d) and possibly (e)); of MUST with the adverbial use of the noun *nede(s)* +(usually) zero-infinitive; and of impersonal BE with *nede*+*to*-infinitive.

Table 11.1 HAVE, MUST, *and* BE *with* nede

Main types	Subtypes	Totals
HAVE + *nede* + infinitive/NP	(a) HAVE + *nede* + PP/NP + *to*-infinitive	9
	(b) HAVE + *nede* + (*for*) *to*-infinitive	78
	(c) *to*-infinitive + HAVE + *nede*	54
	(d) HAVE + *nede* + NP + object	54
	(e) HAVE + *nede* + *to*-infinitive OR NP-object (unclear)	7
	Total of occurrences of HAVE combined with *nede*	202
MUST + *nede(s)* + zero infinitive	(f) *mot(e)(n)* etc. + *nede* + zero (occasionally *to*-) infinitive	131
	(g) *mot(e)(n)* etc. + *nedes* + zero infinitive	96
	Total	227
Impersonal BE + *nede* + *to*-infinitive	(h) *is, was, war, wer(e)(n), be nede* + *to*-infinitive	188
	Grand total of constructions involving *nede*	617

Only combinations with *nede(s)* have been counted, other spellings (*neod(e)*, *need(e)*) being rare. It is important to note in connection with Table 11.1 that the form *nede* occurs in total 4,442 times in the corpus, of which at least 174 instances are verbs, leaving roughly 4,268 nouns. This means that about 14 per cent of all occurrences of the noun *nede* occur in the type of constructions collected in Table 11.1.

To sum up, it is argued that all these synchronically available constructions sharing formal and semantic features with each other co-determined the formal and functional development of HAVE+*to* into a semi-modal auxiliary expressing external necessity.

11.4 Spanish TENER-*que*

11.4.1 Introduction

In this section we will discuss the historical development and the modern usage of Spanish TENER-*que*, literally 'have which', which will turn out to parallel that of HAVE-*to* in a number of respects.[10] Before going into details,

---

[10] A more detailed study of this phenomenon based on the same data is Olbertz (2018).

however, let us first consider some basic properties of TENER-*que*: (i) the relation with its competitors and (ii) its meanings. Consider the following example of TENER-*que* and its competitors (3).[11]

(3) A las once_y_media sería   la reunión con los de la firma
    at the half-past-eleven would-be the meeting with the of the firm
    y   **tenía   que /** **había de / debía** **(de) / había   que**
    and had-he   to   had-he to must-he (to)   there-was to
    presentarles   algo   convincente.
    present[INF]-them   something convincing
    'At half past eleven the meeting with the people of the company would take place and he had to show / there had to be shown something convincing to them.'
    (1982 Lourdes Ortiz, 'Paisajes y figuras')

Example (3) shows that, in addition to TENER-*que*, there are three competing constructions, namely HABER-*de* 'have to', the modal DEBER and its free variant DEBER-*de* 'must',[12] inherited from Latin *debere*, and the impersonal modal construction with HABER-*que*, literally 'there to-be which'. This means that, whereas English HAVE-*to* is the only possession-based modal expression, Spanish has three possession-based modal constructions. However, there are only a few contexts that allow the use of all three of them.

As regards the meanings of TENER-*que*, consider (4) and (5), which illustrate internal (auto-imposed) and external (directive) deontic necessity meanings.

(4) **Tengo que llamar**le   como sea,   **tengo que hablar**
    have-I to   call[INF]-him   how may-be have-I to   speak[INF]
    con   él   pase.   lo_que   pase.
    with   him may-happen   what   may-happen
    'I must call him now, I must talk to him, whatever may happen.'
    (1990 Carmen Rico Godoy, *Cómo ser una mujer y no morir en el intento* [CREA])

---

[11] In order to keep the glosses to a minimum and at the same time provide the necessary morphological information, we have added an appendix listing the relevant parts of the verbal paradigms of the two verbs that are central in this account, viz. TENER and HABER, both for Modern and for Medieval Spanish.
[12] See Eddington and Silva-Corvalán (2011) on the nature of this variation.

(5) Para eso la pagamos, ¿no? [...] **tiene que barrer**,
for that her pay-we not has-she to sweep[INF]
fregar, limpiar los cristales, regar las plantas
mop[INF] clean[INF] the windows water[INF] the plants
y acercarse a Correos.
and approach[INF] to post-office
'This is what we pay her for, isn't it? [...] she has to sweep, to mop, to clean the windows, to water the plants, and to go to the post-office.'

(1995 Adolfo Marsillach, *Se vende ático* [CREA])

The meanings of (4) and (5) could, in principle, also be expressed by HABER-*de* and DEBER(-*de*), but probably not by the impersonal HABER-*que*.

TENER-*que* expresses a different type of external necessity meaning in (6), in which the source of the modality is not the will of an individual (either the subject-referent or someone else) or a social norm, but an inanimate entity incapable of will (cf. Narrog 2012: 46–9).

(6) La carne **tuvimos que tirar**la:
the meat had-we to throw-away[INF]-it
la humedad la había corrompido.
the wetness it had rotten
'We had to throw away the meat: it had gone off due to the humidity.'

(1985 Julio Llamazares, *Luna de lobos*)

This type of modality can also be expressed by HABER-*de* and HABER-*que*, but not by DEBER(-*de*) (cf. Olbertz forthcoming).

In addition, TENER-*que* can express epistemic modality, albeit less frequently than DEBER(-*de*) – see (7).

(7) Me voy, Julio, es ya tarde y **tienes que estar**
myself go-I Julio is already late and have-you to be[INF]
cansado.
tired
'I'm leaving, Julio, it's already late and you must be tired.'

(2013 Álvaro Pombo, *Relatos sobre la falta de sustancia y otros relatos*)

Apart from TENER-*que* and DEBER(-*de*), HABER-*de* is also possible for the expression of epistemic necessity, but the impersonal construction HABER-*que* is not (Gómez Torrego 1999: 3357; García Fernández 2006: 164, 167).

Table 11.2 *Frequencies of verbal expressions of modal necessity in spoken Modern Spanish*

	TENER-*que*	HABER-*que*	DEBER*(-de)*	HABER-*de*	Totals
absolute numbers	816	232	89	5	1,142
percentages	71.45	20.32	7.79	0.44	100

This means that, like HAVE-*to*, TENER-*que* can express any kind of modal necessity. Although, in principle, the same holds for HABER-*de*, in spoken Peninsular Spanish TENER-*que* is over 150 times more frequent than HABER-*de*. Table 11.2 shows the overall frequency relations of the four constructions.[13]

Finally, it is important to note that, whereas Spanish periphrastic verbal constructions (carrying modal and aspectual meanings) are generally constructed with prepositions before the infinitive, either *a* or *de*, TENER-*que* and impersonal HABER-*que* are the only constructions to be conjoined with the infinitive by means of what was originally a relative pronoun. As will become clear in Section 11.4.2, this relative pronoun functioned at first as the 'shared' object of both TENER/HABER and the infinitive (a situation rather similar to the shared object in the HAVE-construction in OE and ME, cf. (1a) above). Later the pronoun loses its object function, and begins to function as an infinitival marker. This 'loss' of its object function is in some ways comparable to the loss of the object noun *need* in the ME construction (cf. points (vi) and (vii) above in Section 11.3) in that in both cases it allowed the finite verb and the infinitive to become adjacent, enabling the grammaticalisation of the original possessive verb into a (semi-)modal auxiliary.

In the following we will first show how TENER-*que* came into existence in Medieval Spanish (Section 11.4.2). Given that TENER-*que* is the youngest of the four competing constructions, we will have to consider the constructions with HABER too (Section 11.4.3 on Medieval Spanish and Section 11.4.4 on the sixteenth to nineteenth centuries), as well as a number of other linguistic facts in order to show how and why TENER-*que* has become the most popular expression of modal necessity in Modern Spanish (Section 11.4.5). We will end this section with a short

---

[13] These data are based on a 443,533-word oral corpus from Alcalá de Henares (Moreno Fernández *et al.* 2002–2007), which contains a total of 1,142 tokens of modal auxiliaries.

summary (Section 11.4.6). The analysis is based on Spanish literary prose mainly from the two online databases provided by the *Real Academia Española: Corpus Diacrónico del Español* (CORDE) for historical and the *Corpus de Referencia del Español Actual* (CREA) for late twentieth-century data.

However, before going into any detail, two preliminary explanations are required. First, Medieval Spanish has two possessive verbs, TENER and AVER (= Modern Spanish HABER). AVER also functions as a perfect auxiliary and loses its lexical function between the fifteenth and the seventeenth centuries, leaving TENER as the only possessive verb. Secondly, whereas the change of constituent order between the OE and ME periods is crucial for the development of semi-modal HAVE-*to*, the corresponding word order change from preferred SOV in Classical Latin to SVO in Romance took place long before the first Spanish documented text (Bauer 2009), which probably dates from the early eleventh century. This means that the documented history of Spanish begins in the period that corresponds to ME rather than OE. This is why the auxiliary, the connecting element, and the infinitive are contiguous in Spanish from the very beginning.[14] It should also be noted that the strict SVO constituent order is what crucially distinguishes English and Spanish on the one hand from Dutch and German on the other (see Section 11.5).

11.4.2 How Did TENER-que Come into Existence?

The following two examples (8) and (9) are representative of the earliest occurrences of TENER-*que* in Medieval Spanish literary prose.

(8) **mucho tengo que** vos **gradescer** por el bien que
    much have-I which to-you thank[INF] for the good which
    de vos me viene
    from you to-me come
    'much I have to thank you for the good things which come to me from you'
    (1482–1492 Garci Rodríguez de Montalvo, *Amadís de Gaula* [CORDE])

---

[14] Although the clitic has always tended to precede finite verbs and to follow infinitives or gerunds – a positioning that became standard by the end of the sixteenth century (Nieuwenhuijsen 2006: 1346) – in the earlier texts the clitic occasionally precedes the infinitive, thus interrupting the construction.

(9) e   vio   los diablos que ponian todos los males   que
    and saw-he   the devils who put   all   the bad-things which
    avia   fecho en una balança de peso   e de la   otra   parte
    had-he done in a   balance of weight and on the other side
    estando los angeles tristes   porque **non tenian que   poner**
    being the angels unhappy because not   had   which put[INF]
    en la   balança
    in the balance
    'and he saw the devils who put all the bad things which he had done on
    the weighing scales and on the other side there were the angels [being]
    unhappy because they had nothing to put on the scales' (literally: 'they
    had not which [to] put on the scales')
    (1400–1421 Clemente Sánchez de Vercial, *Libro de los exemplos por A.B.C.*
    [CORDE])

In both examples, possessive TENER and the verb in the infinitive share both their subject and their object. The referent of the object is the head of the relative pronoun *que*. Example (8) illustrates a minimally headed relative clause, the head being the indefinite quantifier *mucho*, and (9) is representative of the frequent case of a headless relative clause which is typically negated, thus implicating *nada* 'nothing' as a head. The way in which the construction must be interpreted depends entirely on the context, i.e. on the verb in the infinitive and on the nature of the shared arguments. In (8) a necessity reading is the most logical one and in (9) the most obvious reading is that of possibility. This situation is again comparable to the situation in OE and ME where a similar construction containing a shared object and subject could also express both possibility and necessity depending on context; see (1a) above.

Given that negated headless relative constructions analogous to (9) have been attested in Latin already (Lehmann 1988: 208), it is not surprising that we find, even before the first attested cases of TENER-*que*, attestations of a parallel construction in Medieval Spanish with the – by then synonymous – verb AVER (Modern Spanish HABER) – see (10).

(10) non puede ser   que yo non vaya   a aquella isla,   ca
     not can-it be[INF]   that I not go   to that   island since
     non has   que   temer en ir   yo a aquel lugar;
     not have-you which fear[INF] in go[INF] I to that place
     'it cannot be that I do not go to that island, since you have nothing to
     fear when I go to that place;' (literally: 'you have not which [to] fear')
     (1251 Anonymous, *Calila e Dimna* [CORDE])

Both TENER-*que* and AVER-*que* remain infrequent in Medieval Spanish.[15] However, both come to be grammaticalised into verbal expressions of necessity in the nineteenth century or even later, TENER-*que* more rapidly than AVER/HABER-*que*. In order to account for these facts, we must first have a look at the other expressions of modal necessity based on possessive verbs that were in use before AVER-*que* and TENER-*que*.

11.4.3 Other Possession-Based Modal Constructions

Apart from the ubiquitous Latin-based modal DEBER and its Medieval Spanish variant *dever*, the oldest Medieval Spanish prose texts contain examples of AVER followed by the preposition *a* or *de* and an infinitive. Although these two prepositions have basic locative meanings (directional for *a* and source for *de*), they are virtually meaningless in the present context. Both *a* and *de* are in use until the end of the fifteenth century, although with the highly frequent third-person singular present tense form *ha*, the preposition *de* has always been preferred, probably for euphonic reasons.[16] In the sixteenth century the preposition *a* was definitively ousted by *de*. The 'choice' for the preposition *de* may have been on analogy with the older construction SER-*de* 'be to' (Yllera 1980: 96).[17]

In the remainder of this section, we will first consider the grammaticalisation of AVER-*de* and then provide a possible explanation of how it acquired the meaning of modal necessity. Note that in (11) AVER combines with an intransitive verb, i.e. there is no possible possessee argument for AVER. In (12), auxiliary AVER combines with 'itself', i.e. with AVER as a possessive verb, and in (13) it combines with a copular verb.

(11) Et   ssi emienda   deue sser   ffecha a los omnes, quanto
     and   if   atonement must be[INF]   made   to the men   how-much
     más   a   Dios, que nos ffizo, a   cuyo juizio   **auemos**
     more to God   who us made   to   whose judgement have-we
     a   yr.
     to   go[INF]

---

[15] There is a total of eleven cases of AVER-*que* and thirteen examples of TENER-*que* in the present tense in narrative prose between the twelfth and the fifteenth centuries in CORDE, the largest diachronic corpus of Spanish.
[16] In the CORDE juridical prose texts of the twelfth and thirteenth centuries, the preposition *a* prevails in the second-person plural forms *auedes/avedes*, but with the third-person singular form *ha*, the preposition *de* is more than three times as frequent as *a*.
[17] Interestingly, it is by analogy with SER-*de* and AVER-*de* that the Latin-based *deber* also comes to be used with the preposition *de* sometimes, and in the first texts occasionally with *a* (Yllera 1980: 128).

'And if atonement must be made to men, how much more to God, who made us, and to whose judgement we will go.'

(1252–1270 Alfonso X, *Setenario* [CORDE])

(12) E   dixo   que **ha   de aver**   en el   creyente diez_e_seis
     and   said-he that has-it to have[INF] in the believer sixteen
     virtudes
     virtues
     'And he said that the believer has to have sixteen virtues.'

(1250 Anonymous, *Bocados de Oro* [CORDE])

(13) Ca todo aquel   que es mesturero   por fuerça   **ha de ser**
     for all   that-one who is tell-tale   by force   has to be[INF]
     dezidor & asacador   de todo mal
     teller & instigator of all   evil
     'For whoever is a tell-tale, necessarily must be one who tells and instigates all evil.'

(1293 Anonymous, *Castigos* [CORDE])

What motivates this high degree of grammaticalisation is the fact that the construction has its origin as early as Classical Latin. Pinkster (1987: 205–6) shows that the first attested example of the Latin *habere* +infinitive construction is from a text by Cicero dating from 80 BC; the construction becoming somewhat more frequent in the second century AD. The Latin construction had a future-oriented meaning with a modal overtone, such that *habere* could be substituted with a form of *posse* 'can' or of *debere* 'must', the choice between the two being entirely context-dependent.

As regards the semantics of the early construction, it may be that of futurity as in (11) but it may also have a modal meaning, as illustrated in (12) and (13). The future meaning coexists with the modal meaning until early Modern Spanish, and even in twentieth-century texts there are incidental uses of HABER-*de* with a future sense.[18] This may seem strange as there already was a specialised expression for the future in Medieval Spanish, i.e. the combination of an infinitive with auxiliary HABER, which had already fused into a new synthetic form in most contexts. However, the origins of the HABER-*de* construction and the synthetic future are very similar: Latin *habere*+infinitive for what became the modal construction and

---

[18] In Present-day Spanish HABER-*de* is even used as the default form of the future in some American varieties spoken in e.g. Ecuador and Mexico (see also Real Academia Española and Asociación de Academias de la Lengua Española 2009: 2146–7).

infinitive+*habere* for the future (Fleischman 1982: 113; Pinkster 1987: 205–14), which motivates the association of HABER-*de* with the future.[19]

With respect to the modal meaning, (12) and (13) are representative of both Medieval and Modern Spanish HABER-*de* in the sense that they are both expressions of modal necessity, i.e. the meaning no longer depends on the context as in the case of the Latin predecessor. The explanation for this lies probably in the highly frequent collocation of AVER with *menester de* 'need of' followed either by an infinitive or a noun phrase.[20] Consider the following example (14) with an infinitive.

(14) E   despues_que en algunos dias oujere assy bolado **has**
      and after   in several days had-he thus flown   have-you
      menester   de catar   otro   falcon
      need   of watch[INF]   another falcon
      'And after having thus flown for several days, you need to/have to watch a different falcon.'
      (1386 Pedro López de Ayala, *Libro de la caça de las aves* [CORDE])

The perceived analogy of AVER-*de*+infinitive with AVER-*menester-de*+infinitive (or NP) will have strengthened the association of AVER-*de* with necessity in very much the same way as the collocation of HAVE with *nede* +*to*-infinitive in English prompted the necessity reading of HAVE-*to*, as indicated in Section 11.3. In addition, the now obsolete noun *menester* 'need', also occurred as an impersonal construction with the copula *ser* 'to be' (again, just like ME, see (1d) in Section 11.3),[21] but from medieval times onward, until its obsolescence in the nineteenth century, the personal construction AVER/HABER *menester de* was the most frequent collocation.

---

[19] The difference between the two is that infinitive+*habere* is more grammaticalised and probably older: although word order is flexible in Classical Latin, there is a preference for SOV in main clauses, such that the finite verb would be at the end of the clause (Pinkster 1987: 281–3; Bauer 2009), and therefore it is probable that the new future was formed in that period. This difference in periodisation explains why the Medieval Spanish synthetic future is much more frequent in the early texts than HABER-*de*+infinitive: in the thirteenth-century texts of CORDE, there are 6,214 tokens of the third-person singular future against 682 corresponding forms of HABER-*de*+infinitive.

[20] In the *Corpus del Español*, *menester* is one of the most frequent words to immediately follow all forms of AVER in the thirteenth to fifteenth centuries. Only the perfect constructions with the participles *fecho* 'done' and *dicho* 'said' are more frequent.

[21] In the following example the use of *menester* parallels that of *nede* in example (1d) in Section 11.3:
    Agora nos   es   menester de   aver   consejo como ayamos
    now   for-us is   need   to   have[INF]   advice   how   would-have-we
    de   fablar   ante   nuestro   señor   Verenguer
    to   speak[INF]   in-front-of   our   Sir   Verenguer
    'Now we need to have advice on how to speak in front of our Sir Verenguer.'
    (1400–1498 Anonymous, *El baladro del sabio Merlín con sus profecías* [CORDE])

Once the necessity reading of AVER-*de* had been firmly established, the innovative constructions AVER-*que* and TENER-*que* analogically 'inherited' this reading.

On analogy with AVER-*de*, and possibly also motivated by the Latin-based *ser tenudo a/de* 'be liable to' (see Garachana Camarero 2017), TENER-*de* arises in the course of the thirteenth century and gains a certain frequency in the fourteenth century. Consider (15).

(15) Pero antes fablaré con vos **algunas cosas** que
 but before will-speak-I with you some things which
 tengo de fablar.
 have-I to speak[INF]
 'But first I will tell you some things I have to tell.'
 (1300–1305 Anonymous, *Libro del Cavallero Cifar* [CORDE])

Example (15) is entirely parallel to (8)–(10), in that the possessive finite verb and the non-finite verb share both the subject and the object referent. However, in the fifteenth century we already find more grammaticalised instances of TENER-*de* – see (16) and (17).

(16) la mysma obydyencya, amor y acatamiento os
 the same obedience love and respect to-you
 tengo de tener como antes
 have-I to have[INF] as before
 'the same obedience, love, and respect I will have for you as before'
 (1492 Anonymous, *La corónica de Adramón* [CORDE])

(17) yo le dyré que **tengo de yr** allá
 I to-him will-say-I that have-I to go[INF] there
 con más gente.
 with more people
 'I will tell him that I have to go there with more people.'
 (1492 Anonymous, *La corónica de Adramón* [CORDE])

In (16) the finite verb TENER combines with the infinitive of TENER, due to which the first TENER can only be read as an auxiliary. In (17) TENER occurs with an intransitive verb, so there is no object to be shared by both verbs, and therefore a possessive reading of the finite verb is excluded. With regard to the semantics of TENER-*de* in these examples, (16) illustrates its use for the expression of futurity and (17) for that of modal necessity. This means that, in spite of its initially lexical nature, the development of TENER-*de* is entirely analogous to that of AVER-*a/de*: it grammaticalises rapidly and comes to express the same meanings as its predecessor.[22] However, differently from the construction with AVER, TENER-*de* never becomes really frequent (see Table 11.3 in Section 11.4.4 below).

Having considered the competing possession-based constructions, AVER-*de* and TENER-*de*, let us now return to the constructions with a relative pronoun, TENER-*que* and AVER-*que*.

11.4.4 Postmedieval TENER-que and HABER-que

For a better understanding of what happens with TENER-*que*, let us first consider the story of HABER-*que*, which in the course of the fifteenth century disappears in its personal use and takes on an impersonal function instead. This impersonal use arises in the thirteenth century from an existential use of HABER, which begins with the collocation of the third-person singular present tense *ha* 'has-he/she/it' with the now extinct particle *y* 'there', the combination soon being written as *hay*. (Note here again the links between existential possessive verbs and impersonal constructions, as we saw in English too, cf. (iv), (v), and (vii) in Section 11.3.) In the course of the fifteenth century the existential HABER spreads to other tenses. In the same period, impersonal HABER comes to be used with *que*+infinitive in what will gradually become an impersonal expression of modal necessity. Consider the following two examples (18) and (19).

(18) Acábese la misa, que **mucho hay que parlar**
may-end the mass for much there-is which talk[INF]
del sermón.
of-the sermon
'May the mass end soon, for there is much to talk about the sermon.'
(1550 Juan de Arce de Otálora,
Coloquios de Palatino y Pinciano [CORDE])

(19) **Hay que ser** tolerantes con los que están debajo,
there-is to be[INF] tolerant with the which are below
porque si los de debajo se mueven se cae
because if the from below themselves move himself fall-he
el que está encima.
the who is above

---

[22] For more details on the relationship between AVER-*de* and TENER-*de*, see Garachana Camarero and Rosemeyer (2011: 38–46) and Garachana Camarero (2017).

'One must be tolerant with those from below, because as soon as those from below move, the one who is above will fall.'
(1898 Ángel Ganivet, *Los trabajos del infatigable creador Pío Cid* [CORDE])

Example (18) is representative for the use of the HABER-*que* construction until the nineteenth century: an existential construction with a headless relative construction indicating a purpose-like function. To the degree that impersonal SER *menester* 'be necessary' becomes obsolete, *hay que* fills the gap and grammaticalises. In (19) it is followed by a copular construction; *que* is no longer a relative pronoun and the construction functions as an impersonal expression of necessity.

The TENER-*que* construction is still rare in Medieval Spanish, and in the fifteenth century it occurs exclusively in contexts that are compatible with a lexical reading of TENER-*que*, like the cases quoted in (8) and (9) above. In the sixteenth century, however, when TENER-*que* becomes more frequent than TENER-*de*, there are first signs of grammaticalisation – see (20).

(20) Yo **tengo que pescar** anguilas en el río Nilo
I have-I to fish[INF] eels in the river Nile
'I have to fish eels in the river Nile.'
(1542 Anonymous, *Baldo* [CORDE])

In this example (20), *que* can no longer be read as a relative pronoun, because there is an explicit object, *anguilas*, which follows the infinitival verb and cannot be interpreted as the head of a relative clause because *que*, rather than following *anguilas*, precedes the infinitive. Therefore, *que* now merely functions as a nexus between the finite form of TENER and the infinitive, in the same way as *de* precedes the infinitive in HABER-*de* and TENER-*de* and *to* precedes the infinitive in English. In other words, the object (*anguilas*) is no longer 'shared' by the infinitive and TENER as it was in the earlier constructions as in (8)–(10) above – and similarly for English in (1a) – but is now the object of the infinitive only.

In addition, now that TENER-*que* itself can be used without an object, instances with intransitive verbs begin to gradually emerge – see (21).

(21) Cristo **tenía que morir** por el hombre.
Christ had to die[INF] by the human
'Christ had to die by human hand.'
(1613 San Juan Bautista de la Concepción, *Algunas penas del justo en el camino de la perfección* [CORDE])

But, as in the case of HABER-*que*, it is only in the nineteenth century, when TENER-*que* begins to become more frequent than HABER-*de*, that the construction comes to be systematically used with intransitive verbs and other expressions that are incompatible with any other reading than that of modal necessity, such as in (22), where TENER-*que* is followed by the copula *ser*.

(22) Ademas, en el clima cálido **tiene que ser** precisamente el
moreover in the climate warm has to be[INF] precisely the
alimento de carne en menor cantidad que en el clima frio,
food of meat in less quantity than in the climate cold
'Moreover, in the warm climate it is precisely meat that has to constitute a smaller part of the food than in the cold climate.'
(1832 Ventura de Peña y Valle, *Tratado general de carnes* [CORDE])

The comparison with English is again noteworthy. Only after the intermediate object *nede* (as in (1c) above) has disappeared between HAVE and the infinitive, and the original shared object (as in (1a)) has acquired a regular position *after* the infinitive, does HAVE-*to* begin to be used with intransitive verbs. This happens slowly, and only becomes regular in the nineteenth century (cf. Krug 2000: 89–90).

The quantitative relations between the different Spanish constructions in postmedieval written texts from the sixteenth to the twentieth century are represented in Table 11.3.[23] It should be noted that the apparent perseverance of HABER-*de* is due to the fact that Table 11.3 is based on literary texts, to which HABER-*de* has become restricted in the twentieth century (Fernández de Castro 1999: 191–3). The situation is very different in the spoken data, with a much stronger preference for TENER-*que* than in written texts (see Table 11.2 in Section 11.4.1 above).

The two sets of parallel HABER/TENER constructions with *de* and *que*, respectively, had very different fates. In principle, only one of the two continues to be used, in the case of *de* this is HABER, while TENER-*de* has in

---

[23] To keep control over the data, the numbers in Table 11.3 are based on the preterite stems of the auxiliaries, yielding the preterite and the past subjunctive paradigm, which are sufficiently infrequent to allow for a full-fledged count in CORDE and CREA. A count of the more frequent present tense stems would have implied an obligatory random selection of the data, which would have made a quantitative comparison impossible. The 1500–1950 data are from all genres of narrative prose from the diachronic corpus CORDE. The relatively small number of tokens between 1650 and 1800 are due to the reduced literary production of that period. The data from 1950–2000 are a mix from CORDE (1950–1975) and the modern corpus CREA (1975–2000), where only novels have been taken into account.

Table 11.3 *The quantitative relations between possession-based expressions of necessity*

	HABER-*de*		TENER-*de*		HABER-*que*		TENER-*que*		Totals	
1500–1550	37	56.9%	15	23.1%	0	0.0%	13	20.0%	65	100%
1550–1600	115	78.8%	19	13.0%	0	0.0%	12	8.2%	146	100%
1600–1650	381	88.4%	31	7.2%	6	1.4%	13	3.0%	431	100%
1650–1700	26	81.3%	1	3.1%	3	9.4%	2	6.2%	32	100%
1700–1750	7	100.0%	0	0.0%	0	0.0%	0	0.0%	7	100%
1750–1800	85	82.5%	5	4.9%	0	0.0%	13	12.6%	103	100%
1800–1850	193	61.1%	3	0.9%	6	1.9%	114	36.1%	316	100%
1850–1900	414	37.9%	12	1.1%	44	4.0%	623	57.0%	1,093	100%
1900–1950	835	52.7%	10	0.6%	61	3.9%	678	42.8%	1,584	100%
1950–2000	572	19.8%	23	0.8%	197	6.8%	2,100	72.6%	2,892	100%

fact ceased to exist.[24] In the *que*-construction, it is probably due to the specialisation of HABER-*que* to the impersonal construction that TENER-*que* has survived. The question now is: why has TENER-*que* become so popular?

11.4.5 *The Rise of* TENER-que *to the Detriment of* HABER-de

There are at least two reasons why TENER-*que* is replacing HABER-*de*. First, in the seventeenth century HABER definitively loses its possessive meaning, leaving TENER as the only expression of unmarked possession. According to Hernández Díaz (2006: 1064), possessive TENER is already more frequent than HABER in the course of the fifteenth century. Second, HABER becomes the only auxiliary used in the perfect, a process that was completed in the course of the sixteenth century. Whereas HABER is now primarily associated with its auxiliary function, the continuing possessive meaning of TENER allows for the association of modal TENER-*que* with its lexical counterpart, the headed relative clause – see (23a) (cf. Olbertz 1998: 250–3); this construction fully parallels the English one given in (23b). In both Modern Spanish and Present-day English, these are fairly common construction types.

(23) a. **Tenemos** muchas cosas **que contar**nos.
 have-we many things which tell[INF]-us
 'We have many things to tell to each other.'
 (1995 Ignacio Carrión, *Cruzar el Danubio* [CREA])

---

[24] The remaining cases of TENER-*de* in the twentieth century consist of intentional archaisms and quotes from older texts.

b. we **have much to** thank the Romans for
(1993 Robert Rankin, *The Book of Ultimate Truths* [BYU-BNC])

As in (1a) and (8)–(10), the object is shared by TENER/HAVE and the infinitive, and again, as in the older constructions, the examples in (23) may, but need not, be interpreted in terms of necessity.

11.4.6 Summary

The following circumstances may be held responsible for the development of TENER-*que* as a modal expression of necessity and its predominance in this function in Modern Spanish:

i. As in OE, the predominant word order was SOV in Classical Latin. The development into predominant SVO probably took place somewhat earlier than in English, because in Medieval Spanish SVO is standard, so that the order in the new modal constructions is AVER/TENER+nexus+infinitive.
ii. In Latin and Medieval Spanish there are two constructions with possessive verb+infinitive that have a general future-oriented meaning and allow for both a possibility and a necessity reading, i.e. *habere*+infinitive in Latin and the headless relative constructions with AVER and later with TENER in Medieval Spanish.
iii. The first construction mentioned in (ii), inherited into Medieval Spanish as AVER-*de*, has an exclusive necessity reading. This is likely to be motivated by the fact that, from the first Medieval Spanish texts onward and probably long before that in everyday speech, AVER highly frequently collocates with the now obsolete *menester de* followed by an infinitive (or a NP) to express the meaning of 'have a need to (of)'. This situation closely parallels that of ME HAVE+*nede* +*to*-infinitive.
iv. When the second construction-type mentioned in (ii), i.e. AVER/ HABER-*que* and TENER-*que*, begins to compete with AVER/HABER-*de*, thus taking over the necessity reading, *que* no longer introduces a headless relative clause. This is made clear by the fact that there is either an explicit object following, or the infinitive is intransitive. Instead, *que* functions as a nexus between the finite verb and the infinitive similar to *de* in Spanish and *to* in English.
v. Based on the existential use of AVER/HABER, AVER/HABER-*que* becomes an impersonal construction, thus filling the gap left by

ser menester 'be necessary', which has become obsolete in the nineteenth century, leaving TENER-*que* as the only 'personal' necessity construction.

vi. HABER becomes the only auxiliary of the perfect and loses its possessive meaning, leaving TENER as the only possessive verb.
vii. Due to (vi), HABER is primarily associated with the perfect, while TENER-*que* has the advantage of maintaining the association with (weak) possession. This is why TENER-*que* is now about to oust HABER-*de*.

11.5 A Comparison of Developments in English and Spanish against the Background of Dutch and German

There are clearly many similarities between the developments of HAVE-*to* and TENER-*que* in Present-day English and Spanish, even though the Spanish expression has a more complicated history due to the occurrence of more than one possessive verb. In both languages they may express any kind of modal necessity: internal, external (including deontic), and epistemic necessity. This is not the case in Dutch and German, as the examples in (24) show.

(24) a. What time do you have to go to work? (external necessity)
(1991 27 conversations recorded by Betty [BYU-BNC])

   Dutch: **Hoe laat heb je naar je werk te gaan?*
   German: **Um wieviel Uhr hast du zur Arbeit zu gehen?*
   b. Anything that feels this good has to be right ... (epistemic necessity)
(1991 Rosalie Ash, *Love by Design* [BYU-BNC])

   Dutch: **Iets dat zo goed aanvoelt heeft juist te zijn.*
   German: **Was sich so gut anfühlt, hat richtig zu sein.*

In fact, Dutch and German did not advance beyond the medieval stage, where the construction with a 'shared object' (the construction illustrated for English in (1a) and for Spanish in (8)–(10)) could express possibility as well as necessity depending on context and where the possessive verb is still clearly weakly possessive (close to existential). Such a 'weak possessive' construction is also still a possibility in English and Spanish when the object occurs *before* the infinitive, as shown in (23) above and (25). But in English and Spanish this now occurs *next to* the new construction, in which the possessive itself no longer has an object (indicated by the fact that an object, if present, is positioned after the infinitive), as in (26).

(25) a. **Tenía** muchas cosas **que** decir
   had-he many things which say[INF]
   'He had many things to say.'
   (Olbertz 1998: 254)
   b. I **have** a book **to** recommend, and that is . . .

(26) a. Ahora **tienes** **que** saber idiomas
   today have-you to know[INF] languages
   'Nowadays you have to know languages'
   (Olbertz 1998: 256)
   b. If I **have to** recommend a book, it would be . . .[25]

In other words, while English and Spanish have two types with clearly differentiated functions, Dutch and German have only one type of construction, which we have called the weak possessive construction:

(27) a. Ik **heb** niet veel **te** zeggen, zegt oma.
   I have not much to say says granny
   'I don't have much to say, granny says.'
   (2010 *Corpus Hedendaags Nederlands*)
   b. Was ich noch **zu** sagen **hätte**, dauert eine Zigarette . . .
   what I yet to say would-have lasts one cigarette
   'All that I have left to say, takes one cigarette . . .'
   (1972 Reinhard Mey)

The situation in modern Dutch and German shows that the possessive verb construction did not essentially change in these languages, unlike what happened in English and Spanish. Jäger (2013), however, tries to show – probably led by the idea that the grammaticalisation of

---

[25] The differences between the two word orders is clear from the following. Amazon.com has a regular posting called 'I have a book to recommend'. One of the notices found there (www.examnotes.net/index.php?topic=1005192.0;wap2, accessed 10 October 2013) starts as follows: 'For those that have an interest, *there is a book that I would like* to recommend. It is [. . .].' This example shows that obligation is not involved, but weak (existential) possession. An example of adjacent order of HAVE and *to*-infinitive, illustrating that the context indeed implies (external) obligation, comes from the following dialogue: 'What is the one book that you recommend our community should read and why? Can I recommend a film, instead? My movie, "The Keeper of the Keys" is changing lives. It empowers people and encourages them in a time when we all need to know that we are worthwhile. *If I have to recommend a book*, I think "The Magic" from Rhonda Byrne is fabulous.' (http://ideamensch.com/robin-jay/, accessed 10 October 2013)

possessives follows a universal pathway (cf. Section 11.1 above) – that German *haben+zu*-infinitive developed obligative or necessity meaning just like English HAVE-*to*, and that examples of this are already found in the transition period from Old to Middle High German. However, all her examples are of the early type of 'weak possessives'. Consider e.g. her example (Jäger 2013: 158) from Notker's translation of Boethius: *Tér íst fóne diu sâlíg uuánda er dáz fúrder niecht-es ne **hábet ze géronne***, which she translates as 'he is blessed therefore because he has to crave nothing else'. In the philosophical context, which offers advice on how to deal with Fortuna, this in fact means that he is blessed because 'he has nothing to crave', i.e. because 'there is nothing for him to crave anymore'. This also follows from the fact that the original Latin text adds: *quo nihil ultra est* 'through which nothing further exists'. It is clear that the simple adjacency of the possessive verb and the infinitive (as in *hábet ze géronne*) does not *automatically* lead to the new construction. This is a mistake that is often made (see e.g. Łęcki 2010; and comments on Łęcki in Fischer 2015: 130ff.).

While more work will need to be done on the use of weak possessive *haben+zu*-infinitive in Modern German, in a study of Modern Dutch (van Steenis 2013) using the *Corpus of Spoken Dutch*, it was found that weak possessive *hebben+te*-infinitive only (and very rarely) occurs with a necessity sense when the context strongly implies that of all the available possibilities, only one remains, as in (28).

(28) maar   als daar uren   over zijn   en ergens   anders
     but   if there hours   left are   and somewhere   else
     zijn geen uren   dan   **heb** **je**   **te kiezen** of
     are no   hours   then   have   you   to choose   either
     helemaal   geen   uren of daar   inderdaad dus   lesgeven
     completely   no   hours or there indeed   therefore teach
     'but if there are hours left over there and somewhere else there are no hours then you have to choose between no hours at all, or indeed teach there'

(fn000096.225)

Thus, the necessity sense occurs especially in situations where all other possibilities are excluded, as for instance in contract situations, as in the example from German (29) (this is also relevant in (28)).

(29) Der Mieter **hat sich** **verkehrsgerecht zu verhalten** und eine
the renter has himself traffic-adequate to behave and a
materialschonende Fahrweise zu gewährleisten.
material-preserving way-of-driving to guarantee
'The renter must adhere to traffic regulations and drive cautiously in order to avoid damage to the car.'

(www.tks-autovermietung.de/agb/)

Not surprisingly, it is also often found in Dutch in combination with the restrictive discourse marker *maar* 'just/simply', indicating that there is indeed only one possibility left, which turns it into a virtual necessity (30a). We see something similar in German with the adverb *einfach* 'simply' (30b).

(30) a. Daar valt nu eenmaal niets aan te veranderen, **je hebt**
there falls now for-once nothing in to change you have
het maar te accepteren.
it but to accept
'There is no way in which you can change this, you just have to accept it.'

(https://books.google.nl/books?isbn=9460234682)

b. Mag jetzt mies klingen, aber er hat das einfach zu machen,
may now shitty sound but he has that simply to do
schließlich ist er Azubi!
after-all is he trainee
'Now [it] may sound shitty, but he just has to do it, after all he's a trainee.'

(www.mediengestalter.info/forum/18/eure-erfahrung-bitte-seminare-waehrend-der-ausbildung-21902-1.html)

We conclude, pending further research, that Dutch and German have preserved the original weak possessive construction, and that, contextually, a necessity meaning may arise (as was indeed possible all along), but only with a subject that has general reference, implying that the particular situation applies to everyone so that one cannot 'escape' it.

11.6 A Brief Conclusion

We have argued here that the similarities in the development of the possessive verb(s) in English and Spanish are the result of a number of similar, analogically based, circumstances (which were not shared by Dutch and German): notably the fixation of word order to SVO, which led to the regular adjacency pattern of verb and infinitive (with the object, if present, relegated to post-infinitival position), and the highly frequent collocation in both languages with a lexical item expressing 'need', which analogically induced the modal *necessity* meaning into the developing Aux-V construction.

There are clearly also differences. In English the necessity meaning that the construction acquired was further helped along by the similarity with MUST-*nedes* and the subsequent loss of *nedes*, as well as the loss of impersonal BE+*need/neden*, which were used to express external necessity, while in Spanish parallel developments in the other 'necessity'-periphrases with HABER/AVER played a crucial (analogical) role (they all developed a *de*-infinitive, and kept replacing one another in various functions), next to the fact that the remnants of the 'shared object' intervening between the finite verb and the infinitive (i.e. the relative pronoun *que*) functions as an infinitival marker, similar to *de*.

Appendix: Medieval and Modern Spanish Paradigms of TENER and AVER/HABER

This list contains only the forms most frequently used in this chapter. In addition, only indicative forms are given, and the future and conditional forms have also been excluded. The Medieval Spanish forms in this list of verb forms are restricted to the orthographical variants that appear in the chapter.

	Present		Imperfect		Preterite	
	Med. Spanish	Mod. Spanish	Med. Spanish	Mod. Spanish	Med. Spanish	Mod. Spanish
TENER						
1sg.	tengo	tengo	tenie/tenia	tenía	tove	tuve
2sg.	tyenes/tienes	tienes	tenies/tenias	tenías	toviste	tuviste
3sg.	tyene/tiene	tiene	tenie/tenia	tenía	tovo	tuvo
1pl.	tenemos	tenemos	teniemos/teniamos	teníamos	tovimos	tuvimos
2pl.	tenedes	tenéis	teniedes/teniades	teníais	tovisteis	tuvisteis
3pl.	tyenen/tienen	tienen	tenien/tenian	tenían	tovieron	tuvieron

(cont.)

	Present		Imperfect		Preterite	
	Med. Spanish	Mod. Spanish	Med. Spanish	Mod. Spanish	Med. Spanish	Mod. Spanish
AVER/HABER						
1sg.	*(h)e*	*he*	*auie/avia*	*había*	*ove*	*hube*
2sg.	*aues/aves*	*has*	*auie/avias*	*habías*	*oviste*	*hubiste*
3sg.	*ha/ave/á*	*ha*	*auia/avia*	*había*	*ovo*	*hubo*
1pl.	*auemos/ avemos*	*hemos*	*auiemos/aviamos*	*habíamos*	*ovimos*	*hubimos*
2pl.	*auedes/avedes*	*habéis*	*auiedes/aviades*	*habíais*	*ovisteis*	*hubisteis*
3pl.	*auen/aven*	*han*	*auien/avian*	*habían*	*ovieron*	*hubieron*

CHAPTER 12

Modelling Step Change: The History of WILL-*Verbs in Germanic*

Kersti Börjars and Nigel Vincent

12.1 Introduction[*]

Living languages constantly change, but though we have developed an understanding of actualisation – the way in which change spreads through a language (e.g. De Smet 2012) – and propagation – the way change spreads through a population (e.g. Labov 2001), the answer to the question of why change happens in the first place has proven elusive. As McMahon (1994: 225) puts it: 'the actuation problem, sadly, will remain as mysterious as ever' (cf. Walkden 2017). However, in this chapter, we will tackle some of the follow-on questions, which, though still complex, can be more easily tackled on the basis of empirical data: in what ways may the trajectories of change differ even when the prior circumstances in two closely related languages are quite similar? How parallel are changes to form and function? How big are the 'steps' in the changes in the different dimensions and how can they be independently identified? And, once these changes have been identified, how are they best modelled?

In this chapter, we will consider these questions in the light of the development of what we call the WILL-verbs in Germanic (e.g. Icelandic and Swedish *vilja*, German *wollen*, Dutch *willen*, Danish *ville*, English *will*). These can be traced back through Proto-Germanic to the Proto-Indo-European (PIE) root **wel-*, which is widely attested across the whole family in the sense of 'want, desire' and appears to have co-occurred with simple NPs, infinitives, and finite clauses. Latin will serve as a representative example from outside Germanic where the cognate item

---

[*] A version of this chapter was presented at the International Conference on Historical Linguistics in Naples in July 2015. Thanks to the audience on that occasion, especially to Cindy Allen, for their comments, and to Hetty van Enk and Willem B. Hollmann for views on the Dutch data and Tolli Eyþórsson for the Icelandic data. We are grateful too to Emma Moore and an anonymous referee for their comments on an earlier draft.

velle 'to want' may take direct objects ((1a) and (1b)), as well as infinitives (1c) and full clausal complements of both the Accusativus-cum-Infinitivo (AcI) (1d) and the finite type (1e).¹

(1) a. quid vis
 what want.PRS.2SG
 'What do you want?'

    b. quae ego volo
 which.N.ACC.PL 1SG want.PRS.1SG
 ea tu non vis
 that.N.ACC.PL 2SG not want.PRS.2SG
 'Those things which I want you do not want.' (Naev. *com.* 8)

    c. scio iam quid vis dicere
 know.PRS.1SG already what want.PRS.2SG say.INF
 'I already know what you want to say.' (Pl. *Mil.* 36)

    d. volo te uxorem domum ducere
 want.PRS.1SG 2SG.ACC wife.ACC home.ACC lead.INF
 'I want you to take a wife.' (Pl. *Aul.* 149)

    e. si vis ut loquar
 if want.PRS.2SG COMP speak.PRS.SBJV.1SG
 'if you want that I should speak' (Mart. 5.52.6)

In contrast to Romance, where *velle* does not in general develop future uses,² the development of WILL-verbs in Germanic provides fertile ground on which to explore the questions posed in the first paragraph because we find an interesting mix of cases where in some languages the reflex of the PIE root shows little development from the original lexical meaning in the modern language (Icelandic, Swedish, Dutch), while in others it has lost the original meaning and has developed almost exclusively modal or temporal meanings (English), and in yet others it appears to be at an intermediate stage, exhibiting the co-presence of both the original lexical and the diachronically emergent grammatical meanings (Danish). As we shall see, Swedish is a particularly interesting example since in this language

---

¹ In order to make the examples easier to read, we will not gloss for all features, but just those relevant to the discussion in which the example is used. Apart from WILL, DIM(unitive), and PPTCP for past participle, all glosses are as defined in the *Leipzig Glossing Rules* (www.eva.mpg.de/lingua/pdf/Glossing-Rules.pdf).
² Exceptions are some uses of Sardinian *bolli* and Romanian *a vrea*. We will not, however, explore the cross-family dimension in Romance in the present chapter.

there was a stage at which *vilja* did have a future meaning, but this was later lost.³

In the present chapter we contrast developments – or lack thereof – in Dutch and English as representatives of West Germanic with those in Icelandic, Swedish, and Danish as representatives of North Germanic. It is not our intention to provide a detailed analysis of any of these languages, or indeed to provide full coverage of the Germanic languages.⁴ Rather, we aim to compare the global changes within these four varieties with a view to better understanding the nature of the changes and the properties a theory should model if it is to capture both the similarities and the differences between the four historical trajectories. To this end, in Section 12.2, we set out the basic facts relating to the four individual languages, focusing in Section 12.2.1 on the formal and structural properties of the different WILL-verbs, in particular the categorial properties of the verbs themselves and those of their complements, while in Section 12.2.2 we turn to the semantic properties. In Section 12.3, we consider what changes have taken place to lead to the present-day distribution before considering in Section 12.4 how to model the changes within the theoretical framework of Lexical-Functional Grammar (LFG) (see Dalrymple 2001; Bresnan *et al.* 2016; and specifically for its application to diachronic data Börjars and Vincent 2017). Section 12.5 examines some of the steps in the change in more detail, and in Section 12.6 we sum up and draw our conclusions.

Our aim here is to consider general patterns and to compare developments. In each language, WILL displays interesting quirks, but we will not consider these here because they do not affect the general argument. Thus, the past tense of WILL can be used to indicate politeness for instance, as in the Dutch (2a), and all languages allow metaphorical use of WILL, illustrated by Swedish in (2b). The languages also have idiomatic expressions involving a 'desire' reading of WILL, as illustrated from Dutch in (3a), Swedish in (3b), and Icelandic in (3c).⁵

---

³ We will refer to the verb as WILL regardless of language unless the specific form is relevant to the discussion. As will become clear, we do not believe that 'future tense' is an appropriate description of the semantic contribution that the WILL-verbs make in languages such as English and Danish, but we will occasionally use 'future' in an informal sense throughout.

⁴ In particular, we do not discuss the history of German *wollen*, on which see Stevens (1995) and Remberger (2010, 2011). For relevant Norwegian data, see Eide (2005) and literature cited there.

⁵ We were reminded of the use illustrated in (3a) by an anonymous referee.

(2) a. Ik   wou   een tafel reserveren voor morgen   avond,
       1SG   WILL.PST a table   reserve   for tomorrow evening
       alstublieft.
       please
       'I would like to book a table for tomorrow evening, please.'
   b. Mitt hår   vill   inte bli   platt idag.
      my   hair   WILL.PRS   NEG become   flat today
      'My hair does not want to straighten today.'

(3) a. Wou   het maar regenen!
       WILL.PST   it but rain.INF
       'If only it would rain!'
   b. Det vill   gärna   bli   bra!
      it WILL.PRS   readily become.INF   good
      'It really wants to turn out well.'[6]
   c. Það vildi   svo til að þeir léku   allir á   sömu
      it   WILL.PST   so to INF 3PL play.PST   all   on same
      tegund hljóðfæra.
      type   instrument
      'It so happened that they all played the same type of instrument.'

12.2 The Data

12.2.1 Form and Structure

With respect to tense, in Danish, Icelandic, and Dutch, the distinction between present and past form corresponds to the regular present-past time contrast. This is exemplified for Dutch in (4). Present-day Swedish behaves like Danish with respect to form, but with respect to meaning, there is a bump in the trajectory, a point to which we will return in Section 12.2.2.

(4) a. Vandaag wil   ik   een hond kopen.
       today   WILL.PRS   1SG a   dog buy.INF
       'Today I want to buy a dog.'

---

[6] It is difficult to provide an idiomatic English translation for this sentence. It appears for instance in a book title (Göran Valinder and Berit Valinder 2005. *"Det vill gärna bli bra!": bröderna Jacobsson – båtbyggare*. Skärhamn: Båtdokgruppen), where a craftsman is said to have regularly used this phrase whenever he was pleased with the work he had just done.

b. Gisteren   wou   ik   een   hond   kopen.
   yesterday   WILL.PST   1SG   a   dog   buy.INF
   'Yesterday I wanted to buy a dog.'

In English, on the other hand, the distinction in form by and large corresponds to past-present time only in indirect speech (5a) and (5b), and other embedded contexts (5c) and in the expression of past habits (5d) (see Huddleston 1995 for an extended discussion of the present-past correlation). Furthermore, the past form can occur in present-time contexts, as illustrated in (6).

(5) a. He says that he will buy a dog.
    b. He said that he would buy a dog.
    c. We had always expected that he would buy a dog.
    d. As a child he would always stroke other people's dogs.

(6) a. He would buy a dog today if only he had the money.
    b. I would not do that if I didn't have to.

With respect to agreement forms, in Danish finite verbs are generally not marked for person and number, so *ville* is not distinctive in that respect. It does however share with other modal verbs the inflectional idiosyncrasy that the infinitive and the past form are homophonous. In Icelandic and Dutch, WILL shows the same inflectional distinctions as other verbs. There are some irregularities, for instance second-person singular -*t* is optional in Dutch: *jij speelt/*speel* 'you[SG] play' versus *jij wilt/wil* 'you[SG] WILL' (Geerts *et al.* 1984: 444). In English, the WILL-verb patterns with other modals and does not take the third-person singular ending -*s*: **he wills*.

In Icelandic, Danish, and Dutch, WILL has non-finite forms, as illustrated by Icelandic in (7).[7]

(7) a. Það   er   þreytandi   að   vilja   alltaf   vera   bestur.
       it   be.PRS   tiring   INF   WILL.INF   always   be.INF   best
       'It is tiresome always to want to be the best.'
    b. Ég   hef   aldrei   viljað   þetta.
       1SG   have.PRS   never   WILL.SUP   this
       'I have never wanted this.'

---

[7] The form corresponding to the past participle in the other languages is referred to as the supine in Icelandic; the past participle in Icelandic is an agreeing adjectival form. The same terminological distinction is also standardly made in grammars of Danish and Swedish.

English WILL by contrast does not have non-finite forms: *to will*, *has willed*, *is willing*.[8] Structurally, the English WILL is also distinct from lexical verbs in having the so-called NICE properties typical of auxiliary verbs in the language (see for instance Huddleston 2002: 92–102), whereas in the other languages this distinction between auxiliary and lexical verbs cannot be drawn.

Turning to complements, we have already seen in (3), (5), and (7a) that WILL in Dutch, English, and Icelandic can take an infinitival VP; the same is true of Danish: *han vil komme* 'he WILL.PRS come.INF'. In all these languages, the infinitival is bare and is not preceded by a marker such as *to* or *att*.[9]

As the data in (8a) and (8b) show, Dutch and the Icelandic WILL can take a finite complement with a complementiser. In Danish, this construction is rare or obsolescent (Brandt 1999: 76), while, as (8c) demonstrates, in English it is completely ungrammatical.

(8) a. De leraar wil dat de kinderen het boek lezen.
    the teacher WILL.PRS COMP the children the book read.PRS
    'The teacher wants the children to read the book.'

 b. Kennarinn vill að börnin lesi
    teacher.DEF WILL.PRS COMP children.DEF read.SBJV.PRS
    bókina.
    book.DEF
    'The teacher wants the children to read the book.'

 c. *The teacher will that the children read the book.

In Dutch and Icelandic, WILL can also take a nominal complement, as illustrated by Dutch in (9a), but in Danish (9b) and English (9c), this is not possible. Danish WILL can take a pronominal complement as in *Jeg vil ikke det* 'I WILL.PRS not it', but in such instances the pronoun always refers to a verbal constituent.

---

[8] The non-finite forms *to will, willed, willing* do of course exist in the modern language for the separate lexeme WILL meaning 'to cause to happen by force of one's will' but this is a regular denominal formation and not relevant to the present discussion. Similarly, the string *be willing* only occurs with *willing* in its adjectival function and not as the *ing*-form of WILL.

[9] We will not be concerned with the exact category of the infinitival phrase, but refer to it as a VP. An analysis in which it is actually headed by a functional category may be justified for some or all of the languages discussed here, but that level of detail is not relevant to us at this point.

(9) a. Ik   will   een   biertje.
       1SG   WILL.PRS   a   beer.DIM
       'I want a beer.'

   b. *Jeg   vil   en   øl.
       1SG   WILL.PRS   a   beer

   c. *I will a beer.

Dutch *willen* is one of the verbs in the language that takes what is known as the *Infinitivus Pro Participio* (IPP) when it occurs with the auxiliary of the perfect and takes a verbal complement.[10] In such constructions, *willen* occurs not in its participle form, as would be expected, but in its infinitival form. Contrast the examples in (10), where in (10a) we get (obligatory) IPP, whereas in (10b) *willen* occurs in its past participle form because there is no overt verbal complement.

(10) a. Oscar   heeft   haar   nooit   willen/*gewild   kwetsen.
        Oscar   have.PRS   her   never   want.INF/want.PPTCP   hurt.INF
        'Oscar never wanted to hurt her.'

    b. Dat   heeft   Oscar   nooit   gewild/*willen.
       that   have.PRS   Oscar   never   want.PPTCP/want.INF
       'Oscar never wanted that.'

Traditionally, IPP is assumed to be characteristic of – indeed a defining property of – auxiliary verbs.[11] This would mean that WILL is more distinct from lexical verbs in Dutch than it is in Danish and Icelandic. However, IPP is a property of a broad set of verbs in Dutch, namely those that can take a verbal complement and occur in constructions where the verbs immediately follow each other.[12] In fact, for this set of verbs, IPP is the rule rather than the exception (Geerts *et al.* 1984: 523–4), and occurs with

---

[10] We are grateful to an anonymous referee for drawing the relevance of this fact to our attention. We refer to *hebben* as the auxiliary of the perfect even though in these examples the meaning is equivalent to that of the past tense in English (so-called 'aoristic drift').

[11] On this view, a verb like *proberen* 'try' is an auxiliary in (i), but not in (ii) (Geerts *et al.* 1984: 517).

   (i) Ik   horde   dat   Nora   de knoop   heeft   proberen   te   ontwarren.
       I   hear.PST   COMP   Nora   the knot   have.PRS   try.INF   INF   untangle.INF

   (ii) Ik   hoorde   dat   Nora   geprobeerd   heeft   (om)   de knoop   te   ontwarren.
        I   hear.PST   COMP   Nora   try.PPTCP   have.PRS   COMP   the knot   INF untangle.INF
        'I heard that Nora tried to untangle the knot.'

[12] In grammars of Dutch, such a verb is referred to as a 'group-forming verb' (*groepsvormend werkwoord*), and it is in subordinate clauses that the properties are most clearly illustrated (see Geerts *et al.* 1984: 531–2):

infinitival complements with and without the infinitival marker *te* as in the examples in (11). Some of these verbs obligatorily occur with IPP, just like *willen*, and in some cases it is optional.

(11) a. De kinderen hebben mij helpen opruimen.
    the children have.PRS me help.INF tidy up.INF
    'The children helped me tidy up.'

  b. De leraar heeft de ouders proberen te bereiken.
    the teacher have.PRS the parents try.INF INF reach.INF
    'The teacher tried to get in touch with the parents.'

As van der Horst (2008: 881) points out, IPP is an early phenomenon in Dutch; he gives the example in (12) from early Middle Dutch.

(12) Menegen man hebbic helpen slaen.
    many man have.1SG help.INF slay.INF
    'I have helped slay many a man.' (*Ferguut*)

Many verbs show IPP in their earliest attestations in three-verb sequences with the auxiliary of the perfect. The phenomenon is spreading so that a number of verbs have changed from having optional IPP to it being obligatory, and verbs that did not permit IPP now do. If IPP is taken to define auxiliaries in Dutch, this term comes to mean something quite different from the use for other languages. It seems reasonable, therefore, to conclude that the fact that *willen* takes IPP does not set it apart from lexical verbs – in the sense in which we use the term here – that take a verbal complement.[13]

We set on one side here constructions which involve a directional adverbial and what appears to be an elided movement verb as in the Swedish *Ellen vill (åka) till Oslo* 'Ellen wants to go to Oslo'. This

---

  (i) Zij zei dat de kinderen haar **hadden helpen opruimen.**
    she said that the children her have.PST help.INF tidy up.INF
    'She said that the children had helped her tidy up.'
  (ii) Hij zei dat de leraar de ouders **had proberen te bereiken.**
    he said that the teacher the parents have.PST try.INF INF reach.INF
    'He said that the teacher had tried to reach the parents.'

[13] It is interesting to note that varieties of Swedish and Norwegian show a phenomenon that is similar in the sense that a verb takes an unexpected form under the influence of an adjacent form, but here it is the supine that 'spreads'.
  (i) Läraren hade velat hjälpt/ hjälpa barnen.
    teacher.DEF have.PST want.SUP help.SUP help.INF children.DEF
    'The teacher had wanted to help the children.'
The parallel between this construction and IPP is noted by Wiklund (2001: 202).

Table 12.1 *Present tense of Old Icelandic* WILL

		present tense	
		indicative	subjunctive
sg.	1	*vil*	*vilja*
	2	*vill/vilt*	*vilir*
	3	*vill*	*vili*
pl.	1	*viljum*	*vilim*
	2	*vilið*	*vilið*
	3	*vilja*	*vili*

construction also exists in Dutch and Danish as well as in Old English and Old Icelandic.

We turn now to the earlier stages of the languages. We should start by pointing out that though WILL behaves like a preterite-present verb, it was not originally a member of this group, but it goes back to optative forms with present meaning in PIE and it joined the preterite-presents by analogy (Birkmann 1987: 116). There are few remaining texts of Old Dutch and hence in this section we will focus on Old Icelandic and Old English, in both of which WILL had a full range of agreeing forms, as well as infinitival and participial forms, though in both languages the verbs in question were somewhat irregular compared to the general paradigm for lexical verbs. The non-finite forms in Old Icelandic are *vilja* (INF), *viljandi* (PRES. PTCP), and *viljat* (PAST.PTCP), the present tense forms are provided in Table 12.1 (from Gordon 1927: 286). A parallel set of forms can be found for Old English WILL.[14]

The examples in (13) and (14) indicate that present and past forms in Old Icelandic corresponded with present and past time in ways similar to the modern Scandinavian languages.[15]

(13) a. og vil eg mat minn en öngvar refjar
and WILL.PRS.IND.1SG 1SG meat my and no tricks
'I want my meat and no tricks.' (Grettir, 1845)

[14] It is interesting in this context to note that there were other modals in Old English which did not have non-finite forms: **sculan* and **motan* (Traugott 1989: 37).

[15] The Old Icelandic data are from the *Icelandic Parsed Historical Corpus* (IcePaHC).

b. En   þó   vil   eg   að   þú
   and   yet   WILL.PRS.IND.ISG   ISG   COMP   2SG
   látir   Auðun   vera   í   náðum   því   hann
   let.PRS   Auðun   be.INF   in   peace   because   3SG.M
   er   spakr   maðr
   be.PRS   quiet   man
   'I want you to leave Auðun in peace, because he is a quiet man.'
   (Grettir, 1519)

(14) a. en   hann   vildi   fara   aftur til   Þorfinns
       and 3SG.M   WILL.PST.IND.3SG   travel.INF   after to   Þorfinnur.GEN
       vinar   síns
       friend.GEN   POSS.REFL.GEN
       'and he wanted to go back to his friend Thorfinn'   (Grettir, 899)

    b. þeir   Kálfur   og   Þorvaldur   bræður   vildu   að
       3PL   Kálfur   and   Þorvaldur   brothers   WILL.PST.IND.3PL   COMP
       þeir   væru   sáttir
       3PL   be.PST.SBJV.3PL   reconciled
       'The brothers, Kalf and Thorvald, wanted them to be reconciled.'
       (Grettir, 190)

Similar data can be found for Old English.[16]

Turning now to structure, in (15), we see evidence that Old English WILL could take a nominal complement (15a), an infinitival complement without an overt subject (15b) as well as a finite clause (15c). All three complement types can be found in Old Icelandic too, as already exemplified in (13) and (14).[17]

(15) a. þæt   he   geornor   wolde   sibbe   wid
        that   3SG.M   rather   WILL.PST.SBJV.3SG   peace   with
        hiene   þonne   gewinn
        3SG.M   than   conflict
        '... that he wanted peace with him rather than conflict'
        (Or_3:1.54.4.1036)

---

[16] In fact, in Old English there are three different verbs built on the PIE *wel- root. The one that is of interest here is the preterite-present or strong verb *willan* as distinct from the weak verb *willian*, labelled as WILL² in the *Oxford English Dictionary* (*OED*), and the denominal *wilnian*, the *OED*'s WILL³ glossed as 'desire' and which takes an object in the genitive (Lass 1994: 236) and an infinitive introduced by *to* rather than the bare infinitive found with *willan*. We are grateful to Cindy Allen for her advice on this point.

[17] The Old English examples are taken from the *York-Toronto-Helsinki Parsed Corpus of Old English Prose* (YCOE).

b. ic   wille   habban   his dohtra
   1SG   WILL.PRS.IND.1SG   have.INF   his daughters
   Attican and Arthemian to minre gebeodnysse
   Attican and Arthemian to my   company
   'I want to have his daughters Attica and Arthemia for company.'
                                            (ÆLS[Agnes]:310.1931)

c. ic   wille   þæt   min folc   on eallum
   1SG   WILL.PRS.IND.1SG   COMP   my people   on all
   minum   rice   anmodlice   buge
   my   realm   unanimously   bow down
   to Daniheles Gode
   to Daniel's god
   'I want all the people in my realm with one accord to bow down to Daniel's god.'
                                            (ÆHom_22:340.3478)

Earlier forms of both languages also included a construction with a subject and an infinitival verb phrase akin to Present-day English *I want him to leave*, often referred to as AcI in the literature. Examples from English are found in (16) (from Zeitlin 1908: 62–3).

(16) a. Holi scripture wole a man to love al what God wole him love.
                                            (Peacock, 1147)

     b. For he sayd that all such lawes be contrary to the gospel, which wil no man to dye.   (More, 345 H)

The construction existed with WILL also in earlier forms of the Scandinavian languages, though the extent of its use is not entirely clear (see Lund 1862: 381–2, Nygaard 1865: 42–5, Falk and Torp 1900: 200, and Grimberg 1905: 208–10 for the different varieties, though Faarlund 2004 does not mention *vilja* in his section on AcI). Though the examples from English are from Middle English or later, according to the literature it existed in the earlier stages of the Scandinavian languages. Grimberg (1905: 207) even describes *viljan* with AcI as a native construction of Gothic. We return to the issue of non-finite complementation with a subject different from that of the matrix verb in Section 12.4.

12.2.2 Meaning

Within research on grammaticalisation a recurrent strand has involved the search for semantic pathways that are attested across a range of languages and language families. One such is the passage from desire to prediction, set out as in (17) by Bybee *et al.* (1994: 256).

(17) Desire > Willingness > Intention > Prediction

Though we will have reason to suggest a revision of this diachronic trajectory in Section 12.3, it provides a convenient starting point for us to compare the semantics of WILL in the four languages.

The 'desire' meaning is present in Dutch, Danish, and Icelandic and is represented in (18a) by Icelandic. The subject has a desire to read the book, but makes the prediction about the future that it is unlikely to happen. In English the desire meaning has been lost, so that in (18b), the meaning of WILL conflicts with the prediction expressed in the second clause, thereby rendering the sentence infelicitous.

(18) a. Ég   vil   lesa   bókina   en   ég   held
       1SG WILL.PRS read.INF book.DEF but 1SG believe.PRS
       ekki að   ég   muni   hafa   tíma til þess.
       not   COMP 1SG will.SBJV.PRS have.INF time to it
       'I want to read the book, but I don't think that I'll find the time for it.'

   b. #I will read the book, but I don't think I shall find the time for it.

The desire meaning was present in Old English, as illustrated above in (15), and the *OED* gives examples up to the eighteenth century, though those after the fifteenth century take the shape of set expressions of the kind seen in (19).

(19) a. Who wil the curnell of the nut must breake the shell.
       (J. Grange *Golden Aphrod.* sig. Iiij^v, 1577)
   b. You do not make your greatness consist in being able to do whatever you will, but in willing only what may be done.
       (tr. C. Rollin *Anc. Hist.* III. 65, 1735)

In this connection it is interesting to note that the first uses of English *want* to express desire recorded in the *OED* date from the early eighteenth century.

(20) a. All such as want to ride in Post-haste from one World to the other.
(E. Ward *Wooden World Dissected* (1707) 2)
   b. Thieves and Cheats mingle the Flower or Seed among the Food of those, whom they want to defraud.
(G. Lavington *Enthusiasm Methodists & Papists* (1751) III 163)

Before this time the meaning of *want* was 'be lacking, fail' (< PIE *wā- 'lack, be empty' via Old Icelandic *vanta*), a fact which suggests that the rise of the 'desire' meaning for *want* may be linked to the loss of that meaning for *will*.

The WILL-verb is used to express willingness in all the languages we have considered, as exemplified from Danish and English in (21a) and (21b), where it can be assumed that the intended meaning is not that of desire. Example (21c) is instructive; it is taken from an advertising leaflet where the intended meaning is clearly volitional, but in a different context the same string could also mean 'are you willing to make savings?', or indeed express a simple query about how things will turn out financially in the future. It thus serves well to exemplify the way Danish embodies an intermediate stage in the diachronic shifts under discussion here.

(21) a. Vil   du   hælde   vinen   op?
       WILL   2SG   pour.INF   wine.DEF   up
       'Will you pour the wine?'

   b. Will you pour the wine?

   c. Vil   du   også   spare   penge?
       WILL   2SG   also   save.INF   money
       'Do you also want to / Are you also willing to / Will you also save money?'

The next step in the development posited in (17) is intention, which is not always easily isolated from desire or, at the other end of the meaning spectrum, from prediction. It is of course this type of ambiguity that can form the springboard for language change. The Dutch example in (22a) is naturally translated with 'intend to'. However, whereas *van plan zijn* 'intend to' (literally 'be of plan') can be followed by a negation in an example like (22b), this sounds odd when WILL is used, as in (22c). These facts could be taken as evidence that WILL in Dutch is still at a relatively early stage of this development towards the 'intention' meaning.

(22) a. De regering   wil   een beslissing nemen   op basis van
       the government WILL   a   decision   take   on basis of
       de statistiek   die   dit najaar   beschikbaar zal   zijn.
       the statistics REL   this autumn available   will   be
       'The government intends to make a decision based on the statistics
       which will be available this autumn.'

   b. De regering   is van plan   om   vóór   de verkiezingen
      the government   is of plan   to   before the elections
      dit najaar   de pensioenleeftijd   te   verhogen,
      this autumn   the pension age   INF   increase
      hoewel   ze   eigenlijk er   de voorkeur   aan
      even though   3PL   actually there the preference to
      hadden   gegeven om te   wachten.
      had   given   to INF   wait
      'The government intends to raise the retirement age before this
      autumn's election, even though they would actually have preferred
      to wait.'

   c. ?#De regering   wil   vóór   de verkiezingen
         the government WILL   before   the elections
      dit najaar   de pensioenleeftijd   verhogen, hoewel
      this autumn   the pension age   increase even though
      ze   eigenlijk   er   de voorkeur   aan
      3PL   actually   there the preference   to
      hadden   gegeven   om   te   wachten.
      had   given   to   INF   wait

The parallel sentence to (22a) in English, namely (23a), is perfectly acceptable, but here it is difficult to distinguish 'intend' from the 'predict' meaning which has developed in English. The example in (23b), with a first-person subject, provides a context in which an 'intend' meaning is a more likely interpretation than 'predict'.

(23) a. The government will increase the pension age before this
        autumn's election, even though they would have preferred to wait.
     b. I will apologise to everyone I have hurt and then I will try to get
        myself a job.

We turn now to the final stage of the path in (17). On the assumption that you would not expect someone to desire or intend to regret something, but they may predict that they will, the oddness of the sentences in (24) can be ascribed to the fact that in Dutch (24a) and Icelandic (24b), WILL has not acquired the 'prediction' meaning. The examples in (25), on the other hand, show that this meaning has developed in both Danish and English.

(24) a. #Ik   wil   er   spijt   van   hebben.
        1SG   WILL   there   regret   of   have
     b. #Ég   vil   sjá eftir   því.
        1SG   WILL   regret   it

(25) a. Jeg   vil   fortryde   det.
        1SG   WILL   regret   it
     b. I will regret it.

An example like (26) is telling in this respect. It does not refer to a science-fiction world in which robots want to or intend to take over our work, but rather more prosaically to the circumstances that can be expected in future workplaces. Even so, Danish does not go so far as English in allowing impersonal and non-argument subjects, as we discuss below in Section 12.5.

(26) I   fremtiden   vil   robotter   i   stigende   grad
     in   future.DEF   WILL   robot.PL   in   increasing   degree
     overtage   jobfunktioner,   som   danskere
     take over.INF   job function.PL   that   Dane.PL
     i dag   udfører   med   hænder   og   hoved.
     today   carry out.PRS   with   hand.PL   and   head
     'In the future robots will to an increasing degree take over the job functions which today Danes perform with their hands and their heads.'   (*Berlingske* 14 April 2017)

With respect to meaning, Swedish provides an interesting case since Present-day Swedish is much like Icelandic and Dutch in that it appears not to have developed further than possibly intention in (17), so that data parallel to (22) can be found for Swedish, but a sentence like those in (24) would be infelicitous, just as it is in Dutch and Icelandic. However, at an earlier stage, Swedish WILL could have a future meaning. Söderwall (1884–1918), in his dictionary of medieval Swedish, mentions uses that are essentially future, Beckman (1917: 11) describes this use as being less common already at the Old Swedish stage, and Hellquist (1902: 182) states that the future is 'occasionally' formed with *vilja* in sixteenth-century Swedish (see also Björkstam 1919). Details of the demise of the future sense of Swedish WILL are not clear, but Bylin (2017) shows that examples where a future interpretation is the only reasonable one have been in decline since the sixteenth century and in her corpus, there are no unambiguous examples of future use after the beginning of the nineteenth century. She provides the examples in (27).

(27) a. Thet   wil   thå   wara   förseent til   at   anamma
       it   WILL   then   be.PRS   too late to   INF   accept.INF
       noghon godh   lärdom när   man   dragher epter   andan.
       any   good   learning when   one   draws   after   breath
       'It will be too late to learn well when one draws one's final breath.'
                                                            (1529 *Petri*:A 3 b)

   b. Det   wore   sannerligen ingen   ringa   ting
      it   be.SBJV   truly   no   small   matter
      i   hushållningen,   at   vid   Mid-Wintren   kunna
      in   housekeeping   INF   at   mid-winter   can
      weta   hurudant,   och   huru   tidigt slut
      know.INF how   and   how   early   end
      Wintren wil   taga.
      winter   WILL   take.INF
      'It would not be a small thing for the housekeeping to know how and how early winter will end.'   (*Götheborgs Tidningar* 1788: 50:2)

Lagervall (2014: 301–4) shows that Swedish WILL has undergone only minimal structural change from medieval times to the present day. Though grammars of Swedish frequently refer to *vilja* as an auxiliary verb, Bylin (2017) shows that the criteria which are used to identify auxiliaries in Swedish apply to *vilja* only to a very limited extent. It should be noted that this is not a case of degrammaticalisation since the current lexical meaning has not developed from the functional meaning. It would appear rather that a functional meaning developed, but then went out of use. The lexical meaning meanwhile has remained with only slight changes over time, thus yielding an example of what has been called 'retraction' (Willis 2017).

12.3 Diachronic Change

12.3.1 Formal and Structural Change

We can sum up the formal and structural properties of WILL in the languages we have considered as in Table 12.2. Under 'Regular agr

Table 12.2 *Structural properties of* WILL

	Form			Complement		
	Non-finite	Prs-pst distinction	Regular agr distinctions	Noun phrase	Finite clause	Infinitival clause
Icelandic	+	+	+	−	+	+
Dutch	+	+	(+)	+	+	+
Danish	+	+	+	−	(+)	+
English	−	−	−	−	−	+
Old Icelandic	+	+	+	+	+	+
Old English	+	+	+	+	+	+

distinctions', we indicate whether the agreement pattern of WILL parallels that of lexical verbs in the language, not necessarily in specific forms, but in terms of distinctions made.

In terms of form distinctions, WILL in Danish, Dutch, and Icelandic, as well as Swedish, differs little from lexical verbs in the respective languages.[18] With respect to complementation, these languages also behave in a similar way. Furthermore, they share these formal properties with the two early Germanic languages we have considered. If we assume that the behaviour of WILL in Old Icelandic and Old English is representative of WILL in early Germanic, we can conclude from these similarities that WILL in Danish, Dutch, Icelandic, and Swedish has not undergone much change structurally. The most striking differences are that only in Dutch and Icelandic does WILL still permit a nominal complement and that in Danish the finite complement is becoming obsolete. The Dutch agreement pattern also differs slightly between WILL and lexical verbs. English WILL, on the other hand, has undergone major structural changes (see Warner 1993).

---

[18] A referee rightly notes that one respect in which the WILL-verb across the whole family differs from other complement-taking lexical verbs and patterns instead with modal auxiliaries is in the lack of the infinitival marker, whether of the *to* variety as in English, Dutch, and German or the *at(t)* variety as in North Germanic. Even so there are occasional instances of English *will* + NP + *to* + INF as in the strings *wile a man to love* and *wile no man to dye* in examples (16) in this chapter. The explanation for this property is not immediately clear but the fact that it holds true across the whole of Germanic and is independent of the grammaticalisation processes that led to the differential formation of infinitival markers within the sub-families suggests that it should be reconstructed as part of Proto-Germanic morphosyntax and therefore is prior to the developments away from the original 'desire' meaning which are our concern here.

12.3.2 Semantic Change

If we assume that the semantic development has progressed along the path given in (17), we can outline the differences in the changes as in (28).

(28)

There is a sense in which 'willingness' is the odd one out here. The other steps involve a move from the subject's desire to participate in or bring about a particular state of affairs to the subject's plan for making a state of affairs come about, and thence to the speaker's prediction that a particular state of affairs will hold in the future. In a sense this is a development away from the subject's emotional relation to the state of affairs. Willingness, on the other hand, stays in the same dimension; it is still dealing with the subject's desire, it is just a question of not conflicting with the subject's desire, rather than being in line with it. Indeed, Bybee *et al.* (1994: 255) say that they were 'unable to confirm willingness as a use separate and distinct from desire for most of the languages' in their sample. We would argue that willingness is a meaning that naturally arises from any WANT verb, as evidenced by the fact that it is present in English *want*, as in (29). Similarly, Italian *volere*, the reflex of the original Latin *velle* 'to want' referred to in Section 12.1, can display the 'willingness' meaning, as in (30) even though it does not appear to have otherwise developed along the path in (17) in spite of having had many hundreds of years in which to do so.

(29) a. 'Do you want to pass me that beer over there?' my roommate asks as we decorate for Christmas.

(https://twitter.com/mstepanic/status/408429726089232384, 4 December 2013, accessed 21 May 2017)

b. 'do you want to pass me the lunch menu'

(TheCrunchUnderfoot www.mumsnet.com, 2 March 2012, accessed 21 May 2017)

(30) Hai   intenzione   di   stare   lì
     have.PRS.2SG intention   COMP   stand.INF   there
     a   ridermi   dietro   o   mi   vuoi
     COMP   laugh.me   behind   or   me   want.PRS.2SG
     dare   una   mano   davvero?
     give.INF   a   hand   indeed
     'Are you going to stand there giggling or give me a hand?'
                                    (Stephen King, *Christine* p.193, lit.
     'do you intend to stand there laughing at me or will you really give me a hand?')

Examples such as these suggest both that there is a close link between 'want' and 'willing' and that the shift from the one to the other is particularly likely to be triggered in interpersonal contexts. As pointed out by an anonymous referee, it is not unlikely that the willingness meaning develops first in requests, and in this sense *want* has not developed as far as for instance the Dutch *willen*, as illustrated in (31), where (31a) differs from the examples in (29) in not permitting a willingness reading, but for (31b) this is the natural reading.

(31) a. I want to lend you money.
     b. Ik   wil   je   best   geld   lenen.
        1SG   WILL.PRS   2SG   best   money   lend.INF
        'I am willing to lend you money.'

We would then propose to revise (17) as in (32), where the diagrammatic difference in distance between DESIRE and the two immediately following steps is deliberate.

(32)   DESIRE ⟶ INTENTION ⟶ PREDICTION
               ↘ WILLINGNESS

This reconceptualisation of the semantic connections can be contrasted with that proposed in Aijmer (1985), who draws a distinction between the route followed by *will* when it is constructed with human subjects, and hence in all grammatical persons, and the exclusively third-person use in which *will* expresses the potential or capacity of an inanimate object. For her, then, there are two semantic paths, one leading from 'desire' through 'willingness' to 'intention' and thence to future and epistemic uses, and the

Table 12.3 *Desirability and its source as intersecting features*

	Desired	Internal
DESIRE	+	+
INTENTION	−	+
PREDICTION	−	−

other from 'desire' to 'capacity/habit' to 'prediction' and from there to futurity/epistemicity. Ziegeler (2006) takes the argument a stage further and suggests that the instances with third-person subjects – so-called 'omnitemporal' uses – are a necessary intermediate stage in the evolution of *will* as a marker of the future. However, this conclusion does not square with the results of Hilpert's more recent and more wide-ranging corpus study (see Hilpert 2008a: 71–3, and fn.2 on p.199). Here is not the place to go into more detail on this question, but it seems clear that it is necessary to propose, as we do in (32), a bifurcating diachronic route rather than a single trajectory of the kind Bybee *et al.* (1994) advocate.

We will return to a more formal analysis of the change in Section 12.4, but we will first consider the different stages in more intuitive terms, according to which the core concept of desirability can be combined with the source of that desirability, which may be either external or internal to the subject of WILL.[19] In informal feature terms, the three stages left in (32) once willingness has been removed may then be represented as in Table 12.3.

We can then describe the change as an initial loss of the 'desire' component, followed by a development from internal to external to the subject of WILL. In a sense, the involvement of the subject of WILL in the state of affairs represented by the complement of WILL is reduced as this development progresses (note that this change to the role of the subject is unrelated to the type of change commonly referred to as subjectification; cf. Traugott 1989). We can extend this account by incorporating the fourth logical combination of these features, namely [+Desired, -Internal]. A desirability external to the subject of the verb could be seen as a form

---

[19] We use [−Desired] here not as specifically undesirable, just as 'not specifically desired'. The table could alternatively be expanded with a three-valued feature [+/−/u Desired], with [−Desired] indicating something like antipathy or dislike, but that is not crucial to our argument and would take us too far afield at this point.

of weak obligation, and it is interesting to note that OBLIGATION > INTENTION > PREDICTION is also described as a common path by Bybee *et al.* (1994: 258–64).[20] However, since they predict that 'no gram should display obligation and desire as alternate uses' (1994: 257), this path must be separate from the one in (17).[21] In this way we could see the development from obligation to prediction as being different from the one from desire in that the initial change is from external to internal, with the loss of desirability as the second step.

12.4 Modelling Change in Form and Function

One conclusion that emerges from this review of the changes undergone by the WILL-verb in the languages within our sample is that shifts in form and meaning are at least partially independent of each other; the WILL-verb shows little formal change in all the Scandinavian languages considered here, but functionally, there have been changes in Danish but not in Icelandic. This is consistent with more general studies of grammaticalisation. Heine (1993), for example, discusses what he calls the 'overlap model' according to which, from a cross-linguistic perspective, grammaticalisation involves a series of shared starting points and shared endpoints in semantics, syntax, morphology, and phonology (Heine 1993: 87), but the developments within each of these dimensions of linguistic structure and organisation for the most part do not run in parallel with each other. Indeed it is hard to see how they could do otherwise, except by chance, given the (at least partial) structural independence of the different domains of language from each other. The question is then: how are we to model such developments? In what follows we use LFG to sketch an analysis of the stages of the change since this is a formal framework which allows for different types of linguistic information to be represented in separate dimensions, each organised according to its own theoretical primitives and connected by mapping principles rather than derivation. In such an approach it is entirely natural that domains can change at different paces in different languages, as already briefly discussed in Börjars *et al.* (2015: 376).

---

[20] Bybee *et al.* (1994: 263) use FUTURE rather than PREDICTION in this path, even though the latter is used in (17). We can see no obvious reason for this.
[21] A referee points out that in an example like *You **will** listen to what I say*, the stressed use of *will* conveys a sense of obligation. However, such threatening or admonitory uses of *will* are consequent upon the future interpretation and express the speaker's confidence in the desired or feared outcome and as such do not counterexemplify Bybee *et al.*'s generalisation. See Aijmer (1985) and Boye (2001) for more discussion of meanings that can develop once WILL has reached the prediction stage in its diachronic trajectory.

In particular, we exploit the way this approach allows the set of grammatical relations that an item contracts – in LFG terms its f-structure – to be modelled, and hence potentially to change, independently of the syntactic configuration and morphology which overtly realise those relations.[22] That said, there are also limits to the extent of diachronic independence of levels of structure imposed by the very nature of natural languages as functioning sign-systems. Thus, as discussed and exemplified above, the loss of the 'desire' meaning for English *will* entails the loss of complements with *that* and the absence of the later *for-to* infinitival complements just as it also entails the loss of nominal arguments.[23]

The semantic interpretation of a given lexical item within its sentential context belongs to a further and likewise independent domain known as s-structure. There is a considerable literature within the study of grammaticalisation phenomena across languages that takes for granted semantically defined clines such as the one identified in (17) or our revised version of this in (32). There is by contrast a remarkably small literature that seeks to go into semantic detail and show how the stages in such a development are linked to each other, and an even smaller body of literature which deploys the techniques of formal semantics in order to do so. Notable exceptions here are Eckardt (2006) and Deo (2014, 2015), but, as it happens, neither of these includes this particular diachronic sequence within their purview. Within LFG the most usual framework for semantic representation is resource logic or glue semantics (see for example Dalrymple 2001: Chapter 9), but we will not develop the semantic analysis to the level where such a formal system is required. In any case it is not our aim to develop the formal semantic side of the story in any great detail but simply to indicate the desirability of so doing within a full account.

Let us start with the development from desire to intention to prediction. The standard account of the semantics of verbs of wanting, as developed for example by Heim (1992), takes such a verb to articulate the subject's preference for worlds in which the proposition expressed as the complement of the WILL-verb holds true as against those in which it does not. The desiring subject may or may not be co-referential with one of the arguments contained in that proposition; in other words, the subject may have a preference both for situations which involve themselves and for ones which do not. The desired state of affairs can be instantiated by a finite

---

[22] There are different approaches to m-structure within LFG, going back to Butt *et al.* (1996a, 1996b) and Frank and Zaenen (2002); see Dalrymple (2015) for a summary of the issues.

[23] For further discussion of the relation between form and content in diachrony, see Vincent (2014).

complement clause, which may or may not contain a noun phrase that is co-referential with the subject of WILL, as in (33). The distinction between same and different subject can be achieved also with a non-finite clause, as exemplified by *want* in (34), though in Present-day English, this is not an option with WILL.

(33) Oscar$_i$ vill   att   han$_{i/j}$ skall   få   köpa
      Oscar   WILL.PRS   COMP   3SG.M   shall.PRS get.INF   buy.INF
      en hund.
      a   dog

(34) a. Oscar wants to buy a dog.
     b. Oscar$_i$ wants him$_j$ to buy a dog. [where $i \neq j$]

Within LFG the treatment of examples like (33) is clear: *vilja* has the lexical entry in (35). The PRED feature provides a representation of the meaning of the predicate and within angle brackets the functions representing the thematic arguments of the predicate. COMP is a clausal complement that is satisfied by *att han skall få köpa en hund* in (33).

(35) (↑PRED) = 'WILL$_{want}$ <SUBJ, COMP>'

This provides a functional structure which maps straightforwardly onto the semantics that Heim proposes, with SUBJ identifying the 'wanter' or 'preferrer' and COMP the wanted/preferred state of affairs. Extending the same analysis to the examples in (34) involves treating both *to buy a dog* in (34a) and *him to buy a dog* in (34b) as expressing the COMP function, the difference between the two being that the subject of the COMP in (34a) is not present in the c-structure, which is the LFG representation of syntactic structure, though it is present in f-structure and thus equivalent to what in another notation is labelled as *pro*. In the terminology of Bresnan (1982) and subsequent work, this means that the relation between the subject of the WILL-verb and the subject of the embedded COMP in (34a) is one of anaphoric control. A general rule of the kind in (36) allows a pronominal subject to be inserted into the f-structure when the verb is non-finite though there is no corresponding overt material in c-structure (see Bresnan *et al.* 2016: 317).

(36) V[TENSE −] ⇒ (↑SUBJ PRED) = 'pro'

Co-reference between *pro* and the controller in examples such as (34a) is determined by the principle of obviation (Bresnan 1982: 383), which requires a covert subject of COMP to be linked to the nearest argument of the controlling predicate, in this case the SUBJ of the WILL-verb.

An alternative account within the same general spirit is that of Haug (2013), who however revises Bresnan's mechanism for anaphoric control in the light of Landau's (2000) concept of partial control. His analysis involves what he labels 'quasi-obligatory anaphoric control' and which he describes as follows: 'Quasi-obligatory anaphoric control does not involve syntactic specification of the controller but rather a semantic constraint that requires the controller to be a logocenter of the matrix predicate, combined with normal (pragmatic) resolution of anaphora' (Haug 2013: 274). For our purposes, the key feature of both Bresnan's original proposal and Haug's revised account is that the link between the SUBJ of the WILL-verb and the SUBJ of its complement is stated in terms akin to those used to establish co-reference between a pronoun and its antecedent, in other words a semantic/pragmatic type of link. As we shall see, however, with the shift to intention and prediction meanings the constraints on co-reference are stricter and are established syntactically, so that we have here a formal means of modelling what in more informal terms is a type of grammaticalisation.

As we saw in (16), earlier forms of English and the Scandinavian languages did permit the construction type exemplified in (34b) with WILL. This means that these varieties allowed all three options for realisation of COMP: a finite verb with overt SUBJ, a non-finite verb with overt SUBJ, and a non-finite verb with anaphorically controlled *pro*.[24] In modern Icelandic, Dutch, and Swedish, when there are different subjects in main and subordinate clause, a finite construction must be used.[25] When WILL occurs with non-finite complementation, the only interpretation is one in which the subject of WILL is co-referential with the subject of the complement, as in (2), (7a), (14a), and (15b). In such contexts we have the possibility of a different kind of relation, called 'functional control', in which case the complement of WILL has the function XCOMP. An XCOMP is a clausal function which is open in the sense that it contains a grammatical relation (SUBJ) that is not expressed in c-structure. Functional control is then characterised by the fact that the subject of the XCOMP is not free to vary but must equate to a grammatical function of the governing verb, in this case the SUBJ (Bresnan 1982; Bresnan *et al.* 2016: 289–94). This means that WILL in these languages has the PRED value in

---

[24] On the differences between languages in the use of finite and non-finite clauses to express the difference between same subject and different subject constructions with verbs of wanting, see Haspelmath (2013).

[25] Excluding the limited options for verb-less complements in expressions such as *Jag vill honom väll illa* (I WILL.PRS him well/ill).

(37a), with the associated control equation in (37b), which equates the subject of the non-finite complement with that of WILL itself.

(37) a. (↑PRED) = 'WILL$_{desire}$ < SUBJ, XCOMP >'
 b. (↑XCOMP SUBJ) = (↑SUBJ)

With this as our starting point, the next stage in the development, the shift from desire to intention, is naturally modelled as a shift to obligatory functional control. COMP is no longer a possible complement, but XCOMP is the only option, and the subject of the XCOMP is not free to vary arbitrarily but must equate to the SUBJ(ect) of the governing verb. For WILL in its intention meaning, (38) is then the only option.[26]

(38) a. (↑PRED) = 'WILL$_{intention}$ < SUBJ, XCOMP >'
 b. (↑XCOMP SUBJ) = (↑SUBJ)

This is exactly what is needed to characterise the distinction between an intention, which the subject expresses on his/her own behalf, and a desire, which may well involve other individuals or entities. Formulating the shift in these terms is also consistent with the change in complement type from one which permits finite subordinate clauses to one which requires an infinitival clause.

Once we frame the question, as we have been doing, in terms of the argument structure associated with the grammaticalising verb, it is natural to follow the same logic and ask how prediction differs from intention. The answer is that prediction involves a statement about the likelihood of the state of affairs described by a proposition without the intervention of an external subject of any kind. Otherwise put, the syntactic subject of the whole clause is not an argument of WILL, but it functions as the logical subject of the proposition expressed by its complement, that is to say the phenomenon that has come to be known in the literature as 'raising'.[27] In LFG, the fact that the subject of WILL does not form an argument of the predicate is indicated by it occurring outside the angle brackets, as in (39a),

---

[26] It is interesting in this context that English *intend* does permit a different subject in the lower clause in the *for-to* construction:

(i) I intend for United to win the final.

We note that in such examples there tends to be an implicit causative, so that (i) could only plausibly be uttered by their manager or someone else with the power to influence the game. In the words of Setiya (2014: 4), 'intending is always intending to *do* something' (italics his). However, a full discussion of this construction goes beyond the scope of this chapter.

[27] We use this term in its by now conventional sense to identify the class of verbs like *seem* and *appear*. It should be clear however that within a framework like LFG there is no syntactic movement as such.

and as for functional control, with an associated control equation (39b) to ensure that the subject argument of the XCOMP is equated to the formal subject of WILL.

(39) a. (↑PRED) = 'WILL$_{prediction}$ < XCOMP > SUBJ'
 b. (↑XCOMP SUBJ) = (↑SUBJ)

Summing up our discussion so far we see the parallelisms set out in (40), which displays the correspondences between the stages in the semantic trajectory and the LFG-based accounts that we propose for each stage.

(40) Desire > Intention > Prediction

Independently Referring Expression
Anaphoric Subject Pronoun > Functional > Raising
(Quasi-obligatory) Anaphoric Control   Control

We can add a further layer of parallelism here in that English WILL does not have finite complements because it no longer has the desire meanings, but only those meanings that do not involve an independent subject, hence Old English WILL is translated with *want* in (15c), repeated here as (41a). Danish, on the other hand, still has finite complementation because it still has (marginally) the desire meaning as in (41b).

(41) a. ic   wille   þæt   min folc
        1SG   WILL.PRS.IND.1SG   COMP my people
        on eallum minum   rice   anmodlice   buge
        on all   my   realm   unanimously   bow down
        to Daniheles Gode
        to Daniel's   god
        'I want all the people in my realm with one accord to bow down to Daniel's god.'
                                                    (ÆHom_22: 340.3478)
    b. Jeg ville,   at   han   skulle   huske   sangen.
       1SG will.PST COMP   3SG.M   shall.PST remember.INF   song.DEF
       'I wanted him to remember the song.'

In our argumentation so far, a certain level of parallelism between form and function has become clear. With respect to the desire meaning, the proposition expressing the desired state of affairs may involve a subject other than the desirer. At this stage, WILL may take as its complement a finite clause with an independent subject, which may or may not be co-referential with the main clause subject or a non-finite clause with a subject. Once the desire meaning is lost, as it is in English, an independent subject is no longer a possibility with WILL and hence finite complementation is no longer possible.[28] Danish still has finite complementation, though not as productively as the other Scandinavian languages, because it still has – marginally – the desire meaning. However, in more general terms the correlation between types of control and overt syntax exhibits considerable cross-linguistic variation. Thus, English has infinitival expression of both anaphoric and functional control, Italian and French are like Swedish in having an infinitive for functional control and a finite complement for anaphoric, while Romanian and Greek have finite complements for both. Predictably the one combination that is not attested is finite marking of functional control coupled with non-finite marking of anaphoric.[29]

Moreover, with respect to the morphological form of WILL itself, there appears to be no correlation with the semantic development. In Danish, Dutch, Icelandic (modern and old), and Swedish, WILL itself behaves formally in all crucial respects like any other verb in the system. There is then no evidence that the morphosyntactic category of the verb has changed. Nor is there evidence that the category of WILL differs between Swedish and Danish, even though the semantic development of the verb in the two varieties has taken such different courses.

Once we get to the stage of prediction we find ourselves face-to-face with an issue that has been widely addressed in the literature, namely have we moved into the domain of tense or modality? The original discussion in Bybee *et al.* (1994) treats the cline we have been discussing as one of several different routes by which languages may evolve new tense markers.[30] However, the story must be more complex than that. Thus, Hilpert's (2008a) corpus-based investigation of Germanic future constructions confirms one and disconfirms another of the hypotheses that are built into the Bybee *et al.* semantic cline. Confirmed is the notion that intentionality is a cross-linguistically recurrent feature of the futures that develop from verbs of volition; disconfirmed is the idea that modality-based futures go

---

[28] Though there are languages that obligatorily use finite complementation and overt subjects also with same-subject complements of 'want'-verbs (see Haspelmath 2013).
[29] For further discussion of these typological differences, albeit from a different theoretical perspective, see Grano (2015).
[30] From a more formal point of view, Remberger (2011) comes to the same conclusion in her account of the history of German *wollen*.

through a monosemous stage before developing epistemic and speaker-oriented meanings (Hilpert 2008a: 183–4). In other words, there are a variety of different diachronic routes that items with future and futurate meanings can follow and in many languages it will not do simply to refer to a single future. Neither in Danish nor in English is it appropriate, for example, to describe the uses of WILL we have been considering as 'future tense'. WILL is not obligatory for expressing future in either language; both have a range of alternative ways of referring to the time after now. Conversely in neither language is the WILL-verb used exclusively with future reference. We would argue therefore that a description of WILL as a modal of (confident) prediction more appropriately reflects its uses (for a different range of arguments in favour of the same conclusion, see Huddleston 1995).[31]

From the perspective of LFG a further issue which arises once an item like WILL has reached the stage of marking modality and/or tense is the nature of its role within the f-structures which characterise the content of the clause. One possibility, argued for in detail by Falk (1984) and Dyvik (1999) and which we have assumed here, is that such items have their own PRED feature and take an XCOMP complement. The alternative is that they do not have a PRED feature, but contribute semantic content only in the form of features relating to mood or tense. This may be appropriate at the very final stages of grammaticalisation, as indeed Butt *et al.* (1996a, 1996b) argue for auxiliary verbs in some languages, but neither Danish nor English appear to have yet reached that point in their diachronic trajectories.

12.5 More Fine-Grained Changes

In this section we confine the discussion to a comparison of English and Danish though more fine-grained distinctions will also in all probability be required in a full account of the history of the Dutch and Icelandic verbs and of course for the above-mentioned reversal of WILL in Swedish. As we have seen, English and Danish show two stages of development since WILL occurs with the predictive meaning as well as the intentional one.

---

[31] A variety of ways of modelling WILL as a modal have been proposed in the literature, whether in terms of possible worlds (Copley 2009) or force dynamics (Boye 2001). More radically, Jaszczolt (2009) argues that the distinction is not necessary since tense is always supervenient on modality. We will not investigate these alternatives in the context of the present chapter.

However, both languages also demonstrate that the three-stage development outlined in the previous sections involves over-simplification and that we need to take into account smaller intermediate steps. Thus, in English WILL is no longer constrained to take an Experiencer/Agent subject (42a), and indeed may take a non-argument subject (42b) and, in addition, epistemic uses are allowed (42c).

(42) a. That tree will probably come down in the storm.
     b. It will rain before long.
     c. Peter will be in his office now.

The corresponding Danish examples in (43) vary from marginal to unacceptable.

(43) a. #Det   træ   vil   nok   falde   i stormen.
        that   tree   WILL.PRS   probably   fall.PRS   in storm.DEF
     b. #Det   vil   regne   inden   længe.
        it   WILL.PRS   rain.INF   before   long
     c. ?Peter vil   være   på   sit   kontor   nu.
        Peter WILL.PRS   be.INF   on   REFL   office   now

The example (43c) is from Brandt (1999: 62), who comments that such a sentence 'may not be quite impossible'. He nonetheless concludes that Danish *ville* does not in general allow epistemic readings. This too is the conclusion of Hilpert (2008a), who notes that not only does *ville* standardly have Experiencer/Agent subjects but that there is also a preference for it to co-occur with speech-act verbs.

The combination of the WILL-verb with passives is of particular interest in this respect. In English *will* occurs freely with passives as in the examples in (44).

(44) a. That issue will be discussed at the meeting tomorrow.
     b. I expect Bill will be fired.
     c. At the ceremony my sister will be given a medal.

In Danish by contrast there are two passive constructions, one involving a suffixal -*s*, and one involving the auxiliary *blive* 'be, remain'. When the first of these occurs with *ville* the meaning is typically volitional while with the second it is prospective or predictive. Brandt (1999: 119) offers the somewhat macabre minimal pair in (45) (for differences in use between the -*s* passive and the *bli*-passive, see for instance Engdahl 1999).

(45) a. Han   vil   skydes.
       3SG.M   WILL   shoot.INF.PASS
       'He wants to be shot.' [i.e. rather than being hanged]
    b. Han   vil   blive   skudt   (sandsynligvis)
       3SG.M   WILL   be.INF   shoot.PPTCP   probably
       'He will be shot (probably).'

In other words, the shift from volition to intention can move at different rates within different constructions even within the same language.

Data of the kind we have been discussing in this section suggest that not only should the schema in (17) be revised as in (32), but also, as indeed Bybee *et al.* (1994) had already acknowledged, that the route from prediction to futurity needs to be more closely examined (and compare here the conclusions of Remberger 2011).

12.6 Conclusion

In this chapter, we have considered the development of the WILL-verb in a number of Germanic varieties in the light of the cline from 'desire' to 'prediction' as proposed by Bybee *et al.* (1994: 256). Our aim has been to compare the change between a representative sample of Germanic languages, rather than provide an in-depth study of any of the languages. We have argued for a revision of the cline, where 'willingness' is a separate development from 'desire', rather than a step on the way towards the 'intention' meaning. The remaining three global stages in the development, we have suggested, are best analysed as a change in the role the main-clause subject contracts both with respect to WILL and with respect to the subject of the lower clause. In the initial stage, the desired proposition may or may not involve the 'desirer' and hence the two subjects may have the same referent or separate ones, a relation which follows from the concept of anaphoric control (Bresnan 1982; Haug 2013). With the 'intend' meaning, the subject of WILL and the lower non-finite verb obligatorily have the same referent and in our analysis this is accounted for by functional control. Once WILL has acquired the 'prediction' meaning, it takes only one argument – the predicted proposition – and the subject of WILL is an argument of the lower verb only. Over time therefore the subject argument of WILL goes from having the full semantic content to be expected of the initiator or experiencer of the relevant mental state (Heim 1992; Grano 2015) to not being a semantic argument of WILL, but instead taking on the role of semantic subject of the verb in WILL's complement.

The data also show that, although there is a relation between form and function, for instance in that finite complementation is not possible once the verb has reached the 'prediction' meaning, the two dimensions need not develop in parallel. With respect to formal properties, Danish and Icelandic WILL are both indistinguishable from lexical verbs in their respective formal systems. However, in terms of semantics, Danish has developed much further. This means that, as we said at the outset, in order to characterise the changes formally and functionally, we require an architecture that can model these dimensions separately from each other. A parallel correspondence architecture like LFG does this, since it explicitly allows statements of grammatical relations (f-structure) to be made independently of the constituency (c-structure) or morphology (m-structure) of the clauses in question. There is a clear contrast, therefore, between this kind of approach and that proposed for example by Grano (2015: Chapter 4) in his account of English *want* and analogous predicates in other languages, an account in which the syntactic structure has to be expanded to include a range of new functional heads, a silent predicate *have* (required to account for the fact that verbs of volition can have nominal as well as clausal complements), and where the main predicate is then required to move through a series of such positions in order to give appropriate realisation to its argument structure.

We have also shown how within our particular case study there is a need, as indeed already acknowledged by Bybee *et al.* (1994), to break the historical profile down into smaller, semantically defined, steps and to recognise that within a single language as well as across related languages the development can follow different paths, even when the starting points are similar. That said, further research is required to uncover the specific aspects of a given linguistic system that led to a change happening or not happening, or indeed happening and then reversing as the data from Bylin (2017) indicate was the case in the history of Swedish. It will be important too to investigate the relation between the cline studied here and other potential changes for lexical items in this semantic class such as the independent development of German *wollen* in the 'evidential' sense (cf. Remberger 2010, 2011).

In short, we have proposed answers to most of the questions set out in our introduction. One that remains as a puzzle is why changes take place in some languages and not in others, or proceed at different paces within more or less closely related languages. However, by mapping out the terrain associated with WILL-verbs in the way we have, we hope to have made it possible for future researchers to address that question in a more precisely articulated way. Still, McMahon (1994: 225) is right: 'the actuation problem, sadly, will remain as mysterious as ever'.

CHAPTER 13

Possessives World-Wide: Genitive Variation in Varieties of English

Benedikt Heller and Benedikt Szmrecsanyi

13.1 Introduction[*]

In this chapter we investigate regional patterns in the variation between the two major explicit possessive constructions in the grammar of English, the *s*-genitive (as in (1a)) and the *of*-genitive (as in (1b)).

(1) a. the *s*-genitive: [Singapore]$_{possessor}$'s [small size]$_{possessum}$ meant it could be quick to respond to changes in economic conditions
 <ICE-Singapore, w2c-011>
 b. the *of*-genitive: the [size]$_{possessum}$ of [the eyes]$_{possessor}$ is to help them at night. <ICE-Great Britain, w2b-021>

We cannot review here in detail previous research on variation between the *s*-genitive and the *of*-genitive (see Rosenbach 2014 for an exhaustive literature review). Suffice it to say that the *s*-genitive has been on the rise, vis-à-vis the *of*-genitive, since the early Modern English period (Rosenbach 2002) and is spreading right now, particularly in informational registers such as newspaper prose (Hinrichs and Szmrecsanyi 2007; Wolk *et al.* 2013). From near extinction in the fifteenth century, the *s*-genitive has experienced a renaissance and in some registers reached proportions of around 50 per cent (e.g. Jankowski and Tagliamonte 2014), likely because of its newly acquired function as clitic and determiner (Rosenbach 2002: 201–32). These shifts facilitated the emergence of constructions such as the group genitive, where *'s* is attached to complex noun phrases (e.g. *the man in the corner's hat*) – a phenomenon meticulously described by David Denison and collaborators (Denison *et al.* 2010). As far as constraints on

---

[*] Funding from the Research Foundation Flanders (FWO, grant # G.0C59.13N) is gratefully acknowledged. The usual disclaimers apply. We would also like to thank an anonymous reviewer for valuable comments and suggestions.

variation are concerned, we know that animate and short possessors in particular favour the *s*-genitive, while short possessums and possessors ending in a final sibilant favour the *of*-genitive. More generally speaking, the genitive alternation is a positional alternation which complies with the 'Easy First' principle (MacDonald 2013), in that language users tend to place 'easy' (e.g. short, light, or accessible) constituents first; thus, long possessors favour the *of*-genitive, long possessums favour the *s*-genitive (see Szmrecsanyi *et al*. 2016 for more discussion). Possessor animacy and possessor length are typically identified as the most important constraints on variation (see e.g. Hinrichs and Szmrecsanyi 2007: Figure 5).

These are the general patterns, but we also know that the effect that individual constraints have on variant choice may differ across varieties of English. For example, Hinrichs and Szmrecsanyi (2007) report probabilistic differences between written-edited-published British and American English regarding the effect of animacy, possessor thematicity, and possessum length; and Szmrecsanyi *et al*. (2014), an ARCHER-based study, finds significant differences between British and American English concerning the effect of possessor length on genitive choice. But a shortcoming of the literature on probabilistic differences in genitive choice in particular and grammatical variation in English in general is that extant scholarship mostly restricts attention to British and American English. Exceptions include Hundt and Szmrecsanyi (2012), who compare British English to New Zealand English and find differences in the strength of the possessor animacy constraint; and Szmrecsanyi *et al*. (2016), who sketch a probabilistic blueprint of genitive choice in four international varieties of English. But we still need more and more systematic research on the probabilistic grammar of genitive variation in World Englishes.

This volume is the perfect occasion to take the genitive alternation global, as it were. In this spirit, we adopt in this chapter a larger-scale comparative perspective, for the sake of exploring the way international users of English choose between the *s*-genitive and the *of*-genitive. On the methodological plane, we use the variationist method (in the sense of Labov 1972: 188) to identify variable genitives in materials drawn from the *International Corpus of English* (ICE). We specifically consider those ICE components sampling British English, Canadian English, Irish English, New Zealand English, Hong Kong English, Indian English, Jamaican English, Philippine English, and Singapore English. Subsequently, we annotate the genitive observations for a range of pertinent predictor variables (e.g. possessor animacy, constituent length, givenness, etc.), a step that allows us to gauge the extent to which these constraints have differential effects in the varieties under study. Two research questions guide our inquiry: (i) What is the extent to which varieties of English have different genitive choice grammars? (ii) What are the probabilistic constraints that tend to make a difference in a cross-variety perspective?

The research we report here is carried out in the context of a project based at the KU Leuven entitled 'Exploring probabilistic grammar(s) in varieties of English around the world', which is situated at the crossroads of research on English as a World Language, usage-based theoretical linguistics, variationist linguistics, and cognitive sociolinguistics. The project combines the spirit of the Probabilistic Grammar framework (see e.g. Bresnan 2007) with scholarship on World Englishes (e.g. Schneider 2007; Mesthrie and Bhatt 2008). The former assumes that grammatical knowledge is experience-based, dynamic, and partially probabilistic, a view that the project links to the sociolinguistics of postcolonial English-speaking communities around the world. The main aim is to investigate the plasticity of the probabilistic knowledge of English grammar, on the part of language users with diverse regional and cultural backgrounds. We refer the reader to Szmrecsanyi *et al.* (2016) for a programmatic sketch of the project.

This chapter is structured as follows. In Section 13.2, we discuss our methodology. In Section 13.3, we initially present some univariate analyses of the dataset before presenting a multifactorial conditional inference tree analysis. Section 13.4 offers a discussion and some concluding remarks.

13.2 Methods and Data

We adopt the variationist method and are interested in 'alternate ways of saying "the same" thing' (Labov 1972: 188). Hence, we restrict attention to *s*-genitives and *of*-genitives that are 'interchangeable', i.e. that can be paraphrased. For example, the genitive construction in (2) is interchangeable – it could be rephrased as *the activities of the university* – and (3) could in principle be re-cast as *the territory's three universities' vice-chancellors*, or as *the vice-chancellors of the three universities of the territory*.

(2) However, in today's context there are many of our alumni who might like to support **the university's activities** but find themselves in a rather embarrassing position from a pecuniary point of view
<ICE-Canada, w1b-021>

(3) Leading academics, including **the vice-chancellors of the territory's three universities**, as well as prominent professionals are also on the list   <ICE-Hong Kong, w2c-001>

Examples (4) and (5), on the other hand, are not variable and thus are not included in our dataset. The *s*-genitives in (4) are fixed expressions. The *of*-construction in (5) cannot alternate either. It is an example of an appositive genitive, in which the possessor (i.e. *60 seconds per unit*) and the possessum (i.e. *the limit*) are co-referential.

(4) When **the Sovereign's Escort** has come to a halt there as they have now over in front of **the Guards' Memorial** [...] field officer Lieutenant Colonel Lyszinsky will give the command for the final royal salute <ICE-Great Britain, s2a-011>

(5) Longer simulation will approach **the limit of 60 seconds per unit**
<ICE-Philippines, w2a-031>

Consequently, the choice context is defined as the entirety of all genitive occurrences minus the ones that are categorical (Rosenbach 2014). Besides fixed expressions and appositive genitives, we also excluded the following genitive types from our analysis following the guidelines in Wolk *et al.* (2013): partitive genitives, where possessor and possessum are in a part-whole relationship (e.g. *At about the same period of history* <ICE-India, w2a-011>); descriptive or classifying genitives, which cannot be expressed by the respective other genitive variant, but can be paraphrased as a noun modified by an adjective (e.g. *people in positions of trust in the church* <ICE-New Zealand, s1b-011>); dates (e.g. *we're having a thing at Philip Sherlock on sixth of June* <ICE-Jamaica, s1a-031>); and double genitives (e.g. *A painting of Pete's* <ICE-Jamaica, s2b-041>). Apart from that, only instances with a definite possessum were eligible as interchangeable. Examples such as (6) and (7) were, therefore, excluded from the analysis. Re-phrasing the genitive in (6) as **the union treaty's a draft* is not possible. The bare plural in (7) is a similar case; the apparent alternative form *the enterprise's operations* is not ungrammatical, but it refers to the entirety of operations of the enterprise in question rather than to an undefined subset of its operations, as the *of*-genitive in (6) does. Both (6) and (7) cannot be expressed as *s*-genitives because in *s*-genitive constructions, possessors always have a determining function and, in consequence, always render the possessum definite.

(6) the USSR rejected **a draft of the union treaty**
<ICE-Singapore, s1b-041>

(7) And then they also have uh uh Income Statements but uh they are very much related to **operations of the enterprise**.
<ICE-Hong Kong, s2a-021>

The variable context thus defined was studied in nine components of ICE (Greenbaum 1996). Our selection of World Englishes includes – in the parlance of Kachru (1992) – Inner Circle varieties (ICE-Canada, ICE-Great Britain, ICE-Ireland, ICE-New Zealand), advanced Outer Circle varieties (ICE-Jamaica, ICE-Singapore; see Schneider 2007), as well as other Outer Circle varieties (ICE-Hong Kong, ICE-India, ICE-Philippines). We are thus in a position to study genitive variation in a regionally and typologically diverse as well as – crucially – not Inner Circle-centric sample of World Englishes. Each ICE component consists of one million words and covers 600,000 words of spoken English and 400,000 words of written English. The components are further subdivided into a variety of spoken and written registers.

Once all relevant genitive occurrences were identified in the ICE materials, we annotated variable genitives for a range of language-internal variables that previous research has shown to be important determinants of the variation.

Possessor animacy is widely considered to be the most important predictor of the choice between the *s-* and the *of-*genitive (Rosenbach 2005; Jankowski and Tagliamonte 2014). The constraint is so strong that it can be found as a prescriptive rule in many pedagogical grammars (e.g. Murphy 2012). The rule states that if the possessor is animate, the *s-*genitive is to be used (as in *Darwin's disciple* <ICE-Canada, w2a-011>); inanimate possessors, on the other hand, are to be expressed as *of-*genitives (as in *the function of English in India* <ICE-India, s2b-041>). But we stress that possessor animacy is merely one relatively strong force among many factors that influence this syntactic alternation. Recall the genitive in (3), which is realised as *of-*genitive even though its possessor (*vice-chancellors*) is animate. In this specific case, two other factors disfavour an *s-*genitive realisation: (i) the fact that the possessor is longer than the possessum (see the section on length below), and (ii) the fact that the possessor phrase ends in [z] (see the section on final sibilancy below). For the present study, possessor animacy was annotated using a five-fold distinction following Wolk *et al.* (2013), who used a simplified version of the guidelines in Zaenen *et al.* (2004). This distinction includes the following levels: animate (e.g. *doctor*), collective (e.g. *family*), locative (e.g. *London*), temporal (e.g. *today*), and inanimate (e.g. *table*). The annotation was conducted in a semi-automatic fashion: we annotated a big share of our dataset automatically by tapping into the online database that emerged from Kersti Börjars and David Denison's project on 'Germanic possessive *-s*: An empirical, historical and theoretical study' (Denison *et al.* 2010, inter alia). If we could not find a word in this database, we looked it up in the WordNet database (Fellbaum 1998). All automatic annotations were manually checked afterwards.

Constituent length. The genitive alternation being a positional alternation, a crucial mechanism that explains much variability is the principle of end-weight (Behaghel 1909): short constituents tend to precede longer ones. This tendency may help explain the constituent order choices in (8) to (10). In this study, the syntactic weight of the constituents was operationalised as the length in number of characters, following Wolk *et al.* (2013) and Ehret *et al.* (2014). Wolk *et al.* (2013: 395) noted that different operationalisations of syntactic weight are highly correlated and that number of characters, thus, is an appropriate measure.[1]

(8) Beyond **the symbolic significance of these accomplishments** we have brought back inter-faith solidarity   <ICE-Philippines, s2b-021>

(9) And Jimmy Carter [...] walked to his inauguration ceremony to emphasise **the simplicity of republican government**
<ICE-Great Britain, s2b-021>

(10) All of **New Zealand's oil and gas discoveries** to date have been in the Taranaki Basin   <ICE-New Zealand, w2c-001>

In (8), possessor and possessum are of equal length (two words, or twenty characters each).[2] If there is no length difference, we typically find an *of*-construction, which is usually around twice as frequent as the *s*-form. In (9), the possessor is twice as long as the possessum, which makes an *of*-genitive even more likely. In (10), the length difference is reversed; here, the possessum is twice as long as the possessor, which makes the *s*-genitive more likely.

Final sibilancy. If the possessor phrase ends in a sibilant (i.e. [s], [z], [ʃ], [tʃ], [dʒ], or [ʒ]), *s*-genitive usage is less likely thanks to a haplology effect (Zwicky 1987).

---

[1] They report r = 0.976 between number of words and number of characters, r = 0.978 between number of syllables and number of words, and r = 0.993 between number of syllables and number of characters (Wolk *et al.* 2013: 395).

[2] Recall that in interchangeable genitives, possessums have to be definite. Therefore, the definite article in *of*-genitive possessums is a prerequisite and is not counted as part of the possessum phrase.

(11) With the iron will of the Tory gun lobby, and **the spaghetti-like determination of our minister of justice**, we'll soon be on a level playing field with the Americans   <ICE-Canada, w2e-001>

(12) In a bid to stem **Linux's popularity**, Microsoft has allowed the mainland controlled access to its codes   <ICE-Hong Kong, w2b-031>

The possessors in examples (11) and (12) both end in a sibilant. Even though the possessor in (11) is animate and of approximately the same length as the possessum, the *s*-genitive is avoided, possibly among other things for the sake of avoiding the sound clash in *justice's*. *S*-genitives with possessors that have a final sibilant, as in (12), occur very rarely (only six times in our sample of Hong Kong English, for example), and almost exclusively with proper names. The factor was annotated via automatic look-ups of the *CMU Pronouncing Dictionary*. If a word's transcription ended in a sibilant, the factor was coded as *present*, otherwise as *absent*.

Discourse accessibility (a.k.a. **information status**) of the possessor head is another known constraint on genitive variability (e.g. Grafmiller 2014). The possessor head is more accessible if it (i) has been mentioned in the previous context, if it (ii) constitutes a central topic of the text in which it appears, or if it (iii) is a very frequent noun in general. In our research design, GIVENNESS was set to *true* if an instance of the possessor head lemma was found previous to the genitive instance in the respective corpus text. Since corpus texts in ICE are around 2,000 words long, the size of the previous context that was considered thus ranged between 0 and slightly less than 2,000 words, depending on where in the text the genitive is located. For practical reasons, this study only considers previous mentions of the possessor head lemma and does not consider synonymous terms or phrases that might evoke similar concepts. The influence of GIVENNESS as we define it might thus be interpreted as rather conservative measure of the constraint's true potential. Given possessors should prefer the *s*-genitive as this variant then establishes old-before-new order. THEMATICITY represents the degree to which a possessor in question constitutes the topic of a text, i.e. how frequent it is in the corpus text under analysis; possessors with a high degree of topicality are said to be more likely to be realised as *s*-genitives (Osselton 1988) – in a text about Christian theology, for example, the genitive *Christianity's evolution* is more likely (Osselton 1988). We thus determined the number of times a possessor head is mentioned in the corpus text under analysis. OVERALL FREQUENCY of the possessor head has not been studied in the context of the English genitive alternation, but it is known to influence other variation phenomena (see, e.g. Hilpert 2008b on the English comparative alternation). We include overall frequency in the present analysis to gauge its potential influence on the choice between *s*- and *of*-genitive. The value of the factor was determined by consulting the relevant component in GloWbE, the *Corpus of Global Web-based English* (Davies and Fuchs 2015). For all possessors from the Canadian part of ICE, for example, the overall frequency of the respective lemmas in the Canadian component of GloWbE was determined. Frequencies of overall occurrence were subsequently normalised to frequency per million words.

Lexical density. Lexically dense contexts have been shown to favour *s*-genitive usage in some previous studies, as the *s*-genitive is the more compact coding option (e.g. Hinrichs and Szmrecsanyi 2007). We measured lexical density as type-token ratio (TTR),[3] and since TTR is very sensitive to text size, a fixed amount of the immediate preceding and following context of genitive instances was analysed. In each case, we calculated TTR for the surrounding one hundred words, fifty from each side, following Hinrichs and Szmrecsanyi (2007). If a genitive instance was situated at the beginning or towards the end of a corpus text, additional context was taken into account as necessary.

13.3 Results

In our dataset, we find 7,948 interchangeable *of*-genitives and 2,610 interchangeable *s*-genitives (75.3 per cent and 24.7 per cent, respectively). Section 13.3.1 will explore – with an eye towards cross-variety differences – how the distributions of these proportions are predicted by the language-internal constraints that we annotated for (see above) and by language-external factors. Section 13.3.2 will synthesise by presenting a multifactorial conditional inference tree analysis.

---

[3] TTR is defined as the ratio of the number of types and the number of tokens in a text:

$$TTR = \frac{number\ of\ unique\ types}{number\ of\ tokens}.$$

Texts that contain many repetitions (i.e. less unique types per number of tokens) will yield a lower TTR, whereas texts with few repetitions will yield a higher TTR.

Possessives World-Wide: Genitive Variation in Varieties of English 323

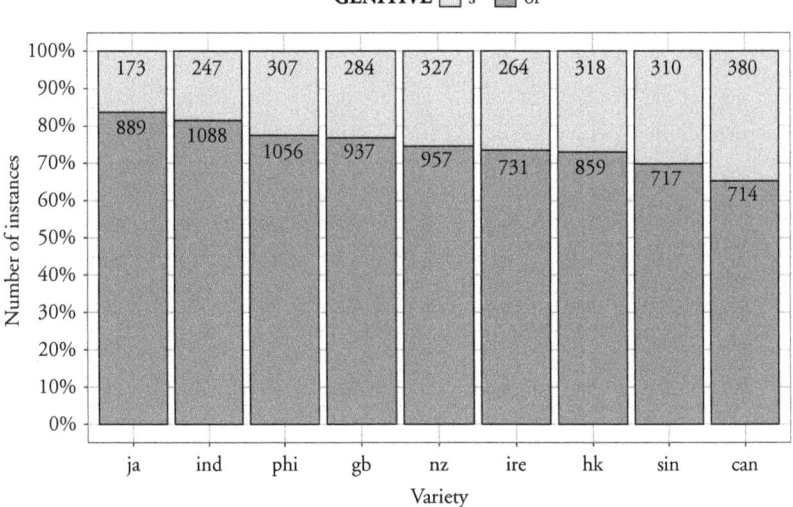

Figure 13.1 Distribution of genitive variants by variety in nine varieties of English
NB. *ja*='Jamaican', *ind*='Indian', *phi*='Philippine', *gb*='British', *nz*='New Zealand', *ire*='Irish', *hk*='Hong Kong', *sin*='Singapore', *can*='Canadian' English.

13.3.1 Genitive Distributions as a Function of Language-External and Language-Internal Factors

Figure 13.1 sets the scene by reporting the distributions of the genitive variants across all varieties subject to investigation in the present study. At the extreme ends of the spectrum, we find Jamaican English, where the *s*-genitive is least popular, and Canadian English, where the *s*-genitive is most popular. On the whole, there is a tendency that the *s*-genitive is more widespread in Inner Circle varieties than in Outer Circle varieties, two outliers (Singapore English and Hong Kong English) notwithstanding.

Next, we turn to a discussion of the role that the difference between spoken and written texts plays. In the dataset as a whole, we do not find significant medium differences (see leftmost panel in Figure 13.2). But a cross-varietal perspective reveals three distinct groups of varieties: one in which the spoken medium favours *s*-genitives (e.g. New Zealand English, Canadian English, Irish English, Singapore English), one in which there seems to be no difference (as in British English and Jamaican English), and one in which the *s*-genitive is less common in spoken texts than in written texts (Philippine English and Hong Kong English).

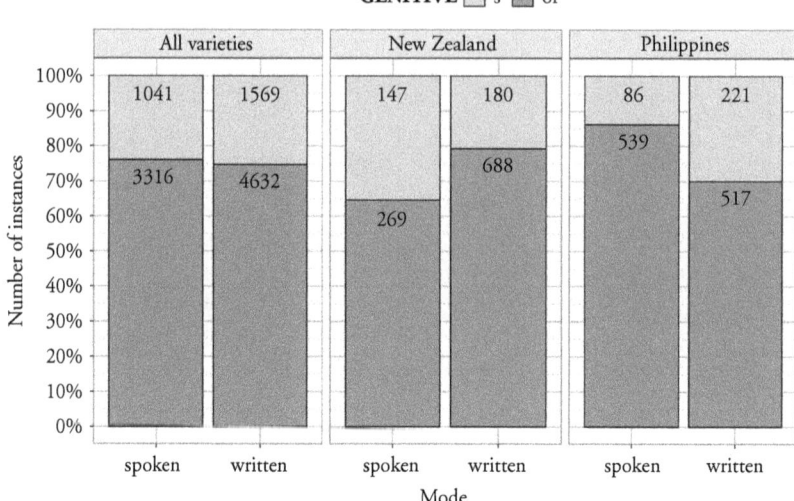

Figure 13.2 Distribution of genitive variants by genre in the entire dataset vs. the distributions in ICE-New Zealand and ICE-Philippines

Figure 13.3 plots the number of *s*- and *of*-genitives as a function of possessor animacy.[4] Animacy has the expected effect across the board: *s*-genitives are attracted by animate possessors and are rare with inanimate possessors. Collective, locative, and temporal possessors are more hospitable to the *s*-genitive than inanimate possessors. But all varieties are not equal: Figure 13.3 also shows that animate possessors in Canadian English quite favour the *s*-genitive, while Hong Kong English *s*-genitives are not particularly much attracted to animate possessors. The varieties not shown in Figure 13.3 (British, Indian, Irish, Jamaican, New Zealand, Philippine, and Singapore English) are all similar with regard to animacy distributions.

Figure 13.4 plots the proportion of *s*-genitives (*y*-axis) as a function of possessor phrase length (*x*-axis). On the whole, we find that, as expected, longer possessors disfavour the *s*-genitive, where they are – in line with the principle of end-weight – placed at the end. However, the relationship has slightly different shapes across varieties. For example, in Canadian English

---

[4] In Figure 13.3 and similar figures that will follow, the plots show cross-varietal differences alongside the effects of the predictors that have been discussed above. We specifically plot the distribution in the entire dataset next to two distributions from varieties that differ substantially from the general trend in opposite directions.

Possessives World-Wide: Genitive Variation in Varieties of English 325

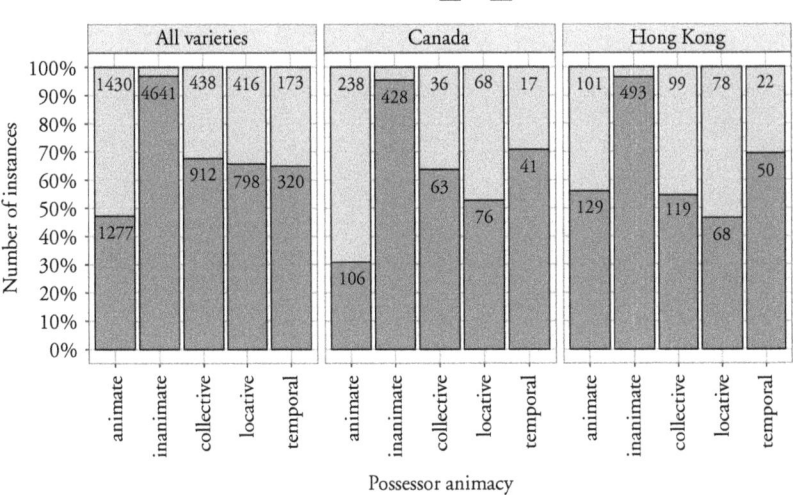

Figure 13.3 Distribution of genitive variants by possessor animacy in the entire dataset vs. the distributions in ICE-Canada and ICE-Hong Kong

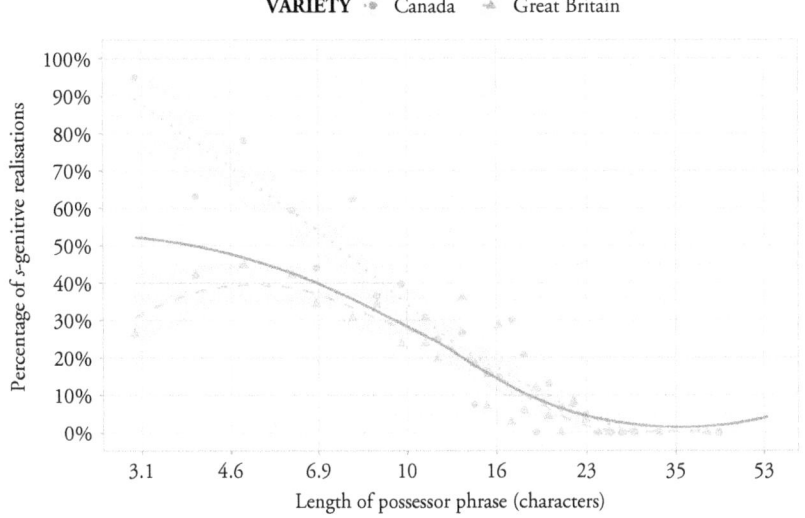

Figure 13.4 S-genitive proportion as a function of possessor length in nine varieties vs. the distributions in ICE-Canada and ICE-Great Britain
NB. Lines are LOESS smoothers (solid line depicts the relationship across all nine varieties in the sample).

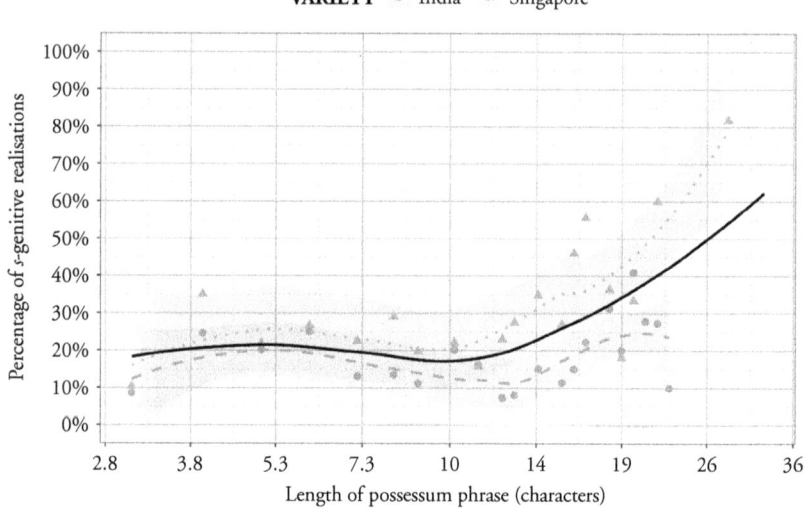

Figure 13.5 S-genitive proportion as a function of possessum length in nine varieties of English
NB. Lines are LOESS smoothers (solid line depicts the relationship across all nine varieties in the sample).

short possessor phrases favour *s*-genitive use more strongly than in all other varieties. In British English, on the other hand, we find a more quadratic relationship: here possessors of medium length (around five characters) are most likely to be phrased in *s*-form. A similar quadratic pattern has been observed by Ehret *et al.* (2014) for British English in the ARCHER corpus. We note that Irish English exhibits a similarly quadratic pattern, and so do – albeit to a lesser extent – Philippine English and Hong Kong English. In the other varieties (i.e. New Zealand, Singapore, Jamaican, and Indian English), the relationship is rather linear. The range of values in Figure 13.4 also shows the importance of the length constraint for the genitive alternation, especially in Canadian English. Here, values range from up to 90 per cent (i.e. almost categorical *s*-genitive use) for very short possessors to less than 10 per cent (i.e. almost categorical *of*-genitive use).

Also in accordance with the principle of end weight is the effect that possessum phrase length has (Figure 13.5). Up until a length of around fourteen characters, possessum length does not seem to make much of a difference, but longer possessums increasingly favour the *s*-genitive. The tendency to code very long possessums with an *s*-genitive is strongest

Possessives World-Wide: Genitive Variation in Varieties of English 327

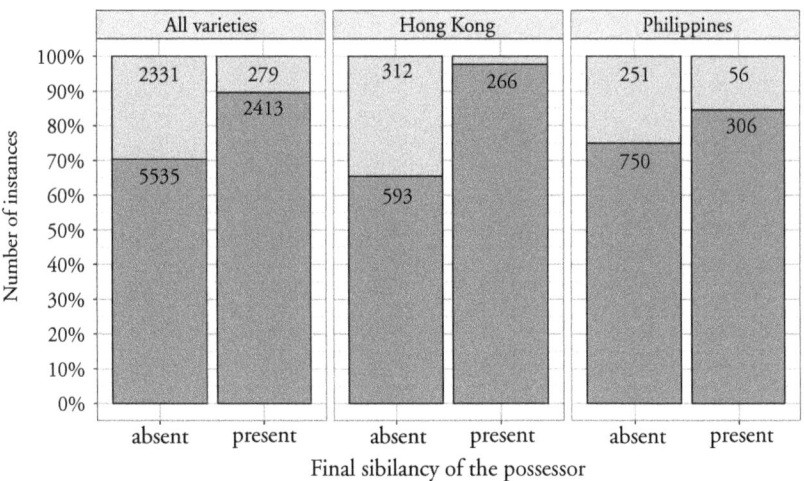

Figure 13.6 Distribution of genitive variants by final sibilancy in the entire dataset vs. the distributions in ICE-Hong Kong and ICE-Philippines

in Singapore English, and weakest in Indian, British, and Jamaican English. The other varieties (Canadian, Irish, New Zealand, and Philippine English) take the middle road. All varieties have in common that possessum length in the lower range (< twelve characters) does not seem to have much of an effect.

Final sibilancy disfavours the *s*-genitive, as it should (Figure 13.6). The effect is strongest in Hong Kong English, where we only find six *s*-genitives with a final sibilant in the possessor. By contrast, Philippine English speakers seem least affected by final sibilancy. Indian and Singapore English are also fairly sensitive to final sibilancy. The other varieties are close to the average.

Figure 13.7 shows that possessors which are discourse-given favour the *s*-genitive, as they should because the *s*-genitive places the possessor (old information) first. The effect is strongest in Canadian English, but fairly absent from Hong Kong English. Also rather unaffected by givenness are speakers and writers of Singapore, British, and Indian English. By contrast, Irish, Philippine, New Zealand, and Jamaican English exhibit rather strong givenness effects.

Thematicity measures the topicality of possessor heads. Thematic possessors have been argued to favour the *s*-genitive, and they generally do in

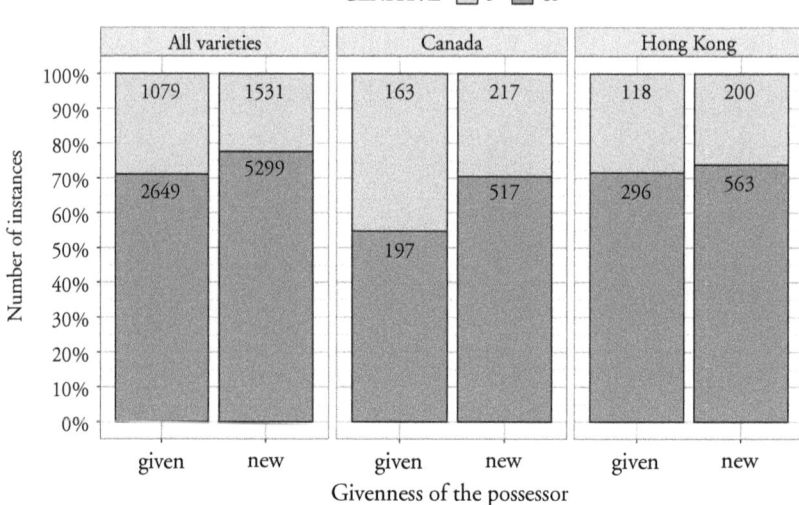

Figure 13.7 Distribution of genitive variants by givenness of the possessor head in the entire dataset vs. the distributions in ICE-Canada and ICE-Hong Kong

our dataset. Figure 13.8, however, uncovers non-linear effects. If the possessor head is very frequent (more than around twenty occurrences per 2,000 words and increasing), we find quite a bit of variability. When possessor heads occur between thirty and eighty times per 2,000 words (rightmost part of Figure 13.8), the factor seems to lose its explanatory power. These complications are partly due to cross-varietal differences. While speakers and writers of Canadian English tend to code thematic possessor heads with the s-genitive, the genitive choices of speakers and writers of Indian English are not much affected by this factor.

In our dataset, the effect of the overall possessor frequency does not have the theoretically predicted direction. The 'Easy First' principle (MacDonald 2013) predicts that 'easy' (which can mean frequent) constituents are placed first, and so we expected that frequent possessor heads would attract the s-genitive. This is not really the case, as Figure 13.9 shows: we find a moderate but significant negative relationship between overall frequency and s-genitive usage. This relationship survives controls for the overall frequency of the possessum. We speculate that the effect is due to a correlation with the factors definiteness (*definite, indefinite*) and noun phrase expression type (*proper noun, gerund,* etc.), which have not been included in this study. Highly frequent possessors that are predominantly

Possessives World-Wide: Genitive Variation in Varieties of English 329

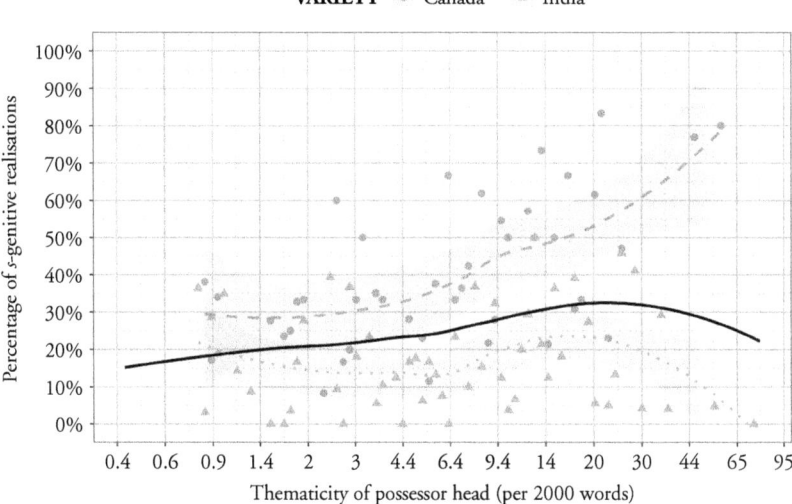

Figure 13.8 *S*-genitive proportion as a function of text frequency of the possessor head in nine varieties of English
NB. Lines are LOESS smoothers (solid line depicts the relationship across all nine varieties in the sample).

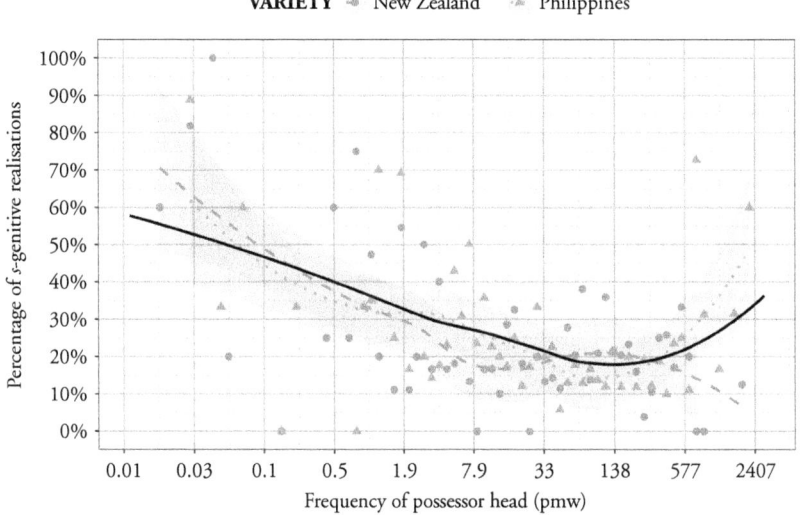

Figure 13.9 *S*-genitive proportion as a function of overall frequency of the possessor head in nine varieties of English
NB. Lines are LOESS smoothers (solid line depicts the relationship across all nine varieties in the sample).

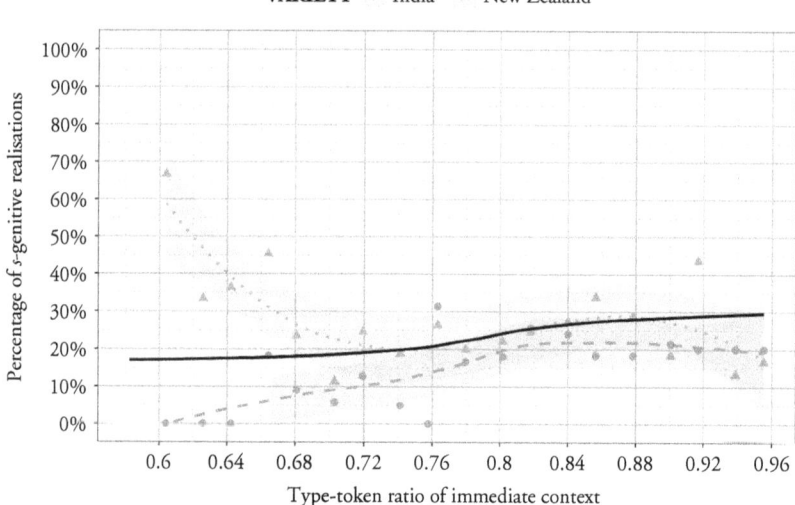

Figure 13.10 S-genitive proportion as a function of type-token ratio of the corpus texts in nine varieties of English
NB. Lines are LOESS smoothers (solid line depicts the relationship across all nine varieties in the sample).

used with *of*-genitives are often indefinite or gerunds. The least frequent possessors are often proper names.

The increase in *s*-genitive use that we find in lexically dense environments (see Figure 13.10) is in line with previous research. The effect is rather weak overall, but we do see differences between varieties, for example between New Zealand English and Indian English. These differences materialise especially in the left, low-density half of the diagram. A pattern similar to New Zealand English can be observed for British English. Jamaican and Irish English are fairly unresponsive to lexical density, whereas Philippine and Hong Kong English show increasing *s*-genitive frequencies in texts with high type-token ratios.

13.3.2 The Multifactorial View: A Conditional Inference Tree

We will now grow a conditional inference tree to model and visually depict how constraints interact to engender genitive outcomes in a multifactorial perspective. Tagliamonte and Baayen (2012) offer an accessible introduction to the technique; suffice it to say here that the algorithm that creates the tree repeatedly splits the data into two parts. The splits are chosen in a way that

Possessives World-Wide: Genitive Variation in Varieties of English 331

seeks to reduce the variability in the outcome variable for the resulting portions. For example, if possessor animacy does affect genitive choice, the algorithm will split the data accordingly (i.e. it will separate genitives with animate possessors from genitives with other levels of possessor animacy). The algorithm will then continue to split the resulting portions recursively until it cannot find any significant differences anymore, or until it has reached the limit of maximum depth. For this analysis we set the significance level to 0.01 and limited the tree to a maximum depth of four levels. With this limit we can still plot the results of our tree and at the same time avoid overfitting our data. Computations were performed using the statistics software R (R Core Team 2014) in conjunction with the *party* package (Hothorn *et al.* 2006).

The plot in Figure 13.11 shows a conditional inference tree that models genitive choice across the nine varieties of English studied. Every branching out from a node indicates a significant split between the portion of the data whose levels are indicated on the left branch and the portion of data indicated on the right branch. The terminal nodes (bars) at the bottom indicate the relative frequency of the *of*-genitive (black) vis-à-vis the *s*-genitive (grey), given the configuration of predictors at higher nodes. For example, the *of*-genitive is particularly popular in the fifth terminal node from the left (n = 1176), which is the set of genitive outcomes we obtain when we – starting at the top of the tree – restrict attention to (i) British, Indian, Jamaican, or Philippine English, (ii) possessors that are longer than 0.167 on a centred log scale (see below), and (iii) inanimate possessors. By contrast, the *s*-genitive is rather frequent in the fourth terminal node from the right (n = 1140). This particular terminal node is about genitive contexts (i) in Canadian, Hong Kong, Irish, New Zealand, or Singapore English, where possessors are (ii) animate and (iii) fairly short.

In the big picture, then, the tree includes the predictors VARIETY, ANIMACY, POSSESSOR LENGTH, POSSESSUM LENGTH, and FINAL SIBILANCY. The other predictors (GIVENNESS, THEMATICITY, FREQUENCY, TTR, and MODE) are not sufficiently important to be included in the top four levels of the tree (recall that we limited the tree to four levels). Most splits divide the data along different levels of ANIMACY, which is represented in six out of fourteen nodes. The data are split four times according to POSSESSOR LENGTH, twice according to POSSESSUM LENGTH, and once each according to VARIETY and FINAL SIBILANCY.

The first, and thus arguably most crucial, split separates British (*gb*), Indian (*ind*), Jamaican (*ja*), and Philippine (*phi*) English on the left branch

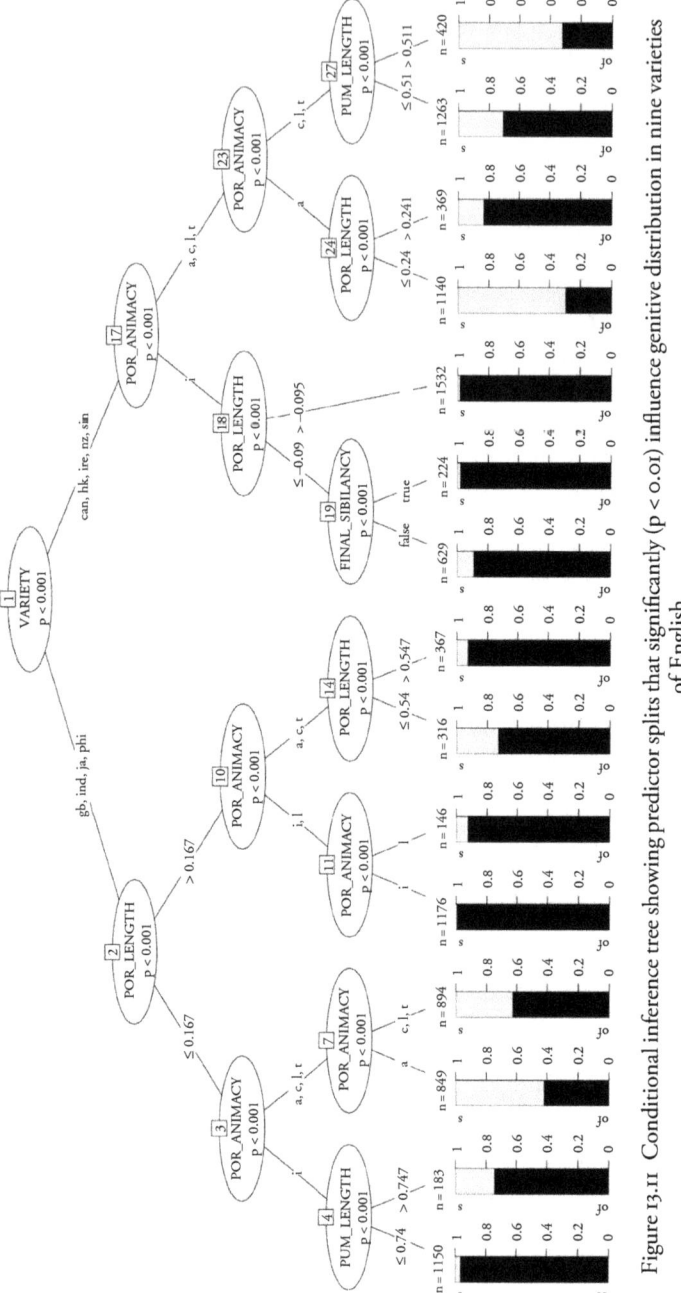

Figure 13.11 Conditional inference tree showing predictor splits that significantly ($p < 0.01$) influence genitive distribution in nine varieties of English

NB. *POR* is short for 'possessor', *PUM* is short for 'possessum'; levels of VARIETY: *can*='Canadian', *gb*='British', *hk*='Hong Kong', *ind*='Indian', *ire*='Irish', *ja*='Jamaican', *nz*='New Zealand', *phi*='Philippine', and *sin*='Singapore' English; levels of ANIMACY: *a*='animate', *c*='collective', *i*='inanimate', *l*='locative', *t*='temporal'.

from Canadian (*can*), Hong Kong (*hk*), Irish (*ire*), New Zealand (*nz*), and Singapore (*sin*) English on the right. This split to some extent reflects the frequencies that we saw in Figure 13.1, with higher *s*-genitive occurrences in the left-branched varieties and lower rates for the right-branched varieties. The varieties under study differ in terms of which split is selected next. The left-branched varieties (*gb, ind, ja,* and *phi*) split according to POSSESSOR LENGTH (node 2). Possessors that are equal or shorter than 0.167 on a centred log scale (which corresponds to thirteen characters in length) constitute a group that contains significantly more *s*-genitives than the group of longer possessors. For the other varieties (*can, hk, ire, nz,* and *sin*), it is ANIMACY that makes a significant difference first (node 17). This second split on the right divides inanimate (*i*) possessors, which favour *of*-genitives, from animate (*a*), collective (*c*), locative (*l*), and temporal (*t*) possessors, which more frequently attract *s*-genitives. The subsequent splits further highlight the importance of POSSESSOR ANIMACY and LENGTH. The two ANIMACY splits that separate non-inanimate from animate possessors (levels *a, c, l, t* versus *i*) (nodes 3 and 17) are followed by splits that separate *a* from *c, l,* and *t* (nodes 7 and 23). In the case of longer possessors in the *gb, ind, ja,* and *phi* varieties (node 10),[5] however, it is the distinction between *i, l* and *a, c, t* that is most important. In all cases, the subgroup with animate possessors contains more *s*-genitives. POSSESSOR LENGTH and POSSESSUM LENGTH influence genitive use in accordance with the principle of end-weight. We further observe that POSSESSUM LENGTH seems to be most important when possessors are inanimate (see nodes 4 and 27). We also note that it is only in the right branch (varieties *can, hk, ire, nz,* and *sin*) that the tree shows a split according to FINAL SIBILANCY, with significantly less *s*-genitives in the presence of a sibilant at the end of the possessor (node 19).

13.4 Discussion and Conclusion

Our point of departure in this contribution was the fact that while variation between the *s*-genitive and the *of*-genitive is one of the best-studied syntactic alternations in the grammar of English, the literature on this variation is deficient because it simplistically restricts attention to variation patterns in Inner Circle varieties such as British, American, and New Zealand English. Genitive variation in Outer Circle varieties, by contrast, has received short shrift. To address this negligence, this study

---

[5] The POSSESSOR LENGTH of 0.167 at node 2 corresponds to thirteen characters.

has endeavoured to explore variation in no fewer than nine international varieties of English, based on data drawn from the *International Corpus of English* (ICE): British English, Canadian English, Irish English, New Zealand English, Hong Kong English, Indian English, Jamaican English, Philippine English, and Singapore English. This sample of varieties is regionally and typologically diverse, covering native, shift, and indigenised L2 varieties. It is this breadth that has enabled us to gauge the malleability of probabilistic genitive grammars on a global scale.

Key findings included the following. First, we saw that the *s*-genitive is by and large more frequent in (native) Inner Circle varieties than it is in indigenised L2 varieties in the Outer Circle. It is well known that contact varieties avoid synthetic structures (Siegel *et al.* 2014), and that morphosyntactic complexity is negatively associated with the proportion of learners (Bentz and Winter 2013), so the hostility in Outer Circle varieties towards clitic *-s* with its inflectional roots (see the chapters in Börjars *et al.* 2013b for more discussion) may very well have to do with the mode of language acquisition in these varieties. Second, on the whole, the constraints on variation that we studied have the theoretically expected effect. Thus, for example, animate possessors always favour the *s*-genitive, long possessors favour the *of*-genitive, final sibilancy consistently disfavours the *s*-genitive, and so on. An exception is overall frequency of the possessor head: ours being the first study to include this factor, we saw that contrary to expectations (consider the 'Easy First' principle proposed by MacDonald 2013), frequent possessors favour the *of*-genitive.

Further, the multifactorial conditional inference tree analysis we utilised to study how the above constraints interact to engender genitive outcomes showed that there are four language-internal constraints that are particularly important to predict the genitive choices that language users make: possessor animacy, constituent length, and final sibilancy. At the same time, the tree suggested that these constraints work in slightly different ways in different varieties of English. In the parlance of Szmrecsanyi *et al.* (2016: 133), then, these are the constraints that are subject to 'probabilistic indigenization': the process whereby stochastic patterns of internal linguistic variation are reshaped by shifting usage frequencies in speakers of postcolonial varieties.

The tree specifically suggested that the varieties under study fall, by and large, into two groups: British English, Indian English, Jamaican English, and Philippine English (Group 1) versus Canadian English, Hong Kong English, Irish English, New Zealand English, and Singapore English (Group 2). Among other things, in Group 1 it is possessor length that appears to be the most important language-internal factor, while in Group 2 possessor animacy is the top-ranked constraint. We add that we also experimented with splitting up the data in terms of a binary Kachru-inspired (Kachru 1992) distinction between Inner Circle and Outer Circle (or English as a Native Language versus English as a Second Language) varieties. This distinction, however, was not selected as significant by the analysis, which may indicate that – in the realm of genitive variation – it is not particularly relevant. What seems to be more significant is the possible role of linguistic conservatism.[6] A post-hoc analysis of *shall* and *upon* in the ICE sample that we investigated reveals a pattern that resembles the split in the conditional inference tree.[7] The link between linguistic conservatism and variant choice, therefore, is a promising topic for future research.

The analysis presented here is in many ways preliminary, and work is underway (Heller 2019) to study the genitive alternation in more diverse materials such as web language, as sampled in the *Corpus of Global Web-based English* (GloWbE), and to utilise more sophisticated analysis techniques such as mixed-effects binary logistic regression analysis to better understand the variation patterns at hand (Heller *et al.* 2017). We are also working on spot-checking the cognitive robustness of the corpus-derived probabilities via rating experiments along the lines of Bresnan (2007) and Bresnan and Ford (2010), who showed that language users' acceptability ('naturalness') intuitions about genitive choices match probabilities as calculated in a corpus-based regression model.

---

[6] We are grateful to an anonymous reviewer for this suggestion.
[7] The frequencies of *shall* and *upon* in the ICE material are as follows: *ind* (fifty-two tokens), *phi* (fifty-two tokens), *ja* (forty-nine tokens), *gb* (forty-three tokens), *hk* (twenty-six tokens), *nz* (eighteen tokens), *sin* (fifteen tokens), *can* (twelve tokens), *ire* (twelve tokens).

CHAPTER 14

American English: No Written Standard before the Twentieth Century?

Christian Mair

14.1 Introduction

In his study *Postcolonial English: Varieties around the World* (2007), Edgar Schneider proposes a sociolinguistic and contact-linguistic 'Dynamic Model' to account for the emergence of new varieties. He goes on to demonstrate this Dynamic Model in sixteen case studies, covering four continents and spanning the entire functional range from L1 Englishes spoken by descendants of European settler-colonists, through L2 varieties serving as languages of education and administration, to new varieties developing in contact with English-lexifier pidgins and creoles. All of these varieties are developing in the same direction, towards more endo-normativity, but the speed of this development is different in different varieties, and none has yet fully reached the end goal. The book concludes with a long chapter on 'The cycle in hindsight: the emergence of American English' (2007: 251–308), which makes the plausible point that American English is the only postcolonial variety which has fully completed the five stages of emancipation from British English which the Dynamic Model postulates. Phase 1, *foundation*, is delimited from 'ca. 1587–1670' (2007: 254). Phase 2, *exonormative stabilisation*, covers the years from 'ca. 1670–1773' (2007: 264) and is in turn followed by Phase 3, *nativisation* ('ca. 1773–1828/1848', 2007: 273). Phase 4, *endonormative stabilisation*, takes us from 1828/1848 to 1898 (2007: 282) and is followed by Phase 5, *differentiation*, which is assumed to have started in 1898 (2007: 291) and thus broadly covers the twentieth and twenty-first centuries.

This chronology reflects a broad consensus among authorities on the history of American English which assumes that:

> British and American English diverged in the nineteenth century because *both* varieties changed. In the prestige dialect of London, words like *dance* and *grass* were pronounced in new ways; the *r*-sound disappeared in some

> places in a word and was kept in others (the first *r* in *river* stayed the same and the second one changed); and *h* vanished in some places (for instance, in *up high*) and erupted in others (as the first sound of *elegant*, though London observers vigorously criticized it). Americans kept some old speechways – for instance, the first vowel in *almond* was sounded as the *a* in *ham* – and introduced new ones in ways that created new words out of old ones – *curse* and *cuss*, *parcel* and *passel*. (Bailey 2004: 13)

In this narrative, the nineteenth century was the period when American English *de facto* took its equal place alongside British English – even if the language-ideological recognition of this process of emancipation may have been delayed. However, from the first quarter of the twentieth century the legitimacy of an American norm alongside the British one was no longer queried seriously. The resulting 'bipolar' standardisation of World English prefigured the present pluricentric constellation, which emerged as the result of twentieth-century waves of decolonisation. These added further standards, with the difference being that none of them as yet enjoys the global recognition and influence of British and American Standard English.

This version of history is reflected in synchronic treatments of British and American English, such as Trudgill and Hannah (2008), which catalogues the many systematic contrasts between the British and American pronunciation standards (2008: 41–58), points to vocabulary differences which 'are very numerous and are capable of causing varying degrees of comprehension problems' (2008: 59), and then goes on to identify the 'relatively few differences in grammar and spelling [... which] tend to be fairly trivial when considered from the point of view of mutual understanding' (2008: 59). Such an assessment is uncontroversial as far as it goes. Where the written language is concerned, however, orthographic and grammatical contrasts are important alongside vocabulary differences, because the phonological plane as the natural and most obvious discriminator between varieties is absent. The point the present chapter will make is that the clear and consistent differentiation of British and American written standards, as defined by orthographic and grammatical norms, went on until well into the twentieth century (and is in several instances still going on today).

There is an enormous literature on general aspects of standardisation of British and American English during the nineteenth and early twentieth centuries, complemented by an almost equal amount of detailed corpus-linguistic studies on present-day orthographical and grammatical contrasts between the two varieties. In view of this, it comes almost as a surprise that not much is known about the precise chronology of the standardisation process and the history of individual variables. The best starting point for such an investigation at present is the collection of papers in Rohdenburg and Schlüter (2009a), which covers an unprecedented range of grammatical variables and, although mainly synchronic-contrastive in orientation, offers detailed historical information on at least some of them. One of the very few studies specifically devoted to the chronological emergence of the Present-day Standard American grammatical profile is Rohdenburg (2009). As the title of this study ('Grammatical divergence between British and American English in the nineteenth and early twentieth centuries') indicates, much in this process was still in flux throughout the nineteenth century, as the author demonstrates in detailed studies of seven grammatical variables.[1]

This chapter will examine the history of a number of variables in order to inform our understanding of the standardisation process. Section 14.2 of the present chapter will briefly introduce the data used and comment on the methodology. Section 14.3 focuses on orthography and traces the chronology of the implementation of the three most characteristic US spellings, namely *-or* for British *-our* (e.g. *favor*), *-er* for British *-re* (e.g. *center*), and single consonant for British double consonant (e.g. *traveler, worshiping*). Section 14.4 will discuss two simple morpholexical variants, namely *toward* (the present preferred US form) as against *towards* (still dominant in British English), and the past participle *gotten*. Section 14.5 will investigate more complex and still ongoing changes in the complementation of the verbs *help* and *prevent* by non-finite verbal forms. Some of these changes lead British and American English into the same direction, if at slightly different speeds. Others, however, have resulted in the standardisation of new regional contrasts between British and American norms of usage for the variables in question. This section thus shows the interplay of historical change, synchronic variability, and standardisation, which is at work today as it has been in the past. The conclusion (Section 14.6) will address the question of whether in view of the very late 'nativisation' of American English spelling and grammar (at least at the level of the standard language), Schneider's chronology of the emancipation of American English should be modified.

---

[1] Reflexive omission (e.g. *launch (oneself) into*), passivisation, *due (to)*, presence of *to be* in passive complements of verbs of direction (e.g. *order them (to be) dismissed*), prepositional gerunds (e.g. *have difficulty (in) doing . . .*), *to-* vs. bare infinitives with *help* (on which see below), mandative subjunctive.

14.2 Data and Methodology

English is a language for which there is an extremely rich corpus-linguistic working environment, which offers coverage of synchronic regional, social, and stylistic variability as well as great diachronic time-depth. The days of researchers struggling with scarcity of data in order to investigate specific instances of synchronic or diachronic variability are largely over. Corpus-based research on the process of standardisation, on the other hand, is still beset with a number of problems. First, as some of the relevant variants are common and others very rare, single corpora usually will be insufficient, and combinations of small and large corpora will have to be used. This introduces problems of comparability of results across different corpora, which need to be considered, although these problems are usually surmountable. More seriously, even corpora which purport to document Standard English (such as the 'Brown family') do so at one remove only. In fact, they do not straightforwardly represent the standard but, like any corpus, are made up of recorded instances of performance, in this case produced by speakers or writers considered capable of using Standard English. Whether these speakers always do what they are capable of is an open question. Some texts in a corpus of Standard English may be regulated even beyond the prevailing standard requirements, for example, because they additionally follow the house-style of a certain publisher. Others – especially, but not exclusively, literary texts – consciously deploy nonstandard features for their own rhetorical purposes. Language standardisation is driven by practical and ideological causes and motivations. Some of it proceeds below the threshold of speakers' and writers' conscious awareness, and some of it is consciously regulated. In this situation, corpus statistics may be a valuable pointer to what is going on, but standardisation and standardness should not be reduced to distributions in corpus data. What the topic of standardisation calls for is a mixed-methods approach, drawing on digital text-technology and statistics as well as traditional philological virtues (such as the careful analysis of individual textual examples in their linguistic and sociohistorical context).

The core data for the present investigation are provided by the extended 'Brown family' of corpora (i.e. LOB, Brown, F-LOB, Frown – already widely used – and their 1930s and 2006 analogues B-LOB, B-Brown, BE06 Corpus, and AmE06 Corpus) and the ARCHER corpus (version 3.2). Where this database is insufficient in size, it is complemented from the *Corpus of Historical American English* (COHA) and the *Google Books Ngram Viewer* project. The above-mentioned linguistic corpora are widely familiar in the English Studies community and do not require further comment here. The *Ngram Viewer* (Michel *et al.* 2011) is a less well-established resource in historical linguistics. It offers basic search facilities for the enormous amounts of text in several languages digitised by the *Google Books* project. With regard to the English-language data, the compilers assert robust usefulness for the period from 1800 to the present, for which it offers much more data than even the large standard historical corpora of English. As the search interface allows separate access to British and American books, this makes the *Ngram Viewer* a convenient tool for the present study. Needless to add, there are deficiencies, the two most important of which are lack of access to individual textual examples and uncertainty about absolute corpus sizes for individual periods.[2]

Apart from caveats to do with corpus practicalities, an element of subjective philological judgement was unavoidable in the choice of variables investigated in the present study. Taken together, however, the results of the individual case studies add up to a plausible language-historical picture on which future research can build.

14.3   1830–1980: One Hundred and Fifty Years of Orthographic Standardisation in American English

This section looks at the chronology of the standardisation processes which have established three types of simplified spellings as the present norm in American English: *-or* (for *-our*), *-er* (for *-re*), and single consonant before vowel-initial suffixes in non-finally stressed verbal bases (e.g. *traveler*). Quoting Milroy and Milroy (1991), Tieken-Boon van Ostade argues that if 'the standardisation process of a language involves "the suppression of optional variability" of that language [...], one would have to conclude that for English only spelling comes close to having a standard' (2009: 37). But as her own account shows, even the standardisation of spelling is usually a long-drawn-out and complex process. For English, it started in the late Middle English period, but as late as the nineteenth century *-or/-our* spellings continued to vary 'in ways that have nothing to do with present-day American or British spelling' (2009: 49).

Schneider (2007: 290–1) and numerous surveys of the history of English (e.g. Bailey 2004: 12–13; Finegan 2006: 392–3) emphasise that the

---

[2] As this chapter is going to press, I have noted the appearance of Gonçalves *et al.* (2018), who have taken a large-scale quantitative 'big data' approach to chart the separation of the British and American norms in the *Google Books* database. Where the variables under investigation overlap, their findings are broadly compatible with the more philological analyses carried out here.

standardisation of American English in the early nineteenth century was helped by Noah Webster (1758–1843), American patriot, lexicographer, and energetic spelling reformer, and a man with a pedagogical mission and mass appeal. The *-or* spellings were among those which he advocated, and the language historical evidence by and large provides evidence for the early success of his efforts. Traditional (subsequently 'British') *-our* spellings were phased out quickly and 'American' *-or* spellings were indeed standardised by the late nineteenth century. Figure 14.1 shows the diachronic tipping point in favour of the contemporary American preferences for three relevant words, namely *colour*, *favour*, and *labour*, in the *Google Books* 'American English' material in the period from 1800 to 1900 (*Ngram Viewer*).

This rapid establishment of an American orthographic norm which is clearly distinct from British usage is a textbook case of endonormative stabilisation – and one that fits squarely into the chronology of nativisation of American English assumed by Schneider. The transition to the *-or* spellings takes place rapidly in the two decades between 1830 and 1850.

If this instance of successful spelling reform was brought about by the widespread use of Webster's *American Spelling Book*, which sold about a million copies annually in the 1820s and had achieved a circulation of forty-two million by 1865 (Schneider 2007: 287), the question remains why other spellings that Webster advocated in the same publication were so much slower to be taken up. Thus, American *-er* spellings became dominant only in the twentieth century, with the diachronic tipping points of individual words separated by many decades. On the evidence of the *Ngram Viewer*, *center* wins out over *centre* in 1905, and *fiber* surpasses *fibre* in 1910; *theatre*, on the other hand, continues to be used at the same rate as *theater* for almost three decades from the 1940s and starts a serious decline only in 1976.[3] Similar observations can be made for the simplification of double consonants. *Traveler* (also one of the spellings advocated in the *American Spelling Book*) overtakes *traveller* in 1915, but *worshipping* continues to be used at equal rates to *worshiping* at the end of the twentieth century. In sum, the foregoing analyses show that the standardisation of localised spelling norms in the United States of America started patchily in the nineteenth century but was fully implemented only in the twentieth century.

[3] All searches were for lower-case forms of the words, so that the high incidence of the 'British' spelling cannot be due to proper names for British theatres, such as the *National Theatre* of London. To be fair, it should be added that *theatre* was a spelling which, unlike *fibre* or *centre*, was tolerated even by Webster himself (Finegan 2006: 393).

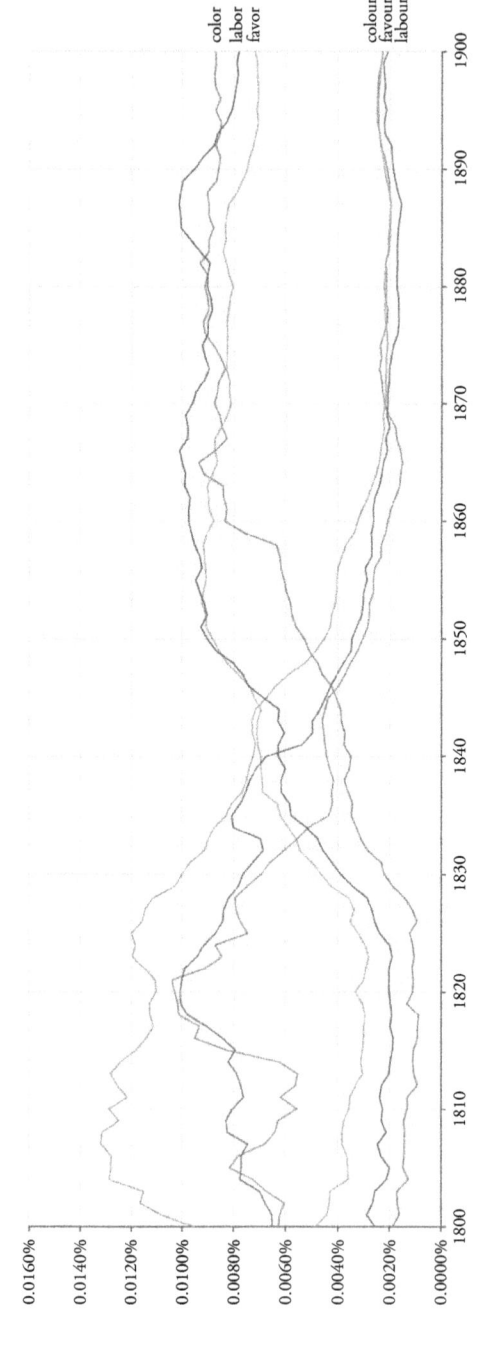

Figure 14.1 Move from *-our* to *-or* spellings in AmE (*Ngram Viewer*, AmE, 1800–1900)

In British English, there was little active intervention. The British *Ngram Viewer* diagram corresponding to Figure 14.1 shows fluctuation rather than change for the nineteenth and early twentieth centuries. The only interesting change during this period was that the *-or* spellings, a marginal option already in 1800, receded even further. The *-our* spellings have remained the clear default option in British English for the past two centuries (see Figure 14.2).

Limited influence from American English becomes evident only from the middle of the twentieth century, when there is a spike in the frequency of American spellings, caused by World War II. In the very recent past, though, American spellings are found at even higher rates in British English, which is a reflection of the default status of American spellings in contemporary transnational and global discourse.

14.4 Morpholexical Variation

A little-discussed but robust indicator of American English is the preference for *toward* rather than *towards* (Algeo 2006: 192; Rohdenburg and Schlüter 2009b: 370). The *Ngram Viewer* evidence (Figure 14.3) is interesting for this item because the diachronic tipping point in favour of the American form happens to be the year 1898, a symbolic demarcator between Phases 4 and 5 in Schneider's chronology of the emancipation of American English.

A corresponding diagram is not necessary for British English, as there is no change in preferences during this period. However, as in the case of *-or*, a gradual increase in the frequency of 'American' *toward* in British English is notable from the 1960s.[4] The Americanisation of (written) British English evidently goes deeper than mere spelling.

The past participle *gotten* figures in virtually every list of supposed present-day grammatical Americanisms, usually accompanied by the mention of the semantic contrast in American English between *I('ve) got a new computer* ('I have it') and *I've gotten a new computer* ('I acquired / obtained it'). What is less often mentioned is that even in contemporary American English *gotten* has not replaced *got*, but is merely a fairly common option. In Present-day Standard British English, *gotten* is used adjectivally, for example in expressions such as *ill-gotten gains*, and of course in the past participle of the common verb *forget*. As the *Oxford English Dictionary* (*OED*) shows with several citations (e.g. David Hume 1761;

---

[4] This is commented on in the Grammarist website: http://grammarist.com/spelling/toward-towards/.

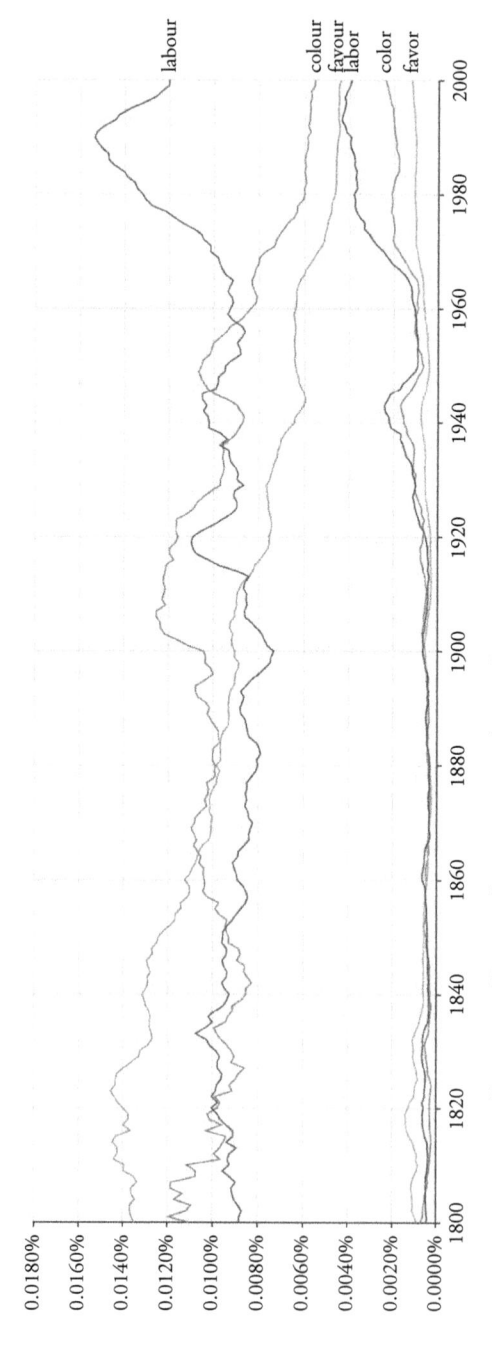

Figure 14.2 Variation between -*our* and -*or* spellings in BrE (*Ngram Viewer*, BrE, 1800–2000)

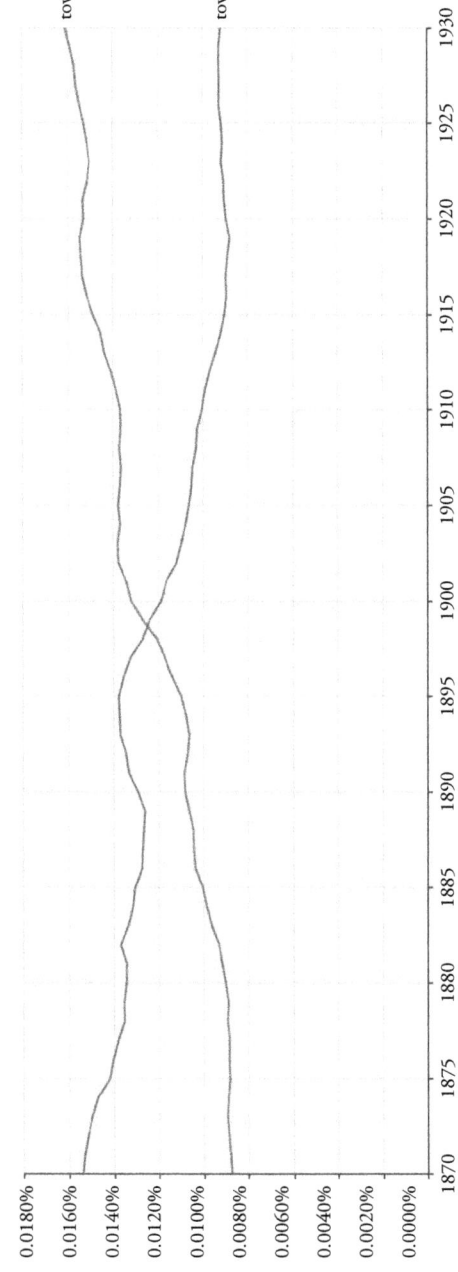

Figure 14.3 The establishment of *toward* as the US norm (*Ngram Viewer*, AmE, 1870–1930)

Samuel Johnson 1781; Richard Chenevix Trench 1860), *gotten* is not infrequently found in eighteenth- and nineteenth-century British writers. As at that time it is certainly no more common in American English, Hundt does not consider its survival in contemporary American English as a true instance of colonial archaism, but describes it as 'a low-frequency colloquial variant that has been gaining ground again rather lately in written Am[erican] E[nglish]' (2009: 22).

In short, it is not really plausible to refer to *gotten* as a grammatical Americanism before the second half of the twentieth century. The frequencies from the Brown family show a rise only from the 1930s, but starting from very low levels: from eight occurrences in B-Brown to sixteen in Brown, twenty-nine in Frown, and forty-eight in the Lancaster AmE06. The eight early occurrences from B-Brown represent the transitive use and use in phrasal verbs such as *get over* or *get back*, with one example representing foreigner talk in a work of fiction.

(1) This unsavory business prompted people to look into boxing to find where and how **it had gotten its bad name**. (B-Brown, A 39)

(2) He **had hardly gotten back to** New York when it was Kentucky Derby time at Louisville, and 'Our Jimmy', of course, had to leave his six million citizens and see the bangtails chase each other around the track. (B-Brown, G 34)

(3) Bu Akba consulted Florian, and Mr. Slappey agreed to take tea with his one-time chief. 'An' I **has gotten** me a swell idea, Bu. I esplains it after they has gone'. (B-Brown, L 13)

This is sufficient material to attest these uses, but insufficient for detailed analysis, in particular of the details of the transition from *got* to *gotten* in the latter half of the twentieth century. For this, we can turn to COHA, which has 585 instances of *gotten* before 1900, and 8,360 after. This is convincing evidence for a steep overall increase in the frequency of the form during the twentieth century. However, the fine-grained analysis of the data still faces a serious challenge, namely the even higher numbers of *got* and the attendant problem of disambiguation. This is why the following analyses are restricted to the forms *had got* and *had gotten*, because this is the environment in which a purely possessive reading can largely be ruled out. Figures 14.4 and 14.5 show the steadily rising frequencies of *gotten* since 1900 and the rise and fall of *got* in this constructional environment (searches for 'had got(ten) [at*]', i.e. *had got(ten)* followed by definite or indefinite articles).

1900	1910	1920	1930	1940	1950	1960	1970	1980	1990	2000
6	7	14	9	14	27	30	35	44	58	75
0.27	0.31	0.55	0.37	0.57	1.10	1.25	1.47	1.74	2.08	2.54

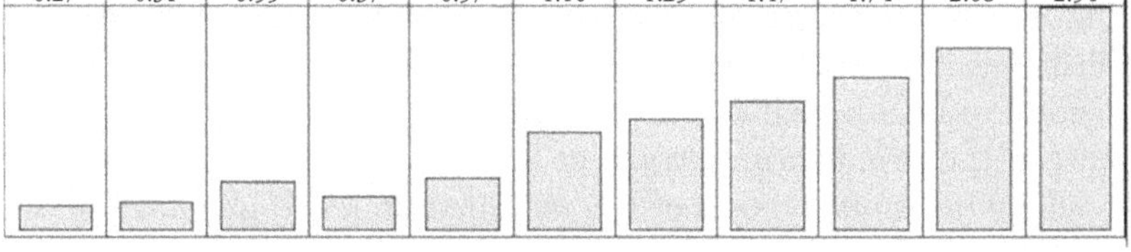

Figure 14.4 Frequency of *had gotten*, followed by article (COHA, 1900s–2000s)

1900	1910	1920	1930	1940	1950	1960	1970	1980	1990	2000
58	44	36	95	83	62	48	34	21	11	14
2.62	1.94	1.40	3.86	3.41	2.53	2.00	1.43	0.83	0.39	0.47

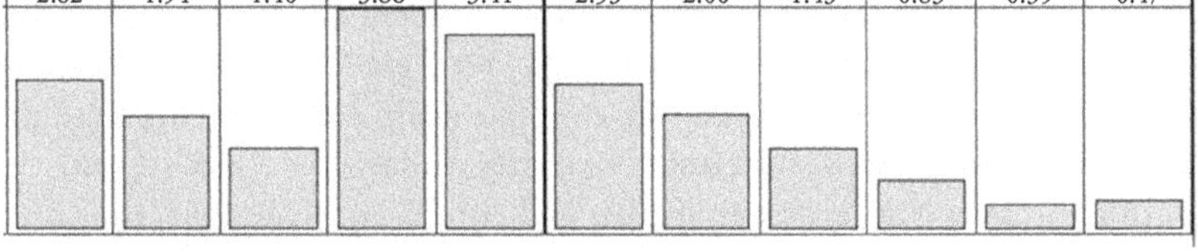

Figure 14.5 Frequency of *had got*, followed by article (COHA, 1900s–2000s)

Note that these figures represent monotransitive uses (*I had gotten the letter*) with fairly high precision and tolerably good recall, but miss copular uses of *get* (*I had gotten angry*).[5] But what the diagrams do show clearly is that the balance did not tilt in favour of *gotten* until around 1970. This is somewhat surprising as a roughly contemporaneous handbook of British and American English (Strevens 1972: 47–8) lists *gotten* as one of the very few salient grammatical Americanisms, suggesting widespread and even obligatory use, whereas the proper interpretation of the facts at the time would have been to argue that the participle form *got* is found in both

---

[5] A search for, say, '[have] gotten|got [j*]' (i.e. form of auxiliary *have*, followed by *got* or *gotten*, followed by adjective) will drastically over-collect as it captures not only *have got(ten) angry*, but also *have got(ten) angry looks*. One way of avoiding this problem is to confine the search to idiomatic expressions such as *get rid of*, where only the copular reading is plausible. COHA has ninety-five cases of [have] *got rid* before 1900, but only three for [have] *gotten rid*. In the *Corpus of Contemporary American English* (COCA) there is a complete reversal: 133 instances of [have] *gotten rid* as opposed to thirty-two cases of [have] *got rid*. Other disambiguation strategies, such as searches for adjectives governing prepositions (e.g. '[have] got|gotten ready to' or '[have] got|gotten tired of') flounder because of the low number of hits, particularly in COHA (e.g. a total of three for the former). A search for 'got|gotten [pp*] to [v*]' (i.e. *got* or *gotten* followed by personal pronoun and the *to*-infinitive) fairly precisely identifies causative uses. Both in COHA and in COCA, all hits for *gotten* cluster in the lowest frequency range for this construction, and even in COCA *got* still dominates *gotten* by a ratio of 645:49.

varieties and *gotten* is available as an additional option in American English. The misperception is easy to explain. For British observers any kind of American usage not attested in British English will be highly salient, regardless of its frequency of use, whereas the American variant identical to British English will tend to go unnoticed. This is why the gap between the two standards tends to be artificially exaggerated in much popular writing on the topic of British-American lexico-grammatical contrasts, which after all is often based on anecdotal observation rather than systematic analysis of large amounts of textual evidence.

In the *Google Books* material we find sufficient amounts of data to even make possible searches for 'minimal pairs' such as *gotten a divorce* (vs. *got a divorce*). With great regularity, the move to *gotten* as the statistical default in such constructions turns out to occur in the 1980s. Figure 14.6 presents the *Ngram Viewer* findings for *get back* and *get over*. (The restriction to the past-perfect contexts again serves to eliminate the noise created by the overwhelming majority of past-tense uses of *got*.)

In contrast to the simple transitive and copula constructions, the crossover from *got* to *gotten* has by and large not (yet) occurred for causative uses, where [have] *got* (somebody) *to talk / agree /* etc. still dominates.

14.5 Complementation of *Help* and *Prevent*

This section revisits an earlier study (Mair 2002) in which I argued that what appear to be straightforward regional contrasts between British and American English often turn out to be more complex phenomena on closer inspection. Long-term diachronic changes such as grammaticalisation, which affect several varieties or even the language as a whole, or variety-internal stylistic differentiation need to be taken into account. Several non-finite-clause constructions were investigated in the 'Brown quartet' of corpora (Brown, LOB, Frown, F-LOB), documenting British and American English in a time-window of thirty years (1961–1991/1992). For *help*, the study showed that there was a regional contrast in 1961, with British English preferring the *to*-infinitive and American English the bare infinitive (see also Kjellmer 1985). By 1991/1992, this contrast had almost been levelled, with both varieties now preferring bare infinitives at slightly different rates. This was not due to straightforward Americanisation of British English. Rather, *help* + bare infinitive showed an increase in both varieties which was related to a long-term development of grammaticalisation. The reverse development was noted for *prevent*, where the 1961 data showed a clear preference for the gerund with *from* (*prevent somebody from*

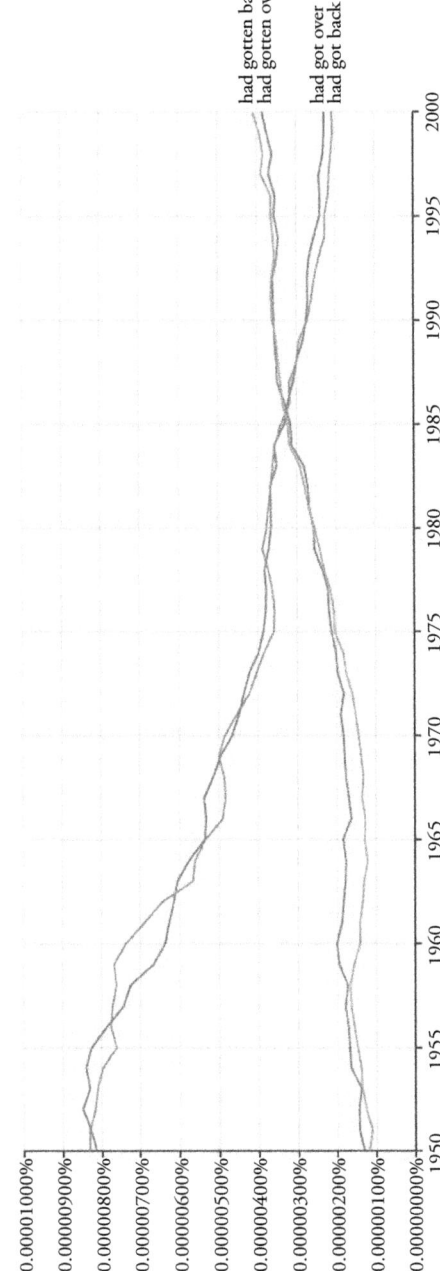

Figure 14.6 *Had got* vs. *had gotten* in *get back* and *get over* (*Ngram Viewer*, AmE, 1950–2000)

doing something) in both varieties. By 1991/1992, however, the variant without *from* (*prevent somebody doing something*) had become an equally frequent option in British English, establishing a regional contrast where previously there had been none.

The complementation of *help* is regularly mentioned as a stable grammatical contrast between British and American Standard English. Quirk *et al.*, for example, argue that '[of] the two constructions with *help*, that with *to* is more common in BrE, and that without *to* is more common in AmE' (1985: 1205ff.; cf. similarly Finegan 2004: 29–30). Trudgill and Hannah claim that 'N[orth] Am[erican] Eng[lish] is also much more likely than Eng[lish] Eng[lish] to delete *to* after *help* when followed by another verb, even when *help* is inflected' (2008: 70).[6] On the basis of a comprehensive corpus-based statistical analysis, Berlage argues:

> Apart from the syntactic parameters NP-length and NP-structure, variation is driven by other language-internal and language-external factors. Multivariate analyses reveal that regional contrasts between BrE and AmE turn out to be the most important factor in a model that is not restricted to the language-internal factors NP-length and NP-structure [...]   (Berlage 2014: 196)[7]

The literature on British-American grammatical contrasts does not give equal prominence to the complementation of *prevent*. However, *from*-less gerunds are mentioned as a grammatical Briticism in Algeo (2006: 246) and Trudgill and Hannah (2008: 71). Quirk *et al.* (1985: 1195), on the other hand, merely state that *from* is optional, thus generalising present-day British usage to Standard English as a whole. The following analysis based on the extended Brown family of corpora, with coverage from the 1930s to 2006, will force us to correct this picture.

14.5.1   Help *(+ NP) (+ to) + Infinitive*

Infinitival complementation with *help* has four variants, here exemplified with one example each from the 1930s American B-Brown corpus: *help* + *to*-infinitive (4), *help* + object + *to*-infinitive (5), *help* + bare infinitive (6), *help* + object + bare infinitive (7).

(4)   Her teachers and the sisters, attracted by the child's poise and promise, encouraged her and **helped to make** the exciting decision that she should go to college.   (B-Brown, G49)

---

[6] On the impact of the form of *help* – inflected or infinitival – on complement choice, see below.
[7] For two further recent multivariate analyses, see McEnery and Xiao (2005) and Lohmann (2011).

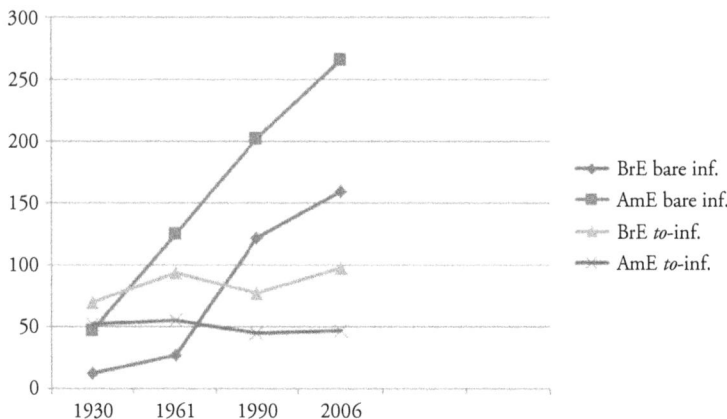

Figure 14.7 *To-* and bare infinitives in British and American English (c. 1930–2006)

(5) I went up there to see if he could **help me to get** a job. (B-Brown, P04)

(6) Perhaps when the answer is found, it may **help solve** another of the pressing social problems of the day – that of Rural Delinquency.
(B-Brown, R02)

(7) '**Will you help us open** Spartan Day at Hollywood-at-the-Fair, a Century of Progress Sunday, Aug. 27?' read the message.
(B-Brown, A42)

Figure 14.7 shows the frequency changes for the bare and *to*-infinitival variants in British and American English from c. 1930 to 2006, based on B-Brown (AmE 1930s), B-LOB (BrE 1930s), Brown (AmE 1961), LOB (BrE 1961), Frown (AmE 1992), F-LOB (BrE 1991), and the two 2006 Lancaster updates (BE06 and AmE06).[8]

As can be seen, both British and American English show some fluctuation without a clear diachronic trend in the use of the *to*-infinitival complement. Bare infinitival complements, on the other hand, show a steep parallel increase in frequency in both varieties. This increase starts from a slightly higher level and is a little more regular in American English. This trend is highly significant statistically for the entire period (see Appendix: Tables 14.6 and 14.7). The analysis of the extended Brown

---

[8] Tables 14.2 and 14.3 in the Appendix document the frequencies of the four variants in the eight Brown corpora and additionally list the small number of relevant examples found in ARCHER. Tables 14.6 and 14.7 provide statistical significance values where appropriate.

family of corpora thus confirms the grammaticalisation hypothesis advanced in Mair (2002) on the basis of the 1960–1990 time window.

Complementation of *help* with infinitives is clearly not a 'closed economy' in which gains for one option mean losses for the other. Figure 14.7 shows clearly that the increase in the bare infinitive is not at the expense of the *to*-infinitive, but driven by other factors. In the 1930s there is a preference (extremely narrow in American English) for the *to*-infinitive in both varieties. In the four most recent corpora this preference has shifted to the bare infinitive in both. Only in 1961 (Brown vs. LOB) was there a temporary and ephemeral regional contrast, misinterpreted as a stable standardised feature. The preference for the bare infinitive is a feature which *help* shares with other auxiliary-like function verbs such as *let* or *make*. Semantic bleaching, another symptom of ongoing grammaticalisation, additionally promotes the increase in frequency of the bare infinitival construction.

The bare infinitival complement with *help* is certainly not an American construction which is spreading to British English. As the *OED* entry for *help* (to be discussed in detail below) shows, it is a sixteenth-century British innovation which was subsequently exported to North America, where it has spread somewhat faster than in Britain. But if the grammar of *help* is so similar in the two varieties, why did so many commentators misinterpret *help* + bare infinitive as a grammatical Americanism? The likely reason was that the statistical distribution in the late nineteenth and early twentieth centuries favoured such a misperception. The bare infinitive was still rare in Britain (at least in written Standard English), but already moderately common in the USA, so that its use might have struck British observers as salient. Like many another piece of linguistic folklore, the misperception has survived into the present in spite of current usage evidence to the contrary.[9]

Let us briefly summarise the grammaticalisation development into which the ephemeral regional contrast between British and American English was embedded. The *OED* lists a sense 4 of the verb *help*, which it attests from 1559 and defines as to 'make (an action, process, condition, etc.) more effectual; to assist in bringing about; to further, promote'. Although the objects in the citations are nominal, this is essentially a causative meaning which is rather far removed from the core sense of

---

[9] Note that, in the same way, other side effects of home-grown grammaticalisation processes, such as the contracted forms *wanna* and *gonna*, are often referred to as incursions from sloppy American speech into good British usage in popular comment.

help ('aid, support'), as examples such as a 1667 citation from Milton make clear: *Thir armor help'd thir harm*. In a modern misreading, this passage might be paraphrased as 'their armour helped against harm'. But the intended meaning in context, in line with the *OED* definition of sense 4, is in fact the opposite: 'their armour was a cause of their harm'.[10]

The core use of *help* with infinitival complements – 'To aid or assist (a person *to do* something)' – is covered in sense 5b and attested from c. 1200. The early citations have infinitives marked by *to* or *for to*. The first bare infinitive is from c. 1535: *I wyll helpe synners turne to the* (i.e. 'I want to help sinners turn to you'). All further nineteenth- and twentieth-century attestations of the bare infinitive happen to be from British sources, too. The *OED* has a further relevant sub-entry 5a, which it explains as a conflation of sense 5b ('help someone to do something'), in which the object is ellipted, and sense 4 ('promote'), in which the nominal object is replaced by an infinitive. The resulting micro-construction is *help* + infinitive (without an object). The early attestations (from c. 1175) all have the *to*-infinitive; the first bare infinitival complement dates from 1548: *To helpe garnishe his mother tongue*. This sixteenth-century variant of the construction is the root of the innovation whose spread through British and American English has been observed in the twentieth-century corpora.

The 1548 *OED* example is also typical in that the verb *help* itself is in the *to*-infinitive, which encourages the use of the bare infinitival variant in the following dependent verb. The tendency to avoid a second *to*-infinitive following *to help* (as in ?*to help* **to** *garnish his mother tongue*) is a special instance of the generalised *horror aequi* principle posited by Rohdenburg in his functional and cognitive model of syntactic variation in Standard English.[11]

Corpus evidence generally supports the claim that the '*to help* + bare infinitive' pattern spearheaded the rise in frequency of the bare infinitive as a whole. The nineteenth-century examples from ARCHER (thirty-five, for all four variants in both varieties for the entire century, see Appendix: Table 14.2) are few, but suggestive. In this small corpus, there are not yet any bare infinitives with *help* in the British data. The small number of

---

[10] In fact, confusion between the two meanings could have arisen in the early Modern English period itself. Compare sense 10a, 'relieve or cure', with the following citation from 1576: *This helpeth poysoning, and comforteth al the members*.
[11] He defines *horror aequi* as a 'widespread (and presumably universal) tendency to avoid the use of formally (near-) identical and (near-)adjacent (non-coordinate) grammatical elements or structures' (Rohdenburg 2003: 236). On *horror aequi* with *help*, see Rohdenburg (2006a: 157–8), Rohdenburg (2009: 316–19), and Berlage (2014: 196–230).

to-infinitival constructions in the British data is unremarkable, instantiating the core sense of 'to aid or assist (a person) to do something':

(8)   Mr L superintended the work and **helpd to get** the Chares in
(ARCHER, BrE, 1846)

(9)   [...] nasty little red onions. You shall **help me to slice** them
(ARCHER, BrE, 1895)

One example stands out as counter-evidence to Rohdenburg's *horror aequi* tendency:

(10) And when she does hear the story, surely it would be better that she should have some knowledge of the world **to help her to understand** it. (ARCHER, BrE, 1893)

The nineteenth-century American data from ARCHER have twelve bare infinitives after *help*, and five of the six potential *horror aequi* cases actually show the tendency applying as predicted. Here are two examples in (11) and (12).

(11) I was Calld up at 5 **to help dress** John   (ARCHER, AmE, 1801)

(12) Maurice & oxen went to **help John Harlow break out** the new road to Keens Mills   (ARCHER, AmE, 1840)

For American English, the much larger COHA makes it possible to check the validity of these preliminary observations. As the lemma frequency of *help* in this corpus is 161,435, of which 128,799 are tagged as verbs, human analysis of all examples is not an option. In a reasonable compromise between precision and recall, the following patterns were therefore retrieved automatically:

- any form of *help* + *to*-infinitive   '[help] to [v?i*]'
- any form of *help* + bare infinitive   '[help] [v?i*]'
- any form of *help* + pronoun + *to*-inf.   '[help] [p*] to [v?i*]'
- any form of *help* + pronoun + bare inf.   '[help] [p*] [v?i*]'

All four searches show the same general trend, which is illustrated for '[help] to [v?i*]' and '[help] [v?i*]' in Figures 14.8 and 14.9. The figures under the decades refer to absolute frequencies and normalised frequencies per million words. For example, in Figure 14.8 the material from the 1850s contains 185 *to*-infinitival constructions, which corresponds to a normalised frequency of 11.23 per million words.

	1810	1820	1830	1840	1850	1860	1870	1880	1890	1900	1910	1920	1930	1940	1950	1960	1970	1980	1990	2000
	9	50	100	151	185	219	321	367	408	442	557	566	573	681	642	639	647	607	591	619
	7.62	7.22	7.26	9.41	11.23	12.84	17.29	18.06	19.81	20.00	24.54	22.06	23.29	27.97	26.16	26.65	27.17	23.98	21.15	20.94

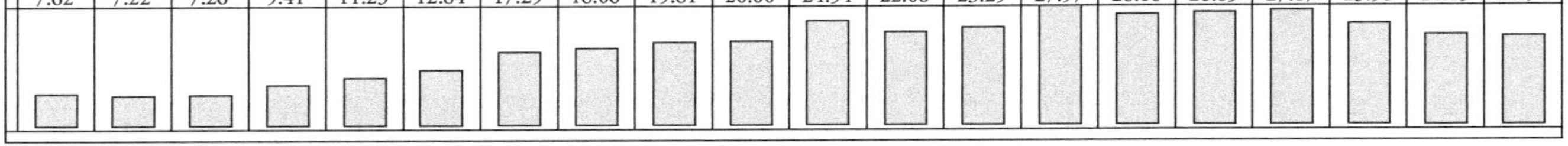

Figure 14.8 *Help* followed by *to*-infinitive, 1810s–2000s (COHA)

	1810	1820	1830	1840	1850	1860	1870	1880	1890	1900	1910	1920	1930	1940	1950	1960	1970	1980	1990	2000
	2	5	32	48	53	82	127	111	173	214	325	409	527	748	972	1073	1243	1749	2167	2758
	1.69	0.72	2.32	2.99	3.22	4.81	6.84	5.46	8.40	9.68	14.32	15.94	21.42	30.72	39.60	44.75	52.19	69.09	77.55	93.28

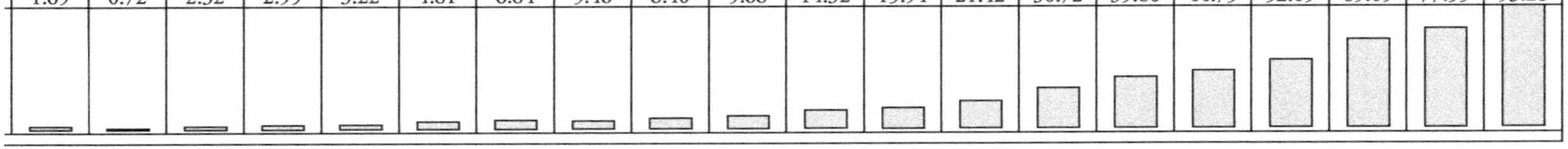

Figure 14.9 *Help* followed by bare infinitive, 1810s–2000s (COHA)

1850	1860	1870	1880	1890	1900	1910	1920	1930	1940
173	211	312	357	397	434	546	558	565	676
10.50	12.37	16.81	17.57	19.27	19.64	24.05	21.75	22.97	27.76

Figure 14.10 *Help* + *to*-infinitive: non-*horror aequi* environments, 1850s–1940s (COHA)

1850	1860	1870	1880	1890	1900	1910	1920	1930	1940
36	45	75	51	89	122	183	242	316	447
2.19	2.64	4.04	2.51	4.32	5.52	8.06	9.43	12.84	18.36

Figure 14.11 *Help* + bare infinitive: non-*horror aequi* environments, 1850s–1940s (COHA)

Help followed by *to*-infinitive increases during the nineteenth century, but then levels off in the twentieth century. *Help* followed by bare infinitive also increases during the nineteenth century, but it starts from low levels. Its increase continues unabated in the twentieth century, however, and from the 1940s it is the more common form of the two.

So far, the twentieth-century trends from COHA helpfully corroborate the picture obtained from the much smaller Brown family corpora. Where COHA breaks new ground is in demonstrating the effectiveness of the *horror aequi* factor during the crucial period of the spread of bare infinitives between the 1850s and the 1940s. Two searches excluding *to* before *help* (for '-to help|helps|helped|helping to [v?i*]' and '-to help|helps|helped|helping [v?i*]' respectively) eliminate the potential *horror aequi* cases in the data.

As Figures 14.10 and 14.11 show, the initial ratio (1850s) of bare vs. *to*-infinitives is 36:173 (17 vs. 83 per cent); the final one (1940s) is 447:676 (39.8 vs. 60.2 per cent). The bare infinitive is clearly increasing its share, but even by the 1940s it is not yet the dominant form.

This is very different in the *horror aequi* environments. *To help* + *to*-infinitive (search for 'to help to [v?i*]') is attested throughout, although at very modest levels (Figure 14.12).

From the very beginning (1850s) and throughout the entire period of observation, bare infinitives outnumber the *to*-infinitives, modestly at first

1850	1860	1870	1880	1890	1900	1910	1920	1930	1940
9	6	8	9	9	5	11	6	3	5
0.55	0.35	0.43	0.44	0.44	0.23	0.48	0.23	0.12	0.21

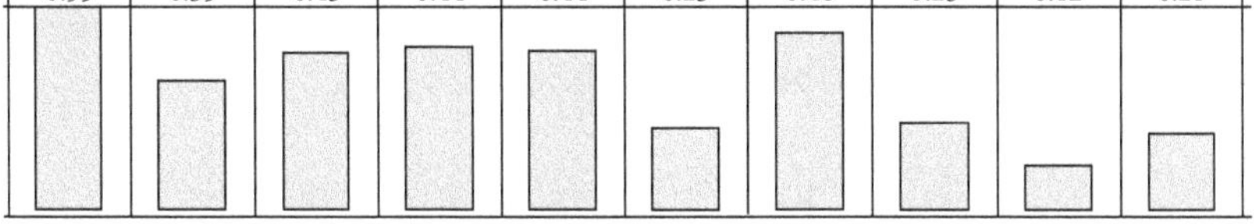

Figure 14.12 *To help* + *to*-infinitive, 1850s–1940s (COHA)

1850	1860	1870	1880	1890	1900	1910	1920	1930	1940
17	37	50	59	84	91	141	166	209	296
1.03	2.17	2.69	2.90	4.08	4.12	6.21	6.47	8.50	12.16

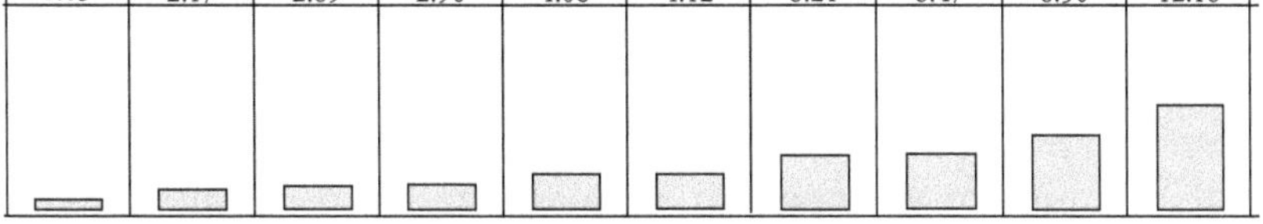

Figure 14.13 *To help* + bare infinitive, 1850s–1940s (COHA)

and drastically later. The data confirm the spearheading role of the *horror aequi* environments in the spread of bare infinitival complements after the verb *help*. There is an additional indirect effect. At least for a limited period of several decades, the infinitive *to help* (i.e. the candidate environment for the *horror aequi* effect) seems to gather momentum under its own steam. The share of the infinitive *to help* as a proportion of all uses of the verb does not remain stable, but increases from 21.7 per cent in the 1850s to 34.6, 38.0, and 37.9 per cent respectively in the 1920s, 1930s, and 1940s (a level at which it remains throughout the remainder of the twentieth century).[12] After computing percentages of the *horror aequi* environment as part of all verbal uses from the frequencies in Figures 14.12 and 14.13 (see Appendix: Table 14.5, for the details), it becomes evident that *to help* + bare infinitive is over-represented in the latter half of the nineteenth century. For example, in the 1870s and 1880s, only roughly a quarter of all tokens of the verb *help* in the corpus are *to*-infinitives, but in the bare infinitive construction, *to help* accounts for 40 and 53.6 per cent of all uses during the same period. Table 14.5 (Appendix) also shows that this divergence is levelled by the 1930s and 1940s. To put it in a nutshell: careful philological analysis of a single sixteenth-century *OED* example (*To helpe garnishe his mother tongue*) suggested *horror aequi* as a factor in the change investigated here.

---

[12] See Appendix: Table 14.4. The figures for the 1990s and 2000s are 39.5 and 38.7 per cent, respectively.

Statistical evidence from nineteenth- and twentieth-century corpus data proves it. What we have not found is any evidence for the frequently made claim that there is a stable regional difference in the use of *help* between British and American Standard English.

14.5.2   Prevent + *NP (+* from*) +* V-*ing*

The variable *prevent* + gerundial complement has the following three variants: *prevent* + noun phrase + *from* + V-ing (13), *prevent* + noun phrase + V-ing (14), *prevent* + genitive / possessive + V-ing (15).

(13)   Small screws **prevent the bearings from coming out** of one end, and the end of the upright pipe, which is screwed into the pipe housing, also helps to hold the ball bearing in place.   (B-Brown, E 16)

(14)   **To prevent the operator slipping** into low gear unless he consciously exerts added pressure on the shifter handle, a spring-backed plunger restrains this action.   (B-Brown, E 32)

(15)   It would, however, **prevent their having to make** a public choice as between other candidates and would help them in getting elected as delegates.   (B-Brown, G 35)

All three variants are exemplified from B-Brown, the 1930s Brown Corpus analogue. Table 14.1 gives the frequencies for the three variants in British and American English in the extended Brown family of corpora, covering the period from the 1930s to 2006.

The *from*-less variant is consistently present (if with some fluctuation)[13] in British English throughout the twentieth century, but has been largely eliminated from American English during the same period (cf. also Ong 2011). The genitive/possessive option is obsolescent in both varieties.

Nineteenth-century British data from the ARCHER corpus show six *from*-less forms out of a total of forty-six relevant uses of *prevent*;[14] the corresponding American ARCHER data have none (out of a total of thirty relevant uses). The much larger COHA solidly attests the usage for the nineteenth century and has some examples even for the twentieth. A search with high precision and tolerably good recall is '[prevent] me|you|him|us|

---

[13] Note that the only statistically significant development in the long term (Appendix: Table 14.6) is a decline in the frequency of *prevent* NP *from* V-ing. The use of the *from*-less variant shows ups and downs which do not build up into a significant diachronic trend.

[14] In addition: twenty-five *from* + V-ing, fifteen with the NP in the genitive/possessive.

Table 14.1 *Complementation of* prevent *in the Brown family of corpora*

	from + V-ing	NP + V-ing	NP (gen/poss) + V-ing	Total
BrE 1930s	53	15	3	71
AmE 1930s	21	3	1	25
BrE 1961	34	7	0	41
AmE 1961	47	0	0	47
BrE 1991	24	24	0	48
AmE 1992	36	1	0	37
BrE 2006	23	15	0	38
AmE 2006	27	0	0	27

them [v*g]'.[15] It yields a total of 170 examples spread out over all sub-periods, with the exception of the 1810s (which has less material than all the others), with a peak in the 1870s (twenty-four occurrences = 1.29 per million). This is a typical instance from the *New York Times*:

(16) Assistant District Attorney Osborne in reply to this holds that it was necessary to distract Jones's mind in this way to **prevent him killing** himself. (COHA, 1902)

The alternative construction with *from* (search for '[prevent] me|you|him|us|them from [v*g]') yields a total of 2,875 results, vastly outnumbering the *from*-less construction in every single decade. Unfortunately, the detailed and in-depth corpus coverage of nineteenth- and twentieth-century developments which we have for American English is not available for British English. Still, the history of the variable is clear in its broad outlines.

The *from*-less construction with *prevent* is a spin-off of the eighteenth-century rise of the gerund (De Smet 2013). It was available as a regular structural option throughout the nineteenth century both in British and in American English. The two varieties parted ways in the early twentieth

---

[15] Note that the search excludes the ambiguous *her*, which especially in nineteenth-century data is likely to represent the possessive rather than objective case. Alternative search strategies, such as '[prevent] [n*] [v*g]' (i.e. forms of the verb *prevent* followed by any noun and V-ing) or '[prevent] * [n*] [v*g]' (*prevent* followed by any word, noun, and V-ing), yield small numbers of additional examples. While thus modestly improving recall, these searches drastically compromise precision, for example by dredging up large numbers of irrelevant hits, such as *what is necessary to prevent big league pitching from deteriorating any further* (COHA, 1973). As the length of object noun phrases correlates with likelihood of *from* (Rohdenburg 2006b), pronominal objects represent the proto-typical environment for *from*-less constructions anyway. For more extended discussions both of search strategies and Rohdenburg's proposal, see Ong (2011).

century, when the *from*-less variant continued increasing in frequency in British English, but decreased to the point of obsolescence in American English.[16] What the corpus data have shown in this case is the emergence of a new grammatical contrast between Standard British and American English. Unlike the bare infinitive with *help*, which is often wrongly listed as such, this one is not widely recorded in the literature yet.

14.6 Conclusion

In Schneider's chronology of the rise of American English, the Spanish-American war of 1898 serves as the symbolic watershed between Phases 4 and 5, endonormative stabilisation and differentiation (2007: 291). If a war is to serve as a signal date for linguistic history, the evidence discussed above suggests that a different one, namely World War I (and the ensuing two decades of political and cultural isolationism), is the more appropriate choice. For one of the variables studied here, *got / gotten*, a case could even be made for World War II, as present-day contrasting British and American preferences were consolidated only during the second half of the twentieth century, with the divergent developments possibly still ongoing.

As Schneider points out, the Spanish-American War of 1898 resulted from a new sense of national self-confidence in the USA, combined with a growing willingness to play a role on the world stage. That a short conflict, which was not very significant from a military point of view and did not even involve Great Britain, should have ushered in the full emancipation of American English is doubtful. The situation is different during and after World War I. Following years of hesitation, the USA entered the War alongside Britain and France in 1917. Mobilisation was not confined to large numbers of troops who went to Europe, but involved millions more on the 'home front', most notably through the idealistic crusade for democracy and the self-determination of peoples advocated by President Woodrow Wilson. But US hopes for lasting peace and a bright future for the world were beginning to falter even during the peace negotiations. The pendulum swung towards disaffection (as, for example, expressed in the literature of the 'Lost Generation'), and the presidencies of

---

[16] This impression is confirmed when one looks at the most recent attestations from COCA in detail. This corpus contains eighteen examples from the 2010–2015 period, which are all genuine in the sense that they exemplify the construction searched for. However, a number of them turn out to be British – either because they were published in Britain or written by British authors (or both): a novel by Alys Clare, articles from the *New Statesman* and *History Today* – or because they come from British or international speakers interviewed in American media outlets: Geoff Dyer (on NPR), Benjamin Netanyahu (PBS).

Wilson's Republican successors, Warren G. Harding and Calvin Coolidge, were characterised by isolationism and withdrawal from Britain and Europe.

The period between the two world wars also saw the end of mass immigration from Europe and the golden age of radio, for which – partly reflecting the isolationist mood at the time and partly reflecting conscious language-political and language-ideological choices – the Inland Northern pronunciation rather than the more British-like New England accent was chosen as the national standard (Bonfiglio 2002).

At least for the standard written norm of American English, it is therefore appropriate to move Phase 4, endonormative stabilisation, forward(s) well into the twentieth century, with a peak in the period extending from World War I to the Great Depression and later developments which are still unfolding. In spite of its late consolidation, however, this American English Standard has not only emancipated itself fully from British English, but also gained global pre-eminence in the concert of World Englishes. It has become a norm of reference and a powerful influence for all other standard varieties of English, including British English, due to the myriad avenues opened up by the United States' 'hard' (politics, military, business) and 'soft' power (lifestyle, media, popular culture).

Methodologically, the present study demonstrates the continued usefulness of combining philology and technology, the detailed study of the individual example and the statistical profiling of large masses of text. In this spirit, the present effort is dedicated to David Denison, a master at this integrative approach to the study of language change and the history of English.

Appendix

Tests for Statistical Significance – Log Likelihood Values

Following the practice in Leech *et al.* (2009), the log likelihood (LL) test was employed to assess degree of statistical significance, using the calculator developed by Paul Rayson at UCREL, Lancaster, UK (http://ucrel.lancs.ac.uk/llwizard.html). Comparability across corpora is distorted in very minor ways by the fact that full certainty about the corpus sizes used for normalisation per million words cannot be obtained from published sources. For LOB and Brown, it seemed reasonable to use the figures given in Leech *et al.* (2009: 26). Leech *et al.* (2009) do not explicitly state figures for the absolute size of F-LOB and Frown, which is why these were obtained from the Manual for the tagged versions of the four original corpora (Hinrichs *et al.*

2007: 12). For the 2006 Lancaster corpora, the Brown standard of 1,000,000 words was assumed, as the only available token frequencies (1,175,965 for AmE; 1,146,597 for BrE – Andrew Hardie, personal communication) included punctuation marks. The calculations presented below are therefore based on the following measures for corpus size:

B-Brown:	1,015,206 words
B-LOB:	1,028,155 words
Brown:	1,013,546 words
LOB:	1,006,863 words
Frown:	1,011,585 words
F-LOB:	1,009,394 words
AmE06:	1,000,000 words
BrE06:	1,000,000 words

Table 14.2 *To- vs. bare infinitives after* help *in British and American English, 1800–2006 (ARCHER and Brown family)*

	help + *to*-inf.	*help* + NP + *to*-inf.	*help* + bare inf.	*help* + NP + bare inf.	Σ
BrE 1800–1849 ARCHER	3	0	0	0	3
AmE 1800–1849 ARCHER	4	1	3	6	14
BrE 1850–1899 ARCHER	2	7	0	0	9
AmE 1850–1899 ARCHER	1	5	1	2	9
BrE 1930s B-LOB	35	35	5	8	83
AmE 1930s B-Brown	31	21	29	18	99
BrE 1961 LOB	57	37	14	13	121
AmE 1961 Brown	37	18	66	59	180
BrE 1991 F-LOB	43	34	78	44	199
AmE 1991/1992 Frown	30	15	103	99	247
BrE 2006 BE06	53	45	74	86	258
AmE 2006 AmE06	37	10	138	128	313

Figures for Brown and LOB are from Kjellmer (1985); those for Frown and F-LOB are from Mair (2002), with minimal adjustments for consistency.

Table 14.3 *Proportion of* to- *vs. bare infinitives after* help *in British and American English, 1930–2006 (Brown family)*

	help + *to*-inf.	help + bare inf.	∑	per cent bare inf.
BrE 1930s	70	13	83	15.7
AmE 1930s	52	47	99	47.5
BrE 1961	94	27	121	23.3
AmE 1961	55	125	180	69.4
BrE 1991	77	122	199	61.3
AmE 1991/1992	45	202	247	81.8
BrE 2006	98	160	258	62.0
AmE 2006	47	266	313	85.0

Table 14.4 *Frequency of* to help *as percentage of all verbal uses of* help, *1850s–1940s (COHA)*

	1850s	1860s	1870s	1880s	1890s	1900s	1910s	1920s	1930s	1940s
help.[v*]	2,169	2,962	3,755	4,016	4,012	4,396	5,193	5,284	4,822	5,475
to help.[v*]	447	651	960	1,073	1,287	1,356	1,801	1,827	1,832	2,074
per cent inf.	21.7	22.0	25.6	26.7	32.1	30.8	34.7	34.6	38.0	37.9

Table 14.5 *Percentage of* horror aequi, *1850s–1940s (COHA), as computed from Figure 14.12 and Figure 14.13*

1850s	1860s	1870s	1880s	1890s	1900s	1910s	1920s	1930s	1940s
32.1	45.1	40.0	53.6	48.6	43.0	43.5	40.7	39.8	39.8

Calculation: (token frequencies for *horror aequi* divided by sum of *horror aequi* + non-*horror aequi* environments) multiplied by 100

Tables 14.6 and 14.7 below: The cut-off LL values for the standard significance levels are 3.54 ($p < 0.05$, visually represented by *), 6.63 ($p < 0.01$, visually represented by **), 10.83 ($p < 0.001$, visually represented by ***), 15.13 ($p < 0.0001$, visually represented by ****). For British English, Table 14.6 gives the LL values for *help* and *prevent*. Table 14.7 for American English only gives the values for *help*, as *prevent* is not attested in sufficient frequency.

Table 14.6 Frequency of non-finite complements of help and prevent in B-LOB, LOB, F-LOB, and BE06

	B-LOB (1930s)	LOB (1961)	LL	F-LOB (1991)	LL	BE06	LL	LL 1930–2006
help + bare inf.	5	14	4.63*	78	****48.91	74	n. s.	****74.17
help + NP + bare inf.	8	13	n. s.	44	****17.73	86	***14.21	****77.77
help + to-inf.	35	57	5.78*	43	n. s.	53	n. s.	*4.22
help + NP + to-inf.	35	37	n. s.	34	n. s.	45	n. s.	n. s.
prevent . . . + V-ing	15	7	n. s.	24	**9.81	15	n. s.	n. s.
prevent . . . + from V-ing	53	34	3.79*	24	n. s.	23	n. s.	***11.35
Corpus size	1,028,155	1,006,863		1,009,394		1,000,000		

Table 14.7 *Frequency of non-finite complements of* help *in B-Brown, Brown, Frown, and AmE06*

	B-Brown (1930s)	Brown (1961)	LL	Frown (1992)	LL	AmE06	LL	LL 1930–2006
help + bare inf.	29	66	***14.86	103	**8.32	138	*5.10	****78.98
help + NP + bare inf.	18	59	****23.07	99	**10.40	128	*3.71	****95.03
help + *to*-inf.	31	37	n. s.	30	n. s.	37	n. s.	n. s.
help + NP + *to*-inf.	21	18	n. s.	15	n. s.	10	n. s.	*3.83
Corpus size	1,015,206	1,013,546		1,011,585				

References

Corpora and Dictionaries

AmE06 = *The American English 2006 Corpus*. Compiled by Paul Baker (Lancaster University).

American Dialect Society Listserve Archive. Available at: http://listserv.linguistlist.org/pipermail/ads-l/.

ARCHER 3.2 = *A Representative Corpus of Historical English Registers* version 3.2. 1990–1993/2002/2007/2010/2013/2016. Originally compiled under the supervision of Douglas Biber and Edward Finegan at Northern Arizona University and University of Southern California; modified and expanded by subsequent members of a consortium of universities. Current member universities are Bamberg, Freiburg, Heidelberg, Helsinki, Lancaster, Leicester, Manchester, Michigan, Northern Arizona, Santiago de Compostela, Southern California, Trier, Uppsala, Zurich. Examples of usage taken from ARCHER were obtained under the terms of the ARCHER User Agreement. Available at: www.projects.alc.manchester.ac.uk/archer/.

B-Brown = *The B-Brown-1931 Corpus*. Compiled by Marianne Hundt (Zürich University).

BE06 = *The British English 2006 Corpus*. Compiled by Paul Baker (Lancaster University).

B-LOB = *The BLOB-1931 Corpus*. Compiled by Geoffrey Leech (Lancaster University), Paul Rayson (Lancaster University), and Nick Smith (University of Leicester).

BNC = BNC*web* (CQP-Edition). Developed by Sebastian Hoffmann (Trier University) and Stefan Evert (Erlangen University). Available at: http://bncweb.lancs.ac.uk/.

Bosworth, Joseph and T. Northcote Toller (eds.) 1882–1898. *An Anglo-Saxon Dictionary*. Oxford: Clarendon Press. T. Northcote Toller (ed.) 1908–1921. *Supplement*. Oxford: Clarendon Press.

Brown Corpus = *A Standard Corpus of Present-Day Edited American English*, for use with Digital Computers (Brown). 1964, 1971, 1979. Compiled by W. N. Francis and H. Kučera. Brown University. Providence, Rhode Island.

BYU-BNC = Davies, Mark (2004–). Based on the *British National Corpus* from Oxford University Press. Available at www.english-corpora.org/bnc/.
BYU-EEBO = Davies, Mark (2017–). *Early English Books Online*. SAMUELS project. Available at: www.english-corpora.org/eebo/.
Cambridge Dictionaries Online. Entry for *if you ask me*. Available at: http://dictionary.cambridge.org/dictionary/british/if-you-ask-me.
CED = *A Corpus of English Dialogues 1560–1760*. 2006. Compiled under the supervision of Merja Kytö (Uppsala University) and Jonathan Culpeper (Lancaster University). www.engelska.uu.se/forskning/engelska-spraket/elektroniska-resurser/a-corpus.
CEECS = *Corpus of Early English Correspondence Sampler*. 1998. Compiled by Terttu Nevalainen, Helena Raumolin-Brunberg, Jukka Keränen, Minna Nevala, Arja Nurmi, and Minna Palander-Collin at the Department of Modern Languages, University of Helsinki. www.helsinki.fi/varieng/CoRD/corpora/CEEC/index.html.
CEN = *The Corpus of English Novels*. Compiled by Hendrik De Smet (KU Leuven). Available at: https://perswww.kuleuven.be/~u0044428/cen.htm.
CLMET3.0 = *The Corpus of Late Modern English Texts, Version 3.0*. Compiled by Hendrik De Smet, Hans-Jürgen Diller, and Jukka Tyrkkö. Available at: https://perswww.kuleuven.be/~u0044428/clmet3_0.htm.
CLMETEV = *The Corpus of Late Modern English Texts (Extended Version)*. 2006. Compiled by Hendrik De Smet. Department of Linguistics, University of Leuven. Available at: https://perswww.kuleuven.be/~u0044428/clmetev.htm.
CME = *Corpus of Middle English Prose and Verse*. Available at: https://quod.lib.umich.edu/c/cme/.
CMU Pronouncing Dictionary. Available at: www.speech.cs.cmu.edu/cgi-bin/cmudict.
CNNE = *The Corpus of Nineteenth-Century Newspaper English*. Compiled by Erik Smitterberg (Uppsala University).
COCA = Davies, Mark (2008–). *The Corpus of Contemporary American English*: 520 million words, 1990–present. Available at: www.english-corpora.org/coca/.
COHA = Davies, Mark (2010–). *The Corpus of Historical American English*: 400 million words, 1810–2009. Available at: www.english-corpora.org/coha/.
CORDE = *Real Academia Española – Corpus Diacrónico del Español*. Available at: http://corpus.rae.es/cordenet.html.
Corpus del Español = Davies, Mark (2001–). *Corpus del Español*: 100 million words, 1200s–1900s. Available at: www.corpusdelespanol.org.
CREA = *Real Academia Española – Corpus de Referencia del Español Actual*. Available at: http://corpus.rae.es/creanet.html.
DOE = *Dictionary of Old English: A to H Online*, ed. Angus Cameron, Ashley Crandell Amos, Antonette diPaolo Healey, *et al*. Toronto: Dictionary of Old English Project, 2016.

DOEC = *Dictionary of Old English Web Corpus*. 2009. Compiled by Antonette diPaolo Healey with John Price Wilkin and Xin Xiang. Toronto: Dictionary of Old English Project. Available at: http://tapor.library.utoronto.ca/doecorpus/.

ENCOW16A = Full version 'A' (web access) of ENCOW16. Available at: http://corporafromtheweb.org/encow16/.

F-LOB = *The Freiburg–LOB Corpus of British English*. The Freiburg-LOB Corpus (original version) compiled by Christian Mair, Albert-Ludwigs-Universität Freiburg. The Freiburg-LOB Corpus (POS-tagged version) compiled by Christian Mair, Albert Ludwigs-Universität Freiburg, and Geoffrey Leech, University of Lancaster.

Frown Corpus = *The Freiburg-Brown Corpus of American English*. The Freiburg-Brown Corpus (original version) compiled by Christian Mair, Albert-Ludwigs-Universität Freiburg. The Freiburg-Brown Corpus (POS-tagged version) compiled by Christian Mair, Albert Ludwigs-Universität Freiburg, and Geoffrey Leech, University of Lancaster.

Google Books = Davies, Mark (2011–). *Google Books (American English) Corpus* (155 billion words, 1810–2009). Available at: https://googlebooks.byu.edu/.

Google Books, Advanced Search. Available at: www.google.ca/advanced_book_search.

Google Books Ngram Viewer. Available at: https://books.google.com/ngrams.

ICE = *International Corpus of English*. Available at: http://ice-corpora.net/ice/.

IcePaHC = Wallenberg, Joel C., Anton Karl Ingason, Einar Freyr Sigurðsson, and Eiríkur Rögnvaldsson 2011. *Icelandic Parsed Historical Corpus*, University of Iceland. Version 0.9. Available at: www.linguist.is/icelandic_treebank.

InternetSlang.com. Entry for *if you ask me*. Available at: www.internetslang.com/IYAM-meaning-definition.asp.

LOB Corpus = *The Lancaster-Oslo/Bergen Corpus*. The LOB Corpus, original version (1970–1978), compiled by Geoffrey Leech, Lancaster University, Stig Johansson, University of Oslo (project leaders), and Knut Hofland, University of Bergen (head of computing). The LOB Corpus, POS-tagged version (1981–1986), compiled by Geoffrey Leech, Lancaster University, Stig Johansson, University of Oslo (project leaders), Roger Garside, Lancaster University, and Knut Hofland, University of Bergen (heads of computing).

MED = *The Middle English Dictionary*. 1952–2001. Ann Arbor: University of Michigan Press. Available at: http://quod.lib.umich.edu/m/med/.

MicroConcord Corpus 1993. Created by Tim Johns to accompany the concordancing programme *MicroConcord*. Oxford: Oxford University Press. www2.fgw.vu.nl/resources/corpora/doc/misc/DocumentationMicroConcordCorpus.pdf.

Moreno Fernández, Francisco, Ana María Cestero Mancera, Isabel Molina Martos, and Florentino Paredes García 2002–2007. *La Lengua Hablada en Alcalá de Henares: Corpus PRESEEA-Alcalá*, 3 vols. Alcalá de Henares: Universidad de Alcalá.

OBC = Huber, Magnus, Magnus Nissel, Patrick Maiwald, and Bianca Widlitzki 2012. *The Old Bailey Corpus: Spoken English in the 18th and 19th Centuries*. Available at: www1.uni-giessen.de/oldbaileycorpus. Version 1.0 (extended version).

OBPO = Hitchcock, Tim, Robert Shoemaker, Clive Emsley, Sharon Howard, and Jamie McLaughlin, *et al.*, *The Old Bailey Proceedings Online, 1674–1913* (www.oldbaileyonline.org, version 7.0, 24 March 2012).

OED = *Oxford English Dictionary*, 3rd edn. (2000–), online. Available at: www.oed.com.

OSS = *OpenSource Shakespeare, An Experiment in Literary Technology*. George Mason University. Available at: www.opensourceshakespeare.org.

Oxford Dictionaries. Entry for *if you ask me*. Available at: www.oxforddictionaries.com/definition/english/if-you-ask-me.

PhraseMix. Entry for *if you ask me*. Available at: www.phrasemix.com/phrases/if-you-ask-me.

PPCME2 = *Penn-Helsinki Parsed Corpus of Middle English*, 2nd edition. 2000. Compiled by Anthony Kroch and Ann Taylor. www.ling.upenn.edu/hist-corpora/PPCME2-RELEASE-4/index.html.

Strathy Corpus = *Strathy Corpus of Canadian English*. Available at: www.english-corpora.org/can/. Project website at: www.queensu.ca/strathy/corpus.

UofV = *The Modern English Collection, University of Virginia Electronic Text Center*. Defunct website at: http://etext.lib.virginia.edu/modeng/modengo.browse.html.

YCOE = Taylor, Ann, Anthony Warner, Susan Pintzuk, and Frank Beths 2003. *The York-Toronto-Helsinki Parsed Corpus of Old English Prose*. Department of Linguistics, University of York. Oxford Text Archive, first edition. www-users.york.ac.uk/~lang22/YCOE/YcoeHome.htm.

Secondary Sources

Aarts, Bas 2007. *Syntactic Gradience: The Nature of Grammatical Indeterminacy*. Oxford: Oxford University Press.

Ackles, Nancy M. 1997. Historical syntax of the English articles in relation to the count/non-count distinction. PhD thesis: University of Washington.

Adamson, Sylvia 1998. The code as context: Language-change and (mis)interpretation. In Kirsten Malmkjær and John Williams (eds.) *Context in Language Learning and Language Understanding*. Cambridge: Cambridge University Press, pp. 137–68.

Adamson, Sylvia 1999. Literary language. In Roger Lass (ed.) *The Cambridge History of the English Language*, Vol. III *1476–1776*. Cambridge: Cambridge University Press, pp. 539–653.

Adamson, Sylvia 2007. Prescribed reading: Pronouns and gender in the eighteenth century. *Historical Sociolinguistics and Sociohistorical Linguistics* 7. Available at: www.let.leidenuniv.nl/hsl_shl/Adamson.htm.

Aijmer, Karin 1985. The semantic development of *will*. In Jacek Fisiak (ed.) *Historical Semantics – Historical Word-Formation*. Berlin: Mouton Publishers, pp. 11–21.

Aijmer, Karin 1997. *I think* – an English modal particle. In Toril Swan and Olaf Jansen Westvik (eds.) *Modality in Germanic Languages: Historical and Comparative Perspectives.* Berlin/New York: Mouton de Gruyter, pp. 1–47.

Aitchison, Jean 1981. *Language Change: Progress or Decay?* [London:] Fontana Paperbacks.

Algeo, John 2006. *British or American English? A Handbook of Word and Grammar Patterns.* Cambridge: Cambridge University Press.

Allen, Cynthia L. 1986. Reconsidering the history of *like. Journal of Linguistics* 22 (2): 375–409.

Allen, Cynthia L. 1995. *Case Marking and Reanalysis: Grammatical Relations from Old to Early Modern English.* Oxford: Oxford University Press.

Allen, Cynthia L. 2007. Variation in the NP/DP in Old English: Determiner and possessive combinations. In Annie Zaenen, Jane Simpson, Tracy Holloway King, Jane Grimshaw, Joan Manling, and Chris Manning (eds.) *Architectures, Rules, and Preferences: Variations on Themes by Joan W. Bresnan.* Stanford, CA: CSLI Publications, pp. 3–20.

Arad, Maya 1999. What counts as a class? The case of psych verbs. *MIT Working Papers in Linguistics* 35: 1–23.

Ariel, Mira 1990. *Accessing Noun-Phrase Antecedents.* London: Routledge.

Auer, Anita 2006. Precept and practice: The influence of prescriptivism on the English subjunctive. In Christiane Dalton-Puffer, Dieter Kastovsky, Nikolaus Ritt, and Herbert Schendl (eds.) *Syntax, Style and Grammatical Norms: English from 1500–2000.* Bern: Peter Lang, pp. 33–53.

Auer, Anita and Victorina González-Díaz 2005. Eighteenth-century prescriptivism in English: A re-evaluation of its effects on actual language usage. *Multilingua* 24(4): 317–41.

Austin, John Langshaw 1962. *How to Do Things with Words.* Oxford: Clarendon Press.

Ayres, Alfred 1883 [1908]. *The English Grammar of William Cobbett. Carefully Revised and Annotated.* New York: D. Appleton and Co.

Bailey, Richard W. 2004. American English: Its origins and history. In Edward Finegan and John R. Rickford (eds.) *Language in the USA: Themes for the Twenty-First Century.* Cambridge: Cambridge University Press, pp. 3–17.

Bain, Alexander 1863. *An English Grammar.* London: Longman, Green, Longman, Roberts, and Green.

Barker, Chris 1998. Partitives, double genitives and anti-uniqueness. *Natural Language & Linguistic Theory* 16(4): 679–717.

Baron, Dennis E. 1986. *Grammar and Gender.* New Haven/London: Yale University Press.

Barðdal, Jóhanna 2008. *Productivity: Evidence from Case and Argument Structure in Icelandic.* Amsterdam/Philadelphia: John Benjamins.

Barðdal, Jóhanna, Elena Smirnova, Lotte Sommerer, and Spike Gildea (eds.) 2015. *Diachronic Construction Grammar.* Amsterdam/Philadelphia: John Benjamins.

Bate, W. Jackson 1971. *The Burden of the Past and the English Poet*. London: Chatto and Windus.
Bauer, Brigitte L. M. 2009. Word order. In Philip Baldi and Pierluigi Cuzzolin (eds.) *New Perspectives on Historical Latin Syntax*, Vol. 1 *Syntax of the Sentence*. Berlin: Mouton de Gruyter, pp. 241–316.
Beal, Joan C. 2010. Prescriptivism and the suppression of variation. In Raymond Hickey (ed.) *Eighteenth-Century English: Ideology and Change*. Cambridge: Cambridge University Press, pp. 21–37.
Beal, Joan C., Carmela Nocera, and Massimo Sturiale (eds.) 2008. *Perspectives on Prescriptivism*. Bern: Peter Lang.
Beckman, Natanael 1917. Hur uttryckes hos verbet framtid i forn- och nysvenskan? En provföreläsning och en önskelista. *Språk och Stil* 17: 1–16.
Beckner, Clay and Joan Bybee 2009. A usage-based account of constituency and reanalysis. *Language Learning* 59(1): 27–46.
Behaghel, Otto 1909. Beziehungen zwischen Umfang und Reihenfolge von Satzgliedern. *Indogermanische Forschungen* 25: 110–42.
Behrens, Heike 2009. Usage-based and emergentist approaches to language acquisition. *Linguistics* 47(2): 383–411.
Behrens, Heike 2017. The role of analogy in language processing and acquisition. In Marianne Hundt, Sandra Mollin, and Simone E. Pfenninger (eds.) *The Changing English Language: Psycholinguistic Perspectives*. Cambridge: Cambridge University Press, pp. 215–39.
Belletti, Adriana and Luigi Rizzi 1988. Psych-verbs and θ-theory. *Natural Language & Linguistic Theory* 6(3): 291–352.
Bentz, Christian and Bodo Winter 2013. Languages with more second language learners tend to lose nominal case. *Language Dynamics and Change* 3(1): 1–27.
Berlage, Eva 2014. *Noun Phrase Complexity in English*. Cambridge: Cambridge University Press.
Bezuidenhout, Anne 2004. Procedural meaning and the semantics/pragmatics interface. In Claudia Bianchi (ed.) *The Semantics/Pragmatics Distinction*. Stanford: CSLI Publications, pp. 101–31.
Biber, Douglas 1988. *Variation across Speech and Writing*. Cambridge: Cambridge University Press.
Biber, Douglas 2003. Variation among university spoken and written registers: A new multi-dimensional analysis. In Pepi Leistyna and Charles Meyer (eds.) *Corpus Analysis: Language Structure and Language Use*. Amsterdam: Rodopi, pp. 47–70.
Biber, Douglas and Edward Finegan 1997. Diachronic relations among speech-based and written registers in English. In Terttu Nevalainen and Leena Kahlas-Tarkka (eds.) *To Explain the Present: Studies in the Changing English Language in Honour of Matti Rissanen*. Helsinki: Société Néophilologique, pp. 253–75.
Biber, Douglas, Stig Johansson, Geoffrey Leech, Susan Conrad, and Edward Finegan 1999. *Longman Grammar of Spoken and Written English*. Harlow: Pearson.

Birkmann, Thomas 1987. *Präteritopräsentia: Morphologische Entwicklungen einer Sonderklasse in den altgermanischen Sprachen*. Tübingen: Max Niemeyer Verlag.
Björkstam, Harald 1919. *De modala hjälpverben i svenskan*. Lund: H. Ohlssons boktryckeri.
Blakemore, Diane 2006. Divisions of labour: The analysis of parentheticals. *Lingua* 116(10): 1670–87.
Bloom, Harold 1973. *The Anxiety of Influence: A Theory of Poetry*. Oxford: Oxford University Press.
Bloom, Harold 1975. *A Map of Misreading*. Oxford: Oxford University Press.
Bock, Hellmut 1931. Studien zum präpositionalen Infinitiv und Akkusativ mit dem *to*-Infinitiv. *Anglia* 55: 114–249.
Bonfiglio, Thomas Paul 2002. *Race and the Rise of Standard American*. Berlin: Mouton de Gruyter.
Börjars, Kersti and Nigel Vincent 2017. Lexical-Functional Grammar. In Adam Ledgeway and Ian Roberts (eds.) *The Cambridge Handbook of Historical Syntax*. Cambridge: Cambridge University Press, pp. 642–63.
Börjars, Kersti, David Denison, Grzegorz Krajewski, and Alan Scott 2013a. Expression of possession in English: The significance of the right edge. In Kersti Börjars, David Denison, and Alan Scott (eds.) *Morphosyntactic Categories and the Expression of Possession*. Amsterdam/Philadelphia: John Benjamins, pp. 123–48.
Börjars, Kersti, David Denison, and Alan Scott (eds.) 2013b. *Morphosyntactic Categories and the Expression of Possession*. Amsterdam/Philadelphia: John Benjamins.
Börjars, Kersti, Nigel Vincent, and George Walkden 2015. On constructing a theory of grammatical change. *Transactions of the Philological Society* 113(3): 363–82.
Boye, Kasper 2001. The force-dynamic core meaning of Danish modal verbs. *Acta Linguistica Hafniensia* 33(1): 19–66.
Brandt, Søren 1999. *Modal Verbs in Danish*. Copenhagen: Reitzel.
Brems, Lieselotte 2011. *Layering of Size and Type Noun Constructions in English*. Berlin/Boston: Walter de Gruyter.
Bresnan, Joan W. 1970. On complementizers: Toward a syntactic theory of complement types. *Foundations of Language* 6(3): 297–321.
Bresnan, Joan W. 1972. Theory of complementation in English syntax. PhD thesis: Massachusetts Institute of Technology. [Published as *Theory of Complementation in English Syntax*. New York: Garland, 1979.]
Bresnan, Joan 1982. Control and complementation. *Linguistic Inquiry* 13(3): 343–434.
Bresnan, Joan 2007. Is syntactic knowledge probabilistic? Experiments with the English dative alternation. In Sam Featherston and Wolfgang Sternefeld (eds.) *Roots: Linguistics in Search of Its Evidential Base*. Berlin: Mouton de Gruyter, pp. 75–96.

Bresnan, Joan and Marilyn Ford 2010. Predicting syntax: Processing dative constructions in American and Australian varieties of English. *Language* 86(1): 168–213.
Bresnan, Joan, Ash Asudeh, Ida Toivonen, and Stephen Wechsler 2016. *Lexical-Functional Syntax*, 2nd edn. Malden, MA: Wiley Blackwell.
Brinton, Laurel J. 1991. The origin and development of quasimodal *have to* in English. Paper presented at the workshop on 'The origin and development of verbal periphrases', 10th International Conference on Historical Linguistics (ICHL 10), Amsterdam, 16 August 1991. Unpublished manuscript. Available at: http://faculty.arts.ubc.ca/lbrinton/HAVETO.PDF.
Brinton, Laurel J. 2008. *The Comment Clause in English: Syntactic Origins and Pragmatic Development*. Cambridge: Cambridge University Press.
Brinton, Laurel J. 2014. *If you choose/like/prefer/want/wish*: The origin of metalinguistic and politeness functions. In Marianne Hundt (ed.) *Late Modern English Syntax*. Cambridge: Cambridge University Press, pp. 271–90.
Brinton, Laurel J. 2017. *The Evolution of Pragmatic Markers in English: Pathways of Change*. Cambridge: Cambridge University Press.
Brinton, Laurel J. and Elizabeth Closs Traugott 2005. *Lexicalization and Language Change*. Cambridge: Cambridge University Press.
Brown, Gillian 1977 (1st edn.), 1990 (2nd edn.). *Listening to Spoken English*. London: Longman.
Brown, Penelope and Stephen C. Levinson 1987. *Politeness: Some Universals in Language Usage*. Cambridge: Cambridge University Press.
Browning, Robert 1846. *Luria*. In *Bells and Pomegranates*, Vol. 8: *Luria; and a Soul's Tragedy*. London: Edward Moxon, pp. 4–20.
Butler, Charles 1634. *English Grammar*. Oxford: Printed by William Turner, for the author. (Facsimile reprint, with an introduction by Albert Eichler. Halle: Niemeyer, 1910.)
Butt, Miriam, Christian Fortmann, and Christian Rohrer 1996a. Syntactic analyses for parallel grammars: Auxiliaries and genitive NPs. In COLING-96 Organizing Committee (eds.) *COLING-96: Proceedings of the 16th International Conference on Computational Linguistics*, Vol. 1. Copenhagen: Center for Sprogteknologi, pp. 182–7.
Butt, Miriam, María-Eugenia Niño, and Frédérique Segond 1996b. Multilingual processing of auxiliaries within LFG. In Dafydd Gibbon (ed.) *Natural Language Processing and Speech Technology: Results of the 3rd KONVENS Conference, Bielefeld, October 1996*. Berlin: Mouton de Gruyter, pp. 111–22.
Bybee, Joan 2003. Mechanisms of change in grammaticization: The role of frequency. In Brian D. Joseph and Richard D. Janda (eds.) *The Handbook of Historical Linguistics*. Oxford: Blackwell, pp. 602–23.
Bybee, Joan 2010. *Language, Usage and Cognition*. Cambridge: Cambridge University Press.
Bybee, Joan L. 2011. Usage-based theory and grammaticalization. In Heiko Narrog and Bernd Heine (eds.) *The Oxford Handbook of Grammaticalization*. Oxford: Oxford University Press, pp. 69–78.

Bybee, Joan L. 2013. Usage-based theory and exemplar representations of constructions. In Thomas Hoffmann and Graeme Trousdale (eds.) *The Oxford Handbook of Construction Grammar.* New York: Oxford University Press, pp. 49–69.

Bybee, Joan L. and Paul J. Hopper (eds.) 2001. *Frequency and the Emergence of Linguistic Structure.* Amsterdam/Philadelphia: John Benjamins.

Bybee, Joan L., William Pagliuca, and Revere D. Perkins 1991. Back to the future. In Elizabeth Closs Traugott and Bernd Heine (eds.) *Approaches to Grammaticalization,* Vol. II *Focus on Types of Grammatical Markers.* Amsterdam/Philadelphia: John Benjamins, pp. 17–58.

Bybee, Joan, Revere Perkins, and William Pagliuca 1994. *The Evolution of Grammar: Tense, Aspect, and Modality in the Languages of the World.* Chicago, IL: The University of Chicago Press.

Bylin, Maria 2017. Hit och dit i prototypkategorin. Historien om *viljas* hjälpverbsstatus. In Emma Sköldberg, Maia Andréasson, Henrietta Adamsson Eryd, Filippa Lindahl, Sven Lindström, Julia Prentice, and Malin Sandberg (eds.) *Svenskans beskrivning 35: Förhandlingar vid trettiofemte sammankomsten, Göteborg 11–13 maj 2016.* Göteborg: Göteborgs Universitet, pp. 67–80.

Cappelle, Bert 2006. Particle placement and the case for 'allostructions'. *Constructions* SV1-7/2006: 1–28.

Chafe, Wallace and Jane Danielewicz 1987. Properties of spoken and written language. In Rosalind Horowitz and S. Jay Samuels (eds.) *Comprehending Oral and Written Language.* San Diego: Academic Press, pp. 83–113.

CHEL IV = Romaine, Suzanne (ed.) 1998. *The Cambridge History of the English Language,* Vol. IV *1776–1997.* Cambridge: Cambridge University Press.

Cheshire, Jenny 2007. Discourse variation, grammaticalisation and stuff like that. *Journal of Sociolinguistics* 11(2): 155–93.

Chomsky, Noam 1981. *Lectures on Government and Binding: The Pisa Lectures.* Dordrecht: Foris Publications.

Christophersen, Paul 1939. *The Articles: A Study of Their Theory and Use in English.* Copenhagen: Einar Munksgaard.

Claridge, Claudia 2013. The evolution of three pragmatic markers: *As it were, so to speak/say* and *if you like. Journal of Historical Pragmatics* 14(2): 161–84.

Coates, Richard 1987. Pragmatic sources of analogical reformation. *Journal of Linguistics* 23(2): 319–40.

Copley, Bridget 2009. *The Semantics of the Future.* London: Routledge.

Craig 1951: *See* SHC.

Creissels, Denis 2013. Control and the evolution of possessive and existential constructions. In Elly van Gelderen, Michela Cennamo, and Jóhanna Barðdal (eds.) *Argument Structure in Flux: The Naples-Capri Papers.* Amsterdam/Philadelphia: John Benjamins, pp. 461–76.

Crisma, Paola 2011. The emergence of the definite article in English: A contact-induced change? In Petra Sleeman and Harry Perridon (eds.) *The Noun Phrase in Romance and Germanic: Structure, Variation, and Change.* Amsterdam/Philadelphia: John Benjamins, pp. 175–92.

Croft, William 1993. Case marking and the semantics of mental verbs. In James Pustejovsky (ed.) *Semantics and the Lexicon.* Dordrecht/Boston: Kluwer Academic, pp. 55–72.
Croft, William 2001. *Radical Construction Grammar: Syntactic Theory in Typological Perspective.* Oxford: Oxford University Press.
Crystal, David 1988. *Rediscover Grammar with David Crystal.* Harlow: Longman.
Crystal, David 2001. *Language and the Internet.* Cambridge: Cambridge University Press.
Culicover, Peter W. 1999. *Syntactic Nuts: Hard Cases, Syntactic Theory, and Language Acquisition.* Oxford: Oxford University Press.
Culpeper, Jonathan and Merja Kytö 2010. *Early Modern English Dialogues: Spoken Interaction as Writing.* Cambridge: Cambridge University Press.
Curzan, Anne 2003. *Gender Shifts in the History of English.* Cambridge: Cambridge University Press.
Curzan, Anne 2014. *Fixing English: Prescriptivism and Language History.* Cambridge: Cambridge University Press.
Cutler, Anne 1979. Contemporary reaction to Rudolf Meringer's speech error research. *Historiographia Linguistica* 6(1): 57–76.
Cutler, Anne 2000. Listening to a second language through the ears of a first. *Interpreting* 5: 1–23.
Cutler, Anne and David Fay 1978. Introduction. In Rudolf Meringer and Carl Mayer (eds.) *Versprechen und Verlesen: Eine psychologisch-linguistische Studie,* new edition with an introductory article by Anne Cutler and David Fay. Amsterdam: John Benjamins, pp. ix–xl.
Cuyckens, Hubert 1999. Historical evidence in prepositional semantics: The case of English *by.* In Guy A. J. Tops, Betty Devriendt, and Steven Geukens (eds.) *Thinking English Grammar: To Honour Xavier Dekeyser, Professor Emeritus.* Leuven: Peeters, pp. 15–32.
Dalrymple, Mary 2001. *Lexical Functional Grammar.* San Diego: Academic Press.
Dalrymple, Mary 2015. Morphology in the LFG architecture. In Miriam Butt and Tracy Holloway King (eds.) *Proceedings of the LFG15 Conference.* Stanford, CA: CSLI Publications, pp. 64–83. Available at: http://web.stanford.edu/group/cslipublications/cslipublications/LFG/20/lfg15.html.
Dancygier, Barbara and Eve Sweetser 2005. *Mental Spaces in Grammar: Conditional Constructions.* Cambridge: Cambridge University Press.
Darwin, Charles 1998. *The Expression of the Emotions in Man and Animals.* 3rd edn. with an introduction, afterword and commentaries by Paul Ekman. London: HarperCollins.
Davies, Hugh Sykes 1960. *Trollope.* London: Longmans, Green and Co. Ltd.
Davies, Mark 2012. Some methodological issues related to corpus-based investigations of recent syntactic changes in English. In Terttu Nevalainen and Elizabeth Closs Traugott (eds.) *The Oxford Handbook of the History of English.* Oxford: Oxford University Press, pp. 157–74.

Davies, Mark and Robert Fuchs 2015. Expanding horizons in the study of World Englishes with the 1.9 billion word Global Web-based English Corpus (GloWbE). *English World-Wide* 36(1): 1–28.

Day, Samuel B. and Dedre Gentner 2007. Nonintentional analogical inference in text comprehension. *Memory & Cognition* 35(1): 39–49.

De Smet, Hendrik 2009. Analysing reanalysis. *Lingua* 119(11): 1728–55.

De Smet, Hendrik 2012. The course of actualization. *Language* 88(3): 601–33.

De Smet, Hendrik 2013. *Spreading Patterns: Diffusional Change in the English System of Complementation*. Oxford: Oxford University Press.

De Smet, Hendrik, Lobke Ghesquière, and Freek Van de Velde (eds.) 2015. *On Multiple Source Constructions in Language Change*. Amsterdam/Philadelphia: John Benjamins.

Deacon, Terrence W. 1997. *The Symbolic Species: The Co-Evolution of Language and the Brain*. New York: W. W. Norton.

Dehé, Nicole and Yordanka Kavalova 2007. Parentheticals: An introduction. In Nicole Dehé and Yordanka Kavalova (eds.) *Parentheticals*. Amsterdam/Philadelphia: John Benjamins, pp. 1–22.

DENG = Sundby, Bertil, Anne Kari Bjørge, and Kari E. Haugland 1991. *A Dictionary of English Normative Grammar, 1700–1800*. Amsterdam/Philadelphia: John Benjamins.

Denison, David 1990. The Old English impersonals revived. In Sylvia M. Adamson, Vivien A. Law, Nigel Vincent, and Susan Wright (eds.) *Papers from the 5th International Conference on English Historical Linguistics: Cambridge, 6–9 April 1987*. Amsterdam/Philadelphia: John Benjamins, pp. 111–40.

Denison, David 1993. *English Historical Syntax: Verbal Constructions*. London/New York: Longman.

Denison, David 1998. Syntax. In Suzanne Romaine (ed.) *The Cambridge History of the English Language*, Vol. IV *1776–1997*. Cambridge: Cambridge University Press, pp. 92–329.

Denison, David 2006. Category change and gradience in the determiner system. In Ans van Kemenade and Bettelou Los (eds.) *The Handbook of the History of English*. Oxford: Blackwell, pp. 279–304.

Denison, David 2012. Introduction to Part V. In David Denison, Ricardo Bermúdez-Otero, Chris McCully, and Emma Moore, with the assistance of Ayumi Miura (eds.) *Analysing Older English*. Cambridge: Cambridge University Press, pp. 247–50.

Denison, David and Alison Cort 2010. *Better* as a verb. In Kristin Davidse, Lieven Vandelanotte, and Hubert Cuyckens (eds.) *Subjectification, Intersubjectification and Grammaticalization*. Berlin: De Gruyter Mouton, pp. 349–83.

Denison, David and Marianne Hundt 2013. Defining relatives. *Journal of English Linguistics* 41(2): 135–67.

Denison, David and Nigel Vincent. 1997. Editorial introduction. *Transactions of the Philological Society* 95(1): 1–8.

Denison, David, Alan K. Scott, and Kersti Börjars 2010. The real distribution of the English 'group genitive'. *Studies in Language* 34(3): 532–64.

Deo, Ashwini 2014. Formal semantics/pragmatics and language change. In Claire Bowern and Bethwyn Evans (eds.) *The Routledge Handbook of Historical Linguistics*. London: Routledge, pp. 393–409.

Deo, Ashwini 2015. Diachronic semantics. *Annual Review of Linguistics* 1(1): 179–97. Available at: www.annualreviews.org/toc/linguistics/1/1.

Dreschler, Gea 2015. *Passives and the Loss of Verb Second: A Study of Syntactic and Information-Structural Factors*. Utrecht: LOT Publications.

Dyvik, Helge 1999. The universality of f-structure: Discovery or stipulation? The case of modals. In Miriam Butt and Tracy Holloway King (eds.) *Proceedings of the LFG99 Conference*. Stanford, CA: CSLI Publications. Available at: http://web.stanford.edu/group/cslipublications/cslipublications/LFG/LFG4-1999/.

Eckardt, Regine 2006. *Meaning Change in Grammaticalization: An Enquiry into Semantic Reanalysis*. Oxford: Oxford University Press.

Eckert, Penelope 2012. Three waves of variation study: The emergence of meaning in the study of sociolinguistic variation. *Annual Review of Anthropology* 41: 87–100.

Eddington, David and Carmen Silva-Corvalán 2011. Variation in the use of *deber* and *deber de* in written and oral materials from Latin America and Spain. *Spanish in Context* 8(2): 257–71.

Ehret, Katharina, Christoph Wolk, and Benedikt Szmrecsanyi 2014. Quirky quadratures: On rhythm and weight as constraints on genitive variation in an unconventional data set. *English Language and Linguistics* 18(2): 263–303.

Eide, Kristin Melum 2005. *Norwegian Modals*. Berlin: Mouton de Gruyter.

Eliot, T. S. 1921. Tradition and the individual talent. In T. S. Eliot, *The Sacred Wood: Essays on Poetry and Criticism*. New York: Alfred A. Knopf, pp. 47–59.

Ellis, Andrew W. 1980. On the Freudian theory of speech errors. In Victoria A. Fromkin (ed.) *Errors in Linguistic Performance: Slips of the Tongue, Ear, Pen, and Hand*. San Francisco: Academic Press, pp. 123–31.

Elmer, Willy 1981. *Diachronic Grammar: The History of Old and Middle English Subjectless Constructions*. Tübingen: Niemeyer.

Emonds, Joseph E. 1976. *A Transformational Approach to English Syntax: Root, Structure-Preserving, and Local Transformations*. New York: Academic Press.

Emonds, Joseph E. 1985. *A Unified Theory of Syntactic Categories*. Dordrecht: Foris Publications.

Engdahl, Elisabet 1999. The choice between *bli*-passive and *s*-passive in Danish, Norwegian and Swedish. *NORDSEM Report 3*. Available at: www.svenska.gu.se/digitalAssets/1336/1336829_engdahl-nordsem-passivechoice-1999.pdf.

Evans, Nicholas 2007. Insubordination and its uses. In Irina Nicolaeva (ed.) *Finiteness: Theoretical and Empirical Foundations*. Oxford: Oxford University Press, pp. 366–431.

Faarlund, Jan Terje 2004. *The Syntax of Old Norse*. Oxford: Oxford University Press.
Falk, Hjalmar and Alf Torp 1900. *Dansk-norskens syntax i historisk fremstilling*. Kristiania: Aschehoug and Co.
Falk, Yehuda N. 1984. The English auxiliary system: A Lexical-Functional analysis. *Language* 60(3): 483–509.
Falk, Yehuda N. 2001. *Lexical-Functional Grammar: An Introduction to Parallel Constraint-Based Syntax*. Stanford, CA: CSLI Publications.
Fellbaum, Christiane (ed.) 1998. *WordNet: An Electronic Lexical Database*. Cambridge, MA: MIT Press.
Fernández de Castro, Félix 1999. *Las Perífrasis Verbales en el Español Actual*. Madrid: Gredos.
Finegan, Edward 1998. English grammar and usage. In Suzanne Romaine (ed.) *The Cambridge History of the English Language*, Vol. IV *1776–1997*. Cambridge: Cambridge University Press, pp. 536–88.
Finegan, Edward 2004. American English and its distinctiveness. In Edward Finegan and John R. Rickford (eds.) *Language in the USA: Themes for the Twenty-First Century*. Cambridge: Cambridge University Press, pp. 18–38.
Finegan, Edward 2006. English in North America. In Richard Hogg and David Denison (eds.) *A History of the English Language*. Cambridge: Cambridge University Press, pp. 384–419.
Fischer, Olga 1988. The rise of the *for NP to V* construction: An explanation. In Graham Nixon and John Honey (eds.) *An Historic Tongue: Studies in English Linguistics in Memory of Barbara Strang*. London/New York: Routledge, pp. 67–88.
Fischer, Olga 1989. The origin and spread of the accusative and infinitive construction in English. *Folia Linguistica Historica* 8(1–2): 143–217.
Fischer, Olga 1990. Syntactic change and causation: Developments in infinitival constructions in English. PhD thesis: University of Amsterdam.
Fischer, Olga 1992. Syntactic change and borrowing: The case of the accusative-and-infinitive construction in English. In Marinel Gerritsen and Dieter Stein (eds.) *Internal and External Factors in Syntactic Change*. Berlin: Mouton de Gruyter, pp. 17–88.
Fischer, Olga 1994a. The fortunes of the Latin-type accusative and infinitive construction in Dutch and English compared. In Toril Swan, Endre Mørck, and Olaf Jansen Westvik (eds.) *Language Change and Language Structure: Older Germanic Languages in a Comparative Perspective*. Berlin: Mouton de Gruyter, pp. 91–133.
Fischer, Olga 1994b. The development of quasi-auxiliaries in English and changes in word order. *Neophilologus* 78(1): 137–64.
Fischer, Olga 1997. The grammaticalisation of infinitival *to* in English compared with German and Dutch. In Raymond Hickey and Stanisław Puppel (eds.) *Language History and Linguistic Modelling: A Festschrift for Jacek Fisiak on His 60th Birthday*, Vol. I *Language History*. Berlin: Mouton de Gruyter, pp. 265–80.

Fischer, Olga 2007. *Morphosyntactic Change: Functional and Formal Perspectives.* Oxford: Oxford University Press.
Fischer, Olga 2011. Grammaticalization as analogically driven change? In Heiko Narrog and Bernd Heine (eds.) *The Oxford Handbook of Grammaticalization.* Oxford: Oxford University Press, pp. 31–42.
Fischer, Olga 2013. An inquiry into unidirectionality as a foundational element of grammaticalization: On the role played by analogy and the synchronic grammar system in processes of language change. *Studies in Language* 37(3): 515–33.
Fischer, Olga 2015. The influence of the grammatical system and analogy in processes of language change: The case of the auxiliation of HAVE-*to* once again. In Fabienne Toupin and Brian Lowrey (eds.) *Studies in Linguistic Variation and Change: From Old to Middle English.* Newcastle upon Tyne: Cambridge Scholars Publishing, pp. 120–50.
Fischer, Olga C. M. and Frederike C. van der Leek 1983. The demise of the Old English impersonal construction. *Journal of Linguistics* 19(2): 337–68.
Fischer, Olga, Ans van Kemenade, Willem Koopman, and Wim van der Wurff 2000. *The Syntax of Early English.* Cambridge: Cambridge University Press.
Fleischman, Suzanne 1982. *The Future in Thought and Language: Diachronic Evidence from Romance.* Cambridge: Cambridge University Press.
Ford, Cecilia E. and Sandra A. Thompson 1986. Conditionals in discourse: A text-based study from English. In Elizabeth Closs Traugott, Alice ter Meulen, Judy Snitzer Reilly, and Charles A. Ferguson (eds.) *On Conditionals.* Cambridge: Cambridge University Press, pp. 353–72.
Frank, Anette and Annie Zaenen 2002. Tense in LFG: Syntax and morphology. In Hans Kamp and Uwe Reyle (eds.) *How We Say WHEN It Happens: Contributions to the Theory of Temporal Reference in Natural Language.* Tübingen: Max Niemeyer Verlag, pp. 17–52.
Freud, Sigmund 1914. *Psychopathology of Everyday Life*, Authorized English edition, with introduction by A. A. Brill. London: T. Fisher Unwin.
Fried, Mirjam and Jan-Ola Östman 2005. Construction Grammar and spoken language: The case of pragmatic particles. *Journal of Pragmatics* 37(11): 1752–78.
Fromkin, Victoria A. (ed.) 1973. *Speech Errors as Linguistic Evidence.* The Hague: Mouton.
Fromkin, Victoria A. (ed.) 1980. *Errors in Linguistic Performance: Slips of the Tongue, Ear, Pen, and Hand.* San Francisco: Academic Press.
Garachana Camarero, Mar 2017. Perífrasis formadas en torno a *tener* en español: *Ser tenudo/tenido ø/a/de + infinitivo, tener a/de + infinitivo, tener que + infinitivo.* In Mar Garachana Camarero (ed.) *La Gramática en la Diacronía: La Evolución de las Perífrasis Verbales Modales en Español.* Madrid/Frankfurt am Main: Iberoamericana Vervuert, pp. 229–86.
Garachana Camarero, Mar and Malte Rosemeyer 2011. Rutinas léxicas en el cambio gramatical. El caso de las perífrasis deónticas e iterativas. *Revista de Historia de la Lengua Española* 6: 35–60.
García Fernández, Luis (ed.) 2006. *Diccionario de Perífrasis Verbales.* Madrid: Gredos.

Geerts, G., W. Haeseryn, J. de Rooij, and M. C. van den Toorn 1984. *Algemene Nederlandse Spraakkunst*. Groningen: Wolters-Noordhoff.
Gentner, Dedre 2010. Bootstrapping the mind: Analogical processes and symbol systems. *Cognitive Science* 34(5): 752–75.
Gentner, Dedre and Laura L. Namy 2006. Analogical processes in language learning. *Current Directions in Psychological Science* 15(6): 297–301.
Gentner, Dedre and Linsey Smith 2012. Analogical reasoning. In V. S. Ramachandran (ed.) *Encyclopedia of Human Behavior*, 2nd edn. Oxford: Elsevier, pp. 130–6.
Gentner, Dedre, Florencia K. Anggoro, and Raquel S. Klibanoff 2011. Structure mapping and relational language support children's learning of relational categories. *Child Development* 82(4): 1173–88.
Giusti, Giuliana 1997. The categorial status of determiners. In Liliane Haegeman (ed.) *The New Comparative Syntax*. London/New York: Longman, pp. 95–123.
Godden, M. R. 2003. Review of David W. Porter's *Excerptiones de Prisciano: The Source for Ælfric's Latin-Old English Grammar*. *Medium Ævum* 72(1): 128–30.
Goldberg, Adele E. 1995. *Constructions: A Construction Grammar Approach to Argument Structure*. Chicago/London: The University of Chicago Press.
Goldberg, Adele E. 2006. *Constructions at Work: The Nature of Generalization in Language*. Oxford: Oxford University Press.
Gómez Torrego, Leonardo 1999. Los verbos auxiliares. Las perífrasis verbales de infinitivo. In Ignacio Bosque and Violeta Demonte (eds.) *Gramática Descriptiva de la Lengua Española*, Vol. 2 *Las Construcciones Sintácticas Fundamentales. Relaciones Temporales, Aspectuales y Modales*. Madrid: Espasa Calpe, pp. 3323–89.
Gonçalves, Bruno, Lucía Loureiro-Porto, José J. Ramasco, and David Sánchez 2018. Mapping the Americanization of English in space and time. PLOS ONE 13(5): e0197741. https://doi.org/10.1371/journal.pone.0197741
Gordon, E. V. 1927. *An Introduction to Old Norse*. Oxford: Clarendon Press.
Görlach, Manfred 1991. *Introduction to Early Modern English*. Cambridge: Cambridge University Press.
Grafmiller, Jason 2014. Variation in English genitives across modality and genres. *English Language and Linguistics* 18(3): 471–96.
Grano, Thomas 2015. *Control and Restructuring*. Oxford: Oxford University Press.
Green, Georgia M. 2011. Elementary principles of Head-Driven Phrase Structure Grammar. In Robert D. Borsley and Kersti Börjars (eds.) *Non-Transformational Syntax: Formal and Explicit Models of Grammar*. Chichester: Wiley-Blackwell, pp. 9–53.
Greenbaum, Sidney 1996. Introducing ICE. In Sidney Greenbaum (ed.) *Comparing English Worldwide: The International Corpus of English*. Oxford: Clarendon Press, pp. 3–12.
Greenberg, Joseph H. 1978. How does a language acquire gender markers? In Joseph H. Greenberg, Charles A. Ferguson, and Edith A. Moravcsik (eds.) *Universals of Human Language*, Vol. 3 *Word Structure*. Stanford, CA: Stanford University Press, pp. 47–82.

Greenblatt, Stephen, Walter Cohen, Jean E. Howard, and Katharine Eisaman Maus (eds.) 1997. *The Norton Shakespeare*. New York: W. W. Norton.
Gries, Stefan Th. and Martin Hilpert 2012. Variability-based Neighbor Clustering: A bottom-up approach to periodization in historical linguistics. In Terttu Nevalainen and Elizabeth Closs Traugott (eds.) *The Oxford Handbook of the History of English*. New York: Oxford University Press, pp. 134–44.
Grimberg, Carl 1905. Undersökningar om konstruktionen ackusativ med infinitiv i den äldre fornsvenskan. *Arkiv för Nordisk Filologi* XXI: 205–35, 311–57.
Grimm, Jacob 1837. *Deutsche Grammatik*, Vol. 4. Göttingen: In der Dieterichschen Buchhandlung.
Gumperz, John J. 1982a. *Discourse Strategies*. Cambridge: Cambridge University Press.
Gumperz, John J. (ed.) 1982b. *Language and Social Identity*. Cambridge: Cambridge University Press.
Gumperz, John J. 2001. Interactional sociolinguistics: A personal perspective. In Deborah Schiffrin, Deborah Tannen, and Heidi E. Hamilton (eds.) *The Handbook of Discourse Analysis*. Malden, MA: Blackwell Publishers, pp. 215–28.
Hale, William Gardner and Carl Darling Buck 1966. *A Latin Grammar*. Tuscaloosa: University of Alabama Press.
Harris, Alice C. and Lyle Campbell 1995. *Historical Syntax in Cross-Linguistic Perspective*. Cambridge: Cambridge University Press.
Haspelmath, Martin 1989. From purposive to infinitive – A universal path of grammaticization. *Folia Linguistica Historica* 10(1/2): 287–310.
Haspelmath, Martin 1998. Does grammaticalization need reanalysis? *Studies in Language* 22(2): 315–51.
Haspelmath, Martin 2013. On the cross-linguistic distribution of same-subject and different-subject 'want' complements: Economic vs. iconic motivation. *SKY Journal of Linguistics* 26: 41–69.
Haug, Dag 2013. Partial control and anaphoric control in LFG. In Miriam Butt and Tracy Holloway King (eds.) *Proceedings of the LFG 2013 Conference*. Stanford, CA: CSLI Publications, pp. 274–94. Available at: http://web.stanford.edu/group/cslipublications/cslipublications/LFG/18/lfg13.html.
Hawkins, Roger 1981. Towards an account of the possessive constructions: *NP's N* and *the N of NP*. *Journal of Linguistics* 17(2): 247–69.
Healey, Antonette diPaolo and Richard L. Venezky 1980. *A Microfiche Concordance to Old English: The List of Texts and Index of Editions*. Toronto: Pontifical Institute of Mediaeval Studies.
Heim, Irene 1992. Presupposition projection and the semantics of attitude verbs. *Journal of Semantics* 9(3): 183–221.
Heine, Bernd 1993. *Auxiliaries: Cognitive Forces and Grammaticalization*. New York/Oxford: Oxford University Press.

Heine, Bernd 1997. *Cognitive Foundations of Grammar*. Oxford: Oxford University Press.
Heine, Bernd and Tania Kuteva 2002. *World Lexicon of Grammaticalization*. Cambridge: Cambridge University Press.
Heine, Bernd, Gunther Kaltenböck, and Tania Kuteva 2016. On insubordination and cooptation. In Nicholas Evans and Honoré Watanabe (eds.) *Insubordination*. Amsterdam/Philadelphia: John Benjamins, pp. 39–64.
Heller, Benedikt 2019. Stability and fluidity in syntactic variation world-wide: The genitive alternation across varieties of English. PhD thesis: KU Leuven.
Heller, Benedikt, Benedikt Szmrecsanyi, and Jason Grafmiller 2017. Stability and fluidity in syntactic variation world-wide: The genitive alternation across varieties of English. *Journal of English Linguistics* 45(1): 3–27.
Hellquist, Elof 1902. *Studier i 1600-talets svenska*. Uppsala: Akademiska Bokhandeln.
Hernández Díaz, Axel 2006. Posesión y existencia. La competencia de *haber* y *tener* y *haber* existencial. In Concepción Company Company (ed.) *Sintaxis Histórica de la Lengua Española*, Primera Parte *La Frase Verbal*, Vol. 2. México: Universidad Nacional Autónoma de México/Fondo de Cultura Económica, pp. 1053–160.
Hilpert, Martin 2008a. *Germanic Future Constructions: A Usage-Based Approach to Language Change*. Amsterdam/Philadelphia: John Benjamins.
Hilpert, Martin 2008b. The English comparative – Language structure and language use. *English Language and Linguistics* 12(3): 395–417.
Hilpert, Martin 2013. *Constructional Change in English: Developments in Allomorphy, Word-Formation, and Syntax*. Cambridge: Cambridge University Press.
Hilpert, Martin 2014. *Construction Grammar and Its Application to English*. Edinburgh: Edinburgh University Press.
Himmelmann, Nikolaus P. 2004. Lexicalization and grammaticization: Opposite or orthogonal? In Walter Bisang, Nikolaus P. Himmelmann, and Björn Wiemer (eds.) *What Makes Grammaticalization? A Look from Its Fringes and Its Components*. Berlin/New York: Mouton de Gruyter, pp. 21–42.
Hinrichs, Lars and Benedikt Szmrecsanyi 2007. Recent changes in the function and frequency of Standard English genitive constructions: A multivariate analysis of tagged corpora. *English Language and Linguistics* 11(3): 437–74.
Hinrichs, Lars, Nicholas Smith, and Birgit Waibel 2007. *The Part-of-Speech-Tagged 'Brown' Corpora: A Manual of Information, Including Pointers for Successful Use*. Freiburg: Department of English, University of Freiburg. Available at: http://clu.uni.no/icame/manuals/FLOB-Manual-tagged.pdf.
Hinterhuber, Hartmann 2007. Sigmund Freud, Rudolf Meringer and Carl Mayer: Slips of the tongue and mis-readings. The history of a controversy. *Neuropsychiatrie* 21(4): 291–301.
Hodson, Jane 2006. The problem of Joseph Priestley's (1733–1804) descriptivism. *Historiographia Linguistica* 33(1/2): 57–84.

Hofstadter, Douglas R. 2001. Epilogue: Analogy as the core of cognition. In Dedre Gentner, Keith J. Holyoak, and Boicho N. Kokinov (eds.) *The Analogical Mind: Perspectives from Cognitive Science*. Cambridge, MA: MIT Press, pp. 499–538.
Hofstadter, Douglas and Emmanuel Sander 2013. *Surfaces and Essences: Analogy as the Fuel and Fire of Thinking*. New York: Basic Books.
Hogg, Richard M. (ed.) 1992. *The Cambridge History of the English Language*, Vol. I *The Beginnings to 1066*. Cambridge: Cambridge University Press.
Hogg, Richard and David Denison (eds.) 2006. *A History of the English Language*. Cambridge: Cambridge University Press.
Holyoak, Keith J. and Paul Thagard 1995. *Mental Leaps: Analogy in Creative Thought*. Cambridge, MA: MIT Press.
Hopper, Paul J. 1991. On some principles of grammaticization. In Elizabeth Closs Traugott and Bernd Heine (eds.) *Approaches to Grammaticalization*, Vol. I *Focus on Theoretical and Methodological Issues*. Amsterdam/Philadelphia: John Benjamins, pp. 17–35.
Hopper, Paul J. and Sandra A. Thompson 1980. Transitivity in grammar and discourse. *Language* 56(2): 251–99.
Hopper, Paul J. and Elizabeth Closs Traugott 2003. *Grammaticalization*, 2nd edn. Cambridge: Cambridge University Press.
Hothorn, Torsten, Kurt Hornik, and Achim Zeileis 2006. Unbiased recursive partitioning: A conditional inference framework. *Journal of Computational and Graphical Statistics* 15(3): 651–74.
Huber, Magnus 2007. The *Old Bailey Proceedings*, 1674–1834: Evaluating and annotating a corpus of 18th- and 19th-century spoken English. *Studies in Variation, Contacts and Change in English* 1. (Issue edited by Anneli Meurman-Solin and Arja Nurmi, *Annotating Variation and Change*.) Available at www.helsinki.fi/varieng/series/volumes/01/huber/.
Huddleston, Rodney 1995. The case against a future tense in English. *Studies in Language* 19(2): 399–446.
Huddleston, Rodney 2002. The verb. In Rodney Huddleston and Geoffrey K. Pullum *et al.*, *The Cambridge Grammar of the English Language*. Cambridge: Cambridge University Press, pp. 71–212.
Huddleston, Rodney and Geoffrey K. Pullum *et al.* 2002. *The Cambridge Grammar of the English Language*. Cambridge: Cambridge University Press.
Hundt, Marianne 2009. *Colonial lag, colonial innovation* or simply *language change*? In Günter Rohdenburg and Julia Schlüter (eds.) *One Language, Two Grammars? Differences between British and American English*. Cambridge: Cambridge University Press, pp. 13–37.
Hundt, Marianne and Geoffrey Leech 2012. 'Small is beautiful': On the value of standard reference corpora for observing recent grammatical change. In Terttu Nevalainen and Elizabeth Closs Traugott (eds.) *The Oxford Handbook of the History of English*. Oxford: Oxford University Press, pp. 175–88.

Hundt, Marianne and Christian Mair 1999. 'Agile' and 'uptight' genres: The corpus-based approach to language change in progress. *International Journal of Corpus Linguistics* 4(2): 221–42.

Hundt, Marianne and Benedikt Szmrecsanyi 2012. Animacy in early New Zealand English. *English World-Wide* 33(3): 241–63.

Hundt, Marianne, David Denison, and Gerold Schneider 2012a. Retrieving relatives from historical data. *Literary and Linguistic Computing* 27(1): 3–16.

Hundt, Marianne, David Denison, and Gerold Schneider 2012b. Relative complexity in scientific discourse. *English Language and Linguistics* 16(2): 209–40.

Hüning, Matthias and Geert Booij 2014. From compounding to derivation: The emergence of derivational affixes through 'constructionalization'. *Folia Linguistica* 48(2): 579–604.

Irwin, Anthea 2010. Social constructionism. In Ruth Wodak, Barbara Johnstone, and Paul Kerswill (eds.) *The SAGE Handbook of Sociolinguistics*. London: SAGE Publications, pp. 100–12.

Jacobs, Andreas and Andreas H. Jucker 1995. The historical perspective in pragmatics. In Andreas H. Jucker (ed.) *Historical Pragmatics: Pragmatic Developments in the History of English*. Amsterdam/Philadelphia: John Benjamins, pp. 3–33.

Jacobs, Roderick A. and Peter S. Rosenbaum 1968. *English Transformational Grammar*. Waltham, MA: Blaisdell Publishing Company.

Jäger, Anne 2013. The emergence of modal meanings from *haben* with *zu*-infinitives in Old High German. In Gabriele Diewald, Leena Kahlas-Tarkka, and Ilse Wischer (eds.) *Comparative Studies in Early Germanic Languages: With a Focus on Verbal Categories*. Amsterdam/Philadelphia: John Benjamins, pp. 151–68.

Jankowski, Bridget L. and Sali A. Tagliamonte 2014. On the genitive's trail: Data and method from a sociolinguistic perspective. *English Language and Linguistics* 18(2): 305–29.

Jaszczolt, K. M. 2009. *Representing Time: An Essay on Temporality as Modality*. Oxford: Oxford University Press.

Jaworska, Ewa 1986. Prepositional phrases as subjects and objects. *Journal of Linguistics* 22(2): 355–74.

Jespersen, Otto 1940. *A Modern English Grammar on Historical Principles*. Part V *Syntax Fourth Volume*. London: Allen & Unwin.

Johnson, Samuel 1755. *A Dictionary of the English Language*. In two volumes. London: Printed by W. Strahan.

Johnstone, Barbara 2000. *Qualitative Methods in Sociolinguistics*. Oxford: Oxford University Press.

Jolly, Julius 1873. *Geschichte des Infinitivs im Indogermanischen*. München: Theodor Ackermann.

Kachru, Braj B. (ed.) 1992. *The Other Tongue: English across Cultures*, 2nd edn. Urbana and Chicago: University of Illinois Press.

Kahneman, Daniel 2011. *Thinking Fast and Slow*. London: Allen Lane/Penguin.

Kaltenböck, Gunther, Bernd Heine, and Tania Kuteva 2011. On thetical grammar. *Studies in Language* 35(4): 852–97.
Keizer, Evelien 2004. Postnominal PP complements and modifiers: A cognitive distinction. *English Language and Linguistics* 8(2): 323–50.
Keizer, Evelien 2011. English proforms: An alternative account. *English Language and Linguistics* 15(2): 303–34.
Ker, Neil R. 1957. *Catalogue of Manuscripts Containing Anglo-Saxon.* Oxford: Clarendon Press.
Kjellmer, Göran 1985. Help to/help ø revisited. *English Studies* 66(2): 156–61.
Klausenburger, Jurgen 2000. *Grammaticalization: Studies in Latin and Romance Morphosyntax.* Amsterdam/Philadelphia: John Benjamins.
Klausenburger, Jurgen 2008. Can grammaticalization be parameterized? In Elena Seoane and María José López-Couso (eds.) *Theoretical and Empirical Issues in Grammaticalization.* Amsterdam/Philadelphia: John Benjamins, pp. 171–82.
Köhler, Anton 1867. Der syntaktische Gebrauch des Infinitivs im Gotischen. *Germania* 12: 421–62.
Kohnen, Thomas and Christian Mair 2012. Technologies of communication. In Terttu Nevalainen and Elizabeth Closs Traugott (eds.) *The Oxford Handbook of the History of English.* Oxford: Oxford University Press, pp. 261–84.
Krug, Manfred G. 2000. *Emerging English Modals: A Corpus-Based Study of Grammaticalization.* Berlin: Mouton de Gruyter.
Labov, William 1972. *Sociolinguistic Patterns.* Philadelphia: University of Pennsylvania Press.
Labov, William 2001. *Principles of Linguistic Change*, Vol. II *Social Factors.* Oxford: Blackwell.
Lagervall, Marika 2014. *Modala hjälpverb i språkhistorisk belysning.* Gothenburg: University of Gothenburg.
Landau, Idan 2000. *Elements of Control: Structure and Meaning in Infinitival Constructions.* Dordrecht: Kluwer Academic Publishers.
Lass, Roger 1994. *Old English: A Historical Linguistic Companion.* Cambridge: Cambridge University Press.
Lau, Phoebe 2015. Semantic change and politeness: A study of verbs of commanding. MSc thesis: University of Edinburgh.
Łęcki, Andrzej M. 2010. *Grammaticalisation Paths of* Have *in English.* Bern: Peter Lang.
Ledgeway, Adam 2012. *From Latin to Romance: Morphosyntactic Typology and Change.* Oxford: Oxford University Press.
Leech, Geoffrey 2013. Where have all the modals gone? An essay on the declining frequency of core modal auxiliaries in recent standard English. In Juana I. Marín-Arrese, Marta Carretero, Jorge Arús Hita, and Johan van der Auwera (eds.) *English Modality: Core, Periphery and Evidentiality.* Berlin: De Gruyter Mouton, pp. 95–115.

Leech, Geoffrey, Marianne Hundt, Christian Mair, and Nicholas Smith 2009. *Change in Contemporary English: A Grammatical Study*. Cambridge: Cambridge University Press.
Lehmann, Christian 1988. Towards a typology of clause linkage. In John Haiman and Sandra A. Thompson (eds.) *Clause Combining in Grammar and Discourse*. Amsterdam/Philadelphia: John Benjamins, pp. 181–225.
Lehmann, Winfred P. 1986. *A Gothic Etymological Dictionary*. Leiden: E.J. Brill.
Levelt, Willem J. M. 2013. *A History of Psycholinguistics: The Pre-Chomskyan Era*. Oxford: Oxford University Press.
Liberman, Mark 2007. WEV. *Language Log*, 3 August 2007. Available at: http://languagelog.ldc.upenn.edu/~myl/languagelog/archives/004781.html.
Lightfoot, David W. 1979. *Principles of Diachronic Syntax*. Cambridge: Cambridge University Press.
Lohmann, Arne 2011. *Help* vs *help to*: A multifactorial, mixed-effects account of infinitive marker omission. *English Language and Linguistics* 15(3): 499–521.
Lombardi Vallauri, Edoardo 2004. Grammaticalization of syntactic incompleteness: Free conditionals in Italian and other languages. *SKY Journal of Linguistics* 17: 189–215.
Longman 1991 = Woolford, John and Daniel Karlin (eds.) 1991. *The Poems of Browning*, Vol. II *1841–1846*. Harlow: Longman.
López-Couso, María José 2007. Adverbial connectives within and beyond adverbial subordination: The history of *lest*. In Ursula Lenker and Anneli Meurman-Solin (eds.) *Connectives in the History of English*. Amsterdam/Philadelphia: John Benjamins, pp. 11–29.
López-Couso, María José and Belén Méndez-Naya 2015. Secondary grammaticalization in clause combining: From adverbial subordination to complementation in English. *Language Sciences* 47(B): 188–98.
Los, Bettelou 1999. *Infinitival Complementation in Old and Middle English*. The Hague: Thesus.
Los, Bettelou 2005. *The Rise of the* To*-Infinitive*. Oxford: Oxford University Press.
Lowth, Robert 1762. *A Short Introduction to English Grammar*. (Facsimile edition, R. C. Alston (ed.) *English Linguistics 1500–1800*. Menston: Scolar Press, 1967.)
Lund, G. F. V. 1862. *Oldnordisk Ordföjningslære*. København: Berlingske Bogtrykkeri ved L.N. Kalckar.
Lyons, Christopher 1986. The syntax of English genitive constructions. *Journal of Linguistics* 22(1): 123–43.
Lyons, Christopher 1999. *Definiteness*. Cambridge: Cambridge University Press.
MacDonald, Maryellen C. 2013. How language production shapes language form and comprehension. *Frontiers in Psychology* 4(226): 1–16.
Mair, Christian 1990. *Infinitival Complement Clauses in English: A Study of Syntax in Discourse*. Cambridge: Cambridge University Press.
Mair, Christian 1997. Parallel corpora: A real-time approach to the study of language change in progress. In Magnus Ljung (ed.) *Corpus-Based Studies in*

English. Papers from the Seventeenth International Conference on English Language Research on Computerized Corpora (ICAME 17), Stockholm, May 15–19, 1996. Amsterdam: Rodopi, pp. 195–209.

Mair, Christian 2002. Three changing patterns of verb complementation in Late Modern English: A real-time study based on matching text corpora. *English Language and Linguistics* 6(1): 105–31.

Mair, Christian 2006. *Twentieth-Century English: History, Variation and Standardization.* Cambridge: Cambridge University Press.

Malkiel, Yakov 1967. Multiple versus simple causation in linguistic change. In *To Honor Roman Jakobson: Essays on the Occasion of His Seventieth Birthday, 11 October 1966*, Vol. II. The Hague/Paris: Mouton, pp. 1228–46.

Mayer-Schönberger, Viktor and Kenneth Cukier 2013. *Big Data: A Revolution That Will Transform How We Live, Work and Think.* London: John Murray.

McEnery, Anthony and Zhonghua Xiao 2005. *HELP* or *HELP to*: What do corpora have to say? *English Studies* 86(2): 161–87.

McGann, Jerome J. 1983. *A Critique of Modern Textual Criticism.* Chicago: University of Chicago Press. (Reprint, with a preface by the author and a foreword by D. C. Greetham, Charlottesville/London: University Press of Virginia, 1992.)

McIntosh, Carey 1998. *The Evolution of English Prose, 1700–1800: Style, Politeness, and Print Culture.* Cambridge: Cambridge University Press.

McMahon, April M. S. 1994. *Understanding Language Change.* Cambridge: Cambridge University Press.

Menzer, Melinda J. 2004. Ælfric's English *Grammar. Journal of English and Germanic Philology* 103(1): 106–24.

Mesthrie, Rajend and Rakesh M. Bhatt 2008. *World Englishes: The Study of New Linguistic Varieties.* Cambridge/New York: Cambridge University Press.

Michael, Ian 1987. *The Teaching of English: From the Sixteenth Century to 1870.* Cambridge: Cambridge University Press.

Michel, Jean-Baptiste, Yuan Kui Shen, Aviva Presser Aiden, Adrian Veres, Matthew K. Gray, The Google Books Team, Joseph P. Pickett, Dale Hoiberg, Dan Clancy, Peter Norvig, Jon Orwant, Steven Pinker, Martin A. Nowak, and Erez Lieberman Aiden 2011. Quantitative analysis of culture using millions of digitized books. *Science* 331(6014): 176–82.

Milroy, James 1992. A social model for the interpretation of language change. In Matti Rissanen, Ossi Ihalainen, Terttu Nevalainen, and Irma Taavitsainen (eds.) *History of Englishes: New Methods and Interpretations in Historical Linguistics.* Berlin: Mouton de Gruyter, pp. 72–91.

Milroy, James and Lesley Milroy 1985. *Authority in Language: Investigating Language Prescription and Standardisation.* London: Routledge and Kegan Paul.

Milroy, James and Lesley Milroy 1991. *Authority in Language: Investigating Language Prescription and Standardisation*, 2nd edn. London: Routledge.

Mitchell, Bruce. 1985. *Old English Syntax*, 2 vols. Oxford: Clarendon Press.

Mitchell, Bruce, Christopher Ball, and Angus Cameron 1975. Short titles of Old English texts. *Anglo-Saxon England* 4: 207–21.

Mitchell, Bruce, Christopher Ball, and Angus Cameron 1979. Short titles of Old English texts: Addenda and corrigenda. *Anglo-Saxon England* 8: 331–3.
Mitchell, Keith 2003. *Had better* and *might as well*: On the margins of modality? In Roberta Facchinetti, Manfred Krug, and Frank Palmer (eds.) *Modality in Contemporary English*. Berlin: Mouton de Gruyter, pp. 129–49.
Miura, Ayumi 2015. *Middle English Verbs of Emotion and Impersonal Constructions: Verb Meaning and Syntax in Diachrony*. New York: Oxford University Press.
Möhlig-Falke, Ruth 2012. *The Early English Impersonal Construction: An Analysis of Verbal and Constructional Meaning*. New York: Oxford University Press.
Motley, Michael T. 1980. Verification of 'Freudian slips' and semantic prearticulatory editing via laboratory-induced spoonerisms. In Victoria A. Fromkin (ed.) *Errors in Linguistic Performance: Slips of the Tongue, Ear, Pen, and Hand*. San Francisco: Academic Press, pp. 133–47.
Murphy, Raymond 2012. *English Grammar in Use: A Self-Study Reference and Practice Book for Intermediate Learners of English*, 4th edn. Cambridge: Cambridge University Press.
Mustanoja, Tauno F. 1960. *A Middle English Syntax*. Helsinki: Société Néophilologique.
Narrog, Heiko 2012. *Modality, Subjectivity, and Semantic Change: A Cross-Linguistic Perspective*. Oxford: Oxford University Press.
Nevalainen, Terttu 2012. Reconstructing syntactic continuity and change in early Modern English regional dialects: The case of *who*. In David Denison, Ricardo Bermúdez-Otero, Chris McCully, and Emma Moore, with the assistance of Ayumi Miura (eds.) *Analysing Older English*. Cambridge: Cambridge University Press, pp. 159–84.
Nevalainen, Terttu and Helena Raumolin-Brunberg 1994. *Its* strength and the beauty *of it*: The standardization of the third person neuter possessive in Early Modern English. In Dieter Stein and Ingrid Tieken-Boon van Ostade (eds.) *Towards a Standard English, 1600–1800*. Berlin: Mouton de Gruyter, pp. 171–216.
Nevalainen, Terttu and Helena Raumolin-Brunberg 2017. *Historical Sociolinguistics: Language Change in Tudor and Stuart England*, 2nd edn. London: Routledge.
Nieuwenhuijsen, Dorien 2006. Cambios en la colocación de los pronombres átonos. In Concepción Company Company (ed.) *Sintaxis Histórica de la Lengua Española*, Primera Parte *La Frase Verbal*, Vol. 2. México: Universidad Nacional Autónoma de México/Fondo de Cultura Económica, pp. 1337–404.
Noël, Dirk 2001. The passive matrices of English infinitival complement clauses: Evidentials on the road to auxiliarihood? *Studies in Language* 25(2): 255–96.
Noël, Dirk 2008. The nominative and infinitive in Late Modern English: A diachronic constructionist approach. *Journal of English Linguistics* 36(4): 314–40.
Nygaard, M. 1865. *Eddasprogets Syntax*, Vol. II. Bergen: Ed. B. Giertsen.
O'Connor, Catherine, Joan Maling, and Barbora Skarabela 2013. Nominal categories and the expression of possession: A cross-linguistic study of probabilistic

tendencies and categorical constraints. In Kersti Börjars, David Denison, and Alan Scott (eds.) *Morphosyntactic Categories and the Expression of Possession*. Amsterdam/Philadelphia: John Benjamins, pp. 89–122.

Oga, Kyoko 2001. Two types of 'of' and theta-role assignment by nouns. In Mamiko Akita and Kyoko Oga (eds.) *Newcastle and Durham Working Papers in Linguistics 6*. Durham: Department of English and Linguistics, University of Durham, pp. 95–108.

Ogawa, Hiroshi 1989. *Old English Modal Verbs: A Syntactical Study*. Copenhagen: Rosenkilde and Bagger.

Ohio 1973 = King, Roma A., Jr. (ed.) 1973. *The Complete Works of Robert Browning: With Variant Readings & Annotations*, Vol. IV. Athens, Ohio: Ohio University Press.

Olbertz, Hella 1998. *Verbal Periphrases in a Functional Grammar of Spanish*. Berlin: Mouton de Gruyter.

Olbertz, Hella 2018. The diachrony of *tener que* and other possession-based modal periphrases in Spanish. In Nildicéia Aparecida Rocha, Angélica Terezinha Carmo Rodrigues, and Suzi Marques Spatti Cavalari (eds.) *Novas Práticas em Pesquisa: Rompendo Fronteiras*. Araraquara: Laboratório Editorial, pp. 1–36.

Olbertz, Hella forthcoming. Periphrastic expressions of non-epistemic modal necessity in Spanish: A semantic description. In Mar Garachana, Sandra Montserrat i Buendía, and Claus D. Pusch (eds.) *From Composite Predicates to Verbal Periphrases in Romance Languages*. Amsterdam/Philadelphia: John Benjamins.

Ong, Teresa Wai See 2011. *Prevent* and *stop* complementation clauses: A corpus-based investigation of 19th, 20th and 21st century American English. MPhil thesis: University of Birmingham.

Osselton, Noel 1988. Thematic genitives. In Graham Nixon and John Honey (eds.) *An Historic Tongue: Studies in English Linguistics in Memory of Barbara Strang*. London: Routledge, pp. 138–44.

Overstreet, Maryann 1999. *Whales, Candlelight, and Stuff like That: General Extenders in English Discourse*. Oxford: Oxford University Press.

Overstreet, Maryann 2014. The role of pragmatic function in the grammaticalization of English general extenders. *Pragmatics* 24(1): 105–29.

Palmer, F. R. 1987. The typology of subordination: Results, actual and potential. *Transactions of the Philological Society* 85(1): 90–109.

Palmer, F. R. 1990. Review of Anna Wierzbicka's *The Semantics of Grammar*. *Journal of Linguistics* 26(1): 223–33.

Panagiotidis, Phoevos 2003. *One*, empty nouns, and θ-assignment. *Linguistic Inquiry* 34(2): 281–92.

Partee, Barbara H. 1997. Appendix B. Genitives – A case study. In Johan van Benthem and Alice ter Meulen (eds.) *Handbook of Logic and Language*. New York: Elsevier, pp. 464–70.

Patterson, Lee 1985. The logic of textual criticism and the way of genius. The Kane-Donaldson *Piers Plowman* in historical perspective. In Jerome

J. McGann (ed.) *Textual Criticism and Literary Interpretation*. Chicago: The Chicago University Press, pp. 55–91.

Paul, Hermann 1909. *Prinzipien der Sprachgeschichte*, 4th edn. Halle: Max Niemeyer.

Payne, John and Eva Berlage 2014. Genitive variation: The niche role of the oblique genitive. *English Language and Linguistics* 18(2): 331–60.

Payne, John and Rodney Huddleston 2002. Nouns and noun phrases. In Rodney Huddleston and Geoffrey K. Pullum et al., *The Cambridge Grammar of the English Language*. Cambridge: Cambridge University Press, 323–523.

Payne, John, Geoffrey K. Pullum, Barbara C. Scholz, and Eva Berlage 2013. Anaphoric *one* and its implications. *Language* 89(4): 794–829.

Penke, Martina and Anette Rosenbach (eds.) 2007. *What Counts as Evidence in Linguistics: The Case of Innateness*. Amsterdam/Philadelphia: John Benjamins.

Pesetsky, David 1995. *Zero Syntax: Experiencers and Cascades*. Cambridge, MA: MIT Press.

Pichler, Heike and Stephen Levey 2011. In search of grammaticalization in synchronic dialect data: General extenders in northeast England. *English Language and Linguistics* 15(3): 441–71.

Pijpops, Dirk and Freek Van de Velde 2016. Constructional contamination: How does it work and how do we measure it? *Folia Linguistica* 50(2): 543–81.

Pinker, Steven 1994. *The Language Instinct: The New Science of Language and Mind*. London: Penguin.

Pinkster, Harm 1987. The strategy and chronology of the development of future and perfect tense auxiliaries in Latin. In Martin Harris and Paolo Ramat (eds.) *Historical Development of Auxiliaries*. Berlin: Mouton de Gruyter, pp. 193–223.

Pishwa, Hanna 1999. The case of the 'impersonal' construction in Old English. *Folia Linguistica Historica* 20(1/2): 129–51.

Porter, David W. (ed.) 2002. *Excerptiones de Prisciano: The Source for Ælfric's Latin-Old English Grammar*. Cambridge: D. S. Brewer.

Postal, Paul M. 1969. On so-called 'pronouns' in English. In David A. Reibel and Sanford A. Schane (eds.) *Modern Studies in English: Readings in Transformational Grammar*. Englwood Cliffs, NJ: Prentice-Hall, pp. 201–24.

Postal, Paul M. 1974. *On Raising: One Rule of English Grammar and Its Theoretical Implications*. Cambridge, MA: MIT Press.

Pylkkänen, Liina 2000. On stativity and causation. In Carol Tenny and James Pustejovsky (eds.) *Events as Grammatical Objects: The Converging Perspectives of Lexical Semantics and Syntax*. Stanford, CA: CSLI Publications, pp. 417–44.

Quirk, Randolph 1965. Descriptive statement and serial relationship. *Language* 41(2): 205–17.

Quirk, Randolph, Sidney Greenbaum, Geoffrey Leech, and Jan Svartvik 1985. *A Comprehensive Grammar of the English Language*. London: Longman.

R Core Team 2014. *R: A Language and Environment for Statistical Computing*. Vienna: R Foundation for Statistical Computing. Available at: www.R-project.org.
Radford, Andrew 2004. *Minimalist Syntax: Exploring the Structure of English*. Cambridge: Cambridge University Press.
Real Academia Española and Asociación de Academias de la Lengua Española 2009. *Nueva Gramática de la Lengua Española*, 2 vols. Madrid: Espasa.
Reinhart, Tanya 2016. The Theta System: Syntactic realization of verbal concepts. In Martin Everaert, Marijana Marelj, and Eric Reuland (eds.) *Concepts, Syntax, and Their Interface: The Theta System*. Cambridge, MA: MIT Press, pp. 1–111.
Remberger, Eva-Maria 2010. The evidential shift of WANT. In Tyler Peterson and Uli Sauerland (eds.) *Evidence from Evidentials*. *University of British Columbia Working Papers in Linguistics* Vol. 28, pp. 161–82.
Remberger, Eva-Maria 2011. Tense and volitionality. In Renate Musan and Monika Rathert (eds.) *Tense across Languages*. Berlin: De Gruyter, pp. 9–35.
Ricks, Christopher 2002. *Allusion to the Poets*. Oxford: Oxford University Press.
Ringe, Don 2006. *A Linguistic History of English*, Vol. I *From Proto-Indo-European to Proto-Germanic*. Oxford: Oxford University Press.
Ringe, Don and Ann Taylor 2014. *The Development of Old English*. Oxford: Oxford University Press.
Rissanen, Matti 1989. Three problems connected with the use of diachronic corpora. *ICAME Journal* 13: 16–19.
Rissanen, Matti 1999. Syntax. In Roger Lass (ed.) *The Cambridge History of the English Language*, Vol. III *1476–1776*. Cambridge: Cambridge University Press, pp. 187–331.
Rissanen, Matti 2008. From 'quickly' to 'fairly': On the history of *rather*. *English Language and Linguistics* 12(2): 345–59.
Rohdenburg, Günter 1995. On the replacement of finite complement clauses by infinitives in English. *English Studies* 76(4): 367–88.
Rohdenburg, Günter 2003. Cognitive complexity and *horror aequi* as factors determining the use of interrogative clause linkers in English. In Günter Rohdenburg and Britta Mondorf (eds.) *Determinants of Grammatical Variation in English*. Berlin: Mouton de Gruyter, pp. 205–49.
Rohdenburg, Günter 2006a. The role of functional constraints in the evolution of the English complementation system. In Christiane Dalton-Puffer, Dieter Kastovsky, Nikolaus Ritt, and Herbert Schendl (eds.) *Syntax, Style and Grammatical Norms: English from 1500–2000*. Bern: Peter Lang, pp. 143–66.
Rohdenburg, Günter 2006b. Processing complexity and competing sentential variants in present-day English. In Wilfried Kürschner and Reinhard Rapp (eds.) *Linguistik International: Festschrift für Heinrich Weber*. Lengerich: Pabst Science Publishers, pp. 51–67.
Rohdenburg, Günter 2009. Grammatical divergence between British and American English in the nineteenth and early twentieth centuries. In Ingrid Tieken-Boon van Ostade and Wim van der Wurff (eds.) *Current Issues in Late Modern English*. Bern: Peter Lang, pp. 301–29.

Rohdenburg, Günter and Julia Schlüter (eds.) 2009a. *One Language, Two Grammars? Differences between British and American English*. Cambridge: Cambridge University Press.

Rohdenburg, Günter and Julia Schlüter 2009b. New departures. In Günter Rohdenburg and Julia Schlüter (eds.) *One Language, Two Grammars? Differences between British and American English*. Cambridge: Cambridge University Press, pp. 364–423.

Rosenbach, Anette 2002. *Genitive Variation in English: Conceptual Factors in Synchronic and Diachronic Studies*. Berlin: Mouton de Gruyter.

Rosenbach, Anette 2005. Animacy versus weight as determinants of grammatical variation in English. *Language* 81(3): 613–44.

Rosenbach, Anette 2014. English genitive variation – The state of the art. *English Language and Linguistics* 18(2): 215–62.

Rosenbaum, Peter S. 1967. *The Grammar of English Predicate Complement Constructions*. Cambridge, MA: MIT Press.

Royster, James Finch 1918. The causative use of *Hātan*. *Journal of English and Germanic Philology* 17(1): 82–93.

Rudanko, Juhani 2012. Exploring aspects of the Great Complement Shift, with evidence from the TIME Corpus and COCA. In Terttu Nevalainen and Elizabeth Closs Traugott (eds.) *The Oxford Handbook of the History of English*. Oxford: Oxford University Press, pp. 222–32.

Rudanko, Juhani 2015. *Linking Form and Meaning: Studies on Selected Control Patterns in Recent English*. Basingstoke: Palgrave Macmillan.

Rydén, Mats 1983. English relatives revisited. *Moderna Språk* 77(3): 209–18.

Sag, Ivan A. 1997. English relative clause constructions. *Journal of Linguistics* 33(2): 431–83.

Said, Edward W. 1975. The poet as Oedipus. *New York Times*, 13th April.

Schäfer, Roland 2015. Processing and querying large web corpora with the COW14 architecture. In Piotr Bański, Hanno Biber, Evelyn Breiteneder, Marc Kupietz, Harald Lüngen, and Andreas Witt (eds.) *Proceedings of the 3rd Workshop on Challenges in the Management of Large Corpora (CMLC-3)*. Mannheim: Institut für Deutsche Sprache, pp. 28–34.

Schäfer, Roland and Felix Bildhauer 2012. Building large corpora from the web using a new efficient tool chain. In Nicoletta Calzolari, Khalid Choukri, Thierry Declerck, Mehmet Uğur Doğan, Bente Maegaard, Joseph Mariani, Asuncion Moreno, Jan Odijk, and Stelios Piperidis (eds.) *Proceedings of the Eighth International Conference on Language Resources and Evaluation (LREC'12)*. Istanbul: European Language Resources Association, pp. 486–93.

Schmidt, A. V. C. (ed.) 1995. *William Langland, The Vision of Piers Plowman: A Critical Edition of the B-Text Based on Trinity College Cambridge MS B.15.17*, 2nd edn. London: J. M. Dent.

Schmied, Josef 1993. Qualitative and quantitative research approaches to English relative constructions. In Clive Souter and Eric Atwell (eds.) *Corpus-Based Computational Linguistics*. Amsterdam: Rodopi, pp. 85–96.

Schneider, Edgar W. 2007. *Postcolonial English: Varieties around the World*. Cambridge: Cambridge University Press.
Searle, John R. 1969. *Speech Acts: An Essay in the Philosophy of Language*. Cambridge: Cambridge University Press.
Setiya, Kieran 2014. Intention. *Stanford Encyclopedia of Philosophy*. Available at: http://plato.stanford.edu/archives/sum2015/entries/intention/.
[Shakespeare, William] 1594. *The First Part of the Contention betwixt the Two Famous Houses of Yorke and Lancaster*. London: Printed by Thomas Creed, for Thomas Millington.
SHC = Craig, Hardin (ed.) 1951. *The Complete Works of Shakespeare*. Chicago: Scott, Foresman and Co.
Siegel, Jeff, Benedikt Szmrecsanyi, and Bernd Kortmann 2014. Measuring analyticity and syntheticity in creoles. *Journal of Pidgin and Creole Languages* 29(1): 49–85.
Siemund, Peter 2008. *Pronominal Gender in English: A Study of English Varieties from a Cross-Linguistic Perspective*. New York/London: Routledge.
Smitterberg, Erik 2008. The progressive and phrasal verbs: Evidence of colloquialization in nineteenth-century English? In Terttu Nevalainen, Irma Taavitsainen, Päivi Pahta, and Minna Korhonen (eds.) *The Dynamics of Linguistic Variation: Corpus Evidence on English Past and Present*. Amsterdam/Philadelphia: John Benjamins, pp. 269–89.
Smitterberg, Erik 2014. Syntactic stability and change in nineteenth-century newspaper language. In Marianne Hundt (ed.) *Late Modern English Syntax*. Cambridge: Cambridge University Press, pp. 311–30.
Söderwall, K. F. 1884–1918. *Ordbok öfver Svenska Medeltids-språket*, Vol. I-III. Lund: Berlingska Boktryckeri- och Stilgjuteri-Aktiebolaget.
Sommerer, Lotte 2015. The influence of constructions in grammaticalization: Revisiting category emergence and the development of the definite article in English. In Jóhanna Barðdal, Elena Smirnova, Lotte Sommerer, and Spike Gildea (eds.) *Diachronic Construction Grammar*. Amsterdam/Philadelphia: John Benjamins, pp. 107–37.
Spradlin, Lauren 2016. OMG the word-final alveopalatals are cray-cray prev(alent): The morphophonology of totes constructions in English. *University of Pennsylvania Working Papers in Linguistics* 22(1): 275–84.
Stefanowitsch, Anatol 2003. Constructional semantics as a limit to grammatical alternation: The two genitives of English. In Günter Rohdenburg and Britta Mondorf (eds.) *Determinants of Grammatical Variation in English*. Berlin/New York: Mouton de Gruyter, pp. 413–43.
Stevens, Christopher M. 1995. On the grammaticalization of German *können, dürfen, sollen, mögen, müssen*, and *wollen*. *Journal of Germanic Linguistics* 7(2): 179–206.
Stirling, Lesley 1999. Isolated *if*-clauses in Australian English. In Peter Collins and David Lee (eds.) *The Clause in English: In Honour of Rodney Huddleston*. Amsterdam/Philadelphia: John Benjamins, pp. 273–94.

Stoffel, C. 1894. *Studies in English Written and Spoken: For the Use of Continental Students*, 1st series. Zutphen: W. J. Thieme.
Stowell, Tim 1989. Subjects, specifiers, and X-bar theory. In Mark R. Baltin and Anthony S. Kroch (eds.) *Alternative Conceptions of Phrase Structure*. Chicago/ London: The University of Chicago Press, pp. 232–62.
Strang, Barbara M. H. 1970. *A History of English*. London: Methuen.
Strevens, Peter 1972. *British and American English*. London: Collier-Macmillan.
Stubbs, Michael 1995. Collocations and semantic profiles: On the cause of the trouble with quantitative studies. *Functions of Language* 2(1): 23–55.
Sundby *et al.* 1991: See *DENG*.
Szemerényi, Oswald J. L. 1996. *Introduction to Indo-European Linguistics*. Oxford: Clarendon Press.
Szmrecsanyi, Benedikt, Jason Grafmiller, Benedikt Heller, and Melanie Röthlisberger 2016. Around the world in three alternations: Modeling syntactic variation in varieties of English. *English World-Wide* 37(2): 109–37.
Szmrecsanyi, Benedikt, Anette Rosenbach, Joan Bresnan, and Christoph Wolk 2014. Culturally conditioned language change? A multivariate analysis of genitive constructions in ARCHER. In Marianne Hundt (ed.) *Late Modern English Syntax*. Cambridge: Cambridge University Press, pp. 133–52.
Tagliamonte, Sali A. 2016. *Teen Talk: The Language of Adolescents*. Cambridge: Cambridge University Press.
Tagliamonte, Sali A. and R. Harald Baayen 2012. Models, forests, and trees of York English: *Was/were* variation as a case study for statistical practice. *Language Variation and Change* 24(2): 135–78.
Taylor, Ann 2008. Contact effects of translation: Distinguishing two kinds of influence in Old English. *Language Variation and Change* 20(2): 341–65.
Thackeray, William Makepeace 1840 [1898]. On the French school of painting. In *The Works of William Makepeace Thackeray: In Thirteen Volumes, with Biographical Introductions by His Daughter, Anne Ritchie*, Vol. 5 *Sketch Books*. London: Smith, Elder and Co., pp. 41–57.
Thackeray, William Makepeace 1850 [1898]. *The Works of William Makepeace Thackeray: In Thirteen Volumes, with Biographical Introductions by His Daughter, Anne Ritchie*, Vol. 2 *The History of Pendennis: His Fortunes and Misfortunes, His Friends and His Greatest Enemy*. London: Smith, Elder and Co.
Tieken-Boon van Ostade, Ingrid 2006. Eighteenth-century prescriptivism and the norm of correctness. In Ans van Kemenade and Bettelou Los (eds.) *The Handbook of the History of English*. Malden, MA: Blackwell, pp. 539–57.
Tieken-Boon van Ostade, Ingrid 2009. *An Introduction to Late Modern English*. Edinburgh: Edinburgh University Press.
Tieken-Boon van Ostade, Ingrid 2011. *The Bishop's Grammar: Robert Lowth and the Rise of Prescriptivism*. Oxford: Oxford University Press.
Tissari, Heli 2003. *LOVEscapes: Changes in Prototypical Senses and Cognitive Metaphors since 1500*. Helsinki: Société Néophilologique.

Tomasello, Michael 1992. *First Verbs: A Case Study of Early Grammatical Development*. Cambridge: Cambridge University Press.
Tomasello, Michael 2003. *Constructing a Language. A Usage-Based Theory of Language Acquisition*. Cambridge, MA: Harvard University Press.
Tottie, Gunnel 1997. Literacy and prescriptivism as determinants of linguistic change: A case study based on relativization strategies. In Uwe Böker and Hans Sauer (eds.) *Anglistentag 1996 Dresden: Proceedings*. Trier: Wissenschaftlicher Verlag, pp. 83–93.
Traugott, Elizabeth Closs 1972. *The History of English Syntax: A Transformational Approach to the History of English Sentence Structure*. New York: Holt, Rinehart and Winston.
Traugott, Elizabeth Closs 1989. On the rise of epistemic meanings in English: An example of subjectification in semantic change. *Language* 65(1): 31–55.
Traugott, Elizabeth Closs 2003. From subjectification to intersubjectification. In Raymond Hickey (ed.) *Motives for Language Change*. Cambridge: Cambridge University Press, pp. 124–40.
Traugott, Elizabeth Closs 2010. (Inter)subjectivity and (inter)subjectification: A reassessment. In Kristin Davidse, Lieven Vandelanotte, and Hubert Cuyckens (eds.) *Subjectification, Intersubjectification and Grammaticalization*. Berlin: De Gruyter Mouton, pp. 29–71.
Traugott, Elizabeth Closs 2016a. On the rise of types of clause-final pragmatic markers in English. *Journal of Historical Pragmatics* 17(1): 26–54.
Traugott, Elizabeth Closs 2016b. Do semantic modal maps have a role in a constructionalization approach to modals? *Constructions and Frames* 8(1): 97–124.
Traugott, Elizabeth Closs 2018. Modeling language change with constructional networks. In Salvador Pons Bordería and Óscar Loureda Lamas (eds.) *Beyond Grammaticalization and Discourse Markers: New Issues in the Study of Language Change*. Leiden: Brill, pp. 17–50.
Traugott, Elizabeth Closs and Richard B. Dasher 2002. *Regularity in Semantic Change*. Cambridge: Cambridge University Press.
Traugott, Elizabeth Closs and Graeme Trousdale 2010. Gradience, gradualness and grammaticalization: How do they intersect? In Elizabeth Closs Traugott and Graeme Trousdale (eds.) *Gradience, Gradualness and Grammaticalization*. Amsterdam/Philadelphia: John Benjamins, pp. 19–44.
Traugott, Elizabeth Closs and Graeme Trousdale 2013. *Constructionalization and Constructional Changes*. Oxford: Oxford University Press.
Trollope, Anthony 1879. *Thackeray*. London: Macmillan and Co.
Trousdale, Graeme 2008. Words and constructions in grammaticalization: The end of the English impersonal construction. In Susan M. Fitzmaurice and Donka Minkova (eds.) *Studies in the History of the English Language IV: Empirical and Analytical Advances in the Study of English Language Change*. Berlin/New York: Mouton de Gruyter, pp. 301–26.
Trousdale, Graeme 2010. Issues in constructional approaches to grammaticalization in English. In Katerina Stathi, Elke Gehweiler, and Ekkehard König (eds.)

Grammaticalization: Current Views and Issues. Amsterdam/Philadelphia: John Benjamins, pp. 51–71.

Trudgill, Peter and Jean Hannah 2008. *International English: A Guide to the Varieties of Standard English*, 5th edn. London: Hodder Education.

Van de Velde, Freek 2014. Degeneracy: The maintenance of constructional networks. In Ronny Boogaart, Timothy Colleman, and Gijsbert Rutten (eds.) *Extending the Scope of Construction Grammar*. Berlin: De Gruyter Mouton, pp. 141–79.

Van de Velde, Freek, Hendrik De Smet, and Lobke Ghesquière 2013. On multiple source constructions in language change. *Studies in Language* 37(3): 473–89.

van der Auwera, Johan and Astrid De Wit 2010. The English comparative modals – A pilot study. In Bert Cappelle and Naoaki Wada (eds.) *Distinctions in English Grammar: Offered to Renaat Declerck*. Tokyo: Kaitakusha, pp. 127–47.

van der Auwera, Johan and Vladimir A. Plungian 1998. Modality's semantic map. *Linguistic Typology* 2(1): 79–124.

van der Auwera, Johan, Dirk Noël, and An Van linden 2013. *Had better, 'd better* and *better*: Diachronic and transatlantic variation. In Juana I. Marín-Arrese, Marta Carretero, Jorge Arús Hita, and Johan van der Auwera (eds.) *English Modality: Core, Periphery and Evidentiality*. Berlin: De Gruyter Mouton, pp. 119–54.

van der Gaaf, Willem 1904. *The Transition from the Impersonal to the Personal Construction in Middle English*. Heidelberg: Winter.

van der Gaaf, Willem 1912. The origin of *would rather* and some of its analogues. *Englische Studien* 45: 381–96.

van der Gaaf, Willem 1931. *Beon* and *habban* connected with an inflected infinitive. *English Studies* 13(1/6): 176–88.

van der Horst, J. M. 2008. *Geschiedenis van de Nederlandse Syntaxis*. Leuven: Universitaire Pers Leuven.

Van linden, An 2010. The rise of the *to*-infinitive: Evidence from adjectival complementation. *English Language and Linguistics* 14(1): 19–51.

Van linden, An 2015. Comparative modals: (Dis)similar diachronic tendencies. *Functions of Language* 22(2): 192–231.

Van linden, An and Jean-Christophe Verstraete 2011. Revisiting deontic modality and related categories: A conceptual map based on the study of English modal adjectives. *Journal of Pragmatics* 43(1): 150–63.

van Steenis, Lindsey 2013. The grammaticalization of *have to* and *hebben te*: A comparative study between English and Dutch. MA thesis: University of Amsterdam.

Verstraete, Jean-Christophe, Sarah D'Hertefelt, and An Van linden 2012. A typology of complement insubordination in Dutch. *Studies in Language* 36(1): 123–53.

Vikner, Carl and Per Anker Jensen 2002. A semantic analysis of the English genitive: Interaction of lexical and formal semantics. *Studia Linguistica* 56(2): 191–226.

Vincent, Nigel 2014. Compositionality and change. In Claire Bowen and Bethwyn Evans (eds.) *The Routledge Handbook of Historical Linguistics.* London: Routledge, pp. 103–23.
Visconti, Jacqueline 2004. Conditionals and subjectification: Implications for a theory of semantic change. In Olga Fischer, Muriel Norde, and Harry Perridon (eds.) *Up and down the Cline – The Nature of Grammaticalization.* Amsterdam/Philadelphia: John Benjamins, pp. 169–92.
Visser, F. Th. 1963–1973. *An Historical Syntax of the English Language,* 4 vols. Leiden: E. J. Brill.
von Fintel, Kai 2000. Whatever. In Brendan Jackson and Tanya Matthews (eds.) *Proceedings of SALT 10.* Washington, DC: Linguistic Society of America, pp. 27–39.
Vosberg, Uwe 2006. *Die Große Komplementverschiebung: Außersemantische Einflüsse auf die Entwicklung satzwertiger Ergänzungen im Neuenglischen.* Tübingen: Narr.
Wales, Katie 1996. *Personal Pronouns in Present-Day English.* Cambridge: Cambridge University Press.
Walkden, George 2017. The actuation problem. In Adam Ledgeway and Ian Roberts (eds.) *The Cambridge Handbook of Historical Syntax.* Cambridge: Cambridge University Press, pp. 403–24.
Ward, Gregory, Betty Birner, and Rodney Huddleston 2002. Information packaging. In Rodney Huddleston and Geoffrey K. Pullum *et al., The Cambridge Grammar of the English Language.* Cambridge: Cambridge University Press, pp. 1363–447.
Ward, William 1765. *An Essay on Grammar.* (Facsimile edition, R. C. Alston (ed.) *English Linguistics 1500–1800.* Menston: Scolar Press, 1967.)
Warner, Anthony 1982. *Complementation in Middle English and the Methodology of Historical Syntax: A Study of the Wycliffite Sermons.* London: Croom Helm.
Warner, Anthony R. 1993. *English Auxiliaries: Structure and History.* Cambridge: Cambridge University Press.
Watanabe, Akira 2009. A parametric shift in the D-system in Early Middle English: Relativization, articles, adjectival inflection, and indeterminates. In Paola Crisma and Giuseppe Longobardi (eds.) *Historical Syntax and Linguistic Theory.* Oxford/New York: Oxford University Press, pp. 358–74.
Weinert, Sabine 2009. Implicit and explicit modes of learning: Similarities and differences from a developmental perspective. *Linguistics* 47(2): 241–71.
Wierzbicka, Anna 1988. *The Semantics of Grammar.* Amsterdam/Philadelphia: John Benjamins.
Wiklund, Anna-Lena 2001. Dressing up for vocabulary insertion: The parasitic supine. *Natural Language & Linguistic Theory* 19(1): 199–228.
Willis, David 2017. Degrammaticalization. In Adam Ledgeway and Ian Roberts (eds.) *The Cambridge Handbook of Historical Syntax.* Cambridge: Cambridge University Press, pp. 28–48.
Wolk, Christoph, Joan Bresnan, Anette Rosenbach, and Benedikt Szmrecsanyi 2013. Dative and genitive variability in Late Modern English: Exploring cross-constructional variation and change. *Diachronica* 30(3): 382–419.

Wood, Johanna L. 2007. Is there a DP in Old English? In Joseph C. Salmons and Shannon Dubenion-Smith (eds.) *Historical Linguistics 2005: Selected Papers from the 17th International Conference on Historical Linguistics, Madison, Wisconsin, 31 July – 5 August 2005*. Amsterdam/Philadelphia: John Benjamins, pp. 167–87.

Yáñez-Bouza, Nuria 2007. Preposition stranding and prescriptivism in English from 1500 to 1900: A corpus-based approach. PhD thesis: The University of Manchester.

Yáñez-Bouza, Nuria 2016. Early and Late Modern English grammars as evidence in English historical linguistics. In Merja Kytö and Päivi Pahta (eds.) *The Cambridge Handbook of English Historical Linguistics*. Cambridge: Cambridge University Press, pp. 164–80.

Yerkes, David 1982. *Syntax and Style in Old English: A Comparison of the Two Versions of Wærferth's Translation of Gregory's Dialogues*. Binghamton: Center for Medieval and Early Renaissance Studies.

Yllera, Alicia 1980. *Sintaxis Histórica del Verbo Español: Las Perífrasis Medievales*. Zaragoza: Departamento de Filología Francesa, Universidad de Zaragoza.

Zaenen, Annie, Jean Carletta, Gregory Garretson, Joan Bresnan, Andrew Koontz-Garboden, Tatiana Nikitina, M. Catherine O'Connor, and Tom Wasow 2004. Animacy Encoding in English: Why and how. In Bonnie Webber and Donna Byron (eds.) *Proceedings of the 2004 ACL Workshop on Discourse Annotation*. Stroudsburg, PA: Association for Computational Linguistics, pp. 118–25.

Zandvoort, R. W. 1949. A note on 'inorganic *for*'. *English Studies* 30(1–6): 265–9.

Zeitlin, Jacob 1908. *The Accusative with Infinitive and Some Kindred Constructions in English*. New York: Columbia University Press.

Ziegeler, Debra 2006. Omnitemporal *will*. *Language Sciences* 28(1): 76–119.

Zupitza, Julius 1880. *Ælfrics Grammatik und Glossar*. Berlin: Weidmannsche Buchhandlung.

Zwicky, Arnold M. 1987. Suppressing the Zs. *Journal of Linguistics* 23(1): 133–48.

Index

abstract noun, 150, 151, 152, 153, 156, 159, 163
accusative, 25, 30, 45, 65, 68, 70, 154, 156, 158, 160, 183
   Accusative and Infinitive (AcI) construction, 160, 161, 165, 284, 293
action noun, 152, 155, 159, 163
adjacency, 69, 70, 259, 260–1, 265, 279, 281
adjective, 30, 33, 34–5, 116, 130, 131, 139, 197, 221–2, 318
   adjectival predicate, 163
adjunct, 54, 68, 70, 75, 156–8, 167
   purpose adjunct, 155, 158, 163
adverbial clause, 156, 157
Ælfric's *Grammar*, 134–46
after, 221–3
agent, 48, 50, 51, 158, 159, 160, 163, 173, 261, 311
American English, 122, 194–6, 208, 248, 316, 336–8, 340–61
analogy, 88, 117–18, 189, 253, 254, 255–8, 260, 268, 270, 271, 291
   abstract structural analogy, 256, 259
   analogical extension, 258
   analogical process, 254
   as default, 257
   concrete, lexical analogy, 256
   paradigmatic analogy, 167, 168
      broad, 149, 153, 163–4, 168
      indirect, 152, 156, 159–63
      narrow, 149, 151, 153, 156, 158–9
   proportional analogy, 258
   semantic analogy, 151, 156, 159
anaphoric control, 305–6, 308, 309, 312
animacy, 26, 27, 28, 108, 121, 158, 177–8, 186–8, 189, 264, 301, 316, 319–20, 321, 324, 331, 333, 334, 335
apodosis, 190, 193, 194, 203–6, 208
apparent change, 214
argument, 132, 155, 156–8, 312–13
   argument structure, 35, 256, 307, 313
   direct argument, 137–41, 144, 145
   shared argument, 267, *see also* shared object

auxiliary, 110, 112, 118, 121, 125, 129, 255, 266, 268, 269, 271, 275, 277, 288, 289, 290, 298, 310, 311
   semi-modal auxiliary, 262, 265
AVER/HABER-*de*, 263–5, 268–72, 274, 275–6
AVER/HABER-*que*, 263–5, 268, 271, 272–5, 276–7
AVER-*menester-de*, 270
Ayres, Alfred, 214–15

backformation, 258
banalisation, 221, 223, 228, 233
bare infinitive, 153, 154, 155, 160, 161, 348, 350–8
biclausal structure, 201, 203, 205, 208, 209
bleaching, 168, 255, 352

case-marking, loss of, 165
case-study, 212, 218, 220, 221
causation, causative, 37, 160, 161, 162, 165, 173, 174, 175–6, 180–2, 184, 188, 189, 348, 352
Cause, 173, 180
   Cause-subject construction, 173, 174, 180–2, 188, 189
change from below, 235, 244, 246
change in an individual, 215–16
chunking, 81, 98, 101, 103
cognitive principle, 254
cognitive status, 212–16
collective noun, 32–5
collocation, 88, 123, 221, 270, 272, 276, 281
colloquialisation, 234, 236, 241, 242, 247
comment clause, 191, 200, 208
complement (COMP), complementation, 30, 40, 54, 56, 63, 64, 66, 68, 69, 71, 72, 74, 75, 76, 78, 79, 111, 190, 194, 198, 199, 200, 201–2, 205, 206, 208, 284, 288–90, 292, 299, 302, 304, 309, 313, 360
   verbal, 149, 150, 156–64
complementiser, 54, 58, 61, 62, 63, 70, 72, 73, 79
   complementising morpheme, 61
   for . . . *to*, 61, 62, 72, 73, 76, 79, 80
conceptual thetical, 192

399

conditional inference tree, 330–3, 334, 335
conjoin, 239, 240–1, 247
conjunctive particle, 62
constituent length, 316, 320, 321, 324–7, 331, 333, 334
construction, 25–9, 51–2
  competing, 263, 265
  constructional change, 88, 100, 101–3, 106, 109, 117, 119, 129
  constructional template, 167
  periphrastic verbal, 265
constructionalisation, 88, 103, 106, 109, 118, 129, 204
context-dependent reading, 269
contextualisation, 232
co-ordination, 31, 56, 171, 235–7, 241–7, 249
  co-ordinator, 86, 235, 244, 247, 248
count noun, 34, 39, 134, 137, 140, 141, 145, 146, 231
courtroom, 107, 237, 242, 245, 247, 248
cultural history, 231

Danish, 283, 284, 286, 287, 288, 291, 294, 295, 297, 299, 303, 308, 309, 310–12, 313
dative, 58, 154, 155
definiteness, 130–4, 136, 137, 138, 139, 140, 143, 145, 146, 328
  definite article, 25, 35, 38, 48, 130–4, 136, 141, 144, 145, 146, 346
  definite NP, 152
  indefiniteness, 49, 53, 330
    indefinite interpretation, 132, 133, 136, 137, 139, 141, 143, 145
  semantic/pragmatic, 134
demonstrative, 25, 131, 136, 145
Denison, David, 3–4, 14, 105, 130–1, 146, 171, 172, 210, 212, 239, 315, 319
dependent desire, 163–4, 166, 167
derivational suffix. *See* suffix
determiner (D), 25, 30, 31, 34, 38, 39, 40, 48, 83, 99, 130–3, 135, 136–46, 315
determiner phrase (DP), 131, 132, 146
diachronic trajectory, 294, 295, 298–303, 304, 310
diffusion, 150–3, 163, 167, 168
direct argument. *See* argument
direct condition, 190, 194, 198, 208
directive, 111, 125, 126, 159, 161, 162, 163, 164–5, 168
discourse, 56, 134, 203
  accessibility, 321–2
  link, 168
  marker, 84, 86, 88, 92, 93, 94, 95, 96, 98–9, 100, 101, 102, 103, 104, 280
double-barrelled sentence, 59, 60

Dutch, 162, 254, 266, 277–80, 281, 283, 284, 285, 286–91, 294, 295–6, 297, 299, 301, 306, 309
Dynamic Model, 336

'Easy First' principle, 316, 328, 334
ellipsis, 193, 201, 203, 206
  reconstruction of, 201
emotion, 151, 171, 172, 197, 300
  duration, 175–7, 184–6, 189
  Target of Emotion, 178, 186–8, 189
endonormativity, 336, 341, 360, 361
end-weight, principle of, 320, 324, 326, 333
entailment, 161, 162
entrenchment, 81
epistemic/hedging function, 191, 193, 197, 206, 208
-er/re, 340, 341
euphemism, 161, 162
Exceptional Case-Marking (ECM) construction, 150, 165, 166, 167, 168
Excerptiones de Prisciano, 135
existential, 259, 261, 272, 273, 276, 277
expansion, 99–103
Experiencer, 170, 171, 172, 173, 174, 176, 177, 179, 180, 185, 311, 312
  Experiencer-object, 173, 174, 182
  Experiencer-subject, 173, 175, 182
extraposition, 67

face, face-work, 97, 98, 197, 207, 208
Face-Threatening Act, 97, 161
familiarity, 100, 134
faulty recollection, 218, 219
felicity condition, 161, 162
final sibilancy, 320–1, 327, 331, 333, 334
finite clause, 55–6, 66, 153, 163, 165, 292, 299, 308
folk etymology, 258
for, 54–80
  For Phrase Formation, 61
  for . . . to. See complementiser
  grammatical sign, subject of, 58
  inorganic, 58, 60
  organic, 58
fossilised expression, 31, 37–8, 49, 50
fossilised inflection, 156
French, 164–5, 309
frequency, 29, 50, 92, 94, 95, 96, 98, 102, 119, 214, 216, 224, 258, 260, 261, 265, 322, 328–30, 331, 334
Freud, Sigmund, 218, 220
f-structure, 304, 305, 310, 313
functional control, 306, 307, 308, 309, 312
future-oriented meaning, 110, 269, 276

gemination, 154
gender, 235, 236, 237, 238, 243–4, 247, 248, 249
　conflict/confusion, 227, 228
　pronominal, 231
general extender, 86, 88, 93, 94, 97, 98–9, 100, 101, 102
generic, 138
　he, 215
genitive, 139, 156, 315–35, 358, 358
　alternation, 25–53, 316, 326
　oblique genitive, 25–6, 27, 30, 52
　s-genitive, 25–9, 31, 45, 48–51, 52, 315–35
genre, 195–6, 234, 235, 237, 241–2, 247
　speech, 86, 195, 234–5, 236–7, 242, 243, 246, 276
　speech-based/related genre, 235, 236, 237, 240, 247, 248
German, 131, 162, 254, 266, 277–80, 281, 283, 313
　Middle High, 279
　Old High, 279
Germanic, 155, 162, 283, 284, 299, 309
gerund, 149, 150–3, 154, 155, 156, 159, 163, 164, 165, 168, 330, 348, 350, 358, 359
givenness, 321, 327, 331
goal, 155, 158, 163, 165
God, 178, 186, 187, 188, 231
Gothic, 150, 155, 156, 158, 293
gotten, 343–8, 360
Government and Binding, 63, 68
gradience, 100, 101, 146
gradualness, 100, 101
grammarian, eighteenth-century, 224–5
grammatical system, 253, 257
grammaticalisation, 85, 100, 102, 105, 106, 109, 119, 127–8, 129, 134, 137, 153, 223, 258, 259, 260, 265, 268, 269, 271, 273, 278, 294, 303, 304, 306, 307, 310, 348, 352
Great Complement Shift, 165
Gregory's Dialogues, 164

HAVE, 255, 265
　+*to*-infinitive, 255, 258–62, 263, 270, 274, 279
help, 152, 348–58, 362–3, 364–5
heuristic tool, 217, 223
historical linguistics, 90, 129, 211, 223–9
HPSG (Head-driven Phrase Structure Grammar), 63
Icelandic, 283, 284, 285, 286, 287, 288, 294, 297, 299, 303, 306, 309, 313
　Old, 290–2, 295, 299
idiom (verbal, prepositional), 30–1, 33, 35, 40, 46, 285
impersonal construction, 116–17, 170–1, 173, 176–7, 179, 186, 189
　modal, 263

impersonal verb, 171–2, 173, 174, 177, 178, 180, 188, 261
inclusiveness, 134
incremental change, 130
indirect condition, 191, 192–3, 194, 195, 200, 201, 208
inference. *See* pragmatics
Infinitivus Pro Participio (IPP), 289–90
inflection (INFL), 155, 287
　that-tense, 63
information-packaging construction, 167, 169
Inner Circle, 319, 323, 333, 334, 335, *see also* Outer Circle
insubordinated *if*-clause, 191, 192–3, 203, 205, 208
interchangeability, 157, 317, 318, 322
internalised grammar, 215, 224, 227
intersubjectivity, 207–8
into-PP, 159, *see also* *to*-PP
irrealis, 163

Johnson, Samuel, 225, 226, 227, 229, 346

L1 Englishes, 336
L2, 223
　varieties, 334, 336
language acquisition, 256, 257, 334
language learning, 254
language/linguistic change, 81, 103, 212, 223, 234, 235, 242, 247, 257, 295
Latin, 116, 134–46, 155, 162, 166, 182, 263, 266, 267, 269, 271, 276, 279, 283, 300
lest, 157
levelling, 258
lexical density, 322, 330
Lexical-Functional Grammar (LFG), 59, 62, 285, 303, 304, 305, 307, 310, 313
literary criticism, 217–20
literate, 235, 236, 243
locative, 31, 37–9, 268, 319, 324
Lowth, Robert, 225, 227–8, 229

metaphor, 34, 37, 42, 159, 227, 258, 285
Middle English (ME), 157, 163, 164, 165, 166, 170–89, 259, 265, 267, 293
　early (eME), 131, 145, 165
　late (lME), 113, 182, 188, 189, 261, 340
modal, 105–7, 109–29
　advice, 110, 119, 121, 125, 126, 128, 129
　comparative, 105–7, 109–29
　core, 110, 112, 128
　preference, 110, 111, 113, 115, 116, 117, 119, 125, 126, 129
modality, 106, 109, 111, 129, 309
　deontic, 110, 120, 124, 125, 126, 129
　participant-external, 110, 111, 125
　participant-internal, 111, 115

Modern English
  early (eModE), 86, 107, 150, 152, 156, 159, 163, 168, 225, 235, 236, 315
  late (lModE), 81, 86, 210–13, 234, 235, 236, 241, 248
motion, verb of, 37, 155
multi-word verb, 30
MUST-*nedes*, 261, 281

necessity, modal, 254, 256, 265, 268, 270, 271, 272, 274, 276, 277, 281
  deontic/directive, 263
  epistemic, 264
  external, 261, 262, 264, 281
  internal, 261
necessity reading, 267, 270, 276
need (*neden*, BE-*nede*), 164, 259, 262, 265, 270, 274, 276, 281
negative purpose, 157
network, 100, 101, 103, 104, 126, 127
  horizontal, 108, 109, 126, 129
  vertical, 108, 109, 129
newspaper, 235, 236, 237, 315
nominalisation, 32, 35, 155, 156
nominalising suffix. *See* suffix
non-argument, 132, 146, 297, 311, *see also* argument
non-impersonal verb, 171–2, 173, 174, 180, 186, 188, *see also* impersonal verb
norm, 223, 224, 229, 235–6, 244, 257, 361

object control, 166
object-raising element, 64
of-PP, 25–53
Old English (OE), 113, 130–3, 134–46, 149, 150, 153, 155, 156, 157, 158, 159, 160, 161, 162, 163, 164, 165, 167, 171, 172, 173, 177, 178, 179–89, 258, 265, 267, 291, 292, 294, 299, 308
-*or*/*our*, 340–1, 343
orality, 235, 236, 241, 243, 247
orthography, 85, 222, 337, 340–3
Outer Circle, 319, 323, 333, 335, *see also* Inner Circle
overlap model, 303

paradigmatic extension, 167
parenthetical, 86, 191, 192, 195, 208
partitive, 29, 48, 50, 52, 175
part-whole, 26, 28, 32, 39–41, 44, 49, 50, 51, 53, 318
passive, 60, 149, 151, 166, 167, 168, 169, 311–12
  passivisation, 30, 174, 182–3, 188
past participle, 166, 167, 255, 289
patient, 35, 174

personal construction, 170, 176–7, 270, *see also* impersonal construction
personal verb, 261
personification, 227
phrasal impersonal, 172, 179, 182, 187, 188, 189
phrase structure hypothesis, 63
pluricentric, 337
politeness, 161, 193, 198, 208, 219, 285
possessive construction, 315
  weak possessive, 259, 277, 278, 279, 280
possessive verb, 254, 255–6, 265, 266, 268, 271, 272, 276, 277, 278, 280
possibility reading, 267, 276, 277
poss-*ing*, 61
pragmatics, 137, 230
  pragmatic implicature, 157
  pragmatic inferencing, 96, 97, 98, 114, 208, 256
  pragmaticalisation, 85, 162
  pragmatic-semantic factor, 253, 255
pre-modification, 222, 223
preposition, 28, 30, 31, 38, 40, 54–80, 142, 143, 144, 145, 146, 265, 268
  prepositional complementiser, 68
  prepositional object (PObj), 132, 134, 137, 141–5, 146, 175, 183, 188
  stranded, 71, 156
  to, 153, 154, 155, 163
prescriptive grammar, 212–16, 224, 319
  vs. descriptivism, 213, 214, 225
present participle, 156, 157
Present-day English (PDE), 109–13, 119, 130, 131, 133, 134, 146, 150, 151, 158, 160, 161, 162, 163, 164, 168, 224, 227, 235, 237, 243, 247
prevent, 348–50, 358–60, 364
Probabilistic Grammar, 316, 317, 334
procedural/pragmatic meaning, 191, 207, 208, 209
pronoun (PRO), 65, 130, 131, 145, 166
  determinative-descriptive, 136
  personal, 25–53, 97, 115, 121, 207, 224–9
proposition, 67, 68, 127, 153, 166, 304, 307, 308, 312
protasis, 190, 203
Proto-Germanic, 162, 283
Proto-Indo-European (PIE), 162, 283, 284, 291, 295
psychological profiling, 232
purpose adjunct. *See* adjunct
purpose expression, 155
purposive (*to*-)PP, 162, 165, 168

qualitative analysis, 27, 103, 211, 212, 229–32, 233
quantificational noun, 32–5
quantitative analysis, 49, 98, 211, 214, 229, 232
que, 267, 272, 273, 274, 276, 281

reanalysis, 58, 61, 130, 131, 257
rebracketing, 255
reduction, 85, 88, 97, 99–101, 102–3, 106, 119, 126, 127, 128, 129, 253
relational noun, 26, 29, 51
relative clause, 142, 212, 215, 275
   adnominal relative, 230
   headless, 267, 273, 276
   minimally headed, 267
relative pronoun, 215, 265, 267
   agreement, 224–9
   relativisation strategy, 215
   restrictive, 214
   who/which contrast, 224, 225, 231
Romance, 255, 256, 266, 284

schema, subschema, 101, 102, 104, 106, 108, 109, 113, 125–6, 128, 129
scribe, 107, 119, 135, 143, 220, 237, 242, 243, 248
semantic pathway, 256, 294, 301
semantic relation, 25–9, 32–53
semantic shift, 161
Shakespeare, William, 115, 117, 225, 226, 227–8, 231–2, 233
shared object, 265, 267, 271, 273, 276, 277, 281
Small Clause, 165, 166
social class/hierarchy, 231, 235, 236, 237, 238, 245–6, 247, 248
sociolinguistics, 211, 317
   'sociolinguistic turn', 213
   'third-wave', 211
Spanish, 174, 262–77, 278, 281
   early Modern, 269
   Medieval, 266, 267, 268, 269, 273, 276, 281
   Peninsular, 265
speakers, role of, 253
special noun, 132, 138, 141
specifier, 131, 146
spoken English, 38, 236, 242
Sprachgefühl, 212
s-structure, 304
stability, 246
stance, 84, 85, 86, 97, 99, 101, 102
Standard English, 82, 235, 337, 339, 350, 352, 353, 358
standardisation, 337, 338, 339, 340–3
subcategorisation frame, 158, 159, 160, 165

subject control, 150, 166, 168
subjunctive, 116, 158, 160, 163, 164
subordinate clause, 55, 60, 61, 79, 203, 259, 306, 307
subordinator, 54–80
   subordinating conjunction, 55
   subordination, mark of, 56, 64–73
suffix, 100, 150, 255, 311
   derivational, 154, 155
   nominalising, 154
Swedish, 283, 284, 285, 286, 290, 297–8, 306, 309, 313
system-mapping, 257

temporal adverb, 184–6
TENER-*que*, 262–77
textual coherence, 167
textual criticism/reconstruction, 220–3
   text-and-context method, 229–32
that-tense. *See* inflection (INFL)
thematicity, 321–2, 327–8, 331
theme, 32, 35–7, 48, 49, 50, 53, 158, 160, 162, 165, 177
to-infinitive, 66, 75, 77, 78, 149–50, 153, 156, 158–64, 165, 166, 168, 208, 261, 348, 350–8
to-PP, 153, 155, 156, 158, 159, 163, *see also into*-PP
toward(s), 343
transitivity, 173–5, 182–3, 188
translation effect, 144, 146
trial proceedings, 235, 236, 247
Trollope, Anthony, 218, 219–20

unaccusative, 36, 37, 174, 182
unidirectionality, 253
universal pathway, 254, 279

V2, 167, 168, 169
variability-based neighbour clustering (VNC), 87, 90, 91, 93, 94
verbal paradigm, 155
volition, 86, 111, 167, 178, 295, 309, 311, 313

Webster, Noah, 341
WILL-verb, 283, 284, 287, 295, 303, 305, 306, 310, 311
word order change, 255, 259
   SOV > SVO change, 260, 266, 276, 281
World Englishes, 317, 319, 361
written language, 235–6, 242, 245, 247, 337

Lightning Source UK Ltd.
Milton Keynes UK
UKHW011510030622
403870UK00018B/426